Death Rays and the
Popular Media,
1876–1939

Death Rays and the Popular Media, 1876–1939

A Study of Directed Energy Weapons in Fact, Fiction and Film

WILLIAM J. FANNING, JR.

McFarland & Company, Inc., Publishers
Jefferson, North Carolina

LIBRARY OF CONGRESS CATALOGUING-IN-PUBLICATION DATA

Fanning, William J.
  Death rays and the popular media, 1876–1939 : a study of directed energy weapons in fact, fiction and film / William J. Fanning, Jr.
      p.   cm.
  Includes bibliographical references and index.

  ISBN 978-0-7864-9922-9 (softcover : acid free paper) ∞
  ISBN 978-1-4766-2192-0 (ebook)

  1. Directed-energy weapons—In mass media. 2. Directed-energy weapons—Social aspects—History. I. Title.

  P96.D57F36 2015
  809'.93356—dc23   2015023948

BRITISH LIBRARY CATALOGUING DATA ARE AVAILABLE

© 2015 William J. Fanning, Jr. All rights reserved

No part of this book may be reproduced or transmitted in any form or by any means, electronic or mechanical, including photocopying or recording, or by any information storage and retrieval system, without permission in writing from the publisher.

On the cover *The Invisible Ray* 1936 (Photofest)

Printed in the United States of America

*McFarland & Company, Inc., Publishers
  Box 611, Jefferson, North Carolina 28640
  www.mcfarlandpub.com*

Contents

Preface 1

Introduction 7

Part I: The Historical Death Ray

1. An Idea Is Born: Harnessing Directed Energy as a Weapon, 1876–1918   21
2. The Catalyst Years, 1919–1924   49
3. The Death-Ray Craze, 1925–1939   76
4. Death Rays and Their Connection to the Second World War   106

Part II: The Death Ray in Fiction and Popular Culture

5. Early Death-Ray Novels and Short Stories   123
6. Death-Ray Novels and Short Stories of the Interwar Years   149
7. Death Rays in Other Media: Movies, Theater, Pulps, Radio and Humor   184

Conclusion 217

Chapter Notes 221

Bibliography 255

Index 265

Preface

For many people the term "death ray" usually refers to a type of science fiction weapon popular from the era of Buck Rogers and Flash Gordon to the present day *Star Trek* and *Star Wars*. Those who have some familiarity with the history of the death ray may also associate it with a few claims made by individuals prior to the Second World War but attribute these to crackpots and con artists. Even scholars of science fiction and those who have written about the history of laser research hold such a view. In any case, such a directed energy weapon prior to 1945 is usually regarded as a fantasy lacking any basis in fact and relegated to the realm of science fiction. As this study will show, however, this is a misconception.

The primary aim of this book is to provide a more extensive treatment of the historical death ray and its place in popular culture prior to the Second World War than has so far been attempted. Although brief descriptions of behind-the-scenes government projects either to construct such a weapon or to evaluate the possibility of doing so are included, the focus of this study is on reports about death rays appearing primarily in newspapers and magazines as well as their use in fiction and other popular platforms. Some information on this subject can be found in a number of works, but the full story of the death ray and its significance has been neglected. An examination of newspapers, magazines, books, and professional journals from that era reveals that wireless energy as a weapon was a news item beginning as early as 1876 and continued to attract considerable attention on up to, and during, the First World War. In the years following, the death ray received even greater scrutiny in the popular media, as claims for its invention multiplied and as some people hoped that it would provide a means of defense against the dreaded aero-chemical menace predicted to wipe out cities and whole populations in the next war. Having already appeared frequently in works of fiction prior to 1914, use of the death ray increased significantly afterward, expanding to the stage, film, and radio. In particular, it became an essential feature of what came to be called "science fiction" during the 1920s and 1930s.

Three main arguments are presented in this study. One is that the historical death ray was an important news story from the late nineteenth century up to the Second World War and owed its popularity not only to the more sensationalist sector of the media but also to statements by government officials, military leaders, and even some mainstream scientists, who often gave credence to such a weapon. As a result, the death ray entered into the culture of much of the industrialized world, its influence reflected in scientific, military, and political commentary, societal news, humor, and fiction. The second argument is that death rays described in the fiction of the period were often based directly or indirectly on news reports and were therefore not simply the product of creative imaginations, a point often omitted in other studies. Some scholars, moreover, assert erroneously that most death-ray claims were influenced by science fiction. In many cases, the descriptions of the fictional death rays seem to come straight from the newspaper accounts themselves, with authors occasionally employing the names of real inventors in their stories. Some writers also refer to the period following the First World War as the "ray-gun era" of science fiction and associate this device primarily with stories about fantastic worlds, futuristic civilizations, and technologically advanced aliens—a gross distortion. This leads to the third argument. Many of the death-ray tales in novels, short stories, films, and plays were set in their own time period, including the 1920s and 1930s, and dealt with contemporary issues: war, espionage, and crime. It is this latter type of fiction and its connection to news reports about real death-ray claims that will primarily be examined. Some in the former category, however, will be included as examples reflecting this relationship. No attempt is made to provide an analysis of the stories as to their artistic merits, as this lies outside the scope of the present work.

This study also demonstrates that the death ray was not simply a fantasy lacking any scientific basis, as some history and literary scholars have long maintained. Prominent military leaders, government officials, and some scientists periodically endorsed its viability, a fact ignored by contemporary skeptics, who usually created straw man arguments, attributing such claims to sensationalist newspapers, crackpots, and the like. Although no death ray capable of serving as a weapon was developed, some directed energy devices actually worked—but at extremely short distances—thus proving to some people that the principle of a wireless energy weapon was plausible. With continued research and experimentation, they asserted, it could be produced. Most scientists, however, maintained that the amount of energy required to project such a ray to distances necessary for military effectiveness lay far beyond the existing technology.

The stimulus for this project was the result of my earlier research into how the "next war" was portrayed in the popular media of the 1920s and 1930s. Many commentators predicted it would be one of inconceivable destruction dominated by airpower, poison gas, and exotic weapons, including death rays. As I delved more deeply into the subject and explored the material on death rays, as well as the fiction associated with them, I realized that there was far more information than could be covered in a chapter or two, my original intention. Another intriguing fact was the sheer number of fictional works that utilized a death ray in contemporary settings with contemporary situations. I continued to uncover more and more storylines that reflected the influence of real news reports about the invention of some type of directed energy weapon. In the early stages of this research, however, I found almost no mention of such a connection in the secondary sources. I then contacted several professors of literature at universities in England, Austria, Germany, and the United States. Although these people had expertise in British, German, and French science fiction of the interwar years, most did not seem to be aware of the death-ray phenomenon at all, let alone its influence on writers. My first effort to share what I had learned was an essay in the journal *Science Fiction Studies* in 2010. Entitled "The Historical Death Ray and Science Fiction in the 1920s and 1930s," a revised version was published in the anthology *Vintage Visions: Essays on Early Science Fiction* edited by Arthur B. Evans (Wesleyan University Press, 2014). As I continued to research this topic, I found that claims for the development of some type of directed energy weapon appeared long before the First World War, with the number increasing significantly afterward. In a similar manner, death-ray fiction became fairly prominent beginning with H. G. Wells's *The War of the Worlds* and expanded considerably during the interwar years.

Terminology

"Science fiction" is a term lacking precise definition, as scholars of the subject disagree on what it means and what it includes. One broad view is that it refers to a work of fiction incorporating any advanced technology, whether imaginary or real. Some writers limit its use to categories that meet more restricted criteria. Since my training is that of a historian and not a literary expert, I have chosen to employ the term sparingly and use instead the label "death-ray fiction" for the majority of works treated in this study. One advantage to this approach is that most of the novels, short stories, films, and other media forms utilizing directed energy weapons were often referred to by literary and movie critics simply as "mystery" and "detective" tales. Not until the late 1920s after the emergence of the pulp magazines did the term "science fiction" catch on. Even then, it was usually not employed to describe mainstream works with death rays in storylines set in the contemporary time period and involving imaginary wars, crime, and espionage. The authors of many of these novels were not referred to as "science fiction" writers. One prominent example is Agatha Christie, whose novel *The Big Four*, with her sleuth Hercule Poirot, includes a death ray employed by one of the villains. Another reason is that in many of these works a death ray plays only an incidental role. In two novels described in Chapter 6, for example, it suddenly makes its appearance at the very end of each story without any warning or even the slightest hint that such a device is wielded by one of the parties. The death ray serves no real purpose—as any weapon would have sufficed—and seems to be more of an obligatory feature.

For practicality, the term "death ray" is used in a generic sense and includes various types of directed energy, or "energy beam," weapons appearing in news reports and in fiction. Most of these were described as utilizing electricity as the damaging force, with others employing radium rays, X-rays, or sound vibrations. Many were claimed to be destructive to all matter they struck, usually having the power to incinerate or to cause explosions. Some energy weapons did not directly harm living things but were depicted as affecting machines only, causing engines to stop functioning or breaking down the molecular integrity of metals such as iron and steel. Others were supposed to be harmful only to living things and to have no effect on inanimate objects. Still others targeted certain functions of humans, leaving them temporarily paralyzed, permanently blinded, or incapacitated in some other fashion.

A Note on Translation

Unless designated otherwise, all translations from French and German are mine.

Sources

Since the subject of this study deals with the death ray and the popular media, most of the information comes from the contemporary sources. In addition to extensive research in libraries, considerable use has been made of online materials. One of the most important is that of the digitized collections of newspaper archives and other scholarly resources now available on the Internet. These include ANNO (Austrian Newspapers Online) from the Austrian National Library in Vienna; British Newspaper Archive; Gallica, the vast digital collection provided by the Bibliothèque nationale in Paris; the National Australia Library Trove; Newspaper Archive; Papers Past from the New Zealand National Library; Scriptorium, Bibliothèque cantonale et universitaire—Lausanne; the Gutenberg Project; the HathiTrust Digital Library; Internet Archive; Pulp Magazine Project; and Google Books.

The following are short references for frequently used sources and databases:

ANNO	Austrian Newspapers Online, Austrian National Library, Vienna
BNA	British Newspaper Archive
FMO	FreeMooviesOnline, www.freemooviesonline.com
Gallica	Gallica, Bibliothèque numérique, Bibliothèque nationale de France, Paris (unless designated otherwise, all newspapers and magazines cited were published in Paris)
GB	Google Books
Hathi	HathiTrust Digital Library
NA	Newspaper Archive
NYT	New York Times
Papers Past	Papers Past, National Library of New Zealand
PMP	Pulp Magazine Project
Scriptorium	Scriptorium, Bibliothèque cantonale et universitaire—Lausanne, Switzerland
Times	Times (London)
Trove	National Australia Library Trove

Some of the online newspaper databases provide two sets of page numbers, the actual and the consecutive, incorporating all the various sections that a newspaper edition may have. The latter also accounts for those pages missing. This system is especially helpful when page numbers are non-existent or illegible. In the citations used in this book, I have listed the actual page number, followed by the database number in brackets when necessary. An example is "To Make the Next War More Horrible Than the Last," *Ogden Standard-Examiner*, 16 December 1923, p. 2 [18], NA.

Introduction

> There is perhaps no figment of the imagination so dear to the writer of fiction who turns his thought to "the war of the future," no speculation so enchanting to the "penny-dreadful" school of "military experts" who, like Mr. Pickwick's Fat Boy, "likes to make yer flesh creep," as the "invention" of some horrible new weapon invented by a professor who has devoted his life to the extinction of war. One reads of battleships dissolving into a thin puddle of metallic scum, of "zones of force" which, when entered by an army, explode the ammunition in their belts, of "death-rays" which can blast all life within a hundred miles of their generation point.—R. Ernest Dupuy and George Fielding Eliot, *If War Comes*[1]

What is significant about this reference to "death rays" by R. Ernest Dupuy and George Fielding Eliot in their 1937 book *If War Comes* is not that they dismissed them as wild claims lacking scientific foundation but that they felt the need to do so. Reports of deadly rays had appeared long before 1914, and the number increased significantly after the First World War in a flurry of newspaper, magazine, and professional journal articles. Although met with skepticism and, later, outright rejection by many in the scientific community, the idea of such a fantastic weapon remained a popular news topic. The 1937 date of the book is also significant, for it indicates that stories were continuing to circulate, including those suggesting several military powers had either already developed, or were at least working on, some type of directed energy weapon. Nor was Dupuy and Eliot's complaint simply that of people who had finally tired of hearing these stories and decided to set the record straight. It was, rather, the lament that previous debunking by scientists on numerous occasions had failed to put an end to them. For example, *Scientific American* carried in its December 1934 issue an essay entitled "The Death of the Death Ray." According to its author: "Death rays we seem to have perennially with us—in the newspapers. Yet there is no known 'death ray,' at least not in the sense which the sensational headlines and accounts intend to convey. Evidently, we are asked to believe every now and then that some new kind of ray, always 'diabolical,' always 'killing,' invariably 'mysterious,' has been hit upon—something to make us shudder about the horror of the wars to be."[2]

But the issue is more complicated than *Scientific American* or Dupuy and Eliot suggested. Aside from the natural human fascination with the bizarre and exotic, even apocalyptic, the ongoing popular interest in the death ray resulted not just from sensationalist articles in newspapers and magazines. Without something more substantial to sustain it, the death ray as a topic would have quickly exited the scene as simply another fad. There are several reasons why it did not. An important one is the fact that some death rays actually worked. Most claims, it is true, were put forward by quacks, con artists, and amateurs whose imaginations surpassed their genuine understanding of the laws of physics and could easily be dismissed as bogus; but several inventors and professional scientists in the 1920s and 1930s produced working models capable of stopping gasoline engines and killing animals, albeit at short distances, usually no more than a few feet. This posed a problem for debunkers of the death ray, for these devices proved in principle that a wireless beam of energy could become a weapon. All that was needed was more research and experimentation. Skeptics who conceded this, however, pointed to the inherent limitation on all such rays at the time: it was then technologically impossible to generate sufficient energy to project them to the distances required for military effectiveness. The law of inverse square holds that the farther a beam of energy travels from its source, the more dispersed, and therefore the weaker, it becomes. That is why some experiments with microwaves, for example, succeeded in killing small animals at close range but were harmless when the distances were greater.

Another reason for the persistence of the death ray as plausible science was the credence given to it publicly by prominent leaders and experts. Government ministers, generals, and even some mainstream scientists periodically announced the existence of death rays or, at least, the possibility that they were in some stage of development. During the interwar years, much of this was purely propaganda, as if no self-respecting great power could admit that it was not engaged in some type of death-ray project or monitoring its development elsewhere. Implying possession of such a weapon would also assuage the fears of the public, already concerned about the dire predictions of aero-chemical attacks on cities and total annihilation in the next war. A few of these officials, however, actually considered the death ray a viable possibility. And although most professional scientists rejected it for the reasons given above, some accepted the basic principle of a wireless energy weapon and believed that it could be created. Their statements to this effect received widespread coverage, lending plausibility to some of the more extraordinary reports and inviting continued speculation by the press.

Claims for various types of directed energy weapons go back at least as far as 1876 and early on were regarded by many as a natural result of scientific progress. During the latter part of the nineteenth century, especially in the 1890s, a number of inventors, including Thomas Edison and Nikola Tesla, advanced the idea that wireless electricity could be adapted to military purposes and possibly end war. Their observations, widely disseminated in the popular media, led to a number of new claims and also influenced writers of fiction. Both during the period leading up to the First World War and while the conflict raged, numerous claims and reports continued to surface about death rays. The most sensational was the press coverage of an Italian inventor named Giulio Ulivi, who in 1913 and 1914 managed to perform demonstrations for military authorities in France, Britain, and Italy, but without conclusive result. It was not until after the First World War, however, that the death ray emerged as a major topic of discussion. The catalyst was the attention given to an Englishman by the name of Harry Grindell Matthews, a proven inventor in his own right, who became a celebrity with his death ray in 1924. The controversy surrounding him even made its way to the floor of the House of Commons, as its members clamored to keep such an amazing weapon in Britain and prevent its sale to a foreign power. Despite Grindell Matthews's ultimate failure to prove that his invention could do all that he claimed, the death ray became a permanent fixture in the culture of the 1920s and 1930s, as more and more stories appeared every year about some new wireless energy device that had a military application. With the rise of Nazi Germany and the increasing fear of another general war, more claims for such weapons invited still more discussion in the popular arena. Even after the outbreak of the Second World War, occasional reports of a German, later Japanese, death ray appeared in the press. In 1945 the public learned that several governments had indeed secretly undertaken projects to develop such a weapon.

The "Next War"

For a better understanding of the death-ray phenomenon, it must be seen within its historical context. As a news item it is inextricably linked to the syndrome referred to simply as the "next war." During the latter part of the nineteenth century, this phrase entered into fashionable usage as a term denoting the inevitability of war between two or more of the great European powers within the near future. The tipping point was the Franco-Prussian War of 1870, for it presaged more than any other contemporary conflict, including the American Civil War, the military consequences of modern technological development. Improved weaponry and the extensive use of railroads and telegraph portended battle on a more destructive scale than previously. By the end of the century, the tremendous expansion of industrialization in many countries led some observers to conclude that the "next war" would be so horrific that it might mean the end of civilization. Others predicted that such a thought might actually make war impossible, as leaders would refrain from unleashing these destructive forces. That seemed less and less a probability, however, with the gradual deterioration of peaceful relations among Europe's major powers after 1900.

During the same period, intellectuals and military visionaries anticipated that this industrial expansion would make war increasingly more about machines than about individual courage and skill on the battlefield or at sea. Indeed, some even prognosticated that technology might dominate the next conflict, as new and fearsome applications of science to warfare continued to appear. Some appreciated the possibilities of the airplane and the airship to extend battle into a new dimension, highlighted by H. G. Wells's 1908 novel, *The War in the Air*, which depicted a massive bombing attack on New York City by German airships. Many of these thinkers, however, regarded different manifestations of energy as the wave of the future, with electricity the most promising. As research into this mysterious force intensified, they saw it going beyond a means to power engines of war or to improve communications. By the end of the nineteenth century and the beginning of the twentieth, a number of scientists, taking their cue primarily from Nikola Tesla, embraced the possibility of wireless electricity as an actual weapon itself. Others speculated that lethal X-rays and radium rays could be harnessed and directed as if they were "shots" from a gun. A few even began to raise questions about the military possibilities of atomic energy, more so after H. G. Wells's publication of *The World Set Free* in 1914.

A number of thinkers, beginning with British soldier George Chesney, reflected on these changes and turned their thoughts to the idea of the "next war" as a promising subject both for fiction and non-fiction. As I. F. Clarke has noted, Chesney's 1871 *The Battle of Dorking*, an imaginary German invasion and conquest of Britain, set the pattern for other next-war scenarios.[3] This led to an entire genre of imaginary war tales involving some or all of the world's major military powers. Many of these carried the theme of a warning to their respective countrymen to take heed and be prepared when the next conflict occurred. The haunting fear of such a future also led to novels and short stories in which individuals discover a means to neutralize all conventional weapons and therefore abolish war. A number of these, discussed in Chapter 5, featured some type of wireless energy "death ray." Non-fiction works likewise appeared frequently, some warning of the dangers to come, others justifying the martial spirit and welcoming a great clash of arms, such as General Friedrich von Bernhardi's *Germany and the Next War* published in 1912.

Despite the devastation wrought by the First World War, the expression "the next war" acquired even greater significance in the aftermath. Not long after the guns fell silent on the Western Front, American journalist and correspondent Will Irwin expressed a widespread sentiment felt on both sides of the Atlantic: "In the two years since the Armistice, a new phrase has entered the discussion of military affairs not only in America but in all the European countries—'the next war.'"[4] Reflected in the title of his book, *"The Next War": An Appeal to Common Sense*, belief in the certainty of another major conflict was a theme that would resonate throughout the 1920s and 1930s.

The causes were quite logical. One of the most immediate was the cynicism in the wake of the Paris Peace Conference. Many political and military leaders, journalists, and scholars did not believe that the Treaty of Versailles provided a strong enough framework for a lasting peace because too many unresolved issues remained from which future wars could arise. Indeed, a number of small conflicts had broken out before the completion of the final provisions of the document. Yet these paled in comparison to one that would again involve the major powers: the likelihood of a German war of revenge, the clash of Anglo-American and Japanese interests in the Pacific, and the new, somewhat still unknown factor, Bolshevik Russia. These concerns, together with Italian frustrations over unrealized territorial acquisitions and the ethnic and nationalistic aspirations in Eastern Europe and the Balkans, left many people with a sense of unease or even foreboding. Skeptics, moreover, did not place faith in the ability of the new League of Nations or in international agreements to maintain peace. Another important reason for this anxiety was the appearance of powerful weapons in the Great War and their continued technological development that was certain to follow. The airplane and poison gas, in particular, were singled out as the means by which civilization could destroy itself in a future cataclysm. Ultimately, many people simply did not believe that humankind possessed the moral and emotional strength to curb its martial nature.

As Irwin indicated, the phrase "the next war" became a commonplace in the realm of military and political discussion in many countries, especially in Europe and America, as well as throughout the colonial empires and dominions. Commentators constantly supplied newspapers and magazines with lurid descriptions of the future conflict they assumed unavoidable. By the time Irwin published his book, thousands of articles on this topic had found their way into newspapers and other print media, reflecting a wide range of concerns. These included those of pacifists and others trying to gain support for the League of Nations and international disarmament, of military leaders wanting to secure continued funds to maintain strong armies and navies to protect their countries, of people—especially the French—who dreaded a German revival, and of those who feared the worst about the future in general and felt compelled to alert the public. In the last few years of peace before Hitler unleashed his armies on Poland, the probability of war increasingly occupied the minds of many Americans and Europeans, but only as the culmination to a fear expressed since the end of the last one.

The image usually presented to the public was the apocalyptic war dominated by the airplane and poison gas. World leaders, prominent military men, and intellectuals began to warn that such a conflict would mean the end of civilization. Some, of course, considered this an exaggerated view of the capabilities of modern weapons and contended that defensive measures would neutralize them to a degree. As a result, a spirited, often vehement, debate over airpower and chemical warfare emerged and continued right on up to the outbreak of the Second World War. Military men provided much of their writing for the professional literature, but they also found a receptive audience for their arguments in the popular media. Almost every day during the 1920s and 1930s, newspaper and magazine articles appeared warning of the dire threat of world destruction posed by aero-chemical means. The most widely accepted scenario, repeated many times over by prominent civilian and military leaders, involved massive air attacks on cities by hundreds, even thousands, of airplanes dropping deadly gas, high explosive, and incendiary bombs, turning great metropolitan centers such as London and New York into "smoking charnel houses," in the words of former British Air Minister Lord Thomson in 1925.

Probably the most sensational picture of the next war, however, appeared in *The Ladies Home Journal* in September 1923. In "World Destruction," author Charles A. Selden intensified the sense of foreboding explicit in the title by saying that his description was based on sober military assessments and not on the fulminations of pacifists. He emphasized, moreover, that the plans of the general staffs in several countries were more horrible than anything envisioned by pacifists and others calling for disarmament. Filling about half the page above the title of the article is an artist's rendering of a son lying dead on the field of battle while his mother, dressed in mourning, weeps over him. These devices, no doubt, were designed to lend credence to his views and to frighten his readers—mostly female it is assumed—even more. According to Selden:

> The next war will last a week—maybe only two days. By the end of that time everybody will be dead.
> From each of the warring nations great fleets of airplanes set out, not to fight each other, not to protect troops and troop ships, but to carry wholesale death, destruction, annihilation to the enemy's cities and millions of non-combatants.
> For three hundred miles from each nation's nearest border the enemy exterminates all life—human, plant and animal—creating a no man's land more barren, more horrible than any that was in France or Belgium....
> For a thousand miles the planes fly with poison gas, with disease germs, with fire bombs, with high-powered projectiles to lay waste cities and towns, to wipe out civilian populations, to shatter morale. Chicago gone and cities under attack as far west as Eau Claire, Waterloo, Kansas City, Fort Smith, Dallas....
> No defense is possible. Our own planes are meantime destroying our enemy as utterly as the enemy is destroying us. It is mutual annihilation.[5]

Despite its hyperbole, Selden's description was not far off the mark from what many others were saying, and some were prominent military commanders such as retired Admiral Sir Cecil Burney, who had been second in command of the British Grand Fleet under John Jellicoe and had led a squadron at the Battle of Jutland in 1916[6]; Field Marshal Edmund Allenby, who had commanded British forces in Egypt and led the campaign in Palestine during the First World War; and the distinguished South African soldier and statesman, General Jan Smuts.[7] Active-duty soldiers such as American general William "Billy" Mitchell made similar statements. One example receiving widespread coverage in the media was his assessment of what could happen to New York City in the event of an air attack with chemical weapons. As quoted in one newspaper: "If phosgene gas were used, 200 tons would be required to be dropped every eight days. This is a very deadly gas and will have almost immediate effect, and will kill every man, woman and child not carefully protected against it."[8] Probably even more sensational was noted British military thinker Colonel J. F. C. Fuller's statement that in a future war a "one-armed cripple sitting in Kamchatka" could by electronic means unleash a gas attack on Britain.[9]

Chemical warfare was a hotly debated issue in and of itself, as scientists and military spokesmen lined up on both sides of the argument as to whether or not poison gases could wipe out whole populations. Debunkers of the gas "bogey" tried feverishly to ascribe the horrors depicted as coming from alarmists who lacked technical expertise, but this was partially a straw man argument. Terrifying descriptions of chemical warfare originated not with sensationalist journalists and pacifists but primarily with revelations from the military about the "Campaign of 1919." The Allies were preparing to launch a great offensive that would include massive aero-chemical attacks on selected German targets, but the cessation of hostilities in November 1918 had cancelled operations. Some of the details of this appeared in the *New York Times*, as a reporter interviewed Colonel William H. Walker of the U.S. Army's Chemical Warfare Service at Edgewood Arsenal, Maryland, shortly after the Armistice. He told the reporter that massive air raids dispensing mustard gas on the enemy's positions would result in the deaths of every living thing, including rats.[10]

Although many scientists and chemical warfare experts tried to downplay the capabilities of poison gas during the 1920s and 1930s, others continually provided a rebuttal and warned that poison gas was indeed the nightmare depicted in the press. Governments also contributed to this fear by initiating programs to provide gas masks for civilians, make homes gas-proof, and build gas-proof shelters to protect the populations of large cities. As a result, much of the public continued to subscribe to the more sensationalist view.

Concerned about the real possibility of war in the near future and its frightening portents, many leaders of the major powers, as well as their peoples, continually hoped for a means to neutralize the aero-chemical threat to metropolitan areas and their populations. In the 1920s some military experts openly admitted that anti-aircraft guns and fighter planes were insufficient for the task and that the only answer was retaliation. This judgment seemed to be confirmed by mock air raids conducted by the major military powers during the 1920s and 1930s. They suggested that if both sides realized they could easily penetrate one another's air defenses and destroy whole cities with poison gas, high explosive, and incendiary bombs, then neither would want to start a war.

This view offered little solace, however, especially when some theorists postulated the idea of the "knockout blow." One nation, it was argued, just might be able to deliver a fatal stroke to its opponent if a surprise attack, without a declaration of war, were launched by massive air fleets. Such a brief window of opportunity for the aggressor could cause such appalling losses that the country attacked might sue for peace within hours or days to avoid further devastation. Although a number of military leaders, including French Marshal Ferdinand Foch, had advanced such a concept, it has been primarily associated with the Italian general Giulio Douhet, who published *Il dominio dell' aria (Command of the Air)* in 1921. He asserted that airpower, spearheaded by bombers, would determine the outcome of future wars. Such credence was given to this superiority of airpower that as late as 1932 Prime Minister Stanley Baldwin sent shivers down the spines of Englishmen with his comment that "the bomber will always get through."

This "next war" syndrome also gave rise to a flood of works depicting the many aspects of what the future would be like. Studies on the probable causes of another conflict, the likely belligerents, and the nature of the fighting appeared early on and continued up to the outbreak of war in 1939. Some examples are Basil Liddell Hart, *Paris: or the Future of War* (1925); John Bakeless, *The Origin of the Next War: A Study in the Tensions of the Modern World* (1926); K. A. Bratt, *That Next War* (1931); Inter-Parliamentary Union, *What Would Be the Character of A New War?* (1931); Ludwig Bauer, *War Again Tomorrow* (1932); L. E. O. Charlton, *War From the Air: Past, Present, Future* (1935); Russell Grenfell, *Sea Power in the Next War* (1938); and Henry Thuillier, *Gas in the Next War* (1939). This does not include the many thousands of articles in newspapers and magazines by journalists, scientists, soldiers, and statesmen, for example, Winston Churchill, whose pessimistic analysis of the next war "Shall We Commit Suicide?" appeared in *Nash's Pall Mall Magazine* in 1924. Its text, in part or in whole, was reprinted many different times in other publications and provoked considerable discussion.

Writers of fiction also capitalized on this concern over the "next war." Novels, short stories, theatrical productions, and films with the leitmotif of annihilation flourished during this time. These also depicted the origins, the likely belligerents, and the nature of the next great conflict. One popular theme was the destruction of civilization and its degeneration into a primitive society. Two prominent examples are Edward Shanks's *The People of the Ruins: A Story of the English Revolution and After* (1920) and Cicely Hamilton's *Theodore Savage: A Story of the Past or the Future* (1922). Airpower and chemical warfare also became a major subject of fiction, with such works as Martin Hussingtree's *Konyetz* (1924),[11] the Earl of Halsbury's *1944* (1926),[12] Major von Helders's[13] *Luftkrieg 1936: Die Zertrümmerung von Paris* (Air War 1936: the Destruction of Paris [1932]); Ladbroke Black's *The Poison War* (1934), and S. Fowler Wright's *The War of 1938* (1936). The same was true with film, with probably the most spectacular depiction of the next war being *Things to Come* (1936), based on the novel *The Shape of Things to Come* by H. G. Wells (1933). Although much of the action deals with a futuristic society that arises from the ruins of a devastating world war, the first part depicting an aero-chemical attack on Everytown (London) was lauded by movie critics as realistically frightening. And a one-act play entitled *Progress* (1922) by St. John Irvine depicted the terrors of poison gas and the nature of the next war as described in newspapers.

Given such a horrific picture of the "next war," it is understandable that many people had a pessimistic view of the future. The image of what massive air raids could do to cities, in particular, was a gloomy one indeed. This was intensified by the acceptance of the inevitability of such a conflict and spurred on by a sensationalist popular press, often drawing sustenance from leading political, military, and scientific authorities. The inundation of "next war" studies and fiction in all its forms also reinforced the public's fears about what might happen. It was in this context that the "death ray" would find a receptive audience.

The Death Ray and Popular Fiction

Although Edward Bulwer Lytton utilized an electrical force called "vril" in his 1871 novel *The Coming Race*, it was not until after the publication of H. G. Wells's *The War of the Worlds* in 1898[14] that directed energy weapons became an important feature of popular fiction. Reports about electricity and its military applications had by this time appeared frequently in newspapers and magazines, giving writers plenty of new material from which to craft their tales. In the period leading up to the First World War, two dominant death-ray storylines were that of imaginary conflict among the Great Powers and that of the good scientist trying to make war impossible through the development of a super weapon. During the First World War, a thematic shift occurred, as much of the death-ray fiction involved the real belligerents (although sometimes with fictitious names) and real situations, such as the British using it to defeat the German zeppelins. The death ray also entered into the realm of crime, as prominent detective storytellers, such as Arthur B. Reeve, placed it in the hands of their fictional villains.

This thematic shift became more pronounced in the 1920s and 1930s, as writers of death- ray fiction turned to an increasing variety of storylines. Some authors chose to write about strange worlds, advanced societies on Earth, and aliens from outer space; many, however, focused on contemporary, and more realistic, topics. Imaginary war tales continued to be popular, but they began to reflect the fears about the "next war" shared by the public and vividly portrayed in the media. One common pattern was that of a conflict between two countries, especially Germany and France, using conventional airpower, armies, and navies. One or both would develop and employ a type of ray weapon capable of arresting gasoline motors, causing ammunition to explode, or incinerating its target. Another popular storyline was that of foreign agents—more often than not German—attempting to steal a death ray or its plans. Most of the narrative, however, was conventional mystery or detective fare, in some cases with only a brief appearance of this weapon. The same was true in tales about criminals using a death ray to facilitate their activities, also a favorite subject with writers. The mad scientist employing a death ray to achieve world power or punish his enemies and the philanthropist attempting to end the scourge of war rounded out the most popular topics.

This increased prominence of the death ray in fiction after the First World War was noted by several commentators. As a writer for the *New York Times* observed in 1928, "Another member of the family 'is likely to storm unless his fireside novel is about death rays carried around in a little black box by a Russian professor who is being shadowed by Bolshevist spies.'"[15] Prominent critic and writer G. K. Chesterton complained about the pervasiveness of such literature because he believed much of it was connected with "next war" anxiety. In one of his essays in 1933, he protested against what he called the "Death-Ray Argument": "We have all read shockers and sensational stories, in which a white-haired and wild-eyed Professor, alleged to be idealistic and instantly recognized to be insane, is at work on producing a Death-Ray or some deadly explosive or destructive machine, so terrific as to lay the nations prostrate with panic, and thus achieve the happy result of imposing peace on the nations of the world."[16] Commentaries such as these attest to the prevalence of the death ray in a considerable body of mainstream fiction after the First World War.

Part I

The Historical Death Ray

1

An Idea Is Born: Harnessing Directed Energy as a Weapon, 1876–1918

The concept of a directed energy weapon stretches back to antiquity with various mythological deities such as Zeus wielding thunderbolts and the legendary mirrors of Archimedes burning up Roman ships, but the idea of a real "death ray" originated in late nineteenth and early twentieth-century scientific research associated primarily with the harnessing of electricity—and to a lesser extent radium and X-rays—and its subsequent application to warfare. Scientists, engineers, and military thinkers in various countries soon anticipated the use of electricity not only as an energy source for war machines[1] but also as the killing agent of new weapons. Discoveries during this period by Thomas Edison, Nikola Tesla, Heinrich Hertz, Henri Becquerel, and Guglielmo Marconi seemed to open the door to the possibility of revolutionizing warfare in this manner. The concept of a wireless, directed energy weapon, moreover, was considered by some scientists and laymen as a logical result of continued progress and therefore enjoyed a degree of respectability.

Probably the first mention of such a weapon occurred in 1876 with the claim made by "Professor" James C. Wingard.[2] Having discovered what he called a "Nameless Force" based on electricity, he announced that he would blow up a fifty-ton vessel on Lake Pontchartrain off New Orleans on 11 May. In addition to representatives of the U.S. military, scientists, and several foreign observers, the general public was invited to watch the spectacular event. A "Nameless Force" committee met with Wingard prior to the demonstration and worked out the details. The target ship was towed to a location, and Wingard, upon being signaled, was supposed to approach to no less than a mile distant before unleashing his weapon. After some time had passed and Wingard's yacht had not arrived, some of the crowd got bored and went home. The committee and official observers then noticed the professor's craft pull up alongside the other ship, and three men scurried over the decks, one going below, before returning to their own vessel and sailing away. Disappointed, the onlookers gave up and returned to New Orleans. The committee held a special meeting and decided to have a team of doctors examine Wingard's sanity if he ever made such a claim again.[3]

This was apparently unnecessary, for the members agreed to give Wingard another chance in June. According to newspaper reports, Wingard was on board a small skiff and directed his apparatus at a schooner a little more than a mile away and destroyed it. Afterward one of the committee members, M. F. Bigney, provided more details to reporters. He said at first he believed the test to have failed, for he saw what appeared to be a little smoke rise from the skiff and then something that seemed to lead from the boat toward the schooner, followed by no explosion. About a minute later, however, the detonation occurred. Bigney added that Wingard had a badly burned hand, which the professor attributed to holding a glass rod connected to the apparatus. The committee congratulated the professor and seemed excited about the possibility of a new invention which would greatly affect the nature of warfare.[4] One note of skepticism arose when a group of newspaper boys got to the schooner afterward and found a pipe with powder inside and a long wire attached, running toward Wingard's boat. The conclusion drawn by the *Galveston Daily News*, which carried the story, was that Wingard had managed to drag a torpedo (mine) below the waterline to the target ship, and the contact had caused the explosion.[5]

This was indeed the case, as Wingard was exposed as a fraud in an unsuccessful attempt to perform a similar demonstration at Boston in 1879. Hours before the scheduled test, a small rowboat in the bay exploded, killing two men. One was Wingard's associate, a man named James R. McClintock, a survivor of the famous Confederate submarine, the *Hunley*.[6] It turned out that he and the boatman were secretly trying to set in place a dynamite torpedo when things went awry. In this case, a premature explosion took their lives and revealed the truth to the authorities. Afterward, the "Professor" had no choice but to admit to the deception.[7]

His folly may have had an adverse effect for a while, as there was little mention in newspapers of any other claims, but the concept of a wireless energy weapon would resurge a few years later. One story did appear in

1878 when the press reported on experiments with powerful night lamps shining on enemy positions, enabling guns to hit their targets more easily. The article omitted the name of the inventor and his nationality but indicated the exercises were conducted near Metz in France, although the city was at the time under German rule as a result of the Franco-Prussian War. As described in an Australian newspaper, this opened the door to developing a weapon far more destructive than rifles and artillery, for then a handful of technicians operating a powerful electric battery could "like Jupiter, hurl the death-dealing bolts throughout the continuous twenty-four hours, and the opposing army will disappear before the destroying fire."[8] In January 1890 reports appeared about a device capable of discharging and directing electrical energy, or "artificial lightning" as it was sometimes called. A New Jersey inventor named Grinnell claimed to have produced a working model of an apparatus having military applications. He had already proved to his satisfaction that it worked by using it to kill flies. With a more powerful dynamo, he asserted that he could increase the intensity and range of this wireless electricity. As quoted in the *San Antonio Daily Light*, Grinnell claimed that "a flash of lightning can be directed against an army a mile or more away and without injury to the party operating the gun, scattering death and consternation among the enemy. With powerful dynamos thousands of soldiers can be killed in a flash, and a number of flashes are enough to destroy an army."[9] One version of the story added a note of skepticism: "He expects to be able to kill an army any fair day in the week. The act of wholesale destruction will have to be suspended on wet days."[10]

Several years later, Thomas Edison became associated with two separate electrical energy weapons. In late 1894 he announced an invention that would revolutionize warfare. Without providing any specific information about how it would operate, he claimed that a machine built at his laboratory could generate 50,000,000 volts per second. According to one expert: "With such an engine of warfare a dozen men could in ten seconds annihilate the largest army put on a field. If directed from a warship at a city of two million population, not a trace would be left in half an hour's time."[11] Later, Edison announced that he intended to give the plans to the U.S. government.[12] In 1895 he also proposed the idea of using jets of liquid charged with electricity and sprayed from nozzles to defend positions against attacking enemy troops. According to the *Manchester Evening News* in England, he told a reporter: "I have invented a machine by which it can be hurled to a great distance and water charged with 5,000 volts and then dashed on an army would sweep it away like chaff."[13]

It should be noted that as early as 1896 several scientists had raised their voices to protest the notion of super weapons utilizing electricity rapidly becoming reality. An article entitled "Electricity in War" appeared in several newspapers in January, including the *Galveston Daily News*, about the same time as Edison's announcement of "spraying electricity" at attacking soldiers. A collection of individual pieces by people with scientific expertise, the article included one strongly criticizing the popular view. Its author, Park Benjamin, was a scientist who had served as editor of *Scientific American* from 1872–1878. In "A Network of Deadly Forces," he commented: "It is necessary to understand that we can not make artificial thunderbolts, that we can not shake ships to pieces by induced vibrations in the cosmic ether, and that we can not send disintegrating currents to them or even drag them upon rocks or shoals by the attraction of powerful electro-magnets."[14]

Such criticism, however, did not undermine belief in the plausibility of electrical energy weapons or lessen press coverage of them. The writer of an article in the London magazine *Lightning* in February 1896 announced that an unnamed inventor had developed a device capable of generating a form of energy waves which could travel for miles and then converge on a target. The resulting explosion was such that it "immediately annihilates every person and everything within an area that can be enlarged to any desired extent by a slight motion of the directing mechanism."[15] In June 1897 Thomas W. Anderson of Worcester, Massachusetts, made the news by claiming to have developed a machine that could direct a bolt of artificial lightning to destroy ships. According to the account in the *Estherville Democrat* of Iowa, Anderson put on a demonstration in which he successfully blew up several tugboats, apparently to the amazement of spectators present. Although the "shot" from his weapon was so far limited to about one and a half miles, he planned to increase its range and also mount the apparatus on warships. Hoping to sell his invention first to the United States government, Anderson was in communication with foreign buyers as well.[16] Newspapers did not report what became of his device or, more important, how he had managed this hoax. Speculation would suggest something similar to Wingard's trick. The following month there was a report that Guglielmo Marconi claimed to have developed a means of wireless remote detonation of gunpowder in warships up to twenty miles away, an assertion that he later denied.[17] Not long afterward an article in *Chambers's Journal of Popular Literature, Science and Arts* kept this idea alive by repeating the claim ascribed to Marconi of wireless electricity capable of exploding gunpowder from a distance.[18]

In early 1898 a story with some importance attached to it surfaced about an American named John Hartman, who was said to have developed a wireless electric gun that could wipe out entire armies. Hartman was a Civil War veteran who had served as an engineer with the Fifteenth New York Infantry. An article in *The World* of New York provided details about his invention, complete with an artist's rendering of the bulky apparatus resembling somewhat a type of searchlight and shown raying to death an army. In an inset, the newspaper featured a description by Hartman himself, who said that he had turned over the plans and design to the U.S. Patent Office in Washington and was simply waiting for an answer. He informed the reader that he managed to adapt the beam of a searchlight to act as a conductor of electricity and performed an experiment on a rabbit some fifty feet away, stunning the creature with a "shot" from his device. He then understood that he could regulate the voltage and either stun or kill.[19] When this story appeared in the journal *Electricity*, reprinted in *The Literary Digest* in February, the writer expressed skepticism: "It is to be regretted that the inventor of this new implement of warfare fails to state what the certain conditions are that make the rays of a search-light a good conductor. Rays of light necessarily pass through the air, and as the latter in a dry state is one of the best dielectrics known, it is rather difficult to see how such an apparatus can accomplish what is claimed for it."[20] What is more significant for this study is the title of the article about Hartman's invention in an English newspaper. *The Northern Daily Mail and South Durham Herald* of Durham referred to his weapon as "The 'Death Ray,'" possibly the first use of the expression to appear in print.[21] Hartman's idea of using the rays of a searchlight as a conductor for a powerful beam of electricity would surface again a few years later.

Despite skepticism toward Hartman's claim, wireless electricity as a lethal weapon nevertheless appeared to be a fashion catching on among inventors, as three months later *The Literary Digest* reported that the U.S. Patent Office in Washington had been receiving a "flood of applications" for new devices utilizing this energy source, some with military applications. Although the Patent Office listed a wide variety of inventions, including a type of rail gun developed by one of its own officials, a General E. W. Serrell claimed to have developed a means of sending wireless electricity to hit ships. Referring to it as a "thunderbolt-wielder," the magazine provided the following description:

> The exact nature of General Serrell's invention is not as yet generally known. It is understood, however, that the device calls for the erection of two towers on opposite banks of a river or bay high enough to allow of a vessel passing

under a cable stretched between them. On the latter will operate the electrical engine of destruction, which will be under thorough control from the shore. In connection with the device, and in order to show the exact position of the vessel, there will be an instrument somewhat resembling the range-finder. When a vessel enters a certain zone, a discharge of electricity will take place, so it is claimed, striking the ship's deck and tearing its way through the water.[22]

The article added that General Serrell had developed this device a few years before and had given the schematics to the government.

Similar stories continued to circulate in 1898, one appearing in newspapers in June under the title "New Weapons." An American electrical engineer named S. H. Short purportedly had the means to use wireless electrical energy as a powerful weapon against targets both on land and under water. According to *The Advertiser* of Adelaide, it would utterly destroy armies, cities, and naval squadrons. In addition, "Mr. Short has a device for exploding submarine mines by electricity without the use of wires, and merely by the dispatch of an intensely powerful current through the salt-water."[23] Another type of weapon mentioned in the article involved using powerful magnets to immobilize enemy warships. There was also a story in connection to the Martian heat ray in H. G. Wells's recently published novel *The War of the Worlds*. According to *The West Australian Sunday Times* of Perth in July, an unnamed "old gent" from "Maoriland" claimed to have invented something similar. He met with a British admiral on board the ship *Orlando* anchored at Auckland to tell him about this weapon. Although the admiral was interested in learning more about it, the newspaper said the old man was unwilling to provide any details as to its properties or how it worked. He simply wanted to tell the naval officer that Armageddon was quickly approaching and, according to the article, he would wait until it "is in full swing, and blast to ashes every man, animal and thing unprotected by the flag of Britain."[24] Since Armageddon did not occur, it is presumed that his heat ray was not needed. The following month, a newspaper reported that science was getting close to solving the problem of how to control the power of electricity for use as a weapon and quoted electrical expert Dr. Emile Berliner as confirmation.[25]

This concept received further support as a result of the work of Nikola Tesla, by this time celebrated as one of the foremost experts on electricity. He proposed that with the proper equipment he could transmit electrical energy for thousands of miles without the need of wires.[26] Envisioning peaceful applications primarily, he believed that this capability could also serve military purposes, for a story reported in the *New York Times* suggested that the oscillator he invented could produce sparks wirelessly in the powder magazines of ships.[27] As one newspaper described it, Tesla could "wreck London, or Paris, or Berlin, or St. Petersburg from his laboratory in New York and no-one need have the slightest suspicion that he is at the bottom of the catastrophe."[28]

Not everyone viewed Tesla's assertion as valid, and some commentators displayed outright hostility to such a notion. A story carried in *The West Australian Sunday Times* of Perth, for example, indicated that Tesla appeared to have plagiarized the idea for such a weapon from Wells's Martians.[29] Later, when reports indicated that Tesla had almost completed a device to blow up ships wirelessly,[30] the writer of an article appearing in *The Western Champion* of Barcaldine, Queensland, expressed considerable doubt as to the inventor's ability to annihilate an entire battle fleet simply by pressing a button. He added that such an artificial bolt would not come close to the energy released in a "single flash of lightning."[31]

Some skeptics employed humor to belittle Tesla's claims. One note of levity about such a weapon appeared in June 1898 in the *Warren Review* of Williamsport, Indiana, in which the writer proposed that "Tesla, if he is the originator of this fearful scheme, should try it on a dog first."[32] This was followed by a commentary in July while the Spanish-American War was in full swing. According to a piece carried in *The National Democrat* of Jeffersonville, Indiana, "We cannot sympathize with a policy that is keeping inventor Tesla in the background and preventing him from coming forward and instantly destroying everything Spanish with his electric heat ray."[33] In its coverage of the story in November, *The Western Gazette* of Somerset, England, mentioned the remarks made by "Dagonet" in the *Referee*:

> It is a gruesome idea ... that a gentleman can sit in his back parlour in New York, smoke his pipe, and destroy the whole world. That is the sort of gentleman who ought not to be left too much alone to get melancholy or morbid. He ought to be kept as cheerful as possible, and every care ought to be taken with his diet and his health generally. What that man could do in a moment of nervous irritability or dyspeptic malice it absolutely paralyses one to think.... It will be no use now for the Martians to come fooling around Wimbledon Common with their black smoke and their heat ray. Tesla, with his electric currents, would dispose of them in ten seconds.[34]

Despite this criticism, Tesla had his supporters and they remained loyal for years. The March 1916 issue of *The Electrical Experimenter*, for example, carried a lengthy article on Tesla's "high frequency oscillator," with the implication that wireless waves for warfare were plausible. The magazine sported on its cover an artist's rendering of the inventor's tower at Wardenclyffe on Long Island sending out wireless waves against enemy warships, exploding them as they approached. According to the writer, H. Winfield Secor, the scientist had claimed that these waves could travel for hundreds of miles and detonate the gunpowder and shells in the magazines of ships far out to sea. They could also be used against land installations wherever ammunition was stored.[35] It was also reported that Tesla collaborated with Michael I. Pupin, a professor at the Massachusetts Institute of Technology, on trying to develop another means of achieving remote detonation. According to the story carried in newspapers, the two scientists had supposedly "perfected a wireless percussion, by means of which explosives could be set off at a distance," blowing up the magazines of ships.[36]

Others, probably influenced by Tesla, made similar claims. In 1899 *The Freeman's Journal and National Press* of Dublin carried a story about an experiment conducted by several people, including Reverend J. M. Bacon and the father-son duo the Maskelynes. They suspended guncotton cartridges from a balloon sent up and then set them off by wireless electric waves. The writer of the article entitled it "The Modern Science of Slaughter," setting the tone for his fear of what such a capability would mean for future wars: "Vast stores of ammunition and explosives can be fired, irrespective of distance or means of communication, in the stores of a factory, fort, or arsenal, or more horrible still, in the hold of a warship."[37] Another newspaper covering the story stated that an additional experiment exploding a powder magazine from ten miles away had been successful as well.[38] Like most other claims of this nature, little was heard of it afterward, with the obvious implication that some sort of trickery had been involved.

The end of the nineteenth century and the dawn of the twentieth were accompanied by more stories involving wireless energy as a weapon. One was the concept of "explosion by concussion" alluded to above. In 1899 French psychologist and physicist Gustave Le Bon announced he was in the process of developing an apparatus that would revolutionize naval warfare. As reported in early July in *The Argus* of Melbourne, "while seated in his operating-room on shore, he will be able to project rays of sufficient strength to annihilate a fleet. The theory is, apparently, that the impact of the projected rays on the ships' sides will result in a series of explosions sufficiently powerful to ignite by concussion all their ammunition."[39] There was also mention of a test in which wireless rays blew up a powder magazine from a distance of ten miles.[40] Such claims no doubt led the writer of one newspaper article in December 1901 to suggest that electricity would become the modern "flaming sword" of Genesis.[41] Apparently still working on his "fleet destroyer," in 1903 Le Bon made another announcement, this time telling the press about an accidental discovery. According to the *Liverpool Herald* of New South Wales, while experimenting with Hertzian rays Le Bon experienced a "rain of fire falling upon him from all the metallic objects in the room."[42] The writer of the article went on to say the scientist believed that metallic mirrors could send this energy over great distances and detonate any explosives they struck. These included gunpowder in the magazines of ships, the shells in the big guns, and the ammunition carried by soldiers.[43] Newspapers also reported on the "Guarini Thunderbolt." While working on a wireless telegraphy device, Professor Émile Guarini of France accidentally got a shock, giving him the idea of utilizing this energy as a weapon. After some time experimenting, he asserted that electrical shocks could be transmitted wirelessly. By using antennae and generating 100,000 volts, he could direct this energy as far as twelve miles and destroy anything it touched.[44]

Commentary on "waves of detonation" continued, accompanied by renewed interest in Hartman's concept of using the beam of a searchlight as a conductor of electricity. In the latter part of 1903, newspapers carried a story, first appearing in London's *Daily Express*, about the British military performing experiments to produce shock waves to detonate explosives, including torpedoes inside submarines. According to the report, "the officers conducting a recent test blew off the head of a torpedo at a distance of 300 ft., the torpedo being 30 ft. under water at the moment of the explosion. In other similar tests the pulsating current acted on the fuse or trigger of the torpedo, setting it off just as effectively as would sudden contact with the side of a ship's hull."[45] Without referencing this story, the writer of an article in the British *Navy League Journal* (also carried in newspapers) followed up on this concept a few years later. He expanded on the "waves of detonation" known to be engendered by lightning strokes and speculated that this force could be harnessed and directed at will. Such a weapon would make an enemy helpless, as it could explode the cartridges carried by soldiers as well as render guns and torpedoes vulnerable.[46] The two foregoing articles also dealt with the idea of using a searchlight as a conductor for powerful electric currents. The former included a story about a Hungarian scientist having successfully developed something akin to it to destroy a target. *The Advertiser* of Adelaide compared the weapon to that of Wells's Martians.[47] The writer for the *Navy League Journal* also discussed the possibility of developing heat rays along similar lines to neutralize airships, considered at the time a real threat to naval vessels in a future war.[48]

Electricity, however, was not the only source considered for a directed energy weapon, as radium emerged as another possibility. Research with this element by Pierre and Marie Curie had by this time become well known. Gustave Le Bon proposed that it, too, could be manipulated to emit rays capable of exploding gunpowder at a distance.[49] He elaborated on this idea more over several years as evidenced by newspaper articles in 1909, in which Le Bon suggested radium might end war within the next fifty years. He added that he had been working with Professor Branly on experiments with Hertzian and radium rays. Although both types penetrated stone walls three feet thick, Le Bon claimed that the radium emanations "disintegrated them." If someone managed to harness this energy, he believed, "the radiations directed in parallel waves would penetrate the arsenals, casements, fortresses, or powder magazines, destroying everything in their passage. Buildings would crumble and fall."[50] Whole fleets lying at anchor could be destroyed in this manner as well. The same newspaper article also included Dr. Wilson Hartwell's vision of what radium rays could do to a great city like New York:

> Imagine ... that great American city resting, as it thinks, secure upon its island. Suddenly a dirigible or an aeroplane comes swiftly and silently in from over the sea, perhaps loosed from an aerial fleet at rest somewhere beneath the horizon. It circles for a moment, and then from its bow there shoots out a narrow shaft of white light. This is from its radium condenser, and it is directed against the Metropolitan tower. The crowds stand amazed, thinking perhaps, it is some new form of amusement provided for them. Then suddenly the tower, shining new with intense radiance of this directed energy, breaks and crumbles before their eyes. Down it goes crashing among them, while a coruscation of blinding sparks shoots from its sides where the radium ray has penetrated. Down it will fall, crumbling like a monster of stone under an annihilating force. From one play to another the balloon may go, directing the ray upon whatever its guiders choose, and everything will crumble under its touch. In a few hours New York could be made a wilderness.[51]

What is significant about this report is that it links two prominent scientists, Hartwell and Édouard Branly of France, to the possibility of a ray weapon. Branly, however, later became a strong critic of its viability, especially after the announcement by Harry Grindell Matthews in 1924 that he had invented a wireless ray capable of arresting airplane engines in flight. Nevertheless, this underscores the point that the concept of such a weapon enjoyed a degree of respectability in the years leading up to the First World War.

Russian Prince Ivan R. Tarkhanoff also supported the view that radium could be a powerful weapon. A professor of physiology at the military academy in St. Petersburg until 1895, he served as a *privat-docent* until his death in 1908. The *New York Times* commented on his lecture in 1904 at the Military Association in the capital: "When large quantities of radium were available, the Prince continued, the whole system of modern warfare would be revolutionized, as powder magazines, whether in forts or in the holds of vessels, would be at the mercy of radium rays, which could explode them at long distances."[52]

Another type of device reported in newspapers evoked the specter of Archimedes. In 1901 an article on miscellaneous inventions included one by an unnamed German scientist who claimed to have developed an apparatus designed to harness the sun's rays. Instead of burnished metal mirrors used by the ancient Greek genius, the German allegedly put together a complex structure of glass mirrors from which the solar rays would converge on a single point with terrific heat.[53] This concept would resurface after the First World War.

Regardless of the energy source, the idea of some type of ray adapted for war purposes continued to gain credibility. English scientist Harry Cox, for example, predicted that a ray would be found "potent enough to blow up a battleship."[54] Remote detonation, furthermore, seemed closer to reality with the mysterious explosion of the French warship *Iéna* in 1907. A reporter on the scene shortly afterward was told by a naval officer the cause was the instability of the type of powder used for the shells, as it was known to self-ignite after a long time. He added, however, that the rumor was already circulating about a short circuit being the cause of the explosion.[55] The *New York Times* picked up on this quickly and ran a story suggesting *wireless* electric sparks were responsible.[56]

The following year a newspaper article appeared in which the writer speculated on the cause of the *Iéna* explosion—and that of several other ships—in the overall context of wireless detonation as a means of revolutionizing warfare. The story began with an account of a demonstration at the Royal Institution in London, in which a wireless burst of electricity traversed the Lecture Hall and burned up a copper coil at the other end of the room. The inventor, a Mr. Poulsen, did not have the intention of developing this into a weapon, content simply with utilizing the powerful dynamo to enhance telephony. The writer of the article, however, used this as an example to show that wireless electricity may have been the cause of the destruction of the *Iéna*, the Japanese battleship *Mikasa* in 1905 during the war with Russia, and the Brazilian *Aquidaban* in 1906. He added that even the USS *Maine* might have fallen victim to the same type of force. The writer also cited a recent address by Nikola Tesla to a scientific audience in New York, in which the celebrated electrical wizard asserted that he could destroy an entire fleet in this manner. The case of the *Mikasa* the writer found to be particularly compelling: "on the shore, some distance away, were three mysterious strangers with an apparatus 'like that of a photographic camera,' to quote the words of a witness at the subsequent court of inquiry. This apparatus they were seen to be manipulating. Shortly afterwards the *Mikasa* suddenly exploded like a giant bombshell."[57] Fearing that the power of "vril" described by Edward Bulwer Lytton in *The Coming Race* in 1871 (see Chapter 5) and the Martian "heat rays" of H. G. Wells were now possible, the writer suggested that Britain should consider doing away with its fleet. The sensational testimony of one witness notwithstanding, the Japanese government's official conclusion was that the *Mikasa* blew up because of faulty powder.[58]

The plausibility of ray warfare nevertheless continued to receive support. In April 1909, Lewis Nixon, a leading American shipbuilder who had designed the USS *Oregon*, expressed his belief that "a discovery may be made any day that will enable one battleship to discharge a tremendous volume of electricity at a ship perhaps five miles distant and instantly kill every one on board."[59] At the same time an editorial comment in an English newspaper summed up the prevailing view that wireless energy weapons might become a reality, with the horrors inflicted on civilization greater than even those imagined by Wells.[60] The following year another story appeared about the development of an electric ray for warfare. The perceived technological advances with such weapons led one commentator to suggest that the next war would be directed by an electrician or an engineer. Heat rays "will be sent out that will wither the invaders into ashes, or an electric shock will go through their lines and the destruction of Sennacherib will be repeated, not a soul being left to tell the tale."[61] This view was echoed in 1910, as described in the *Albany Advertiser* of Western Australia: "Distance is no object. The army may be miles away; it may be marching drawn up in battle array or in camp—it will be all the same to the electrician who directs the ray, and who will be able to sweep thousands of men into eternity between two whiffs of a cigarette."[62] More support for such a weapon's power appeared at this time in a report of an unnamed inventor who allegedly used his death ray to kill a horse. As described in one newspaper: "The brute staggered as though dazed by a blow from some thunderous, some unseen hand, then fell stone dead. The same thing would have happened had the rays been doubled or trebled. And the fate of the horse might be the fate of an army corps."[63]

One strong endorsement of ray warfare's plausibility came from

William Russell, the vice-president of the American Wireless Association. In June 1912 newspapers carried his comments about the different applications of wireless electricity for war. In addition to communications, he spoke of the possibility of developing some type of gun capable of concentrating electrical energy and directing it at airships and battleships. He went further by raising the alarm that the Germans were apparently already working on such a capability. Russell described what this would mean if mounted on an airship:

> Imagine a fleet of these destroyers flying over a ship in action! One points its electric gun at an enemy's ships. He presses the button, and zip, puff! nothing but silence; the once present ship is no more!
> It has been completely volatised and turned into gases and vapor—or into its original element—so quickly that the imagination is stunned at the rapidity of the action....
> A city would be wiped off the map as if by a gigantic invisible hand, and in a dark night, the enemy's airships hovering over us in darkness, we could not have any chance of defence.[64]

Although a few scientists, like Park Benjamin, had rejected the notion of a wireless energy weapon, others, including many of those with electrical expertise, were more optimistic. They shared the public attitude that such a development would be a natural result of the prodigious expansion of scientific progress over the last fifty years. It was just a matter of time.

The Case of Giulio Ulivi

That time had apparently come in 1913 and 1914 when newspapers and magazines reported on stories about an inventor named Giulio Ulivi. A thirty-three-year-old Italian engineer who had been living in Asnières, France, since 1907, he had earned some notoriety for his inventive talents. He attracted considerable notice in 1913 by claiming he was working on a device that could explode gunpowder by means of invisible infra-red rays, or "F-rays." General Joseph Joffre, chief of the French general staff, became interested and even visited with Ulivi to learn more about his work. The Italian inventor said that he could detonate explosives from ten miles away; but, after a request by Joffre to extend the range to fifteen miles, Ulivi announced he had succeeded in attaining a distance of twenty miles. Naturally, Joffre and other French military leaders wanted to see a demonstration, and arrangements were made for a series of tests off the coast near Le Havre in August. Ulivi received permission to operate his device from a ship flying a British flag so that the French military could not seize his invention under the cloak of national security, and a wealthy Englishman's yacht, the *Lady Henrietta*, was subsequently made available for the exercise.[65] In addition to Joffre and members of his staff, others present included General Curières de Castelnau of the war ministry and the chief of the wireless service, Commandant Gustave Ferrié. So important did Joffre consider the possibility of such a technological breakthrough and the advantages it would give France that he delayed his departure for Russia, where he was to attend a series of military maneuvers.[66]

According to newspaper accounts, there seemed to be some confusion about the results of the tests carried out over several days. Some reports indicated Ulivi had made a favorable impression on the French officers while others suggested that they had some suspicions about what they had seen. The *New York Times* quoted from an article in the French newspaper *L'Éclair* to describe what took place. According to *L'Éclair*, in one test Ulivi successfully detonated ten submarine mines spaced out at six-hundred-yard intervals. Astounded by what he had seen, Joffre supposedly then asked Ulivi if he could explode gunpowder and ammunition stores in a fortress, to which the Italian responded affirmatively. Ammunition was then brought to an old fort and placed inside where it was shielded by concrete. Manipulating levers, he once again directed his F-rays at the target and easily detonated it.[67] American consul John Hall Osborne also attended these exercises and was impressed with the results.[68]

Problems began when the French officers asked technical questions. Ulivi was unable to answer some of them, gave responses not conforming to well-known scientific principles, and even seemed not to understand the technological nature of some of the queries. He also contradicted himself several times. Suspicion, or at least disappointment, grew when Ulivi came up with excuses for why he could not perform more tests there if they were under military supervision. For example, one officer wanted to provide explosives that he would make himself. Ulivi finally agreed to comply with the army's requests, but on three succeeding days his apparatus "broke down" and he was unable to perform any demonstrations.[69] According to *L'Éclair*, the French officers returned to Paris greatly mystified by what they had seen but especially concerned over the bit of a letdown after they had had their hopes so high for a weapon that could radically affect their military strategy. As things turned out, Ulivi did not conduct any more tests for the French army and went back to Asnières. He then packed up and traveled to England to hawk his wares to the military there.[70]

Details of Ulivi's dealings with the British are not altogether clear. Several newspaper articles stated that he was negotiating with the authorities there but had told them Italy had the first option to acquire his invention.[71] One report indicates he met with two naval officers, an Admiral [Edward] Charlton and a Captain [W. C. M.] Nicholson, but that nothing resulted from their discussions.[72] Ulivi himself later told the press he had signed an agreement with Nicholson but would not divulge the details. Another revelation by the Italian inventor was his surprise to learn that the second mate on board the *Lady Henrietta* for the French trials was a British naval officer who reported back to the Admiralty on all he had witnessed.[73]

In any case, newspapers described an exercise in which the British damaged the old light cruiser *Terpsichore* in the Solent off the coast at Portsmouth in October. *Die Neue Zeitung* of Vienna said that the British placed Ulivi's invention on board the *Vernon* (commanded, incidentally, by Captain Nicholson) and directed the rays at the *Terpsichore* located eight miles distant, detonating the ammunition and turning the vessel into a wreck. The newspaper article also mentioned the explosion having to be triggered with the aid of some mysterious apparatus placed on the ship.[74] Other sources provided slightly different versions. The *Times* simply reported that two submarine mines placed under the hull of the vessel had been detonated by electricity from one of the nearby launches of the *Vernon*. The Portsmouth correspondent said details about the event remained confidential and any unofficial stories had no validity.[75] There was no mention of Ulivi, F-rays, or any type of wireless beam involved in the test. French electrical engineer Henri Murat, writing in *Le Journal Général de l'Algérie, de la Tunisie et du Maroc* of Algiers, stated that the Royal Navy had used a wireless device to blow up the *Terpsichore* but added it had nothing to do with Ulivi, suggesting the British had developed their own wireless energy weapon.[76] *The Register* of Adelaide said it was uncertain as to whether or not Ulivi was present but reported that Winston Churchill and other members of the Admiralty were there.[77] The *New York Times* also confirmed the British had used wireless rays but had exploded a mine placed under the hull of the ship, which suffered considerable damage without sinking. As for a connection to Ulivi, this newspaper said only that it was unclear if the British had used his F-rays.[78] An article in the *Galveston Daily News* the following year, however, reported Ulivi's device was employed to explode a mine under an old cruiser.[79] The version found in *The Western Gazette* of Somerset, England, simply confirmed that a wireless device had been used. According to this paper: "From what transpired, however, it seems that the light cruiser Terpsichore, having had all her watertight compartments closed, was towed to the Solent. There a mine, well charged with explosives, was secured to the ship's hull several feet below the waterline. From a distance—how far is not known—this mine was exploded by means of the concerted electrical rays."[80] *The Western Gazette* added that the damage to the ship was such that it took five tugboats to prevent it from sinking and tow it back to the harbor. In 1936 a newspaper article said Ulivi had successfully detonated a submarine mine in the Solent but balked at performing another demonstration under British supervision and therefore left the country.[81] In any case, Ulivi failed to persuade the naval authorities to do business with him, and he went home to Italy.

Although branded a fraud by some, Ulivi found a receptive audience in his native land and resumed his work. The Italian government even provided him with a new laboratory in Florence. In February 1914, with the assistance of Admiral Pietro Fornari of the Italian navy, Ulivi put on a demonstration in which he successfully exploded two torpedoes placed in the Arno River. In May he performed another, exploding mines in the river. Among the onlookers was the well-known seismologist Padre Guido Alfani, who was impressed by the demonstration and believed that Ulivi had actually managed to harness wireless electricity as a weapon.[82] Since he demanded total control over such tests, critics continued to call him a charlatan. Admiral Fornari, however, wanted to give Ulivi the opportunity to prove conclusively that the F-rays were genuine and not a hoax.[83]

In the meantime, according to the newspapers, a soap opera-like drama unfolded. Ulivi asked Admiral Fornari permission to marry his daughter, Maria Luisa. In fact, he had renamed his rays "M-rays" in honor of his bride-to-be. The admiral consented but on condition that Ulivi conduct the supervised tests before the wedding. The inventor protested, insisting on the marriage first. At this point, Alfani contacted Fornari and advised him not to trust Ulivi. The scientist, who had been favorably inclined to the inventor as mentioned above, had visited his laboratory and become skeptical at what he had seen. He then asked Ulivi to perform a simple test for him by exploding some gunpowder at a range of only three meters. If he could do that, Alfani would use his influence to promote Ulivi to the scientific community. At first agreeing to do so, Ulivi managed to find excuses for not going through with the test. Subsequently, when Fornari would not budge on the marriage issue, Ulivi postponed the demonstration several times and then suddenly eloped with the admiral's daughter.[84]

Many people suspected Ulivi of being a fraud, but it was not until the somewhat comical episode of his elopement that they learned how he had supposedly managed his trickery. According to a story in the *New York*

Times, Ulivi had succeeded in detonating sea mines by a simple textbook understanding of chemistry. He had bored a hole in each mine, put sodium inside, and then placed a small amount of cotton wool into the opening. When water came into contact with the sodium, it ignited, setting off the explosion. The cotton wool acted as a "timer," for water would have to soak through it to reach the sodium. In this manner, Ulivi could predetermine the time each mine would detonate, and all he had to do was direct his rays in the right direction at the approximate moment.[85] Ulivi's apparatus and how he operated it did lend support to this explanation of a hoax. According to the description given by the *New York Times*, the device consisted of two parts. A locator-sender would generate electric waves that would find the explosives and then "bounce back" to a telephonic headgear worn by Ulivi.[86] He would then manipulate his F-rays and direct them to destroy the target. In this manner, he could know approximately how much time he had before the sodium-doctored mines would go off and simply be seen pushing levers and buttons until the explosions occurred. Some of the accounts, indeed, indicated that Ulivi often took more time "looking" for a few of the explosives with his locator-sender than he did for others. His insistence on always controlling the demonstrations and refusing to submit to tests supervised by others further seemed to substantiate these charges of fraud.

This explanation could not, however, account for every type of test ascribed to Ulivi and was not accepted by much of the press. For example, as described above, he had been asked by Joffre to explode ammunition inside a fortress and apparently did so to the satisfaction of the French. As for his experiments with bombs and torpedoes in the Arno River, the sodium theory can explain some of the demonstrations but not others. Several magazines and newspapers in June and July 1914 included an account by a reporter from the *Corriere della Sera* of Milan who described the munitions used. As reported in *The Labor Digest*, a commentary on this from *Scientific American* described them as containing powder "inclosed in a capsule of gutta percha and this in fiber, which another portion of the story suggests was waxed cord. Outside there was a sphere of porcelain, this encased in asbestos cardboard, and finally to inclose the whole, a jacket of wrought iron."[87] Although *Scientific American* remained skeptical toward the Italian reporter's account, it seems unlikely that Ulivi would have taken measures designed to interfere with his deception of using sodium to ignite on contact with water. The *North China Herald* of Shanghai, for one, discounted the sodium hoax theory altogether.[88] An article first appearing in *The Daily Chronicle* of London and carried in several newspapers, furthermore, stipulated that in the demonstration on 14 May Admiral Fornari placed in the river "corded metal bombs" he had fashioned himself.[89] Another explanation for a hoax appeared in a 1915 article in the *Tages-Post* of Linz, Austria. According to this newspaper, Ulivi had secretly attached wires to the mines and connected them to an electric battery, thereby exploding them using conventional technology.[90]

Despite accusations that his F-rays were a hoax, Ulivi weathered the storm. One newspaper, the *Illustriertes Österreichisches Journal* of Vienna, carried the story about his accomplishments with the M-rays without mentioning the allegations of fraud or even how F-rays became M-rays.[91] A number of newspapers acknowledged the skepticism toward him but asserted that he was apparently on to something with the concept of a wireless energy weapon.[92] For example, the *Washington Post* ran a story in June 1914 saying that his weapon could greatly revolutionize warfare and that several foreign powers, including Japan, had approached him about his invention.[93] The following month the same newspaper had another article depicting the power of wireless rays as an accepted reality. The author, Rudolf Hensingmüller of the University of Heidelberg, revived the view that wireless transmissions were responsible for several disastrous explosions on ships at sea, in particular, the French battleship *Liberté* in 1911. More than two hundred men lost their lives in that tragedy. Hensingmüller argued that none of these tragedies appeared to be deliberate acts but were simply unfortunate accidents. He believed that wireless transmissions from sending stations had exploded the gunpowder and ammunition in the magazines. The author cited as support Ulivi's demonstrations in Florence. Acknowledging the criticism directed at the Italian inventor, Hensingmüller still regarded Ulivi's work as genuine.[94] Electrical engineer Henri Murat, mentioned above, indirectly lent support to Ulivi in a letter to the French Naval Ministry back in 1908, in which he asserted not only the *Iéna* disaster but the mysterious explosions on board *La Couronne* and *Latouche-Tréville* as well were caused by wireless electrical sparks. The naval authorities replied that they were not interested. The gist of his detailed scientific explanation provided to the French navy, however, appeared in an article in August 1913 in *Le Journal Général de l'Algérie, de la Tunisie et du Maroc* and was used to substantiate the plausibility of Ulivi's work.[95] In 1915 Frederick T. Jane, the founder of the famous publication on naval warfare, also suggested wireless energy as a possible cause for the mysterious explosion that sank the *Princess Irene* and attributed this to the Germans. The newspaper article included a reference to Ulivi and his experiments.[96]

1. An Idea Is Born 39

Well into the war, Ulivi continued to be regarded by some as a genuine inventor of F-rays. In July 1915 an article entitled "Italy's Terrible Secret" appeared in newspapers, including the *Raleigh Register* of Beckley, West Virginia. The writer mentioned that Ulivi had performed a demonstration in Rome for the king of Italy just prior to the outbreak of the World War, using his F-rays to detonate successfully five bombs in the Tiber River. The article included a remarkable statement about Ulivi describing the use of a special "firing charge that the wireless spark would ignite...." and "that he was working on a device that would make it possible to explode ammunition magazines at any distance without the necessity of preparing charges for that purpose."[97] Three years later, newspapers carried F. H. Randall's article in the *Illustrated World* describing the results of a demonstration in Rome in which an "unnamed" Italian scientist detonated explosives along the Tiber River. Randall also said that the scientist directed his ray to a three-inch piece of hardwood, which "in an instant ... was seared and broken as if it had been broken by lightning."[98] The author then speculated on the military application of this "canned lightning," as he called it. He predicted this weapon would sweep airplanes from the skies, warships from the seas, and armies from the battlefields. The same story under the title "Frightful Arc Ray New Weapon of War," also appeared in newspapers with an artist's rendering of a night battle scene in which two barely visible soldiers direct a flash of lightning at an enemy position.[99] In October at the 5th Congress of the Spanish Association for the Progress of the Sciences, in Valladolid, General José Marva lent support to Ulivi's work in mentioning other experiments concerning remote detonation with ultra-violet rays, this time by an American named Gibbon and a collaborator named Buw. Marva indicated progress had been made in this field and Ulivi's accomplishments, if true, would certainly be "a marvelous discovery."[100] In a book published in 1916, author B. F. Miessner described the controversy over the Italian's demonstrations for the French and British military establishments. Although not endorsing Ulivi, he left open the possibility that something might result from the F-rays. Miessner was a member of the Institute of Radio Engineers and worked with the U.S. Navy as an expert radio aide.[101] Garrett P. Serviss, an amateur scientist and author of the novel *Edison's Conquest of Mars* (see Chapter 5), provided indirect support to Ulivi in an article in *Popular Science Siftings*. He believed that wireless remote detonation of ships was possible, suggesting incidents of mysterious fires and explosions on board ships prior to the war may have been due to sparks caused by wireless waves.[102] In 1917 an article appeared about an Italian inventor who had conducted experiments under military auspices with "V-rays," adding he had "proved that the explosives in an enemy's magazine or on board a hostile warship can be 'set off' at a distance of miles."[103] Although the source had the wrong letter of the alphabet and did not name the inventor, it could have been none other than Ulivi. As a postscript, one report added more intrigue to the story of Ulivi by mentioning that he had sold his F-ray device, possibly to Germany.[104]

Ulivi also managed to help his public image as a serious scientist. In 1916 he announced the invention of a device, which he called the "Scotoscopia," employing infra-red rays to penetrate the darkness and detect ships at sea. One newspaper reporting the story still labeled Ulivi as the inventor of the F-rays.[105] He also developed luminous paint. Instead of fading into obscurity, he would appear off and on in the news for several years to come.

Although not made public until later, Ulivi got another opportunity to experiment with his F-ray, or *radioballistica* as it was often called in the Italian press. In 1917, when he was serving in a medical unit of the Italian army, interest in his device was apparently rekindled, for a private business syndicate managed to get him temporarily released to go to the Somaini Cotton Mill in the little town of Lomazzo, some thirty miles north of Milan. The director at Somaini, Adolfo Hilzinger, was in charge of overseeing Ulivi's experiments. In order to avoid attention from the press, the inventor took on the pseudonym "Signor Planta" and was given a special room in which to work. After several months during which Ulivi's *radioballistica* played havoc with the electrical system at the plant as well as in the town, Hilzinger informed him that the operations would have to end because of the financial damages already accrued and the potential for even greater losses. Both Hilzinger and Ulivi wrote reports detailing the experiments carried out at the Somaini plant, with Ulivi's including a justification for the research and the validity of the principle of a wireless energy weapon. In the end his work there ended up in obscurity for a time, as Hilzinger informed the business and military leaders of the problems.[106] In 1921, however, *The World* of New York obtained a copy of Hilzinger's account and incorporated it in an article written by Arthur Bennington. It subsequently appeared in other newspapers as well.[107]

In addition to the saga of the Italian inventor, newspapers during this time reported on other claims of projecting electrical energy as a weapon. A bizarre story appeared in July 1913, in which twenty-three-year-old W. L. Cummings was arrested in Salt Lake City for threatening to kill a wealthy society girl named Dorothy Bamberger if she did not pay him one thousand dollars. His murder weapon was a "wireless death device."[108] As recounted in the *Indianapolis Star*, state and federal authorities took Cummings and his apparatus into custody before he could carry out such a heinous crime. Electricians tested the device by placing it in a vault shielded with steel and concrete, after which they set up in another room the bell and incandescent globe found with the apparatus. When they turned on the electric current, the bell rang and the lamp lit up.[109] One report in late 1913 concerned a Danish engineer named Victor Harhorn, who was allegedly in Berlin working on a ray to detonate explosives. The owner of an automobile factory in the German capital, the Dane had supposedly developed a type of wireless ray described by *The Western Gazette* of Somerset as being "similar to but not an imitation of the 'F' rays." The article added that his work was under the supervision of the German government.[110] According to a brief story in the *New York Times* in March 1914, a Spaniard by the name of Iglesias Blanco supposedly performed a test similar to that of Ulivi in which he exploded buried dynamite by wireless means.[111] Just prior to the outbreak of hostilities in Europe, American inventor Bernays Johnson, already noted for his wireless telephone, announced that he had developed a "Z-ray," which he claimed could melt steel and explode the powder inside cartridges. He hoped that this new weapon would bring about an end to war.[112]

The First World War

The start of the First World War did not put an end to stories about new claims for some type of death ray. Soon after the fighting began, a most sensational piece appeared in the *Washington Post*. In an artist's drawing, two men are looking out a window, one watching as the other manipulates some controls. Outside, an airship explodes while a warship is about to be engulfed by a huge funnel wave rising hundreds of feet in the air. The article claimed that the inventor of melinite (unnamed but must refer to Frenchman Eugène Turpin) had succeeded where Ulivi failed in harnessing the F-rays. It furthermore stated that he had given the secret to the French government.[113] In October newspapers carried an article about explosives and war gases that included a brief notice about a German inventor referred to simply as "Herr Hartman." He had allegedly offered his device—a searchlight capable of serving as a conductor for electricity—to the German army and navy authorities. According to reports, he successfully killed two hundred sheep in a demonstration using 25,000 volts of electricity at a distance of six miles.[114] The following year, a report about another wireless electrical weapon appeared in newspapers. According to the account in the *Beatrice Daily Sun* of Nebraska, Charles F. Billows of St. Paul, Minnesota, invented such a device to kill rabbits up to a distance of one hundred and seven feet. After failing to interest the British and French in his ray, he claimed to have given it to the Germans. As Billows told the press, "I believe it was used in the present Russian campaign.... I believe Russian powder stations were set off by our machine."[115]

More stories appeared in 1917. In its May issue *Popular Mechanics* featured an article about a bright young Irishman from Belfast named Alexander Corr. He had gained the attention of the British government for his discovery of a new aniline dye and was awarded a money prize and given a post in London to continue his research. He then supposedly worked on a ray that could destroy zeppelins and blew out a window and part of a backyard wall in an experiment. Later, after a zeppelin raid in which the Germans reported losing one of their airships over London, the author said that the gossip among certain British artillery officers was that Corr's ray was responsible.[116] In June 1917 Dr. A. C. Cowperthwaite of Los Angeles told the press that he was working on a gamma ray based on radium that could be used as a powerful weapon for the United States. The writer for the *Oakland Tribune* commented that the professor might soon make the Martian heat ray of H. G. Wells a reality.[117]

Besides wireless electricity, reports about a device similar to that of Archimedes resurfaced. In December 1914 as the Western Front had degenerated into the nightmare of trench warfare, a story about a fantastic weapon appeared in newspapers. Entitled "The Last Gunpowder War," the article described a plan to mount on airships devices consisting of lenses and mirrors to concentrate the rays of the sun into powerful beams of heat energy. The result would be total annihilation of fortresses and cities; even men would "shrivel into nothingness."[118] Although envisioning commercial uses only, Dr. W. J. Harvey of the Royal College of Science in Toronto explained to the *Illustrated World* magazine in 1917 that he had managed to harness the power of the sun. This article, appearing in the December issue, was accompanied by photographs and described small mirrors mounted on frames resembling modern solar panels. These could gather sunbeams and concentrate them in any desired direction. Harvey claimed that he could generate any temperature desired and that he had successfully vaporized water and burned a hole through a wooden shingle at a distance of fifteen feet. His apparatus had allegedly melted a metal bar in forty-three seconds as well.[119] As the next chapter will show, this idea continued as one of many proposals on how to develop a wireless energy weapon.

In addition to ongoing reports of some type of death ray being invented during this time, several writers made predictions about the use of directed energy weapons in the "next war." In 1914, shortly after the outbreak of hostilities in Europe, Irish author Shaw Desmond penned for the London magazine *Ideas* "The Invisible War of 1950," a summary of which appeared in the *Warwick Examiner* of St. Lucia, Queensland. In addition to more advanced airplanes, submarines, and remote-controlled dirigibles and torpedoes, he believed that wireless rays would play a significant role in future warfare. He referenced Ulivi without naming him, acknowledging his failure, but believed that future scientists would succeed in harnessing his N-rays (another alphabetical error). Desmond's scenario suggested that much of the fighting might be done by technicians sitting in control centers: "by pressing a button in London, for instance, the military man of the future will be able to set going the high-powered explosives stored within a radius of five hundred or five thousand miles as the case may be. It may no longer be a dream to forecast the time when Berlin or St. Petersburg can be laid in ruins from these lands, or vice-versa. This will be the last word in invisible war."[120] *The Electrical Experimenter* of November 1915 offered another type of ray, this one shot from a machine called the Radium Destroyer. Complete with an artist's rendering on the cover, the magazine speculated that on the basis of scientific progress with radium and the atom such a powerful machine could become reality within a century. In the article a hypothetical warlord has been presented with a weapon mounted on an armored vehicle capable of jumping over obstacles. After a demonstration, the warlord decides to conquer the world and orders the manufacture of more destroyers. The official designation for the actual weapon is the "Radium-K-Ray." In the ensuing conflict the warlord's destroyers quickly overrun the defensive positions of the hypothetical enemy, and his general then orders a town in their path to be evacuated in order to demonstrate the futility of resistance. As described by the magazine: "Destroyers line up on the hills and spray the unlucky city with their fearful rays. Within five minutes the entire city, houses, churches, bridges, parks and everything else have gone up in a titanic Vapor cloud; only a vast crater in the ground where the thriving city one [sic] stood remains."[121]

Several other predictions, these not quite so far into the future, appeared at this time as well. In 1915, the writer of an article recounted in *The Western Champion and General Advertiser* of Barcaldine, Queensland, stated that scientists considered it quite reasonable to expect one day soon the use of wireless waves to detonate explosives. He added that they were currently experimenting with heat rays as hot as an acetylene torch. The effects would be such that "fortresses of steel and stone would melt, the biggest guns would crumble into pools of steel, and whole regiments of men might, with one blast, be shriveled into ashes."[122] Three months later, the same newspaper mentioned Thomas Edison reaffirming his earlier prediction that wireless electric waves would be able to detonate ammunition from a distance.[123] In 1917 previously cited Garrett P. Serviss repeated the notion that electric waves could disable an enemy fleet by either blowing up the powder in the magazines or by putting the electrical systems in disarray.[124]

A few stories about death rays in the First World War did not appear publicly until after the conflict,[125] three of them involving soldiers of the British Empire. In 1921 Ferdinand Tuohy contributed an essay on the "next war," which appeared in the *Syracuse Herald* of New York. Although much of the information was derived from Will Irwin's book, Tuohy added a brief story about a Canadian soldier attached to the British Third Army in 1916. He had supposedly developed a death ray with which he claimed to have killed rabbits and chickens. He managed for a while to maintain his hoax until it was learned that the creatures had succumbed to poison.[126] In 1936 newspapers ran an article about an electric death ray involving an Australian engineer, a veteran of Gallipoli serving on the Western Front. As described in *The Mercury* of Hobart, Tasmania, he convinced his superiors that his invention would work, and they promoted him to the rank of major and sent him to headquarters, where he was housed at a French chateau with armed guards. There he put on a demonstration in which he directed his ray at some rabbits and killed them. Later it was learned that he had placed an electrically charged wire above the heads of the animals, and his ray of "visible" light caused them to raise their heads and be electrocuted.[127] The other death-ray story from the First World War involved an enterprising young British soldier who also managed to hoodwink the army for a while. According to an article in the *Times* in 1937, Field Marshal Sir Archibald Montgomery-Massingberd provided this tidbit of information in the course of an evening when he presided over a lecture given by J. B. S. Haldane, a prominent authority on chemical warfare. The former chief of the Imperial General Staff (1933–1936), Montgomery-Massingberd was chief staff officer for the British Fourth Army when a corporal convinced his superiors that he had invented a death ray. Known as someone with a creative and talented mind, he effected this hoax by providing photographs of his apparatus, which he said could kill mice. Excited about the military advantages of such a weapon, the Army gave him money, a lieutenancy, and a place where he could continue his experiments. Only later did someone with scientific credentials expose the man as a fraud. Montgomery-Massingberd did not relate what punishment was meted out or how this incident influenced the government's view of such claims when others announced their death rays.[128]

Although not greatly publicized in the media until afterward, there were also rumors about the development of a death ray by the Germans as well as the use of such a weapon by others during the First World War. In 1921 the British War Office had in its possession a number of reports about German electromagnetic waves that could both kill and set off explosives. But a team of distinguished scientists that included Ernest Rutherford decided to dismiss these claims for lack of scientific proof.[129] When the press got hold of the story later, however, rumor became fact. In an article in 1924, the *Manchester Guardian* stated that the war had ended just in time, for the Germans would have used this new weapon to annihilate the British forces facing them.[130] Writing for *Popular Mechanics* in June 1927, Harold T. Wilkins claimed that during the war unnamed parties were working on a device capable of exploding ammunition wirelessly and causing airplane engines to stop.[131] In 1933 *Popular Mechanics* expressed this as fact, asserting that lethal rays were indeed deployed against opposing aircraft and that "the full story of their use in the war has yet to be revealed."[132] One possible source for some of these rumors was that the Inventions Department of the British Air Ministry had received during the war a number of bizarre suggestions, including one for heat rays to be used against zeppelins and electric beams to cause enemy airplane engines to halt.[133]

A few weeks after the signing of the Treaty of Versailles, a most remarkable story about a British ray appeared in the *New York Times* magazine section on Sunday, 20 July 1919.[134] Written by American naval historian and journalist Edgar Stanton Maclay, the article was entitled "Burning Glasses," a revised version of his essay "'Burning-Glasses,' Dundonald's Destroyer?" published in *The North American Review* in March 1915. In the latter piece, Maclay described the development of a weapon based on the idea of Archimedes and his polished mirrors that supposedly set fire to Roman ships during the siege of Syracuse. He said that he had discovered a late eighteenth-century British pamphlet about a contraption consisting of individual mirrors arranged on a frame and so positioned as to concentrate the rays of the sun into a powerful beam of heat energy. With such an apparatus it would be possible to set fire to wooden sailing vessels, explode the powder magazines, and incinerate almost anything. Maclay speculated that this was the basis for a secret weapon invented by British admiral Thomas Cochrane, later Tenth Earl of Dundonald, who perfected it and proposed its use to a select committee in 1812 during the Napoleonic Wars. Although concluding that the device worked quite well, the committee members decided that it was beyond the bounds of civilized warfare and ordered it to be kept secret. Maclay went further and linked the "burning glasses" to the F-ray and similar weapons reported in the news, suggesting that the principle of wireless heat rays held great potential.[135]

In the 1919 *New York Times* article, Maclay turned speculation into fact. Repeating much of the information about the history of the "burning glasses" and Dundonald's unsuccessful attempt to gain permission to use his invention, Maclay asserted that the British navy had in its possession during the recent war a weapon that could have effectively ended the German submarine threat. The authorities decided, however, that unleashing it would be too terrible for civilization. This weapon was none other than Dundonald's, kept secret for more than a century. According to Maclay, the old admiral had been able to mount his invention on a ship, thereby extending its application beyond a stationary position. The author provided a vivid and horrific description of its capabilities, as it

> would instantly kill any human being touched by it, explode any magazine of powder reached by it and set on fire any wooden structure or inflammable material that felt its scorching breath. It was more deadly than the gas bomb and more far-reaching in its effect than the German liquid fire. At a distance of a mile or more, it would set fire to a town, and at closer range it would mow down a line of advancing troops faster and with more deadly effect than any type of machine gun employed in the late war.[136]

The newspaper article also displayed an artist's sketch of the "burning glasses," but mounted on a modern dreadnought rather than a wooden vessel of Cochrane's era. The important aspect of the image is that similar versions were later reproduced in stories of death-ray claims and shown in newspapers and magazines without any reference to Maclay's article in the *New York Times*.

Why Maclay created such a fantasy remains unclear, for his story misrepresents well-known facts, even in his time. The overall historical framework he used was correct, but the single most important feature was false: Lord Dundonald developed a form of chemical warfare based on sulfur—not "burning glasses."[137] Two newspaper articles in May and June 1915 had in fact mentioned the old admiral's weapon as a form of chemical warfare. The first appeared in the *Washington Post* under the title "Gas in War Old Secret," and stated that the Germans had gotten the idea of using poison gas from Lord Dundonald.[138] The second article, found in the *North China Herald* of Shanghai, mentioned that a chemistry professor at the Royal Naval College had been making public comments about the rejection of Dundonald's "secret" plan, "a combined attack by smoke-screens and asphyxiating gases."[139]

More important, Dundonald's weapon had ceased to be a secret in 1854. Shortly after the outbreak of the Crimean War, the admiral, now nearly eighty years old, proposed its use to capture the formidable Russian fortresses at Sevastopol and Kronstadt. This time the whole affair, including the story of the 1812 committee, was out in the open, debated in the House of Commons, and reported in newspapers both in Britain and abroad. The public knew of "Dundonald's Plan," or "Dundonald's Destroyer," but it did not know exactly what it was, although there was considerable speculation. The *Illustrated Times* of London, for example, referred to it as an "explosive machine."[140] The London newspaper *The Patriot* was actually close to the truth with a story in August 1855, stating that "Lord Dundonald's plan consists in destroying the enemy by blasts of poisoned air."[141] *Harper's New Monthly Magazine* overshot the mark by some degree, suggesting that "Lord Dundonald has invented a shell, loaded with cacodyl or some analogous substance, and that he calculates to poison the defenders of Cronstadt with its fumes."[142] Despite Dundonald's entreaties, a committee appointed by Prime Minister Palmerston turned down the request and ordered the exact nature of the weapon continue to be kept secret. In 1908 the secret got out, probably with the publication of the private papers of Lord Palmerston's Secretary of State for War, Lord Panmure, for these included Dundonald's memoranda of August 1855 detailing his plan.[143]

Maclay, however, may have been influenced by newspaper articles that substantiated his claim. In 1915 and 1916 there were reports that Britain had a secret weapon, or plan, to stop a German invasion of the island, and it was the one devised by Dundonald. Probably the most widely circulated story was the one written in 1916 by noted American war correspondent Mary Boyle O'Reilly, who said that it was a powerful weapon, quoting Dundonald himself: "This plan will obliterate every ship from the sea, every enemy fortress and army from the land, instantly and irrevocably as a child rubs pencilings from a slate."[144] She also mentioned that spies for years had been trying to obtain the secret but that it was safely locked away in a vault and known to only three people at any one time: the reigning monarch, the war minister in time of war, and each succeeding Earl of

Dundonald. Maclay may have also been influenced by a sensational article appearing before the war, one that greatly increased the destructive power of the admiral's weapon: "That England should shudder with horror at the thought of destroying one-third of the population of a continent in a few hours is second in interest to the fact that, if England should employ it against the Teutons, it would mean perhaps the eventual annihilation of all humanity and perhaps of all animal life on the face of the globe."[145] Heightening the mystery, the article said the secret was locked up in the Tower of London.

Whatever the reasons for this far-fetched story, it does not appear that any naval authority or historian wrote to the *New York Times* to refute it. One could easily surmise that it did not deserve even this type of recognition since Maclay had created such a fantasy. The fact that the newspaper gave it top billing in the magazine section, however, does raise questions as to why no one responded, especially since Maclay was a well-known historian and not some crackpot trying to sell a sensational news item to a tabloid. Even in September 1919, a newspaper article appeared repeating the gist of the story from the *New York Times* without any mention of criticism.[146] In October, however, *Munsey's Magazine* had a brief review of Maclay's article, pointing out that the historical record was quite clear about Dundonald's weapon being a form of chemical warfare. *Munsey's* did not offer any explanation as to where the historian had obtained the information for such a bizarre story.[147] As late as 1924, a reference to Lord Dundonald's invention appeared in a newspaper article about a new death-ray claim. Recounting some of the basic information, the writer failed to mention the nature of the weapon but added that the plans are "supposed to be safely locked in the British archives."[148]

The idea of some type of wireless energy weapon received considerable attention in the popular media during the period leading up to the First World War and continued once the great conflict began. Given the tremendous advances in various fields of scientific endeavor, the "death ray" appeared to some as a more or less plausible consequence of research with electricity and other energy sources and therefore enjoyed a degree of credibility. It was also associated primarily with making war impossible. In the aftermath of the Great War, the death ray would be seen more and more as a means of neutralizing the aero-chemical threat and protecting cities and civilian populations from total annihilation. It would also come under increasing fire from mainstream scientists.

2

The Catalyst Years, 1919–1924

Although reports about directed energy weapons had appeared frequently before and during the First World War, the death ray received its greatest publicity and had its greatest impact during the interwar years of 1919 to 1939. Private individuals, government officials, and even military agencies periodically made announcements regarding a ray device that would put an end to war or at least give their nation a decided advantage in any future conflict. The most important stage in the development of this fascination with such an exotic weapon was the period 1919–1924, punctuated by two important stories. One was press coverage of French commercial airplanes flying over Bavaria allegedly being targeted by a German ray that forced them to make emergency landings. The other was the sensational saga of the British inventor Harry Grindell Matthews.

Publicity about death-ray claims prior to, and during, the First World War had made this type of weapon not seem so unusual to people in the years immediately following despite the fact that no proof existed of such a device having actually been created. For example, the writer of one newspaper article in 1920 stated: "Ray warfare is a virgin field. It was a source of worry to more than one general staff during the late war. It was realized that the first nation whose inventors discovered the military use of rays would wield a weapon before which the world would be compelled to accept any terms which were imposed upon it."[1] As late as 1935, the *La Crosse Tribune and Leader-Press* of Wisconsin reminded its readers: "Back in the World war we were accustomed to pictures showing the death beam directed against armies."[2] Although focusing greater attention on the aerochemical threat, the popular media nevertheless included wireless energy weapons in the panoply of "next war" fears during the 1920s and 1930s.

New reports and commentaries on the possibility of lethal rays for the battlefield appeared a little more than a year after the signing of the Treaty of Versailles. One was an October 1920 article in the *New York Times* about a weapon based on the same principle as Maclay's "burning glasses." Without referencing Maclay, Cuthbert Hicks, a former member of the British Air Ministry, discussed the role of airpower in future wars. In addition to bombs and gas, he mentioned the possibility of "light" weapons mounted on airplanes. According to Hicks, a concentration of sunlight by means of a lens would produce enough heat to destroy any target. In this way, he said, an entire city "would be reduced to ashes in no time."[3] This idea of a weapon harnessing the power of the sun did not go away, but death rays produced by electrical energy continued to take center stage in the press.

One such announcement appeared in the summer of 1920 in a report published in the journal of the Royal United Service Institution in Britain, a think-tank made up of representatives from the armed forces (established in 1831 at the behest of the Duke of Wellington). A study on what to expect in the next war, it focused primarily on the changes that had already taken place and those anticipated for the near future. One contributor was General Ernest Swinton, instrumental in the development of the tank, who discussed among other things ray warfare:

> I imagine from the progress that has been made in the past that in the future we will not have recourse to gas alone, but will employ every force of nature that we can; and there is a tendency at present for progress in the development of the different forms of rays that can be turned to lethal purposes.
> We have x-rays, we have heat rays, we have light rays. H. G. Wells, in his "War of the Worlds," alludes to the heat rays of the Martians, and we may not be so very far from the development of some kinds of lethal ray which will shrivel up or paralyze human beings if they are unprotected.[4]

Writers soon picked up on Swinton's comments, which were reprinted in many sources for some time to come, and by 1921 were using them as support for the concept of such a weapon. One important work suggesting this as a real possibility was Will Irwin's *"The Next War": An Appeal to Common Sense*, in which he quoted the above passage by Swinton.[5] Other references to killing rays can be found in the popular literature of 1921, including Joseph K. Hart's piece, "The Next War," in *The Survey*. The *Literary Digest* issue of 12 November featured an article entitled "Aerial Navies and Armies of Chemists," listing many of the new and fantastic weapons being proposed and developed. According to it, the British already possessed electrical rays that could explode ammunition at great distances and kill the enemy. The next month's issue had an article entitled "'Viper' Weapons," showing a cartoon with "The Modern God of War" holding among other weapons an "X-Ray Killing Outfit." In his book *The Riddle of the Rhine: Chemical Strategy in Peace and War*, Major Victor Lefebure of Britain mentioned the "'electric' death-dealing ray."[6] The most sensational reference to rays that year, however, was in the December 1921 issue of *Popular Science Monthly*. Entitled "Civilization Must Abolish War or War Will Destroy Civilization," the brief article was accompanied by an artist's depiction of how the next war would be fought. It included a drawing of a large apparatus generating some type of destructive ray wrecking a city. The caption reads "At least one great power is known to be at work on a machine by which lethal rays can be directed at the enemy's military and civil centers."[7]

In addition to Swinton, other prominent soldiers commented on the real possibility of death rays. One was French general Eugène Debeney, commandant of the military school at Saint Cyr and newly appointed chief of staff of the army. During the First World War he had held several important posts, culminating in command of the French First Army from December 1917 to the end in 1918. In January 1921 he gave his views on the "next war" to Wythe Williams of Philadelphia's *Public Ledger*. Although asserting that a variety of weapons, including poison gas, would play important roles in a future conflict, he noted that some type of device generating wireless electric rays might prove dominant.[8] In September the *New York Times* printed more of his observations. In an article entitled "The War of Tomorrow," Debeney described what would happen if such a weapon were unleashed in a future conflict: "Under the attack of these electric waves the airplane will fall as though struck by a thunderbolt, the tank will burst into flames, the dreadnought will blow up, poison gas will be dispersed."[9] In a 1923 article in the *Revue des Deux Mondes*, French general Bernard Serrigny gave tacit endorsement to such comments by acknowledging that progress with various weapons, including *"rayons électriques,"* could be expected in the future.[10]

Debeney's statement appeared somewhat prophetic, as new claims for death rays and commentaries on their use in the next war flooded the press. Not long afterward, for example, an employee of the Shaw Wireless Company at Randwick, Australia, announced that he had successfully destroyed metal with an electric ray. Although the distance in his experiment was only two feet, Raymond Allsop believed that with an extended range in future warfare it would prove lethal to an enemy's aircraft, field guns, and battleships.[11] A description of the next war carried in the *Joplin*

Globe in June 1922 included the prediction that "Giant guns with hundred mile ranges will fire electric heat blasts, setting fire to the cornfield and towns in the enemies' country."[12] Writing for the September 1923 issue of *The Nineteenth Century and After*, Professor A. M. Low of Britain described how wars would be fought one hundred years from that time. In discussing the probable development of military technology, he anticipated the dominance of wireless electrical energy, adding that he had already successfully destroyed "a wire at a distance of more than a yard"[13] and that with greater energy one should be able to destroy airplanes. Two articles in *The Argus* of Melbourne commented on Low's salient points, emphasizing the possibility of a "hydro-electrocutor" (high pressure jets of electrified water) as well as mounting ray devices on aircraft. One added that a Mr. G. Russell claimed to have already developed a hydro-electrocutor during the war but had tried unsuccessfully to get the military in both Australia and the United States interested in adopting it.[14]

Newspapers and magazines increasingly carried stories appearing to have scientific endorsement for the plausibility of ray weapons. At a meeting of the American Institute of Electrical Engineers in October 1923, President Harris J. Ryan, a professor of electrical engineering at Stanford University, announced that a new weapon for future wars might result from a discharge of high-voltage electricity. The former vice president of the organization, Professor Robert Sibley, said afterward that "in some future war our scientists may be able to hurl a devastating bolt of lightning across the ocean."[15] The November issue of *Popular Mechanics* also provided an article claiming scientific support for death rays:

> Electricity is to be a strong factor in future wars according to statements made by British experts who see in the discoveries of science a terrible power of destruction from mysterious waves of electric current sent through the air from hidden sources. Motors of airplanes and seacraft will be halted by special waves of wireless broadcast for thousands of miles, and even infantry and cavalry might be thrown into confusion or utterly destroyed by strong jets of water charged with electricity and mixed with acids.... Heat generated wirelessly will shoot out unseen over wide areas, destroying all life without warning.[16]

A newspaper story in December displayed a photograph of a forty-two foot arc of electricity generated by one million volts at the Westinghouse laboratory in Trafford City, Pennsylvania. The caption under the picture included the prediction by scientists "that such man-made lightning bolts will be used in the next war to destroy in one flash whole armies, fleets and cities."[17] The article also mentioned that an Italian scientist by the name of L. G. V. Rota was working with electric currents from the earth and could melt metal up to sixty miles away and possibly knock out radio stations up to a distance of two hundred miles.

Germany, in particular, became a source of death-ray rumors receiving considerable attention in the press. One story circulating in newspapers in late 1921 concerned reports of the Germans having invented an electrical device that could be mounted on airplanes and "kill anything on the earth within a wide circle."[18] The source was Count Luckner, a former commandant of a Danish naval station, whose claim first appeared in the *Berlingske Tidende* of Copenhagen. Several months later, an article came out asserting that German scientists were secretly working on a "?-ray." The Interallied Disarmament Commission had acknowledged the rumor but said it could not act without more information. The writer of the article went on to say that other governments were supposedly trying to develop some type of military ray.[19]

German possession of such a weapon appeared to have become reality in 1923 as bizarre tales circulated in Europe about airplanes flying over a region of Bavaria mysteriously experiencing sudden engine problems, forcing the pilots to make emergency landings in Germany. All were French commercial aircraft of two lines—Paris-Rumania and Paris-Strasburg-Prague-Warsaw. Many people, especially in France, believed rumors that the Germans had created something to interfere with the magneto of an airplane motor and were deliberately targeting French aircraft. One of the first incidents to receive attention in the media, however, was not accompanied by any reference to a ray. In May 1923, German authorities seized a French airplane forced down near Nuremberg and allowed the passengers and pilot to continue their journey by train to Strasbourg. Despite French protests, the German government justified its actions on the grounds that no agreement existed with France permitting its planes to fly over German air space. According to *Le Matin*, however, such incidents did not start until after the French army had begun its occupation of the Ruhr, suggesting these actions were simply a retaliation.[20]

As more information came to light, stories continued to circulate about a possible mysterious German ray, increasing press coverage and spawning more rumors and inviting considerable speculation. One example was a brief news item in *The Daily Chronicle* of London, subsequently carried by other papers, including the *Queensland Times* of Ipswich, Australia. Entitled "Death-Dealing Ray," the article mentioned rumors of Russo-German collaboration on trying to develop such a weapon, an allegation spurred on by unnamed "air experts."[21] Without saying so, the writer was referring to the 1922 Treaty of Rapallo and the clandestine activities of the Reichswehr and the Red Army, for by now it was widely accepted, at least by the media, that the Soviet Union was helping Germany evade some of the military restrictions of Versailles in exchange for technical expertise.[22]

Most of the attention, however, continued to focus on the French airplane mystery. In an article for the *New York Times* in July 1923, reporter Cyril Brown provided a fascinating tale related to him by an unidentified source who had attended a reception at the Belgian legation in Berlin three months before. According to Brown, it all started when several of the guests, including the French consul and a Polish colonel, told his informant that the Germans had developed a wireless means to interfere with the magnetos of airplane and automobile engines, having already experimented successfully in stopping cars on Potsdamerstrasse in Berlin. As rumors began to fly, according to Brown's source, they attracted the attention of the French general staff, which wanted to know if the Germans had indeed perfected some type of ray capable of halting gasoline engines. Stories then circulated that the electric waves could also set airplanes on fire. The *pièce de résistance* of the article, however, was the assertion that the whole thing was bogus, a pure fabrication. Skeptical of the "ray" stories, Brown's informant traced their origin to what he believed was the ultimate source: a Hungarian woman living in Germany and married to a German citizen. Having decided to leave her husband, she tried to get a visa to come to France. To convince French authorities to grant her request, she told them the Germans were responsible for the mysterious emergency landings of French aircraft. In an attempt to get her back, her husband, an engineer with the Siemens-Schuckert Electric Works, had revealed to her the secret of a ray that could stop airplanes. As proof the woman had made up this story, Brown's informant added that an investigation into the five incidents involving the French aircraft revealed normal mechanical problems responsible—not a mysterious ray.[23]

Brown's article raised more questions than it answered. For example, he provided no other supporting evidence that this Hungarian woman, if she existed at all, had made up such a story for the French. There was also no explanation as to why the woman's husband might have thought that revealing a defense secret would make her want to stay with him, nor is there any mention of what happened to her. It is possible that the informant could have fabricated the whole thing, but Brown appears to have accepted it without reservation, having not supplied any corroborating information from other sources. It is somewhat curious, moreover, that newspaper and

2. The Catalyst Years, 1919–1924   55

magazine articles about the French airplanes forced down over Bavaria continued to appear throughout 1923 and on into 1924 without any reference to Brown's piece in the *New York Times*.

Some of these articles, however, expressed strong doubt about any type of wireless, electrical waves being responsible for the emergency airplane landings in Germany. One skeptic was Frenchman Charles Nordmann, a frequent contributor of articles on military aviation. Writing in *Le Matin* in August 1923, he rejected the "ray" explanation, for he pointed out the view generally accepted by scientists that any type of wireless beam would have no effect on a properly shielded engine.[24] French aeronautical engineer E. Nicolet also expressed skepticism in a piece for *L'Écho de Paris* in December 1923. He asserted that all eight instances of engine failure could be attributed to normal mechanical problems and not the result of a mysterious ray developed by the Germans. He went on to explain in technical terms why such a weapon was virtually impossible. Although Nicolet admitted the plausibility of an electric beam disrupting the ignition system of a motor, he argued that to project it over a long distance would require huge amounts of energy. This, he said, was beyond current technological capabilities.[25] French inventor F. Honoré, writing for *L'Illustration* the same month, also discounted the "ray theory" because only twelve airplanes (according to his information) out of more than six hundred flights had experienced difficulties.[26]

Despite the skepticism of many scientists and aviation experts, the popular media continued to generate sensationalism and confusion about the story during the latter part of 1923. In a lengthy article in the *Dundee Courier* of Scotland in September, the writer, identified simply as "WS," acknowledged that no effective military ray had yet been proved to exist but asserted that it was highly probable for such a weapon to be perfected sooner or later. One reason for his optimism was that, as he said, scientists had already proved theoretically that telluric currents (rays emanating from the earth) could "melt heavy masses of metals at a distance of 60 miles."[27] Perhaps, he added, the Germans had succeeded in controlling such a power. A slightly different slant came from a correspondent for London's *Daily Chronicle*, who wrote that the Germans' aim was not simply to disrupt the magnetos of airplanes. Instead, they sought to develop a powerful beam capable of guiding pilotless "flying bombs" to a designated point, presumably over a city, and then shutting off the engines, causing the explosives to do their nasty work below.[28] Another view was that the Germans had dirigibles emitting wireless signals to disable airplanes. As reported in the *Mansfield News* of Ohio, the French secret service now believed this rumor to be true. The article included an artist's drawing of a dirigible crew operating a ray gun and targeting an airplane.²⁹

The writer of one piece in the *New York Times* seemed oblivious to what had been going on for quite some time. In a front-page article on 22 November, he reported a British newspaper had recently set off a controversy by asserting that the emergency landings of eight French airplanes flying over Bavaria had been caused by a German ray. He also said the editor of *La Liberté* had that day published a story dismissing the possibility of a German wireless beam while putting forth an equally sensational claim. The editor stated that the principle of such a capability was real, for he had actually witnessed a French inventor's successful experiments in stopping the motors of three cars on the streets of Paris. In an even more bizarre twist, the *New York Times* article added in tantalizing fashion a report about a French lieutenant who had supposedly developed a similar apparatus only to have his proposal squelched by a jealous superior officer.³⁰ As was often the case, the *New York Times* did not provide sources or any more details, leaving the reader to wonder what happened to the lieutenant's alleged invention.

The following day this newspaper carried two somewhat contradictory stories. In one the writer said that American army officials did not believe the reports because investigations in both France and Germany revealed nothing to substantiate the claims. The other article repeated the gist of another story from *Liberté*, in which a spokesman for the French Air Ministry confirmed that the French airplanes in question had simply experienced normal mechanical difficulties. According to his information, the Germans were experimenting with wireless rays but had been successful so far only in halting automobile engines in close proximity to the generating device. He went on to say that the French government was greatly interested in pursuing the possibility of developing some type of electronic means of stopping airplane engines and "is in touch with successful experiments which are being carried along similar lines."³¹ With a single statement to the press he dismissed one rumor but lent credence to another, equally sensational one, a point not missed by the press.

Some of the media now presented the story about a mysterious ray as an established fact. One such assertion appearing in December in *The Register* of Sandusky, Ohio, was that the French minister's comment had put to rest any skepticism toward the feasibility of such a device.³² Another newspaper article cited as support for this view Sir Oliver Lodge, a prominent British physicist, who had said that it would be possible to develop a means to interfere with the magneto of an engine.³³ The same month

Popular Mechanics featured an article also strongly suggesting that the claims of French airplanes brought down by immobilizing rays were in fact true. According to the magazine, there were thirty such incidents and, more important, British scientists believed that some type of ray capable of damaging aircraft had actually been developed. The writer repeated the conventional view of a ray designed to interfere with the ignition system of the airplane engine but added the possibility of some type of reflector concentrating heat energy on the target. *Popular Mechanics* claimed that a pilot of one of the airplanes in question had reported finding a "mysterious hole in the oil tank, and the solder on the piping ... melted."[34]

Support for the allegations concerning the airplane mystery also came from a related story of a purported German experiment with rays. This occurred sometime in the fall of 1923 and involved the radio station at Nauen. Located not far from Berlin, this facility had been set up prior to the war and had become Germany's main sending center for wireless radio communications. As reported in the *Los Angeles Times* and circulated in many local U.S. newspapers in November and December, a group of people was invited to the installation but warned that their cars might stop running. As the motorcade approached Nauen, the engines of the cars did indeed stop. The explanation was that powerful radio waves had "killed" the magnetos.[35] A later newspaper article retelling the story added more intrigue to the mystery by mentioning that the motorists had been told of future experiments on the engines of airplanes, electric trains, and submarines.[36] According to another newspaper, the German government had apparently wanted to keep this secret safe, for the director at Nauen was livid that the story had leaked out and subsequently tried to downplay the incident. Reporters were told that the cars had been prepared in advance for receiving the wireless signal, and therefore this did not represent anything new. According to the newspaper, however, a German technician had informed the passengers in the cars that Nauen had a new and powerful ray.[37]

The French airplane mystery had another strange twist, one that included Giulio Ulivi popping up again in the news. In one article appearing in 1923, the writer described the controversial story of French airplanes being forced down over Bavaria but added new information as well as some highly speculative assertions. Among those were that the French had come to believe the rumors surrounding the transmitting station at Nauen and the alleged incident involving the experiment stopping car engines. According to unnamed French secret service agents, "The Germans have invented or discovered a new vibration of tremendously high frequency, capable of being transmitted by wireless."[38] The writer went on to speculate that such a weapon could be mounted on dirigibles and used to take down airplanes. In support of this assertion, he added statements by scientists Oliver Lodge and A. M. Low that gave credence to the plausibility of a ray capable of short-circuiting the magnetos of gasoline engines. For more confirmation, the article mentioned that Ulivi was continuing to conduct experiments in Italy, suggesting his F-rays were still taken seriously by many people: "Ulivi's projector is said to have a range of fourteen to fifteen miles, and an airplane, dirigible, battleship, or any other engine of war containing gases which comes within its range, according to some claims, is immediately annihilated by an explosion or series of explosions."[39] The newspaper cited an interview in which Ulivi explained how his F-rays worked and how his principles were in accord with accepted laws of physics. The article also displayed artists' renderings of wireless ray weapons being operated by military personnel and directed at enemy aircraft and ships at sea, the latter vulnerable to rays exploding the powder in their magazines.

One of the most comprehensive descriptions of the story involving the French airplanes appeared in the February 1924 issue of *The Literary Digest* under the title "Can Aero Engines Be Stopt by a Mysterious Ray?" The article made reference to many of those that had appeared in the *New York Times*, French newspapers, and other sources. It did not, however, mention Brown's "Hungarian woman theory." Although retelling much the same story found in previous writings, including objections to such a ray device raised by scientists and aviation experts, *The Literary Digest* added another provoking piece to the puzzle. This was the claim by Professor Oswald Flamm, a preeminent German scientist and naval construction expert. In an interview for the *New York Tribune*, according to *The Literary Digest*, Flamm confirmed Germany had developed "a certain new force." He explained that German physicists had discovered a marvelous new power—certain mysterious rays which had the remarkable property of being able to put land artillery, battleships, airplanes, and all moving motors out of action at a considerable range and perform other uncanny feats on various kinds of mechanisms employed in modern warfare. To substantiate this claim, Flamm also described a test of this ray in South Germany similar to the one at Nauen mentioned above. Traveling in four cars, he and several other scientists had arranged for all of the automobiles to be halted at a precise spot along the road. The chauffeurs, who had been kept in the dark about the experiment, got out and tried to determine why the engines had stopped, but they could not find any reasonable mechanical cause.[40] *The Literary Digest* added, however, that Flamm's reputation had not protected him from criticism in this matter. Dr. Lee de Forest, one of the leading American experts on radio, commented that "Flamm's other name is Flimm."[41] De Forest had been in Germany shortly after the stories began about the French aircraft. He rejected the idea of a mysterious ray as the cause, for he had concluded the incidents were due to normal mechanical problems and the type of wireless signal supposedly responsible was beyond the reach of current technology. Although media speculation continued, another story soon eclipsed the airplane mystery and took center stage.

Harry Grindell Matthews

The "death ray" phenomenon received its greatest media attention with the claims made by the English inventor Harry Grindell Matthews, for they provoked widespread public discussion and even became a topic for debate on the floor of the House of Commons. Grindell Matthews had served with a constabulary unit in South Africa during the Boer War and had afterward become engaged in the developing phenomenon of radio telephony. In 1912 he received an invitation to Buckingham Palace to demonstrate for Queen Mary a wireless telephone that he had invented.[42] In 1920 he announced that he had succeeded in making film with sound and was looking into the possibility of television. With these and other accomplishments, Grindell Matthews established a reputation for himself as a credible inventor with some degree of notoriety.

One of his most impressive feats before the death ray, however, occurred in December 1915 during the First World War, when he successfully demonstrated remote control of a power-driven model boat and wirelessly exploded a mine. This was a classified event not revealed until the publication of *The Moon Element* in 1924 by Grindell Matthews's assistant, E. E. Fournier D'Albe,[43] whereupon the story quickly appeared in newspapers. Among the dignitaries present at this demonstration were Admiral Lord Fisher, the architect of Britain's naval reform prior to the war, First Lord of the Admiralty Arthur Balfour,[44] and the Chancellor of the Exchequer, Reginald McKenna, along with army and other naval representatives. The purpose of the secret exercise was to prove that remote control was possible and could lead to the development of a guided aerial torpedo to combat the German zeppelin menace. The event took place on Penn Pond in Richmond Park in London on 7 December. A model power-driven boat,

Dawn, served as the platform for the test. Grindell Matthews attached a selenium pilot to one of the funnels, enabling the vessel to be controlled by a searchlight. After about three quarters of an hour navigating here and there on the pond, the *Dawn* fired its small gun by remote control. In a second test, a mine outfitted with a selenium relay and a lens four inches in diameter was exploded by means of a searchlight beam directed at it. The visitors were greatly impressed by what they had witnessed and, as a result, Grindell Matthews received £25,000 from the British government. The deal made to him included the promise of £250,000 once he successfully developed the remote-controlled aerial torpedo, but this invention did not come to fruition.[45] Nevertheless, the inventor had established himself as a credible scientist.

When Grindell Matthews announced in late 1923 and early 1924 that he was working on a wireless means of transmitting considerable power over great distances and that it could be used as a formidable weapon, especially against aircraft, people took notice. Public concern over terrifying descriptions of the devastating impact of airpower in the "next war" and the recent reports of French airplanes being forced down over Germany by some type of invisible ray heightened interest in his claims. In fact he said he began work on his version as a result of reading about the airplane mystery in the newspapers. One of Grindell Matthews's first public appearances came on 15 April 1924 when he was the keynote speaker at a luncheon of the Foreign Press Association held at the Café Royal in London. Citing overwork and shyness at public speaking, he had one of his colleagues read his address. He reviewed for his listeners his work for the British government during the Great War, explaining in some detail how he had accomplished the feat of remote control and how he intended to improve upon harnessing the transmission of electrical energy over great distances. He made reference to the idea, already proposed by others,[46] of creating a path of conductivity through the air along which electricity would travel. In his address he did not speculate on how this could be used as a weapon, suggesting merely that it might "make war impossible."[47]

He had, however, on other occasions made more specific claims as to what his invisible ray could do and had performed demonstrations for laymen. According to *Time*, Grindell Matthews stated that it had the potential to stop airplane engines and even to set fire to the wings. He also asserted "that in the near future machine guns will be found only in museums."[48] As reported in the *Mercure Africain* of Algiers, one of Grindell Matthews's assistants told the press that this "heat ray" (*rayon thermique*) could destroy an airplane in about five seconds and annihilate an army just as easily.⁴⁹ The inventor's demonstrations and statements had apparently impressed some people with the potential of this device.

News of his claims reached Winston Churchill, who was anxious about the growth of airpower and the destruction that could be visited on cities and civilian populations in a future war. In a letter to his close friend and scientific advisor, Professor Frederick Alexander Lindemann, and dated 21 April 1924, Churchill wrote: "I wish you would make enquiries about the man who is said to have discovered a ray which will kill at a certain distance. I meet people who say that it can actually be seen to kill mice etc. It may be all a hoax, but my experience has been not to take 'No' for an answer."⁵⁰ The possibility of such a weapon and his concerns about the near future led Churchill to publish the essay entitled "Shall We Commit Suicide?" for *Nash's Pall Mall Magazine* in September. In it, he warned of the increasing terror of the application of science to warfare and referenced death rays.⁵¹

News of Grindell Matthews and his diabolical invention had also reached beyond the British Isles. In addition to extensive coverage by American and French newspapers, a somewhat detailed account of his claims appeared in the *Berliner Tagblatt*, which was reproduced in the Viennese newspaper, the *Neue Freie Presse* on 10 April. The German reporter had obtained his information from several British papers, including the *Star* of London. He included the story about Grindell Matthews having killed a mouse at a distance of sixty-four feet (the length of his laboratory) and that of an assistant straying too close to the ray and losing consciousness for twenty-four hours. The reporter also told his readers the full power of the apparatus was such that "the rays could be sent out to a height of five English miles and to a radius of 50 miles so that within this area nothing could live."⁵²

Interest in his "death ray" increased, for newspapers reported that Grindell Matthews had managed to attract the notice of business enterprises in England and in France. One was the Chantiers du Rhône Company, an engineering firm in Lyon. Eugène Royer, its director and an inventor himself, was offering Grindell Matthews an opportunity to work in the most up-to-date facilities to develop his ray into a potent military weapon. A French syndicate had supposedly put up 3,000,000 francs to fund the project.⁵³ At the invitation of Royer, Grindell Matthews traveled to France and took a tour of the plant before going on to Paris. His notoriety was such that *Le Matin* referred to him as a "Jupiter moderne."⁵⁴ In his hotel in the French capital, the inventor held an interview session for the press. To a reporter from the *New York Times* on 20 May, Grindell

Matthews described his relationship with the French company, emphasizing that this was strictly a business offer from the private sector and that the French government was not involved. According to Grindell Matthews, he was still free to deal with anyone and that he hoped ultimately to gain the collaboration of both the British and French governments.[55]

In the interview, Grindell Matthews also described in a little more detail the capabilities of his ray. According to him, it "may become possible to put the whole of an enemy army out of action, destroy any force of airplanes attacking a city or paralyze any fleet venturing within a certain distance of the coast by the invisible rays."[56] He claimed that his apparatus was limited to four miles but that with continued experimentation he should be able to expand its destructive radius to about eight miles, far less than that mentioned in the *Berliner Tagblatt*. Grindell Matthews underscored the importance of such a device by reminding the reporter—and therefore the public—that London had been subjected to bombing during the Great War and that his invention could make the island nation safe from air attack in a future war. The reporter then asked him about the rumors concerning the Germans and their possession of some type of mysterious ray. Grindell Matthews said he believed that the stories were true but added that the Germans had not managed to control it well because they utilized too much electrical energy—two hundred watts of power. He said that he would limit his experiments to one hundred watts.[57] His stay in France was interrupted, however, because of pressing concerns in London.

News of his claims had by now invited a discussion of the death ray in Parliament. In the House of Commons on 23 May, several members queried William Leach, the Under-Secretary for Air, regarding the government's position on working with Grindell Matthews. Although Leach divulged only that the government was in communication with him,[58] events moved quickly. The Air Ministry had in fact been in contact with the inventor as far back as February and had offered him the opportunity to give a demonstration, but he had declined it.[59] While in Paris, however, Grindell Matthews had been persuaded by one of his supporters to return to London to visit with Air Vice-Marshal Sir Geoffrey Salmond, the Air Member for Supply and Research on the Air Council. This meeting took place on Saturday, 24 May, and Grindell Matthews agreed to conduct a demonstration for representatives of the armed forces and government at his laboratory.[60]

He performed for his special visitors on the following Monday. Grindell Matthews used his apparatus to turn on an Osglim electric lamp and to stop the engine of a small motorcycle at a distance of about fifteen yards. One of those present was Major Harry E. Wimperis, Acting Director of Scientific Research at the Air Ministry, who reported back to Salmond. According to the *Times*, he and the others did not seem that impressed, for such a limited demonstration scarcely resembled the claims made in the press by the inventor.[61] One reason for this lack of enthusiasm was that Wimperis and two others had stepped in front of the ray and suffered no ill effects. The inventor told the press later that they had not placed themselves in the direct path and that the power being generated at the time was insufficient to harm a human.[62] Another reason for the Air Ministry's coolness toward Grindell Matthews and his death ray was that, according to one of its spokesmen, Britain already possessed a ray capable of stopping an airplane engine—a remarkable admission—but that a means to shield the motor from it had also been developed. Indicating that this knowledge would probably become available to other countries, the representative said the Air Ministry was hoping that Grindell Matthews's ray could penetrate any shield.[63] *Le Matin* had a different version of the results of the tests, however, saying that Wimperis seemed pleased with Grindell Matthews's efforts, giving the inventor the impression that he could expect a favorable decision by the government. It added, however, that he had that evening received notification of a request for another demonstration.[64]

Officials at the Air Ministry asked Grindell Matthews to perform it under their supervision. They wanted him to use his device to stop the engine of a larger motorcycle to be supplied by the government. If all went well, he would receive £1000. The government would then have the option of two weeks to decide if it wanted to do business with him. Grindell Matthews was not satisfied with such an arrangement and once again departed for France,[65] supposedly because of the more lucrative deal with the Chantiers du Rhône Company.

A somewhat comical episode occurred at this juncture. Grindell Matthews had already found three English investors willing to back him financially, and they had signed a contract. When these men learned that he was now trying to do business with others, they got a judge to issue an injunction forbidding Grindell Matthews to leave the country. Arriving at his home and finding him gone, they hurried to the airport at Croydon, only to see his plane lifting off the runway bound for Paris. Other visitors to his residence that day were Major Wimperis and Wing Commander J. T. A. Bowen, sent by the Air Ministry to see if some kind of deal could be arranged. They, too, had just missed him.[66]

Yet the saga of Grindell Matthews and his death ray continued to take twists and turns, always keeping him in the public eye. Over the next several weeks, he seemed to play a little game, keeping the press and the British public guessing as to what country would get his death ray. He continually stated that he hoped he could do business with the British government but that he also had to consider a deal with the Chantiers du Rhône Company. Grindell Matthews would indicate that an English firm would manufacture his weapon but then there would be reports that he was going to do business with the French after all. Later, rumors would circulate that he was secretly negotiating with American representatives.

These developments made Grindell Matthews and his "death ray" an even greater *cause célèbre* in the press and in Parliament. Given the "next war" state of mind and the imagined terrors, people certainly did not want to see a weapon of such potential being sold to a foreign country. A newspaper campaign ensued to keep the secrets of the death ray in England.[67] In the House of Commons, Under-Secretary Leach replied to questions as to why the government was not at present doing business with Grindell Matthews. Leach said he really had no information beyond what was in the official announcement released to the press. He simply reiterated for the members that Grindell Matthews had failed to provide the necessary demonstration requested by the Air Ministry. Lord Curzon asked him if it were true that the Royal Air Force already had a ray that could accomplish what had been witnessed in Grindell Matthews's laboratory. Leach answered in the affirmative,[68] but his reply did not mean that Britain had such a weapon. He meant simply that stopping a gasoline motor and lighting an electric lamp wirelessly from a short distance could be accomplished rather easily.

By this time many people, including prominent scientists in Britain and the United States, had begun to speak out, expressing considerable skepticism about Grindell Matthews's claims. In a letter to the *Times*, Lord Birkenhead expressed strong doubt about the ray's capabilities and stated that the government should certainly not finance Grindell Matthews until the strictest scientific standards had determined the credibility of such a device. He also commented scornfully: "That an unknown amateur should stumble upon an epoch-making discovery is about as likely as that a child of five should defeat either a champion chess-player or Mlle. Lenglen."[69] Sir Richard Gregory, president-elect of the Southeastern Union of Scientific Societies, addressed its twenty-ninth congress, taking issue with Grindell Matthews and his supporters. He said that the inventor had not accomplished anything that any physicist could not do, referring to the short distance traversed by the ray. Much of Gregory's concern, however, was with the attitude of the newspapers and the general public who "seemed to blame scientific people for adopting the attitude of being absolutely incredulous of anything until it was proved. Scientists were not prepared to give a Stock Exchange quotation on a box of mysteries."[70] Physicist W. L. Severinghaus of Columbia University labeled Grindell Matthews's rays "fishy," while Professor R. W. Wood of Johns Hopkins scoffed at the idea that rays could bring down airplanes and zeppelins. Wood even later offered to test the death ray and let a panel of scientists evaluate the results.[71]

French scientists also weighed in on Grindell Matthews, some as far back as April. One was Paul Langevin, quoted by *Le Figaro* early that month as being extremely skeptical of his claims, saying that physicists were well aware of some of the simple operations with rays accomplished by the Englishman but that stopping the magneto of airplane engines was out of the question.[72] One Frenchman was willing to give Grindell Matthews a fair hearing before passing judgment despite his initial skepticism. This was Georges Urbain, a professor at the Sorbonne.[73] Most were not so accommodating. Édouard Branly, regarded as one of the foremost physicists in France, said in an interview for the *New York Times* the current level of scientific development was such that no known ray could produce the results claimed by the Englishman. When asked by the reporter if it would be possible for someone, such as Grindell Matthews, to make a scientific breakthrough, Branly responded, "No. Moreover, when scientists make a discovery of such tremendous importance as that claimed by Mr. Matthews they do not make so much noise about it before they have proved it."[74] The French inventor F. Honoré also raised some doubts. Writing for the magazine *L'Illustration* in May, he described a meeting with the Englishman when he was in Paris. After seeing the standard performance, one of Honoré's colleagues asked Grindell Matthews if any British scientists had been present at one of these demonstrations. The answer was "Yes, all the outstanding scientists!"[75] Honoré then asked pointblank for some names, but Grindell Matthews would not divulge any, leaving the Frenchmen skeptical as to his claims.

An article in *The New Republic* in July provided an analysis of the reasons for the "death-ray" phenomenon as well as an explanation for why it was a pipe dream. Entitled "The Myth of the Death Ray," its author was none other than E. E. Fournier D'Albe, Grindell Matthews's assistant at the time of the demonstration of remote control mentioned above. By now he had broken with his former colleague and had joined the ranks of the critics. He expressed the view shared by others that the widespread support for Grindell Matthews by the British press and public rested on fear. The all-too-vivid memories of the Great War and the horrors foretold for the next one made people want to believe that some new device, some new weapon, would protect them from such devastation. D'Albe also said that previous reports of French airplanes flying over Germany experiencing engine problems allegedly the result of an invisible ray had reinforced this hope even more. He went on to acknowledge that some killing rays might have been generated and proved effective on small animals or objects such as motorcycle engines but that they had been so only at close ranges. The central limiting factor was the amount of energy that must be generated to project a ray at a distance sufficient for it to be useful as a weapon. D'Albe concluded his article with a firm rejection of the need for concern:

> There is no Ray Peril.
> And even if it should ever arise, there would be no need for panic. All known radiations have been discovered by physicists working serenely in their laboratories, with no hope of reward except a rare prize and the appreciation of their fellows. It is they who are the pathfinders. And if an enemy of mankind should find a new path and use his knowledge to the detriment of his fellow-men, the physicist would soon find a way of neutralizing his activities.[76]

Grindell Matthews, however, had many supporters. In the *Time* article in April previously mentioned, the magazine added that Nikola Tesla and Professor Bergen Davis of Columbia University considered such a device possible.[77] A piece in *The Outlook* on 30 April also suggested that the basic idea of a wireless transfer of concentrated energy was plausible despite some of the sensationalist exaggerations in the press.[78] Austrian naval captain Emo Tescovich agreed. As reported in the *Neue Freie Presse* of Vienna, he said that although scientists had to remain skeptical until it was actually proved, one should keep an open mind and not dismiss it out of hand.[79] *The World* newspaper of New York sent one of its reporters, Arthur E. Mann, to England to witness one of Grindell Matthews's standard demonstrations—stopping a motorcycle engine and killing a mouse. As for its application on the battlefield, Grindell Matthews told Mann that one would not have to kill the enemy, for "it would be quite easy to graduate the electric power used so that hostile troops would only be knocked out long enough to effect their capture."[80] The magazine *Popular Mechanics* was also favorably disposed to Grindell Matthews, as evidenced by an article entitled "'Death Ray' Is Carried by Shafts of Light" in its August

1924 issue. It seemed to accept the inventor's assertion that some type of beam produced a path of conductivity for an electrical charge that could be transmitted over a great distance.[81] *Popular Science Monthly* sided with him as well, for one of its writers, Frederic Mortimer Delano, went to Britain to witness one of the inventor's demonstrations and returned impressed. In his article, "Man's Most Terrible Invention," appearing in the August issue, Delano described what was the standard fare dished up by Grindell Matthews to all his visitors: stopping a motorcycle engine, exploding a small amount of gunpowder, turning on a light bulb, and killing a mouse. As usual, the Englishman did not divulge any technical data about his ray other than it produced a carrier beam permitting electricity to flow from the apparatus to the target. Delano acknowledged that it was too soon to tell if a genuine death-ray weapon would become reality, but he believed that the principle of wireless transfer of energy was established. Developing the ability to project it at a great distance would be the challenge.[82]

Probably the most favorable attention given to Grindell Matthews was a lengthy article appearing in the *New York Times* on 1 June. Author Samuel J. McCoy presented a fairly balanced account of the issue by providing both the concerns expressed by a number of prominent scientists and the plausible arguments supporting the idea of a death ray. In addition to R. W. Wood of Johns Hopkins and W. L. Severinghaus of Columbia, McCoy cited other skeptics such as Max von Laue, a Nobel Prize winner for physics, and Michael I. Pupin, head of the Department of Electro-Mechanics at Columbia. The most important part of the article, however, was the author's interview of Dr. Alfred N. Goldsmith, head of the Department of Electrical Engineering in the College of the City of New York and Chief Radio Broadcasting Engineer for the Radio Corporation of America.

Goldsmith described for McCoy the five known rays, their properties, and to what extent they could be the force in Grindell Matthews's invention. The five were ultraviolet, X-rays, radium, heat, and high frequency or radio frequency electric field. Goldsmith dismissed X-rays and radium but regarded the ultraviolet ray as the most likely one used by Grindell Matthews because of its ability to be a conductor of electricity—the damaging force. It was by now a well-established scientific principle that ultraviolet light ionized the air as it passed through, providing a path of conductivity for electrical current. Other possibilities included the radio high frequency, with Goldsmith citing the experiment conducted at Nauen described above, and "artificial lightning." Regarding the latter, Goldsmith referred to the work of Giuseppe Faccioli at Pittsfield, Massachusetts, who had been able to generate 2,000,000 volts of electricity and produce a lightning bolt fourteen feet in length.[83] Goldsmith also reminded McCoy of the work of Tesla, especially his experiment in Colorado Springs years earlier.

One example given by Goldsmith to lend plausibility to some type of weapon generated by a ray was an incident that occurred in Times Square the previous winter. He said that a truck advertising heaters had mounted a large reflector emitting heat and pointed it at pedestrians as it cruised back and forth. Despite the fact that it was a chilly day, Goldsmith said that they became noticeably uncomfortable from the heat of the reflector. A much more powerful reflector could therefore be used as a weapon. According to Goldsmith, "It is strictly possible that the wings of an unwary aviator approaching too close might be made to burst into flames by its means."[84] Goldsmith was willing to keep an open mind about Grindell Matthews's claims, but he did say that the Englishman should disclose the details of how his device worked—which was what scientists normally did.

In response to the rising criticism directed against him, Grindell Matthews issued a statement to the press in early June, claiming that the British government had reneged on the original agreement, which called for one demonstration only. He said that it then requested three more—one for each of the representatives from the armed forces—and that he had complied. He charged that the government then dragged matters out and did not get back to him with an offer in a timely fashion. Since he had also already promised to talk to the French, the British government's actions left him no choice but to leave without having settled anything.[85]

While the spotlight was on Grindell Matthews and his dealings with the British and the French, rumors circulated that he was also trying to make a deal with the Americans. According to the *New York Times*, he had supposedly been in contact with the Navy Department, an allegation denied by U.S. authorities. The article speculated that American naval attachés in London and Paris had simply been looking into Grindell Matthews's claims as a matter of routine, for they were supposed to be alert to any military developments, and their activities had given rise to the rumors.[86] At the same time another newspaper story alleged that army personnel had been monitoring the situation. As reported in *The Coshocton Tribune* of Ohio, not only were they doing so but an American scientist had already developed such a device capable of killing "animal life at a distance of 40 feet." Furthermore, a spokesman for the U.S. Army, Colonel W. I. Westervelt, stated that "Rays similar to those invented by Professor Matthews and the French so-called thermic ray are clearly understood in the United States."[87] The matter became less clear when *Le Matin* ran a story in which Grindell Matthews claimed to have received offers from the

United States and Germany for his death ray. *Le Matin* printed the text of a letter from a Lawrence Timpson, who told the British inventor that he was acting on behalf of the American government. Grindell Matthews declined this offer but made no comment regarding the German proposal, indicating simply that he had not planned to sell his invention to any foreign government.[88]

Not long after, Grindell Matthews did travel to the United States to talk with unnamed parties there. On his arrival in July, however, he told the press that he was not there to sell his device to the United States government, nor to any other government except that of Britain. His purpose, rather, was to locate some "electrical records" and to recuperate from his failing vision. He claimed to have lost the sight in one eye and was losing it in the other one as well. When asked about the military applications of his death ray—a term he considered inaccurate, Grindell Matthews repeated his earlier claims that the electric beam could stun armies and set fire to cities. He still declined, however, to divulge the properties of his invention on the grounds that he needed to protect its secrets for the time being until he had enough proof "to convince electrical experts that I have discovered a new force."[89] Despite his initial comments to the press about the reason for his visit to the United States, one newspaper reported that some American scientists tested his ray on Long Island. It failed even to kill the mosquitoes inhabiting the marshes.[90]

The possibility of doing business with the Americans received another setback when, according to a story in the *Times* in September, J. Frederick Richardson presented to a select committee of the U.S. House of Representatives a report in which he attacked the very concept of a death ray. Richardson had gone to Europe for the purpose of gathering information and ascertaining the veracity of claims made for this device. He concluded that no such weapon existed or any known form of energy that could be harnessed for the purpose of stopping the engines of airplanes. Richardson also commented in his report that the stories about a ray forcing French aircraft to make emergency landings in Germany had no basis in fact.[91]

Despite criticism that his death ray was either a hoax or just bad science, Grindell Matthews continued to attract favorable attention from the press. After his first visit to the United States, he went to the island of Flatholme off the coast of France to continue his research. During this time, he had a film made showing the death ray in operation in his laboratory. As reported in the *New York Times* on 3 November, the motion picture, which had opened at the Rialto Theatre, showed stills of Grindell Matthews turning on a light bulb, causing a small amount of gunpowder to flash, killing a rat in a cage, and stopping a motorcycle engine. At the end of the film, a picture from the Great War of an airplane crashing in flames was used to depict how the death ray could be effective as a military weapon.[92] Commenting on his research activities on Flatholme, newspapers included a picture of two men in protective suits setting up the death ray for a demonstration.[93] One article entitled "Will 'Death Rays' Destroy Armies and Make Aircraft Useless?" alleged that Grindell Matthews and his assistants had increased the range of the machine to three thousand feet. Furthermore, he announced that he was planning to return to the United States in December to put on a demonstration that would include using his weapon to kill a cow or a horse. An added feature would be an American pilot—with parachute—flying his plane as a target for the death ray.[94] Although a second trip to the United States in December 1924 did not produce anything significant, Grindell Matthews returned to Britain in early 1925 and announced that he had sold his death ray to "unnamed" American buyers.[95] As with his other claims about financial deals, this one did not materialize either.

Although Grindell Matthews ultimately failed to do business with the British, French, or Americans regarding his death ray, he nevertheless remained in the public eye almost up to the time of his death in 1941. During this period, he continued to be regarded, at least by the press, as a serious inventor who had created a death ray, for many subsequent newspaper articles on the "next war" and scientific developments mentioned him in this manner. Spending much of this time in seclusion in Wales, Grindell Matthews also expanded his inventive repertoire, working on aerial torpedoes to defend Britain against air raids, speculating on a rocket plane capable of going to the moon, and trying to develop a means of detecting submarines. Aside from these projects, he ensured continued media attention by real inventions: a luminaphone which played music by light, a phonofilm (the first device to produce talking movies), and a powerful searchlight beam to project images in the night sky or against buildings.[96] Yet, almost every newspaper article about his other activities still described him as the inventor of the death ray despite the fact that he had not been able to produce anything that could actually serve as a weapon.

The Impact of Grindell Matthews

The death-ray phenomenon did not end with the failure of Grindell Matthews; rather, it seemed as if the publicity surrounding him acted as a catalyst for others to come forward with new claims. A few inventors had already been at work when his story attracted the attention of the media, but others appear to have been more in the "copycat" category to get their names in the newspapers. There were also claims bearing a degree of official imprimatur, as a number of governments apparently did not want to admit that they were not diligently at work on some type of military ray or, at least, following its development elsewhere.

In addition to statements by British and French officials suggesting that their governments already possessed some type of death ray or were closely monitoring its development, two other countries quickly followed suit. The most dramatic salvo was fired from Germany. As reported by the *Chicago Tribune* on 24 May 1924 and circulated in many other newspapers, Reinhold Wulle, a journalist-turned politician, informed the Reichstag to the effect that Germany already had "death rays that will bring down airplanes, halt tanks on the battlefields, ruin automobile motors and spread a curtain of death like the gas clouds of the recent war...."[97] Wulle had received information about a weapon supposedly invented by German Otto Conrad and a Belgian assistant named Van Carneghem.[98] Not to be outdone, Russia leaked that it, too, had a death ray. According to an article in the *New York Times* on 28 May, an engineer named Grammachikoff had developed a device that could destroy aircraft. Tests supposedly conducted at an air base convinced the Soviet government to begin construction of stations equipped with the ray as a means of anti-aircraft defense. Another capability ascribed to this ray was that of taking out electrical systems on board ships at sea. The article also mentioned there was apparently German assistance with the project,[99] a result of the not-so-secret collaboration between the two countries. There would also be a report several years later that a German scientist working for the Russians had developed a similar device.[100]

Some of the stories about death rays emanating from the Soviet Union went beyond the merely questionable to the preposterous. As reported in *The Advertiser* of Adelaide, an electrical engineer in Kiev claimed that his ray could light a cigarette at a considerable distance and that it could melt a sheet of lead at eighty-five feet. In addition, an electrician serving in the Soviet navy was allegedly reprimanded for lighting cigarettes of fellow sailors with his ray when matches were forbidden. He was then imprisoned for setting fire to a canvas tent from ninety-eight feet away.[101]

Stories also surfaced about another Englishman's invention of a death ray, this one concerning Dr. T. F. Wall, Lecturer in Mechanical and Electrical Research at Sheffield University. Announcements appeared in the newspapers even before Grindell Matthews had performed his demonstration for the representatives of the British armed forces, and some of these suggested that the government was considering doing business with Wall. One report indicated that the Japanese were also interested in finding out more about his work.[102] Articles carried in numerous newspapers during the last few days of May revealed a similarity between Wall's claims and those of Grindell Matthews in that his invention would also be capable of halting airplane motors and killing human beings. Wall had even already applied for a patent regarding his ability to transmit wireless energy.[103] In a later statement to the press, however, Wall modified the capabilities of his invention, stating that the ray could probably kill humans but not be able to halt gasoline engines. He continued to assert that his device would be able to defend Britain against air attack and underscored the importance of such a weapon by mentioning that the Germans were assiduously working along the same lines. Wall had studied in Germany before the war and had recently made contact again with some of his friends there who told him that the Germans did possess a ray capable of short-circuiting an engine at a distance of five miles.[104] The connection of a death ray to Wall was modified even further in October. According to a newspaper article, he had shifted his focus to unlocking the power of the atom, and he believed that his death ray would be the best means of generating sufficient energy to accomplish this.[105] By 1925 Wall was apparently disassociating himself from his death ray using electricity and looking more into the possibility of atomic rays serving a military purpose.[106]

Other death-ray inventors came forward in late May and early June. According to one newspaper article, Thomas Frederick John Truss of Sheffield had applied for a patent back in 1906 but the process had stalled. In addition to his earlier work, he had two notebooks containing more recent research and written in Greek characters. This was supposed to help keep his secrets safe. Unfortunately for him and for the defense of Britain, he told the police on 31 May that burglars had broken into his home and stolen all his papers. The *Dundee Courier* bestowed some credibility on Truss by stating that he had once worked with a Professor John Tyndall in conducting research with heat rays.[107] Two other British inventors associated with wireless weapons, William Prior and a man named Raffe, were also mentioned in passing in the newspapers but with little specific information. A brief article in the *Western Daily Press* of Bristol did describe Prior's device as being capable of remote detonation of explosives, and indicated that he planned to give a demonstration for the Air Ministry.[108]

2. The Catalyst Years, 1919–1924

At the same time, a British engineer named John H. Hamill told the press that he was negotiating on behalf of a German scientist to sell a ray to the American military. He claimed that this man, who had to remain anonymous, was the one responsible for successfully stopping the engines of those French airplanes flying over Bavaria the previous year. An additional feature of the German's invention was that ray-generating devices could be mounted on airplanes, thereby greatly increasing their firepower. Hamill said that he had offered to demonstrate this ray to American authorities but that they wanted more time to consider matters. As a result, he said that he might have to go elsewhere and that he had been in contact with a Japanese admiral. One interesting note about this story is that Hamill criticized the work of Grindell Matthews, saying that his claims were ludicrous—no doubt to increase his chances for business by eliminating the competition. Crediting Nikola Tesla as the pathfinder in harnessing the power of electricity, he nevertheless said that scientists were working on means to expand the principles established by him. Hamill asserted that the German scientist's ray operated on a new principle to project electrical energy in concentrated form over a great distance.[109]

One death-ray claim at this time involved a device using lenses and mirrors to concentrate the sun's energy, reminiscent of Maclay's story in the *New York Times* about Lord Dundonald. As described in the *Evening Telegraph and Post* of Dundee, Scotland, in July 1924, a "Professor" Marcel Moreau of California, assisted by his father, had developed an extremely powerful weapon that could generate a temperature of 15,000 degrees Fahrenheit. Directed at a battleship a mile away, the heat ray could burn a hole right through it. The contraption consisted of fifteen hundred mirrors and twenty-two magnifying lenses. According to the article, Moreau had actually constructed three different models, with the two smaller ones having more limited capabilities, including benefits to medicine, such as treating cancer. The two men conducted much of their experimentation in Death Valley, where the sun's rays were the most intense.[110]

Aside from reporting on contemporary announcements, the press dug up stories of claims going back even to pre-war years. Although expressing considerable skepticism, the editors of *The Pathfinder* mentioned one about a French scientist who had supposedly discovered just before the Armistice a "demon ray" more powerful than the one claimed by the British.[111] And in an interview for a newspaper, an Australian army captain named Geake commented on the publicity surrounding Grindell Matthews's ray, which he said was not a novel idea. Geake, who was in charge of the research section of the army during the war, said that he and his staff had tried to develop a ray to stop the engines of tanks. When they discovered how easy it was, they dropped the project because they knew that the Germans would quickly catch on and develop one themselves. Captain Geake also said that engines without magnetos, such as those using diesel, would not be affected by such a ray. He did sympathize somewhat with Grindell Matthews, for he was not sure if the British War Office had been fair in its dealings with the inventor since all too often those at the upper command levels did not appreciate new ideas.[112]

French newspapers commenting on Grindell Matthews in the spring of 1924 asserted that several inventors had already developed something similar. *Le Matin* ran a story on 18 April naming seven dating back to 1908. One of the men, a Monsieur Caldine, was said to have electrocuted mice with his apparatus in 1915, while a Lieutenant Peyvel had supposedly developed in 1917 an electric rifle emitting deadly rays.[113] *Le Phare de Majunga* of Tananarive reported that two Frenchmen, V. A. Hencocque and Henri Schmidt, were prepared to prove with documentation that they had invented a *rayon ardent* in 1915.[114] In June *Le Matin* featured on its front page an interview with a Monsieur Charbonneau, labeled the "father of the infrared ray" because of his research in that area. According to Charbonneau, Grindell Matthews had probably utilized the high frequency, ultrashort wave first pioneered by Tesla. In fact, he said that scientists had known for quite some time how to use this to do all the things demonstrated by the Englishman. Charbonneau even claimed that he had tried in 1918 to develop a means to project electricity as a weapon.[115]

There was also a story in *Le Matin* about an Englishman named E. Mason, who had developed a death ray in 1916 and had tried unsuccessfully to interest the British War Office. According to the article, Mason said his device "could stop internal combustion motors and set fire to inflammable materials."[116] Information about Mason was not altogether clear. The *Nottingham Evening Post* in June 1924 named a George Mason as the man who had been experimenting since 1912 with a ray whose capabilities were identical to those described in *Le Matin*,[117] while back in 1915 a report by W. R. Bennett, carried in the *Sunday Times* of Perth, Australia, mentioned an unnamed English scientist who claimed to have developed a death ray. It, too, had been submitted to the British War Office for evaluation, but no word was as yet forthcoming. Bennett, however, described this ray as possessing more formidable capabilities than the one mentioned in *Le Matin*. It was "more malign ... than a whole fleet of dreadnoughts: a ray which, evolved and directed by one who knew how, might paralyse armies as easily and swiftly as though lightning had blasted their ranks."[118]

The "mystery" of the French aircraft forced down over Bavaria, echoes of Giulio Ulivi, and, especially, the publicity surrounding Harry Grindell Matthews all provided the stimulus for the subsequent wave of stories about death rays that would continue on up to the outbreak of the Second World War. As the next chapter will show, claims for ray weapons of all kinds were made both by individuals and governments, with announcements appearing frequently in the popular media and inviting considerable debate as to their authenticity.

3

The Death-Ray Craze, 1925–1939

The events of 1923 and 1924 with the French airplane "mystery" and the saga of Grindell Matthews opened the floodgates to more death-ray claims that would continue right on up to the Second World War—and beyond. Some were made by private individuals acting alone, many of whom were nothing more than quacks and con men, but there were also those by serious inventors, often with semi-official endorsement. Governments, too, got into the act, periodically releasing statements suggesting that they were supporting some type of research involving death rays. As the fear of another war intensified in the mid–1930s with the rise of Nazi Germany, some of these were seen as propaganda efforts by several of the major powers as a deterrent to a would-be enemy. Despite repeated statements by many scientists who considered the death ray beyond the limits of current technology, stories about its success continued unabatedly during this period, providing the popular media with plenty of fuel to stoke the fires of "next war" anxiety.

Throughout the 1920s and 1930s most of these claims were put forward by individuals usually working alone, occasionally in pairs, in their home workshops. Although some were hucksters who saw opportunities for profit, many were simply amateurs with far greater imagination than genuine understanding of the laws of physics. Like those of previous years, most would attract media attention for only a brief period before fading into obscurity. In 1926, for example, Maurice Francill, described as an "American radio wizard," announced he had created a "radio death ray" that would make war impossible. He told an audience at a radio exposition in Atlanta that he would offer to demonstrate his device on condemned prisoners.¹ There does not appear to be any evidence of state governors asking for his services. Two years later the *New York Times* had a story about a new death ray reportedly developed by unnamed German "scientists" (a ubiquitous but loosely applied term in many cases). According to the article: "If the German reports are correct, the machine operates through a series of waves that when directed at enemy planes put the motors completely out of commission. Neutralized zones would be established in which no plane could 'live' once it had penetrated the zone of death."² Several French newspapers, including *L'Action française*, published in March 1929 the gist of an article from the London *Sunday Chronicle* in which two American "scientists," likewise unnamed, had developed another death ray. Although limited to a range of one hundred meters, this apparatus supposedly could generate one million volts of electrical energy.³ A month later C. H. Melsone-Smith, an engineer with the Pacific Gas and Electric Company in San Francisco, informed the press that Hector M. Hassell, a former wireless instructor in Seattle, had invented a death ray.⁴ According to the description given by Melsone-Smith: "Any one who got in the path of the ray would be instantly snuffed out, the chemical composition of his blood would be changed, and the life cells disintegrated."⁵ An article in the *Lowell Sun* of Massachusetts the same day included an announcement about John T. Martin, the president of the Marjohn Mines Company, having shown stockholders a film of Hassell's ray, which the former employee had developed for use in the mining industry.⁶ In August newspapers ran a story about Dr. Richard Moldinke, an old, bewhiskered New Jersey scientist, who had discovered a "secret formula" of a death ray.⁷ Another American was also reported in 1929 to have developed such a weapon. The *Charleroi Mail* of Pennsylvania featured on its front page the story about Eugene T. Sergi, a twenty-six-year-old employee of the Allenport mill of Pittsburgh Steel Products Company, who had created a device capable of dispensing both rays and deadly gas. Having supposedly started work on his death ray at the age of sixteen, his invention was apparently ready, for his attorneys had sent the necessary patent documents to Washington. In the meantime, the newspaper indicated that professors of science and engineering from Chicago and Pittsburgh might come to Charleroi because of their interest in Sergi's death ray.⁸ And in November of the same year, the Martin brothers of San Francisco announced they had filed for patents on a device capable of discharging an energy beam of three million volts.⁹

Similar news reports continued on into the next decade without letup. One of the first was the case of a German engineer named Youg, who claimed to have invented a ray that could cause a gun to discharge. He planned to make it available to police as an aid in foiling criminals.[10] Another story was that of German engineer and chemist Ludwig Nudl, formerly with Mercedez Benz and the Bosch Company, who was now living in Melbourne, Australia. According to newspapers in 1930, he had developed a ray that completely incinerated a rat, cut through steel sheets, and stopped the ignition systems of moving cars.[11] Two years later a German named Josef Karl Schlosz teamed up with Englishman Cyril Henry Grantham to get permission from the local authorities to demonstrate their death ray at the seaside resort of Blackpool, located north of Liverpool. The plan was to explode a balloon anchored by a cable and floating some six hundred feet above the beach. Schlosz told the press what he and Grantham hoped to accomplish: "The experiment will show what little chance belligerents will have in the next war when by means of the invisible death ray Zeppelins, aeroplanes and balloons will be brought to the ground in flames. By merely operating the death ray, ships will be sunk through the explosion of their own ammunition, and batteries will be blown up without the least difficulty."[12] It does not appear that the demonstration took place. In 1935, there was a brief story about John Kalsey, identified simply as a research worker, who was supposedly building a laboratory in Palo Alto, California, in order to develop a "life or death" ray. Kalsey revealed only that he planned to harness power from the sun.[13] In Ireland, an engineer from Dublin, who wished to remain anonymous, claimed to have invented a ray lethal to living creatures. As reported in the *Nottingham Evening Post* in December 1935, a Mr. Charles Sinclair of Grove Park witnessed a demonstration, saying that the engineer used his ray to kill a flock of low-flying birds.[14] In 1938 Ladislas Papp and Etienne Kokai, two Hungarian inventors from the city of Szeged, reported they had developed an electrical device that could project a lethal ray and kill animals, liquefy glass, and melt steel.[15] Nothing more was heard from them or their invention. One Hungarian was apparently not fortunate enough to exit quietly. According to a "filler" in the *Ogden Standard-Examiner* of Utah in 1936, an eighteen-year-old student in Budapest committed suicide because he was distraught after being unsuccessful in developing a death ray.[16]

Although not a fatality, an English lad of seventeen became the subject of a strange story unfolding in newspapers in 1936. First reports indicated that he had been admitted to Saint Bartholomew's Hospital in London because of stress related to his research with a death ray. According to the accounts, Frank Manning was trying to split infra-red rays into cosmic rays, the effect of which he knew "would kill a man at 3000 yards and stop an aeroplane engine at a mile."[17] Shortly afterward the story changed somewhat, for the young man's father told reporters his son was suffering from "mystery rays" accidentally discovered while working on a television transmitter and receiver. Young Manning began experiencing fainting spells and memory loss. One man assisting him in this research was apparently not exposed to the rays but told reporters that one of Manning's friends was doing so and had also begun to feel ill. A spokesman for the Marconiphone Company offered as a possible explanation that the young men may have been subjected to ultrashort waves, whose physiological effects on humans were still not well understood.[18]

Not long before the start of the Second World War, two unnamed inventors contacted the *San Antonio Light*, which had published an article about a new death ray recently discovered. The men informed the newspaper that they had just developed one far superior and that it would protect the good citizens of San Antonio from Hitler.[19] As these examples indicate, some of the reports involved individuals who enjoyed brief notoriety but then disappeared from the news for lack of concrete results.

Although many of these death-ray claims were submitted by unnamed sources or persons with questionable scientific credentials, occasionally they were associated with some type of official government recognition and therefore acquired a degree of legitimacy, as the example of Grindell Matthews demonstrates. In May 1925 the U.S. Trade Commissioner in Berlin, William T. Daugherty, sent to the Commerce Department a summary of an article about a German death ray called the "heliotaueb." The report stated that "its mysterious waves are capable of paralyzing life for six hours over a distance of forty miles and to an altitude of more than 45,000 feet."[20] A version of the story carried in *Le Gaulois* claimed the device was more powerful than the one of Grindell Matthews and added that the U.S. War Department had expressed interest.[21] At about the same time the French government was apparently looking into an ultraviolet ray for air defense. A report based on laboratory experiments indicated it could cause metal to turn red hot.[22] In a 1925 issue of *Popular Science Monthly*, Truman Stevens invoked the mantra of officialdom in referring to death rays in general: "Scientists, inventors, and military men in active touch with the development of armaments practically are unanimous in the belief that a war of the future will be one of almost inconceivable annihilation. Death swifter than light, riding on waves of electricity and obedient to the will of master minds, they say, will blot out great cities, and even nations, almost in a breath."[23] He cited as one of his authorities the previously mentioned A. M. Low, who had suggested the development of electricity as a weapon back in 1923. In 1926, there was a story about another inventor named Scott, this one a James K. Scott of California, who was reported to have demonstrated his death ray to the U.S. War Department. No word of the results was mentioned. As described in the *Nottingham Evening Post*, its effective lethal range was seven miles. The newspaper added that an unnamed Italian inventor claimed to have one that could kill at seventeen miles.[24] David Sarnoff, the vice president and general manager of the Radio Corporation of America and famous pioneer of broadcasting, suggested that continued research with X-rays and heat rays might one day yield powerful weapons of war. A lieutenant colonel in the Army Signal Corps Reserves at the time, he delivered this message when he spoke at the Army Industrial College in Washington in July 1926.[25] Earlier that year, newspapers reported that A. N. Boyka of the Russian Magnetic Observatory had developed a device to generate heat rays capable of destroying aircraft out to a range of twenty-five miles, a weapon which he said would be made available to the Red Army.[26] Like so many reports in newspapers that failed to acknowledge other connected stories, this one did not mention anything about the Grammachikoff ray supposedly being utilized by the Soviet military. There was a story in 1929 about a ray device capable of remote detonation located somewhere in Melbourne. Although turned down by the Australian Defence Department, an unconfirmed report indicated that the British government was interested in it.[27]

As if a forecast of the Holocaust, there was also a story in 1929 about an anti–Semitic German electrical engineer who promised that his death ray would "purge Berlin of its Jewish population in three minutes."[28] According to newspapers, Albert Brühahn, a member of the veterans group the Stahlhelm, had supposedly developed the plans for a death ray during the World War and in early November 1918 had attracted the interest of German military authorities. They allegedly gave him 26,000 Marks to continue his research, but this ended abruptly with the Armistice. Afterward, during the early years of Weimar, retired Lieutenant General Oskar von St. Ange formed a consortium of Silesian nobles to develop this weapon and gave the inventor a credit of 60,000 Marks to get started. The consortium also made arrangements for Brühahn to use the facilities at the University of Breslau where he would receive help from scientists there. After some time had elapsed and nothing substantial was achieved, the stockholders grew suspicious and investigated. Brühahn was arrested and put on trial for fraud. Convicted, he received a sentence of fifteen months in prison. According to *La Tribune Juive* of Strasburg, Brühahn's plan was to herd all of the Jews of Berlin on to the field at Tempelhof Airport and have an airplane fitted with the death ray unleash its lethal beams on them.[29]

Other death-ray stories bearing some type of official imprimatur continued on into the 1930s. One evoked memories of Giulio Ulivi. In 1931 German scientist Kurt Schimkus announced that he had developed a chemically produced ray. Claiming its effective range to be five hundred feet, he said it was designed to explode artillery shells and other types of ammunition. According to a story in the *New York Times*, Schimkus had successfully detonated submarine mines below the surface of the water as well as cartridges placed underground.[30] As reported in *The Pathfinder* magazine, the German government showed little interest and Schimkus went to the United States to try to sell his device. He supposedly demonstrated it to representatives of the U.S. Army and Navy at the Great Lakes Naval Training Station near Chicago, but nothing came of it. Afterward, it was rumored that local gangsters had at first been interested but seemed disappointed that Schimkus's weapon was not labeled a "death ray." The scientist had called it an "anti-war machine."[31]

Other stories alleging official government involvement continued. A news report in 1934 stated that successful tests of a death ray had been observed by General Victor Denain, the French minister of air,[32] without saying what came of them. In late 1935 and early 1936 newspapers carried a story about a scientist named L. G. Anderson of Melbourne, whose ray had attracted the attention of the U.S. Navy Department. Offering him a job at the experimental laboratory in Lakehurst, New Jersey, the Navy expressed interest in the possibility of this beam as an aid in radio control of aircraft—not as a weapon. Anderson, however, claimed that it was a veritable heat ray with tremendous military potential. Citing his assistant, Roy McIvor, an American engineer who died in 1927, as the one who first suggested the idea, Anderson said he had perfected it. He claimed to have turned glass tumblers into powder and caused motors to stop, all at short range. He envisioned that with further research and experimentation, this ray would be able to put aircraft and motor vehicles out of action as well as disrupt wireless communications of an enemy. At the time of the interview, Anderson had not decided to accept the Navy's offer, preferring instead to make his research available to the Australian or British governments.[33] And in September 1936 *Le Madécasse* of Madagascar had a story about a Canadian chemist who claimed to have given his death ray to his country's war ministry. He also indicated that he could sell it to Ethiopia, despite the fact it had just been conquered by Italy.[34]

Shortly afterward, two other sensational claims about a death ray connected with government assistance appeared in newspapers. One in 1935–1936 was about a New Zealander from Auckland named Victor Penny, a garage attendant who reportedly had considerable expertise in electricity and radio. Having attracted the attention of the New Zealand Ministry of Defence, he became an overnight celebrity after he was assaulted and robbed of important papers, allegedly by foreign agents. Guards were posted in the hospital while Penny recovered, and others were sent to watch over his house where his invention was kept. He was later transferred to a government facility on Somes Island in Wellington Harbor in order to conduct experiments. The only information made known to the public was that he was working on something concerning radio. Rumors nevertheless circulated that he had developed a death ray capable of causing airplane engines to shut down. Eight months later, a newly elected government ended the research after an investigation revealed that nothing substantial had been achieved. Penny would not divulge any details about his work for the government but continued to maintain that his invention was real.[35]

Two and a half years later, there was a report that a farm boy in Wisconsin had invented an electric ray capable of wreaking havoc on all electrical equipment within a radius of eight miles. H. E. Taylor, at that time president of the National Inventors' Congress, told the press that members of his organization had witnessed a test in which car motors suddenly stopped when struck by the ray. The story seemed preposterous, especially when it was revealed that the invention was based on an "old battery-operated radio set," but a newspaper went further by claiming that the United States Congress had ordered the War Department to send armed guards to Wisconsin to protect whatever secrets might be revealed.[36]

A most bizarre story alleging a death ray with official connections to appear in the press was that of Charles Sidney Way, who supposedly sold his device to the Spanish government in 1937 for £40,000. Although it had a limited range, some reports indicated that it was used in Valencia against General Francisco Franco's forces and had allegedly brought down one of his airplanes.[37] An added bit of drama was that Way shortly afterward committed suicide. According to one newspaper, an investigation revealed that he did so because another woman he had been seeing jilted him when she found out he already had a wife and children.[38] The French *Journal des Mutilés et Combattants*, however, told a different tale, one involving a hoax. It reported that Way did not follow through with a demonstration of his weapon and departed unexpectedly from Valencia, leaving behind a box containing some worthless junk that was supposed to be his death ray. The magazine added that he then tried to interest the British in his device but, failing to achieve this, took his own life.[39]

In 1938 a story appeared about an Englishman named Arthur Coxhead of Maidenhead, who had allegedly developed a powerful death ray and was going to demonstrate it to interested representatives of the British War Ministry. As described by *The People* magazine and repeated in the *Dover Express and East Kent News*, he was a seventy-year-old former antique dealer who had become an autodidact scientist. Living on a small country estate, Coxhead had worked for eight years on a weapon that would end war. The power of this ray was superior to most others described in the news over the years: "Mr. Coxhead claims that with it he could destroy an entire continent either by fire or water within a few hours. Directing it at London, he could set the whole city ablaze from end to end or produce a storm of such violence that the streets would be flooded."[40] Coxhead even told the reporter from *The People* that he had recently generated a powerful storm over Dover. As for destroying battleships, he said that his ray would heat the steel bulwarks to such a high temperature that the ammunition in the magazines would explode. Like many other such stories, this one, too, was quickly forgotten. Although often sensationalized in the press, government involvement in most of these cases turned out to be nothing more than a willingness to investigate some reports to see if any death-ray devices showed promise.

Deceptive claims appearing to be directly supported by a government occasionally showed up in the press as well. One example was a brief description of a device reported in the *San Antonio Light* in 1927. Entitled "Quartz 'Death Ray' May Revolutionize Methods of Warfare," the story was limited to a series of photographs with captions below. The first frame shows a man—later identified as scientist H. C. Williams—holding quartz crystals. The caption reads as follows: "Naval experiments to develop a 'death ray' with quartz crystals (shown above) and violet rays interest U.S. leaders." The second frame, with a man operating a device, has this caption: "The new radio activity may revolutionize warfare. By pressing a button like this ships can be sunk."[41] The remaining pictures and statements elaborate on the weapon's capabilities and reinforce the notion that there is official involvement in its development. Nowhere, however, is there any specific link to the Navy Department or its representatives.

Another example was that of the "Electro-tank," a revival of Thomas Edison's earlier suggestion about using electrified jets of liquid to spray at attacking troops. In 1935 *Modern Mechanix and Inventions* magazine carried a story about such a contraption and displayed a picture of it on the cover. The article starts off by linking such a machine to a real development at two major universities. Robert J. Van deGraff of Princeton is described as the inventor of a 7,000,000-volt generator built at the Massachusetts Institute of Technology, which would be installed in an armored vehicle. There is an artist's sketch of a bulky, high-silhouetted, one-man contraption with a huge globe on top from which the gunner directs a high-pressure nozzle. There is also a cross-section diagram showing the internal parts: the engine, the generator, and the water tank. The magazine described it as the "newest war machine" which "will revolutionize offensive warfare."[42] Such a vehicle, however, would have been too impractical for the modern battlefield for several reasons, including the fact that it would have been an easy target for enemy fire.

Implying a degree of official recognition of death rays was one thing, but the media also featured views of military spokesmen and others with some expert status who contradicted mainstream scientists and other skeptics. Generals Swinton and Debeney have already been mentioned, but their observations had appeared before the scientific community felt sufficiently challenged, especially by Grindell Matthews, to respond openly and so vigorously. In 1926 *The Reader's Digest* carried American John Bakeless's comments about the death ray from his book *The Origin of the Next War: A Study in the Tensions of the Modern World*. As a former colonel on the army general staff, his words carried some weight: "The device might be made so simple that pointing it and pressing a button would suffice to bring fleets of airplanes tumbling from the skies while the enemy's tanks, motor lorries, artillery transports could be stopped simultaneously. The prospect opens an alluring possibility of bringing war literally to a halt at a cost no greater than a few broken necks for aviators."[43] A year later, French general Frédéric Canonge mentioned a *rayon destructeur* in an article published in *Revue militaire française*, implying that it existed.[44] In January 1931, Henry Rhodes, editor of the *Chemical Practitioner*, sided with the death-ray enthusiasts, stating that "Researches are being carried out with invisible rays of such power that they will be capable of exterminating whole populations."[45] In "New Weapons for the Next War," appearing in the November 1931 issue of *Modern Mechanix and Inventions*, retired American army colonel Jay Earle Miller referred to newspaper sensationalism about death rays, stating that none had lived up to the claims. He went on, however, to mention a related type of device that produced an "electric rhythmic wave" capable of exploding gunpowder at a distance by breaking down its molecular stability.[46] The following year, Major General H. L. Gilchrist, Chief of the U.S. Army Chemical Warfare Service, told a group of officers at Fort Benning, Georgia, that death-ray experiments were being conducted at the University of Virginia.[47] In 1933 the *New York Times* ran a story about Dr. J. W. M. du Mond of the California Institute of Technology telling a group of scientists how X-rays could be developed for use against aircraft by halting the engines. The article did not say how the other scientists reacted to this assertion.[48] In early 1935 an article appeared about death-ray research at the British Institute of Radiologists. According to one of its staff members, "From our experiments it seems that a death-ray which will kill a human being instantly and at any distance [sic]; it is only a matter of transmitting ultra short waves with sufficient power. There is no limit to the distance the waves can travel—with terrible effect."[49] Another newspaper carrying this story added more information. Not only did the rays kill a rabbit and some flies but left no trace of the creatures. One of the Institute's officials said "It is quite possible to visualize the time when the death ray, if it got into the wrong hands, would become a frightful weapon."[50] In March 1935 newspapers reported on Professor R. C. Chadfield of the Leicester College of Science and Technology in Britain, who announced that he had developed a death ray that killed painlessly.[51] Although not endorsing it as fact, Professor G. Russell Harrison of the Massachusetts Institute of Technology said that a death ray was theoretically possible. He agreed with other scientists that the range of any such ray would be greatly limited.[52] There was also a report about Guber de Saentis, a high-level officer in the Swiss army, who was working at the Jungfrau Research Institute located on that mountain. According to French journalist Charles Reber of *L'Intransigeant* who visited the installation in 1936, part of the defensive system being developed at the Jungfrau and the Mönch was a death ray capable of disrupting the magnetos of airplane and automobile engines. De Saentis allegedly utilized cosmic rays and, from a station set up to detect enemy aircraft, carried out successful experiments at ranges of several miles.[53]

One of the most sensational death-ray stories related by a government official appeared in 1934. Herbert T. Fitch, a retired detective of the Special Branch of Scotland Yard, was also known as the "King's Shadow" for his service as personal bodyguard to Edward VII and George V. He shared his memoirs in serialized form in newspapers before his death in 1935, after which the collection was published as a book in 1936. Under the general title "Dicing with Death," one installment bore the label "Attempt to Sell the Death-Ray." Fitch said a brief story about a death ray had appeared in British newspapers two years before, generating quite a discussion in the press, but had been pulled after only a few days. Having been involved in the investigation, he explained what happened and why the story disappeared from the newspapers. According to him, it concerned two brothers who were working on a death ray. Although at liberty to reveal the details of the case now, Fitch concealed their true identities and referred to them as the "Wright Brothers." According to the detective, the elder brother, "John," had just stumbled upon the final adjustment that turned the apparatus into a lethal machine but was accidentally killed by it. This occurred after he had tried several times to obtain assistance from the British government. His younger brother, "Fred," believed that had John been given a chance to demonstrate their work, better facilities, equipment, and other support would have been forthcoming; and John would still be alive. Blaming the government for the death of his brother, Fred contacted agents of an unnamed foreign country "unfriendly" to Britain and offered to demonstrate it, possibly offering it for sale. By this time, the British government had become interested and sent an official who had earlier communicated with John to speak with the surviving brother, but Fred would not relent, such was his anger. Fitch had been assigned to go with the official and remain in the small town to keep an eye out for the foreign agents for whom Fred was going to perform a demonstration of the death ray. At the last minute, possibly out of a sense of patriotic duty not to let this weapon get into the hands of an enemy, Fred smashed the death ray, in the process killing himself. Fitch told his readers that the death ray was real and described a test on a small model airplane carried out by Fred: "The ray not only fused the magneto of the model; it brought the aeroplane to the ground from a height of about 100 feet, a mass of twisted, half-melted metal and smoking canvas."[54] He added that British scientists had tried in vain to learn how this death ray worked but that the apparatus was too damaged to yield up its precious secret.

Although not scientists or military personnel, two others should be mentioned because of their status within their communities. This also underscores the fact that speculation about death rays had become a topic of interest even at the local level. One was Dr. Daniel Webster Kurtz, president of McPherson College, whose training was in theology. In November 1921 he spoke at the bankers' convention at the Hutchinson, Kansas, Chamber of Commerce, telling his listeners about the terrible weapons of the next war and lending his endorsement to their reality. As reported in the *Hutchinson News*, one described by Kurtz was an electric ray lethal to humans out to forty miles.[55] The other person was Dr. Sergius V. Algin, a pathologist and X-ray physician at the Indiana County Memorial Hospital in Indiana, Pennsylvania. Speaking at the local Kiwanis Club celebrating

"Nurses' Night" in 1937, he informed his audience of two capabilities of death rays. According to him, they could be "charged with a mixture of H2O and directed against the gasoline tanks of airplanes, making the planes unable to proceed."[56] He added that death rays could be conductors of poison, such as potassium cyanide, with horrific effects on people struck by them.

These and other reports no doubt made directed energy weapons seem at least plausible to many people. A lengthy newspaper article in September 1935 suggested as much. As reported in *The Daily Mail* of Hull, England, scientists in many countries, including the major military powers, were known to be experimenting with death rays; and it was just a matter of time before their efforts would be crowned with success.[57] The following January, Hanson Baldwin, the noted military analyst and frequent contributor to the *New York Times*, echoed the belief that some type of ray to stop airplane engines was possible. In "The Terror That Rides the Air," he acknowledged the lack of success so far but said that scientists were nevertheless at work on developing such a weapon.[58] Although expressing skepticism about a death-ray claim by an engineer in Massachusetts two years later, an Ohio newspaper observed: "But if such a ray has not yet been discovered it very likely will be. After the invention of radio we are prepared to believe almost any prophecy in the domain of electricity, and it should surprise nobody to learn that some sort of electronic impulses have been discovered which will destroy life at long range."[59] Comments like these made it more difficult for skeptics to convince people that the death ray as a viable military weapon was not possible at the time.

Some claims made for death rays started in a modest fashion before acquiring the lethal properties and greatly expanded capabilities accompanying them. In June 1928 a German physicist named Erich Graichen, employed by the Siemens Halska Electric Company, announced that he had developed a ray that could treat blindness and cancer but that long exposure to it could be deadly. An article carried in the *New York Times* focused mostly on this healing aspect of his work but added sensationalism with the title: "Finds a 'Death Ray' Fatal to Humans."[60] By October, however, Graichen had begun to assert that his invention was a veritable death ray to be employed in warfare. One newspaper carrying this story was the *Davenport Democrat and Leader* of Iowa. Without revealing its exact properties, the German explained that his ray was created from several combinations, including X-rays and cathode rays, and was capable of widespread destruction. He envisioned a fleet of pilotless, radio-guided airplanes mounted with his death ray utterly wiping out cities and their populations. As described by Graichen:

> The ray could be turned on a city entirely invisible to its inhabitants not with the purpose of immediate destruction but creating a disturbance of the electrons, charging the buildings, the streets, every mechanical object with "radium activity" until a point is reached in which the city begins to "ooze" electrons and "radium rays."
>
> Every living being within the city would be destroyed. No living being could approach the area of the city for a long time without instant death.[61]

Another scientific discovery whose application was for healing also gave rise to speculation about a weapon. Although widely reported in the media, including some of the scientific journals, the *New York Times* ran the story under the title "Tests of Death Ray Aim at Saving Lives." The opening sentence reads "The most potent death ray yet devised by man...."[62] Researchers at the University of Illinois in Urbana in February 1936 announced that they had developed a neutron beam shot from a "gun." Experiments were made to see if this could aid in fighting leukemia and possibly other forms of cancer such as Hodgkin's Disease. The neutron beam had shown the capability of killing white corpuscles of the blood. Since leukemia is a condition involving an abnormal growth rate of white cells, a controlled level of neutron radiation was thought to hold promise. Dr. P. G. Kruger, the director of the project at Illinois, told the press that the neutron beam was fourteen times more lethal than X-rays. For that reason, scientists involved in the experiment had to be at least fifty feet away from the gun to avoid danger. The gun was actually a powerful magnet that generated "the lethal rays by whirling electrical particles, ions of heavy hydrogen, in the magnetic field."[63]

Sometimes articles about death rays appeared in which the title and the opening few paragraphs focused on the sensational but then proceeded to describe what had actually been accomplished and the scientific reasons for healthy skepticism. One such was "The 'Death Ray' and the Next War," in the American Weekly section of the *San Antonio Light* in December 1935. It also suggested official sanction, for the subtitle was "Science Already Has Produced in the Laboratory Radiant Beams of Withering Heat or Deadly Penetration Which the Army Experts Are Trying to Develop for Long Range Destruction of Warships, Airplane Squadrons and Advancing Armies." Accompanied by images showing the death rays destroying attacking enemy airplanes, the article takes up three pages in the newspaper and provides a brief historical sketch of developments up to that time. The writer states that the publicity surrounding Harry

Grindell Matthews provided the most important stimulus to the idea of creating a death ray, although acknowledging that the Englishman's device failed to convince experts.[64]

On a number of occasions, news stories distorted research by prominent scientists and described their work as new types of death rays. One example was that of Dr. W. D. Coolidge of the General Electric Company and inventor of the Coolidge X-ray tube used by doctors in hospitals and elsewhere. In 1926 he developed a new cathode tube that harnessed killing rays. In experiments widely reported in scientific journals as well as in many popular magazines, he managed to destroy bacteria and insects and cause some physical injury to a rabbit. Given the limited range of the cathode tube's rays, no more than three feet, this device could not be considered a weapon. Even with increased voltage, the distance would not extend to more than a few yards.[65] The press, however, did not confine itself to such a modest accomplishment. The *Waterloo Evening Courier* of Iowa featured a photograph showing one of Coolidge's assistants holding the device, with the caption below describing it as "the forerunner of a military death ray."[66]

A similar example was press coverage of the work of Professor Abraham Esau at the University of Jena in Germany, also noted for his research with the cathode tube. In February 1929 a brief announcement appeared in newspapers in which he had supposedly extended the range of ultrashort waves to two hundred and fifty miles. According to *The Advertiser* of Adelaide, which obtained the story from the *Thüringer Allgemeine Zeitung* of Erfurt, they were lethal to germs and small animals.[67] An article the following May, however, corrected this distortion although the title "Death Ray" suggested otherwise. The story in the *Canberra Times* described the true killing range as three meters and focused on the use of ultrashort waves to destroy bacteria. Professor Esau himself discussed only the benefits to medicine provided by his work and did not link it to any military use.[68]

In another instance, Professor Robert W. Wood of Johns Hopkins University attracted attention from the media in 1927 with his research into the effects of high-frequency sound vibrations. During the First World War, he had worked at a French naval arsenal at Toulon with several scientists, including Paul Langevin, in an attempt to develop a means of detecting German submarines by utilizing inaudible sound waves. Their efforts led to some success, but Wood made an accidental discovery in the process. One day he noticed that fish in an experimental tank had died when they came into contact with the sound waves. When Wood put his hand into the water, he said that he got a "sensation of disintegrating and most intolerable pain."[69] It was not an electrical shock but heat produced by the sound waves.

After the war, he and Alfred E. Loomis, a wealthy New York banker and amateur scientist, began conducting experiments with high frequency oscillating current and quartz crystal. In one test Wood killed a minnow in two minutes with vibrations of 300,000 cycles. Although unable to dispatch a mouse after fifteen minutes' exposure, he did notice its blood corpuscles were reduced sixty-five percent, the result weakening the animal.[70] The effect was only temporary, but later experiments showed that red corpuscles placed directly into a solution and subjected to the sound waves were destroyed.[71] Wood and Loomis also expanded their research with sound beyond a liquid confinement. Placing a mouse between two metal plates, they generated short radio waves that killed the creature in approximately thirty seconds. An examination revealed that the blood had coagulated throughout its body. When queried by the press, Wood did not make any claim for this discovery to be applicable as a military weapon,[72] especially since he had earlier debunked Grindell Matthews and his death ray.

Others, however, did. For example, the *Dallas Morning News* ran a story entitled "Perfecting a New Death Ray." The sound waves, according to the newspaper, "comprise the so-called 'death ray' and can operate only through a solid or liquid medium. No living matter, plant or animal, when placed in the path of this 'ray' has managed to survive."[73] *Popular Mechanics* followed suit in an article in May of that year entitled "Can Inaudible Sounds Kill?" The subtitle was "American Inventor's Death Ray, Employing Ultra-Audible Sound Waves, May Spell Doom for Submarine Crews."[74] Although accurately describing the research of Wood and Loomis, *Science News Letter* referred to the "'death-noise' instead of a 'death-ray.'"[75] The most outlandish comment about their work, however, was a newspaper article announcing that Wood had "invented a new deadly ray which is said to be effective at long range."[76] Yet two years later, an unnamed science writer cited by the *Auckland Star* commented on the real possibility of a death ray based on sound waves to cause physiological injury.[77]

Reports in 1932 indicated that experiments using sound waves as a destructive force were still being conducted. *Modern Mechanics and Inventions*, without mentioning Wood and Loomis, described a recent experiment using sound at Johns Hopkins University, an experiment that certainly presaged a military application. According to the article, the effect of the sound waves "instantly converted glass into a thin white powder, oil into thin vapor, and wood into a burst of flame."[78] The magazine also stated that representatives of the U.S. Army had observed the tests and concluded that this force could be an effective death ray capable of rendering obsolete conventional weapons, including airplanes. The article is accompanied by a drawing of the proposed ray machine mounted on a flatbed army truck. It is shown as a generator attached to a dish emitting sound waves and operated by one man. There is also a scale indicating the different levels of sound, with 300,000 decibels listed as fatal.

The work of Wood and Loomis was not the first, or the last, to be associated with the possibility of using sound as a type of death ray, for the concept had appeared as early as 1920, with stories continuing to surface in later years. These, too, often received a stamp of credibility because of the status of some of the sources. Former British Air Ministry official Cuthbert Hicks, in the *New York Times* article "A World Ruled From the Air" mentioned in Chapter 2, also claimed that sound waves could be harnessed as a weapon. He used the analogy of how certain notes played on a musical instrument such as a piano could shatter glass and imagined this principle applied to an apparatus that could concentrate sound vibrations at enormous levels and direct them to a target. Mounted on airplanes, such devices, he contended, could cause buildings to collapse and even "destroy the brains and ears of humanity."[79]

Another proponent of this force was an inventor who claimed to have worked with Grindell Matthews. A. J. Roberts of New Zealand had served as a captain in the British naval flying service and as a liaison officer with Britain's air and submarine forces during the war. Currently employed by the Schumann Circus in Copenhagen, he told a local newspaper that Grindell Matthews's ray was in reality a combination of the vibrations of light and sound—not electricity. To advance his credibility as an expert, he told the *Politiken* that in 1908 he had gone to Britain under the auspices of the Australian government "with the first wirelessly-navigable torpedo."[80] Roberts told another newspaper that while working with Grindell Matthews he had developed the capability of using sound to explode bombs and mines. He also belittled the claims of the English inventor, saying that he, too, could cause a motorcycle engine to stop.[81] A few months later, Roberts addressed a group of technicians in Hamburg, repeating his criticism of his former colleague and promising to demonstrate his own death ray sometime.[82] He apparently did not.

Claims for sound as a weapon continued throughout the 1920s. In 1925 Howard Coonley, the civilian director for the U.S. Army Chemical Warfare Service in the district for New England, spoke at a gathering of the Women's Republican Club of Massachusetts, telling them that sound waves could be deployed as a weapon of war.[83] The following year, *Le Matin* ran a story originally reported by the Riga correspondent of London's *Daily Telegraph* about a Russian scientist and a weapon utilizing sound. Identified simply as Dr. Goldman of the University of Kiev, he supposedly had developed an apparatus capable of killing living creatures by means of powerful sound waves directed over great distances.[84] Two years later, there were reports of a new French death ray described as not electrical in nature. The *New York Times* ran the story in February 1927 about tests using some type of device that successfully blew up sections of trenches and started fires. The inventor was a French army engineer, and the experiments had been carried out at a base in Montpellier.[85] The *Popular Mechanics* article "Can Inaudible Sounds Kill?" mentioned above also referred to this story, its inclusion suggesting that it might be based on sound. This particular ray was said to detonate mines and to start or put out fires with neither "wireless nor any form of electric current...."[86] In 1929 an Englishman named John Morgan Symes, a wireless engineer living in Guilford, announced that he had perfected a small, working model of a device that used sound waves to kill. As reported in the *San Antonio Light*, Symes claimed that the vibrations "would shatter the ear drums and the blood corpuscles, yet nobody would hear them. Death would come to them so suddenly they would know nothing at all about it."[87]

Sound as a weapon continued to receive attention into the 1930s and even after the start of the Second World War. In an article for *Popular Mechanics* in 1935, Thomas E. Stimson asserted that research into ultra-high frequency had yielded results suggesting the use of sound to disable electric-current generators and to harm body tissue. He referred to a recent announcement by Marconi that airplane motors could be knocked out in this manner. As for use as a weapon against humans, Stimson said that research focused on discovering the frequencies that could disrupt the molecules of a person's body and cause death.[88] Frank Thone, a death-ray debunker, refuted the "sound weapon" idea in an article in *Science News Letter* in 1935. Having written about the experiments conducted by Wood and Loomis, he pointed out that the only known manner in which sound had a lethal effect was in water or some other type of fluid. (Thone apparently overlooked the article written by Wood himself describing the experiment with the mouse placed between two metal plates.) Wood and Loomis, he added, had shown that the effects of the destructive force were limited to simple organisms and to a range of only a few inches.[89]

That did not put a stop to endorsements of sound waves as a weapon.

Hiram Percy Maxim, for example, described their power in his "Next War" series for *Popular Mechanics* the following year. After mentioning their effect on organisms in water, he added: "Directed at persons they create violent nausea and a long list of disabilities, some of which are fatal. Directed at large structures of light weight, such as airplane wings and propellers, they create vibrations violent enough to wreck the structure. By altering the frequency of a given structure, they will actually 'fiddle the bridge down,' so to speak."[90] The power of sound received further support in an article appearing in *Science Digest* in August 1940. According to writer Douglas W. F. Mayer, ultra-sound waves could set off explosives and radio waves could cause a rise in body temperature to 300° F, resulting in death of an organism.[91]

Although not a death ray as such, another similar weapon appeared in newspapers in 1934 and 1935. According to reports, a Frenchman named Edmond de Christmas developed a machine that intensified light so brightly that it could temporarily blind a person, even causing permanent eye damage. Applied as an anti-aircraft defensive system in and around a city, it could render attacking air fleets helpless at night, as the pilots would become disoriented, lose control of their planes, and crash. This "light" gun could also be used against enemy ground forces, likewise blunting their assault on a defensive position.[92] One newspaper article provided more detail about this invention. It supposedly worked by firing cartridges that generated extremely bright light for a few moments, with the intensity and concentration increased tremendously by a reflector.[93] Another effect of this light, according to de Christmas, was that it could also paralyze a person temporarily, a most bizarre example of which was reported in many newspapers in October 1934. It concerned tests being conducted in France. As described in *The Advertiser* of Adelaide: "Military experts, while experimenting with a 'death ray' [this bright beam of light], accidentally turned it on to villagers who were participating in folk dances. The results were astonishing. The dancers stopped, rigidly maintaining their dancing attitudes. The ray was immediately switched off and the dancers recovered unharmed."[94] What gave the story some legitimacy, despite its absurdity, was that reports indicated that the French air minister and a representative of Marshal Philippe Pétain were present.[95] With such a weapon, one wonders if the French could have avoided defeat in 1940—at least, if they had counterattacked the Germans at night.

One of the most important stories to stimulate press excitement over death rays in the 1930s was the announcement by the aged electrical wizard Nikola Tesla in 1931 that he was working on a new power source that no one else had ever contemplated. This was not an obscure story buried in the newspapers, as evidenced by the fact that *Time* sported his picture on its cover.[96] By 1934 Tesla clarified that he had developed a powerful death beam, which he believed would ultimately make war impossible. His announcement was carried in numerous publications, including *Newsweek*, the *New York Times*, and *Time*, as well as local and foreign newspapers. Without divulging many details, Tesla did state that he had the capability of directing a silent beam of "highly charged particles driven by an enormously repellent electrical force of 50,000,000 volts."[97] This energy beam would be capable of destroying an attacking air force of 10,000 planes at a distance of 250 miles. It could also annihilate instantly an invading enemy army of 1,000,000 men.[98] Tesla stated that the ray's delivery system would have to be completed by four other inventions which he would develop. The weapon would then become operational from generating stations located at strategic sites along the U.S. borders. Tesla emphasized that his ray was primarily defensive in nature since these power stations could not be moved, but he indicated that a smaller version of the device could be placed on board ships, giving the United States dominance at sea.[99] Although not ruling out the possibility of creating such a weapon, French physicist Jacques-Arsène d'Arsonval stated that no one, including Tesla, had actually succeeded yet.[100] Likewise skeptical because of previous claims of death rays and their rejection by most in the scientific community, officials at the United States Bureau of Standards decided to evaluate Tesla's idea anyway. His reputation and earlier work were such that they could not afford to dismiss outright the possibility of a scientific breakthrough. But after running exhaustive tests the Bureau of Standards could not find any known energy source that could do what Tesla had claimed for his death ray.[101] A few months later, Tesla clarified to some extent that his ray would operate more as an invisible wall of dust particles. According to a story in *Popular Mechanics*, experiments along theses lines were already being conducted in Europe. In fact, the magazine claimed that successful tests had shown the feasibility of such a weapon. Tesla described these "force rays" as "particles, possibly dust of some sort, microscopically fine, driven electrically and projected into walls miles high and 100 miles each in length."[102] As will be seen in the next chapter, Tesla's idea of a "defensive curtain" would become linked to the development of radar.

Occasionally, a story would appear about a death ray proven to work. Henry Fleur, an inventor living in San Francisco, claimed to have developed an apparatus that could kill and then persuaded several men to finance the project. After some time had passed and dissatisfied with Fleur's progress, the investors brought charges of grand theft against him. In May 1936, the case went to trial in the courtroom of Judge George Steiger. In a dramatic turn of events, Fleur received permission to demonstrate his death ray, and the court reconvened at his home laboratory. In front of a startled judge, jury, and group of attorneys, Fleur promptly dispatched several insects and reptiles from ten feet away with his "death ray." According to the *Fort Worth Star Telegram*, which ran the story on the front page: "The snake was killed in eight and one-half minutes, the lizard in four minutes, and the termites in just 35 seconds."[103] It took the jury only four minutes to acquit the inventor. Afterward Fleur was asked if his device could be used to kill human beings. He replied that it could with increased power but that he had no plans to continue research in that direction. He also explained to reporters how his death ray worked: "a bombardment of ultrashort electrical waves which I send down a beam of light does the work. These waves are attuned to the normal bodily vibrations of the animals to be destroyed. The ultrashort waves increase the vibrations to such an extent that the individual molecules in the body of the animals simply explode."[104]

A curious fact about this story was the apparent ignorance on the part of reporters about Fleur's earlier notoriety regarding a death ray. A number of newspapers had featured the San Francisco inventor and his death ray back in 1930. At the time it was hailed as a new and revolutionary means of combating insects that destroyed millions of dollars in crops each year. The report included a somewhat detailed description of how the device worked, pointing out it generated "cold" rays that froze the insides of the pests. According to the *Hamilton Evening Journal* of Ohio, Fleur put on a demonstration for a group of farmers in which "he directed his ray against a tree covered with fruit pests and killed them in half a second. The same ray swept another tree and annihilated thousands of red spiders, ants and aphis [sic]."[105] The writer of the newspaper article went on to speculate about the application of Fleur's invention to warfare: "An enemy army is slowly advancing. The army reaches a point seven miles from its objective. Suddenly a mysterious light bathes the soldiers in its rays. Every man feels the clutch of an icy hand. They drop one by one, as the 'cold' death comes. The ray could pierce walls, the thick armor of battleships and the heights of space which usually protect airplanes from field artillery."[106]

Although less sensational in its presentation, a story about Professor Jacques Brettmon, a radiologist at the University of Paris, appeared in the *New York Times* in May 1935. Brettmon claimed that he had developed a death ray made up of short waves and ultraviolet radiation. He cautioned, however, that it was limited in range and that the application of such a ray for military purposes was not yet feasible. According to Dr. Brettmon, he had succeeded in dispatching a mouse, but at the cost of approximately $2,000. He speculated that even if the power of the ray could be increased it would still probably not be able to kill a human. As to the future, he said, "some one may hit upon the right combination of rays to make the death ray a reality. It is not impossible, but I think it is many years off."[107]

Unlike the accounts of Fleur and Brettmon, as well as some serious inventors who were guilty only of bad science, many of the death-ray claims were indeed the products of con men and quacks whose contraptions were downright laughable. In 1925 *The Daily Northwestern* of Oshkosh, Wisconsin, had a story about an unnamed inventor who tried to convince British naval authorities that his death ray could blow up battleships. The Admiralty decided to let him prove it and placed a vessel at his disposal. Since the Royal Navy apparently had set certain parameters for the demonstration, the man decided that discretion was the better part of valor and quietly departed the country. An attempt by him to interest another power produced the same result, as the inventor would not submit to close supervision by the authorities. In the same article, the newspaper also described one of the first death-ray claims after the First World War clearly exposed as a hoax, in this case an Englishman who asserted that his device could kill animals. This man, likewise unnamed, selected a cow and sent it to its death in view of witnesses. The unfortunate animal did not succumb to the death ray; rather, it was electrocuted with the aid of unseen wires and electric current operated by the inventor.[108] Bovine sacrifice showed up again in connection with another death ray. Although this occurred in late 1940, it is one of the more absurd stories and is worth telling. As described in the *Wisconsin State Journal* of Madison, ninety-one-year-old Milton McWhorter claimed to have killed a bull at a distance of two and a half miles with a device that utilized X-rays. In addition to saying that the U.S. military was interested in his invention, McWhorter mentioned that his death-ray apparatus depended on a mysterious material obtained only in Sweden. The energy source, however, was quite simple, as his machine worked by "plugging it into an ordinary light socket."[109] One death-ray inventor set his sights lower and, instead of trying to interest a government in his machine, tried to con the family physician. In 1931 Englishman Harry Smith bilked Dr. Thomas Dixon Cook out of £1355 in a scheme to extract electricity from the air. He also said that he had developed a ray to stop gasoline engines of cars and airplanes. Arrested for fraud, Smith was sent to jail.[110]

One highly questionable death ray was one that could do just about anything. A man identified only as a Mr. Ibbotson, a masseur and osteopath from Burnley, England, claimed in 1926 to have invented a new ray quite different from anything else because of its myriad capabilities. It could go through six feet of lead and serve as an electrical gun shooting a seven-inch bullet into a wall. But it would do much more. As described by one newspaper, his ray would act as a remote control for a boat, "turn steel into powder," and "weld brass and steel together." If that did not pique one's interest, it should be noted that it would also "petrify silk." The concluding sentence of the article said it all: "While a staff of operators demonstrate his inventions on music halls, Mr. Ibbotson will continue his experiments at home."[111]

One wild claim resulted in part from an instance of official information about what could be called a "plague ray." In 1933 Professor O. A. Newell, head of the research department at the National League of Health in London, announced the results of successful experiments using wireless waves to produce fatal diseases, including anthrax. Without providing details as to how this was accomplished, Newell gave a brief description of the project. A team of twenty-two doctors and scientists, accompanied by sixteen volunteers from the army and the RAF, participated in the experiments. When subjected to these waves, the men supposedly developed diseased bacteria in their blood. The good news was that the scientists had also developed wireless rays that could block the harmful waves. Lending more official support to this story was that Colonel Sir Augustus Fitzgeorge, a cousin of Queen Mary, had initiated the study prior to his death in October 1933.[112] Four years later, in the summer of 1937, Anthony Holder, an Englishman and former professor of natural sciences, announced that he had developed a radio death beam capable of all sorts of mischief, including the transmission of electrical energy, poison, and disease germs. As described in *La Tribune de Madagascar et Dépendences* of Tananarive, the secret, at least as much as Holder would divulge at the time, lay in his discovery that "chemical substances such as gas all possessed their own particular wavelength, enabling them to be transported through the air like a song or the solo of a violin."[113] Holder maintained that his radio beam could therefore direct these lethal waves to any specified target and that it could kill, stop airplane engines, disrupt all electrical equipment in a selected area, and penetrate armor and fortified bunkers. The weapon could also be mounted on airplanes and greatly extend the range of destruction, "spreading death over great distances, destroying towns and armies in little time at all."[114]

A death-ray drama reported in the press in 1929 about a con man involved espionage in addition to the weapon and its alleged capabilities. A Belgian by the name of Antoine-Joseph Delattre went to Paris ostensibly to sell to the French government secret documents of a death ray stolen from an unnamed foreign country adjacent to France. The device was described as capable of halting airplane engines. According to the version in an Australian newspaper, he did meet with the Intelligence Department of the French War Office but without result. The authorities there were highly suspicious since he did not ask for any sum of money; he simply wanted them to find him a job. Five days later, Delattre was found unconscious in the Bois de Boulogne.[115] According to Parisian newspapers, after regaining consciousness in the hospital, he told police that he was a twenty-four-year-old officer of radiotelegraphy in the Belgian merchant marine and that he had been attacked by assailants who stole his documents. The police, however, were suspicious of the whole affair, especially after contacting Belgian authorities and learning that he was a known liar, fraud, and possibly a drug dealer. He also had a criminal record, having been arrested on more than one occasion. French police concluded that his wounds were self-inflicted and the whole story of the incident in the Bois de Boulogne a fabrication.[116]

Similar attempts by deceitful or incompetent people to interest governments in their death rays continued to appear. One notorious charlatan was the Polish engineer Zbigniew Dunikowski. Claiming he had developed a secret ray capable of making gold, he was arrested for fraud by French police and in 1933 a court sentenced him to two years in prison.[117] After his release in 1935, he announced that his ray was capable of destroying airplanes and armies. Several people witnessed a demonstration at his home in San Remo, Italy, in which he used his device to set on fire the toy airplane of his young daughter. Dunikowski then tried unsuccessfully to have his case reopened by offering his discovery to the French government.[118] In November 1934 newspapers mentioned a German ray in a story dealing with possible horrors in the next war. According to reports from France, a German refugee had offered his device to the French government, which took possession of it and was currently conducting experiments. Instead of a "death ray," however, it was described as a "stunning ray," for that was the alleged effect observed when it struck animals and humans at a distance of a little less than a mile away. A type of pistol fired cartridges containing a special powder—the source of the weapon's effectiveness. When the cartridges exploded, according to the article, they set up "impulses, which leave the pistol at regular intervals uninterruptedly."[119] Although the writer of the article, John L. Coontz, expressed skepticism toward military rays in general, he acknowledged that such a weapon as this would be invaluable if it became reality. This story received further notice when the January 1935 *Modern Mechanix and Inventions* featured a photograph of the German inventor holding his pistol, which looks more like a child's plastic toy.[120] Later that year, another death-ray article appeared in this magazine about a Frenchman, described as a "well-known scientist." According to the story, Henri Claudel of Bourges had invented a device that had the capability of killing anything up to a distance of about six miles. Experiments had supposedly been conducted on small life forms. A photograph shows Claudel with a flimsy contraption that looks more like a one-armed water sprinkler and, like the German pistol, without a visible means of power.[121] The photographs of the German and the Frenchman even made the two men look more like quacks than real scientists or inventors to be taken seriously. In October of the same year, Harry May of London unveiled his death ray at the California Pacific International Exposition in San Diego.[122] The article in *Modern Mechanix and Inventions*, accompanied by a photograph of May with his device, did not include information about any demonstration for the public, but the official program listed this as a feature presentation. Included are statements such as "The Secrets of Army Authorities laid bare before your eyes...." and "It Destroys Everything before your view."[123]

Three contemporary studies of mysterious rays and other fantastic weapons widely discussed in the popular media presented a fairly balanced view of the phenomenon. In 1931 Russian mathematician and science writer N. A. Rynin published *Radiant Energy: Science Fiction and Scientific Projects*, part of his multivolume work on recent scientific achievement. In examining some of the death-ray claims, including those of Grindell Matthews, Rynin explained what the inventors asserted their devices would do, how their work stacked up against the known laws of physics, and what seemed plausible. He also took a look at the research of mainstream scientists such as Coolidge and Wood. Although Rynin remained skeptical toward Grindell Matthews and some of the others, he left open the possibility that some type of wireless energy could be developed for military purposes. In particular, he cited the research of Phillips Thomas of the Westinghouse Company, described more fully below. But Rynin also lent a degree of credibility to a far-fetched tale.

This was an early story about experiments with remote detonation by Mikhail Mikhailovich Filippov. A well-educated Russian—law degree from the University of St. Petersburg, degree in math from the University of Odessa, and a Ph.D. in philosophy from Heidelberg—Filippov dabbled in a variety of intellectual pursuits. He wrote a number of works on philosophy, translated Charles Darwin into Russian, and edited *Nauchnoe obozrenie* (Scientific Review) from 1894 until his death in 1903. According to *The Modern Encyclopedia of Russian and Soviet History*, Filippov died in an accident while conducting experiments with explosives. In *Radiant Energy*, Rynin added sensationalism to the story. He claimed that some people believed Filippov had developed a means of setting off explosions by some type of remote control, the range reportedly reaching several thousand kilometers. Rynin also said that Filippov died under mysterious circumstances and that the Tsarist secret police then removed from the laboratory all of his notes and equipment. Rynin concluded: "I think that the deceased anticipated the ideas that only now attract the attention of the scientists and that the solution of the problem of remote energy transmission, that he perhaps had found, is near."[124] A story published in 1906, however, had already described Filippov's activities and his death in an intriguing fashion. As reported in the *Ada Evening News* of Oklahoma, he died from an accidental dose of prussic acid during an experiment. A greater mystery, according to the paper, was that he had developed some "death-dealing engines" and was supposed to present these plans to the St. Petersburg Academy of Science but had died before he could do so.[125]

The other contemporary works dealing with death rays were undertaken by two Germans, Max Seydewitz and Kurt Doberer. Having become ardent anti–Nazis, they left Germany and went first to Czechoslovakia. Seydewitz was a book publisher and editor who had also been a member of the German Socialist Party until his expulsion in 1931. After the Second World War, he served as Communist governor of Franconia and mayor of Dresden. Doberer had a degree in engineering but also dabbled in writing fiction. In 1936 they co-authored a book entitled *Todesstrahlen und andere neue Kriegswaffen* (Death Rays and Other New War Weapons). A year later Doberer published *Elektrokrieg: Maschine gegen Mensch* (Electro War: Machine Against Man, but published in 1943 as *On the Way to Electro War*), a more in-depth study of death rays. The purpose of their writings was twofold: to separate fact from fiction regarding exotic energy forces and new military technology and to warn the world about the danger to peace posed by Hitler. They based their conclusions on the contemporary level of scientific knowledge, and their speculations reflected what they believed was within the realm of possibility. At the outset they emphatically stated that no real death-ray weapons existed despite all the claims over the years reported in the press. The authors, however, accepted the principal concept of such an energy device, for experiments had shown that it could be created in the laboratory, albeit with an extremely limited range.

Seydewitz and Doberer considered the first serious work in the direction of the death ray to be with ultrashort waves. They regarded the experiments of Abraham Esau (mentioned above) at the University of Jena as an important beginning, for in 1929 he created an ultrashort wave beam generated between two plates that killed flies immediately when they flew into its path. They pointed out that researchers in the United States in 1930 had employed the same method to kill a dog, an ape, and an ox.[126] According to Doberer in his book published the following year, the cause of death in each case was "heart failure, decomposition of the blood, and changes in the cortical substance of the brain."[127] He also referred to a successful experiment in the summer of 1932 at the Westinghouse Company in Pittsburgh, in which these waves were employed to boil sausages.[128] Seydewitz and Doberer also acknowledged Philipp Lenard of the University of Heidelberg and W. D. Coolidge for their work with the cathode tube, which was a veritable death ray although its effectiveness was limited to only a few feet.

On the subject of individual inventors and their claims, Seydewitz and Doberer remained skeptical, regarding many of them as nothing more than con artists trying to take advantage of the public's fear of devastating air raids predicted for the next war. For example, they cited several instances that fell into this category, naming the previously mentioned Dunikowski as one of the most blatant. In *On the Way to Electro War*, Doberer included this account from the Yugoslavian newspaper *Vreme*:

> Belgrade, January 5, 1937. As the special correspondent of the "Vreme" reports from Serajevo [sic], the engineer, Rajko Siljak has invented a Death Ray. The reporter himself piled up a heap of straw on the road. Siljak directed his apparatus upon it, and a few seconds later the straw was consumed by the flames. Siljak intends to make a large-scale model of his apparatus and give a public demonstration, in the course of which he will ignite any inflammable material desired by remote ignition.[129]

Apparently, the media event did not take place. Another example of a questionable story was that of a Danish engineer named Ravn, who in 1935 claimed to be able to knock out airplane engines from 50–60 miles away.[130] According to a newspaper article from Danzig quoted by Doberer: "Danzig, September 6, 1935. The Danish engineer, Rawn [German spelling], the inventor of the much-discussed Death Rays, was to-day the victim of a mysterious burglary. All the plans and devices which he used for experimental purposes in connection with his invention have been stolen. According to the Paris 'Liberté,' this theft is supposed to have been carried out by military espionage agents of a foreign power."[131] As Doberer said, time and time again, many of these inventors made claims, put on a few demonstrations for laymen, and then suddenly theft of their work, pressing business elsewhere, or some other matter sent them into obscurity. Likewise, reports of their discoveries, as the example of Ravn shows, often took a circuitous path: invented in one country, reported by a foreign newspaper, but published in yet another locale.

Doberer apparently overlooked the fact that the story of Ravn had first appeared in May, with a news article stating that he had conducted experiments from 1914–1916 at the Danish Navy Station, where he developed his ray. According to the *Nottingham Evening Post*, a document issued by the Danish Army Technical Department confirming this research was supposed to be on file. It was also alleged that Ravn had later worked for the Germans, prompting a question to Nazi Luftwaffe chief Hermann Göring as to whether or not the Third Reich possessed such a weapon. Göring answered evasively, leaving it up to the world press to wonder, i. e. to fear, that Germany did have such power. It was that following August when Ravn was supposed to take his ray to England that the plans were stolen.[132] Doberer's point was well taken nevertheless. He also contended that with time and proper research the death ray could become a military weapon. It would come about, however, through the efforts of professional scientists working in laboratories at universities and other institutions—not by individuals tinkering away in their home workshops.

Doberer and Seydewitz did not mention it, but the June 1928 issue of *Radio News* magazine carried a story about the ultrashort wave entitled "The Radio Gun—The Silent Weapon of the Future," with the subtitle "How Concentrated Radio Impulses Might be Made to Act as 'Death Rays.'" The cover shows crews operating two radio guns against attacking infantry. The article made reference to Grindell Matthews, acknowledging that nothing came of his invention, but went on to tout the ultrashort radio wave (microwave) as a possible energy weapon. As proof of its potential, the magazine mentioned successful experiments using these waves to cook apples and kill rats. The article then strayed beyond the realm of contemporary technology by listing a number of stupendous capabilities for the radio gun that made it an invincible weapon against airplanes, warships, and armies.[133]

A more detailed description appeared in several local U.S. newspapers not long afterward. All included the same image that graced the cover of the magazine. In "How the Radio Gun Will Broadcast Death Waves with Speed of Light," the story in the *Sandusky Register* of Ohio provided information on the work of Dr. Phillips Thomas, a noted research scientist with the Westinghouse Company and former professor at Princeton. He explained in a paper entitled "Power by Radio" that such a weapon could be developed by generating a radio wave ten centimeters in wavelength and shooting it through ionized air. The result would simply be an electrical stroke projected over a great distance to kill any living thing it touched. Thomas admitted that the ten-centimeter wavelength was then technologically impossible but that recent work suggested hope in its future realization. It would be the veritable death ray so long discussed in the media.[134]

Newspapers in 1931 and 1932 carried several stories about different types of death rays. One was in reference to work with short-wave radio waves at the General Electric Company. According to *The Mail* of Adelaide (1932), in 1928 experiments there had resulted in killing rats and rabbits from a distance of ten feet, in which the animals were "broiled to death." The newspaper also mentioned that an Austrian inventor (unnamed) had claimed to have caused metal to glow white hot from a mile away.[135] Earlier, in its story about this man, *The Advocate* of Burnie, Tasmania, in 1931 had added that "it is an open secret that every War Office is experimenting on these lines."[136] The most detailed description of one of these death-ray claims, however, was the effect of the so-called "death whisper" of Robert Wood and Alfred Loomis discussed above. According to *The Mail* of Adelaide, vibrations at 700,000 times per second had a devastating impact on both machines and animals: "It [the death whisper] would bore holes instantly through aeroplanes, and probably set them alight, as it has a strong heating effect. At a distance beyond its shaking and heating effect it would kill by 'de-blooding' (smashing the corpuscles in the blood vessels of any human beings it met)."[137]

One of the most fantastic stories about death rays appeared in 1932 in the *Ogden Standard Examiner*, for it mentioned several different claims, evoked images of world annihilation, and raised the specter of government secrecy and mystery surrounding new weapons. Complete with an artist's rendering of a city in ruins and rampaging Martian war machines à la H. G. Wells, the full-page article focused primarily on the invention of a new death ray by engineer Lester P. Barlow, described as the "bomb wizard" because of his work with explosives for the Allies in the World War. According to the article, Barlow, now a pacifist, had developed a death ray of such tremendous power that he believed it would make war impossible.

He wanted first to brief four members of the U.S. Congress who would, if convinced of the device's capability, then arrange for him to present his discovery to the disarmament conference at Geneva. In case of rejection, he would then offer it to other powers, possibly even Mussolini's Italy or Stalin's Russia. Barlow asserted that his weapon had a range of one thousand miles.[138] The article went on to make reference to the work of Marconi and others, but the most sensational piece concerned a secret death ray possessed by the British: "for over a decade the world has heard recurrent rumors that in a London vault known only to a handful of high officials of the British Empire, lies a set of death-ray plans that if put into operation would lay waste to entire countries."[139] According to the paper, a British inventor had allegedly offered his death ray to the government during the war, but the authorities decided not to deploy the weapon. In a cloak-and-dagger conclusion, the man then disappeared and was rumored to have been murdered by German agents. The British still possessed the secret but had refused to use it. This smacks of Maclay's assertion about Lord Dundonald's "burning glasses" mentioned in Chapter 1, but the writer of this article made no reference to it.

One of the few recurring death-ray stories, other than that of Tesla's claims, involved Dr. Antonio Longoria of Cleveland. In July 1934 reports appeared about this Spanish-born American inventor who claimed to have accidentally discovered a new ray capable of killing on a large scale. According to the *Montana Standard* of Butte: "Merely by slowly sweeping the ray from left to right, permitting it to linger over each individual soldier for a tenth of a second, slaughter such as this world never before has witnessed would be extremely simple."[140] The effective range was about twenty-eight miles, restricted only by the earth's curvature. Longoria claimed that his ray—produced by electrical energy—destroyed the red corpuscles in experiments on rabbits and mice. Identified as an advisor to the U.S. War Department during the World War, Longoria described himself as a pacifist who would make his invention available to the government only in the event of a direct threat of attack on the United States. Shortly afterward, according to *Time* in its July 1934 article on Tesla, President Albert G. Burns of the Inventors' Congress told members attending the meeting in Omaha that he had personally seen Longoria's device in action. It instantly killed the small animals exposed to its lethal rays, turning the blood of cats, dogs, and rabbits to water.[141] He added, however, that the United States government had banned an exhibition of the ray.[142] Two years later, *Time* had another story about Longoria. Although reminding readers of the previous feats of this inventor, the magazine added that his invisible ray could also weld metals.[143] In 1938 Longoria spoke about his death ray at the National Inventors' Congress meeting again in Omaha. The professor reviewed for his audience his experiments with this ray and its destructive effects on small animals. He claimed that the government had then asked him to keep his invention confidential for the time being. In October 1939, shortly after the start of the Second World War, the *New York Herald Tribune* interviewed Longoria, who revealed that "he could set up his death-ray apparatus 'in four or five hours through the use of any high-grade X-ray machine' but that this would be done only if 'the United States were invaded without cause.'"[144] This was followed by an article in *Popular Science Monthly* in the February 1940 issue, in which Longoria announced that he had destroyed his death ray machine. According to this account, he had supposedly demonstrated its lethal effect on pigeons in flight some four miles away.[145]

As Europe drew closer to war and most of the nations' focus was on conventional weaponry and manpower, the death ray nevertheless continued to be news. In late summer 1938 as the Czech Crisis involving the Sudetenland intensified, there was a report that a retired American army major had developed a new death ray and had given it to the U.S. government. With the sensationalist headline "Army Gets Death Ray that Cuts Steel and Withers Human Bodies" emblazoned on its front page, the *Lowell Sun* of Massachusetts went on to announce that the government had already conducted tests with it and was impressed with the results. In an interview, inventor Major Arthur W. Marchant, now a construction engineer, said the ray had been discovered by accident, for he wanted to try to cut through steel with an electrical force rather than with acetylene. As he and his crew began to experiment with it, they managed to cut steel at a distance of three hundred yards.[146] As with so many other announcements about death rays, this one, too, soon exited quietly.

The start of the Second World War did not mark the end of the saga of the death ray, as reports continued to appear from time to time in newspapers. Many concerned the development of German, and later Japanese, energy weapons, but the Allies always dismissed these as enemy propaganda. The lack of concrete, visual proof of any such devices being deployed in battle seemed to confirm for many people that death rays all along had been nothing more than a fantasy. As will be seen in the next chapter, however, governments took them more seriously than their public statements suggested.

4

Death Rays and Their Connection to the Second World War

Beginning in 1930, news stories about death rays increasingly became more firmly linked to efforts by the major powers to develop them as a weapon for the next war. Reports of military experiments to stop the engines of automobiles appeared in Germany, Britain, Italy, and elsewhere in Europe. These were usually accompanied by official denials of any such undertakings, but at the same time these governments periodically released statements suggesting—even declaring openly—that their scientists were indeed working on rays for military use. Shortly after the end of the Second World War, the public learned that Britain's development of radar was the result of an attempt to create a death ray and that both Germany and Japan had funded projects for such a weapon.

The idea of a defensive "curtain" along the lines proposed by Nikola Tesla in 1934 came up on more than one occasion afterward. In March 1935 the *New York Times* had a story about a British committee (described below) set up to examine the nation's ability to defend itself against air attacks. In the course of its investigation, the committee welcomed suggestions from the public. Several inventors claimed that they could stop an invading air fleet "by spraying into the air at a given height invisible layers of minute metal particles that derange aero engines."[1] A year later a member of the House of Commons asked Prime Minister Stanley Baldwin if any improvements had been made to Britain's air defenses since the status report to Parliament in November 1932. After replying in the affirmative, Baldwin was then queried about a new defensive measure: "Is there any truth in the Press statements which are now appearing that a so-called 'invisible curtain' has been designed which will render air attacks upon this country impossible?" Baldwin responded, saying "I could not answer that question, but I should advise every hon. member to accept with great reserve any statement on the secret processes that may or may not be designed."[2]

Some took his reply to mean that Britain did have such a weapon, as news items continued to appear in the press that seemed to confirm this belief. At the end of April, newspapers ran a story about a British war correspondent, Linton Wells, who had been told unofficially that such a ray was real. Covering the Italian war in Ethiopia for the New York *Herald Tribune*, he had stopped off in Egypt where he met a "high-ranking officer" of the British Egyptian forces, who said "I've heard something about a ray of some sort which would burn Musso's (Mussolini's) pants off if he ever came buzzing around here."[3] In June *Le Madécasse* had an article entitled "Le mur invisible" (The Invisible Wall) about secret British research to create a wall of rays that could cause engine trouble as soon as an airplane tried to penetrate it. According to the article, an experiment conducted with a squadron of planes had indeed produced such a result. Now openly discussing this remarkable breakthrough, British scientists asserted that this new power would completely revolutionize aerial warfare. They even spoke of "surrounding England with this invisible palisade that would guarantee its security, without airplanes and without [anti-aircraft] guns."[4] The writer of the article also reminded readers of the news stories about French airplanes forced down over Germany in 1923 and raised a question about a recent French airplane crash in the Mediterranean. Since the cause of the accident was still a mystery, the "rayon mortel" could be the answer. A few months later, a "high official" of the Air Ministry leaked that Britain already had rays that could throw up a screen to disable enemy bombers and kill their crews. At present the altitude limit was several thousand feet but that "within five years an impassable barrier of invisible rays will protect the British Isles from invading airplanes no matter how high they fly."[5] More followed, as a spokesman for the Air Ministry told the press in December that a successful test resulted in paralyzing an engine of a bomber, forcing the pilot to make an emergency landing. He added that the effective range of the ray was now 25,000 to 30,000 feet and could kill the crew or explode the plane's ammunition.[6]

In more dramatic fashion, Sir Thomas Inskip, the first Minister for Coordination of Defence (a position created in 1936 by Prime Minister Baldwin), openly informed the House of Commons in August 1937 that

British scientists were at work on a new weapon that would completely protect the island and its civilian population from any air attacks. According to Inskip: "The scientists who are working on the ray are convinced that within a very few years, provided they can work unhindered, they will reach protective perfection" and that this new power will mean that "no air fleet could invade the country; no ship could land a man; no army could march."[7] His announcement to Parliament also provoked the concern of a writer for *Pearson's Magazine.* Since most leading scientists had publicly rejected the notion of a death ray, he wondered why the minister would say such a thing: "What, then, is the ray which is hinted at by Sir Thomas Inskip? Is it one of those closely guarded secrets which only military and air experts know of, and which is still unknown to the majority of scientists?"[8]

Inskip's announcement had not appeared out of the blue. As mentioned above, there had already been newspaper stories of inventors recently offering their talents to the British government. In 1935, it was revealed that a Scottish-American named Paul Humphrey MacNeile had been working secretly in Holland on an infra-red ray that could detect the heat of airplane engines at a great distance. He had shown his device to the British military, but no word was yet known about its fate.[9] Another story was about a thirty-six-year-old Londoner who had supposedly demonstrated a ray device for members of the Scientific and Research Department of the Air Ministry. According to reports, the apparatus resembled a searchlight on a swivel tripod and operated by sending out infra-red rays combined with a secret ray developed by the inventor. In the test, he allegedly stopped the engine of a car, suggesting that it could be used as an effective anti-aircraft measure.[10]

As it turned out, the British were secretly working on radar, the development of which is described below. The government made such announcements about "invisible walls" and "rays" for two reasons. One was to reassure the public that Britain was safe from air attack in the event of another general European war, the other, according to a press release in July 1945, a deception to cover the real work going on with radar.[11] These statements, however, also bestowed a degree of credibility on the continuing claims of death rays being invented.

A side note on this concerns Basil Liddell Hart, the well-known military analyst and writer who frequently advised the British government. He was not brought into the loop on radar until 1939, but in 1937 he wrote a paper for Inskip, in which he suggested starting a rumor that Britain had developed a means to counter the air attack. The secret of its falsehood would be shared with a few select individuals. In this way he believed that it might have a wholesome effect on a would-be enemy (Germany). Somewhat later that year, two men who were privy to the secret of radar, Air Marshal Sir Wilfred Freeman and Group Captain Jack Slessor, "unwittingly told Liddell Hart ... that they were anxious about Inskip spreading the idea that we might have a death ray or similar device as a defence against air attack."[12]

Soon after Inskip's remarks, newspapers reported that a number of people were continuing to spread the familiar rumor of British scientists working on some type of death ray to combat the aerial threat. The London correspondent for the *Devon and Exeter Gazette* of Devon, however, told his paper that a superior air defense would be ready within the foreseeable future and that it involved improved anti-aircraft batteries, searchlights, and other conventional means. He suggested that statements made by Inskip and Winston Churchill had given rise to more "romantic" explanations.[13] Several months later, noted American lecturer and journalist Dorothy Fuldheim nevertheless told members of the Elyria Foreman's Club in Elyria, Ohio, of rumors indicating a British ray capable of halting enemy airplanes before they could reach London.[14] Such stories continued on into 1938, as *Le Matin* reported in November that British scientists had presented to Minister Inskip a report on their recently developed *barrière de la mort* capable of stopping an army on the battlefield.[15] As late as August 1939 newspapers indicated that officials of the Air Ministry had witnessed a demonstration of a radio wave emitter capable of causing airplane engines to stop functioning. According to the *Auckland Star*, the apparatus was mounted on a swivel tripod and looked like a searchlight.[16]

British—and French—concern about air defense certainly increased whenever there were new rumors of German devices capable of immobilizing gasoline engines. In October 1930, there was a story about Czech motorists returning from Germany reporting that they had experienced sudden engine failure on a four-kilometer stretch of road near the town of Riesa in Saxony. Some forty vehicles, including trucks, were involved. As described in *Die Neue Freie Presse* of Vienna, the motorists, unable to find any normal mechanical reason for this occurrence, then encountered a Saxon policeman who informed them that they would be able to resume their journey at 3:00 p.m. The cause, according to the officer, was a test being conducted by the Saxon authorities. At precisely that time all of the motor vehicles started and their drivers resumed their journeys.[17] The unofficial explanation involved the use of electro-magnetic rays disrupting the magnetos of the cars. Former French premier Paul Painlevé commented on the incident, expressing doubt that a ray could stop a car unless the vehicle had a receiving unit.[18] The story also appeared in national and local newspapers in the United States. According to the *New York Times*, the German War Ministry flatly denied the allegations that it was conducting any military tests with an invisible ray, and the *Reno Evening Gazette* added that a total of four hundred and forty cars had been disabled.[19]

Five years later a similar event was reported, this time with Austrian motorists in southern Germany. According to a Viennese businessman, "I was driving my own car, going from Linz to Munich. Almost exactly 20 miles beyond the German frontier my motor suddenly stopped. I made an immediate and exhaustive investigation. There was plenty of petrol, and everything was in perfect order."[20] He went on to say that another motorist behind him, a business acquaintance from Graz, experienced the same thing. A policeman came up and told them not to worry, for their cars would soon start up again, which they did five minutes later. The Viennese businessman asked friends in Munich what was going on and was informed that military tests were responsible.[21]

Earlier that spring more rumors of a successful German ray had circulated in the press. On its front page in March, the *New York Times* featured a story entitled "Reich Burns Oil in Planes; Would Foil Radio Beams," with the subtitle "Report That It Has Perfected Device to Stop Ignition Motors Is Revived—Diesels' Employment in Bombers Seen." In the article, writer Frederick T. Birchall explained to his readers that German civil aviation was reportedly switching to diesel engines for its aircraft since they operated more efficiently than gasoline ignition motors. This development acquired greater concern amid rumors that the Germans had invented a means to halt airplanes in flight. The diesel engine, which does not employ ignition and is therefore unaffected by a ray, would be ideal for use in bombers.[22] The next day, however, the *New York Times* had a piece entitled "Experts Doubt Ray Can Stop Airplane," in which several men, including Dr. Alfred N. Goldsmith, pointed out the difficulties of using such a ray to target an airplane and explained that proper shielding would most probably protect the engine anyway.[23]

Stories about such a German weapon nevertheless continued to appear in the press. In April the Parisian newspaper *La Croix* carried an article, first published in London's *Sunday Chronicle*, about a Z-ray. According to reports, apparently endorsed by German sources, it could "build up an invisible wall against France" and cause "bridges to collapse, the mouths of cannons to melt, motors of airplanes to stop in midair, and

4. Death Rays and Their Connection to the Second World War

... pulverize wireless stations, railroad tracks, and the plate armor of tanks."[24] This claim was viewed by some as simply an example of the propaganda efforts of several countries to convince others that they had achieved some success in gaining military superiority. It should be noted also that the press seemed to have forgotten about the Z-rays of Bernays Johnson prior to the First World War.

Although not connecting this story to the Z-ray, rumors surfaced in July that a German scientist in Bavaria was the inventor of a ray capable of disabling a gasoline engine at a range of two miles. According to the Berlin correspondent for the London *Evening News*, a Bavarian government spokesman had confirmed for him the validity of the report.[25] The newspaper article, carried in *The Mercury* of Hobart, Tasmania, added that an aeronautical expert by the name of Nigel Tangye, who had visited Germany and spoken with "a world-famous pilot, who now holds an important post in the German air ministry...," had actually witnessed the demonstration of the ray.[26]

Other reports also endorsed the possibility that Germany had a death ray. In 1933 the crash of a Lithuanian airplane led to rumors of foul play by the Reich. According to the *Nottingham Evening Post*, a Captain Darius and a Mr. Girenas had almost completed their Atlantic flight when their craft went down about four hundred miles from their destination of Kovno. Allegations of a German ray being responsible, however, were quickly suppressed by the Lithuanian government, and its official investigation concluded that "bad weather conditions and fatigue" accounted for the tragedy.[27] The same year a story about the French airplanes being forced down over Bavaria ten years earlier surfaced again. According to the *Muswellbrook Chronicle* of New South Wales, the incidents had never been fully explained and, consequently, remained a mystery.[28] There was also a related commentary on a book entitled *Mysteries of the Great War* by Harold T. Wilkins published in 1935. According to *The Argus* of Melbourne, the author mentioned that a squadron of French planes had been forced by some type of unknown means to land inside German lines, suggesting a death ray.[29] Appearing in American newspapers in July 1935 was a sensational account of the development of a death ray two years before at the Charlottenburger Technische Hochschule in Berlin. As described in the *Indiana Evening Gazette* of Pennsylvania, the apparatus "was capable of killing a small animal at a distance of 50 yards."[30] Another sensational story in August 1936 was reported by British journalist Trevor Kennard. According to his sources, the Germans had developed a ray capable of projecting an invisible wall four miles high impenetrable by airplanes.[31]

A similar story in January 1937 appeared first in the French paper *Oeuvre* but was then picked up by others. According to *Oeuvre*'s Geneviève Tabouis, the Germans were in the process of erecting installations in the Saar Valley which could generate death rays as a defense against aircraft. She also claimed that the Germans had developed an artificial fog which could be used to protect vital areas from air attack.[32] In 1938 another story appeared about ray installations along the frontier but added that German aircraft were being equipped with the ray devices as well.[33] The plane in question was the new Heinkel H-60, which would emit an ultrashort wave capable of causing engine failures. The German planes, according to the Radio Nazionale Agency of Italy, used "heavy-oil engines" unaffected by the rays.[34] The sheer number of stories about Germany possessing some type of ray capable of causing engine failure led to speculation that this alleged military superiority might be the cause for Hitler's aggressive behavior.[35]

As for Italy, work on a death ray was associated with the famous inventor Guglielmo Marconi. In 1931 he announced that birds and mice accidentally struck by beams from his ultrashort wave radio had been killed and that he might look into the possibility of utilizing them as a weapon.[36] In 1932 and again in early June 1935 rumors circulated that Marconi was indeed working on some type of "war ray" and had even demonstrated it for Mussolini. Over the course of the next several months, reporters' speculation turned into probability and, for some, reality. In September 1935 Marconi announced that he was experimenting with a death ray that would aid in air defense. Although American scientists remained skeptical, they had to acknowledge the remote possibility because of Marconi's credentials and past accomplishments. Even if an ultrashort wave radio flash were capable of doing what Marconi suggested, scientists such as A. N. Goldsmith believed that it would be fairly easy to shield a motor against it.[37] According to *Popular Mechanics*, reports indicated that Marconi had succeeded in creating a high-energy beam that could short circuit an airplane's ignition system, causing it to fall out of the sky. The article, however, went on to say that such claims had to be regarded with skepticism, for scientists still did not know how to generate enough energy for any type of beam or ray to be effective at great distances.[38]

During this period a number of American local newspapers reported on Marconi's death ray and seemed in general favorably inclined to accept the possibility of the inventor's success. *The Times and Daily News Leader* of San Mateo, California, for example, stated that military establishments in Europe were taking it seriously enough to begin work on countermeasures.[39] In October the *New York Times* lent support to the possibility that his work had paid off when it reported that a strange event occurred during Marconi's demonstration for Mussolini. Motorists traveling along the highway between Rome and Ostia suddenly experienced engine failure. After considerable effort to try to start their cars, they succeeded suddenly without any explanation as to what had happened.[40]

One self-styled evangelist named Nicholas Pirolo railed against Mussolini as the "Anti-Christ" at the time of the invasion of Ethiopia and referenced Marconi's "radio ray" as one of Il Duce's diabolical weapons. He described it as "a 'lightning death ray,' a super physical 'radio beam' capable of doing incomparable damage to life and property. It is designed to stop enemy airplanes in flight, put out lights by airplane control, stop ignition systems and exert a force capable of destroying whole fleets of ships in a very short time."[41] Pirolo added that he had been told Marconi's invention was capable of annihilating Britain's entire Royal Navy.[42] Before his death, however, Marconi told a reporter that he had been unsuccessful in developing an effective military ray.[43]

Linked to the reports of Marconi's work, as well as to the rumors about German rays, were several news items about other "ray" developments in Britain. These often included some rather strange stories. One such appeared in the French North African paper *Le Progrès de Sidi-Bel-Abbès* in August 1935. Traveling through Wales, a man and woman with their little boy stopped along the highway. The child went for a walk, and when he did not return after a certain period of time his parents went looking and found him lying unconscious. He remained quite sick for about two days before recovering. Inquiring of the local authorities as to what could possibly have caused this, the parents learned that there had been some experiments with a death ray in the vicinity. Further details were not available for security reasons. A short time later, a child was found dead near the same spot. The article gave some credence to a "ray," mentioning that of Marconi and of the Germans as fact.[44] One newspaper had a story about an anonymous British scientist who said that he had invented a ray similar to that of the Italian but had been able to develop a defense against it as well. Interviewed by a reporter, the scientist said that he had received funding from a wealthy donor—now dead—who told him to remain anonymous and to give the results of his research to the British government. The man claimed to have stopped the motors of cars with his ray and caused engine problems for airplanes, forcing them to land. A more powerful transmitter would enable him to protect London from air attack in a future war. His weapon was not limited to such modest capabilities, however, for this scientist told the reporter that it could transmit disease germs, destroy crops and food supplies, and project poison gas. Probably even more astounding was his claim that he could generate stratospheric conditions over a city, suffocating the entire population. Britons and those in the Dominions could now rest assured, for the secrets were in the hands of the prime minister and his cabinet.[45]

As some of the above stories indicate, reports of car engines mysteriously stopping appeared frequently during the 1930s. There were more in 1937 and 1939 about motorists experiencing this phenomenon as they traveled along country roads in Britain. As the London correspondent for the *Devon and Exeter Gazette* wrote in March 1937, he was told by a resident living on the Salisbury Plain that a number of cars suddenly lost power and stopped without any apparent reason. After some time had passed, a policeman came by on a bicycle and told them that everything would be "O.K. in ten minutes."[46] The correspondent suggested that the military was conducting secret experiments with a ray. The *Bath Weekly Chronicle and Herald* reported in August 1939 that "invisible rays" were being blamed by motorists for the sudden and mysterious loss of power to their car engines as they passed near Colchester, Droitwich, and Lewes. One driver in the vicinity of Colchester claimed that a soldier of the Royal Engineers approached him while he was trying to figure out what caused his motor to stop and told him "O.K.—you can go ahead now."[47] The newspaper added that a number of complaints of this nature had been submitted to the War Ministry over the past several years but had either been ignored or openly "pooh-poohed." One story about car motors stopping, however, came from Denmark and did not involve official connections. In 1939 after a series of unexplained breakdowns on a road between Odense and Kewteminde on the Island of Funen, rumors circulated about a mysterious man seen on the island who was experimenting with electricity, possibly the same person who was believed to have invented a death ray.[48]

The start of the Second World War did not mark the end of the death ray as a news item, as stories continued to circulate that both belligerents and non-belligerents had either developed such a weapon or were feverishly trying to do so. Although many Americans hoped to avoid being drawn into the conflict, they expected their government and military agencies to keep up with scientific advances and not be caught unprepared; and the popular media made certain that the general public was kept informed. In Britain and France there was genuine concern that the Germans were secretly working on new types of weapons, including a death ray. Despite the fact that none of the claims made for such an energy weapon throughout the interwar period had panned out, people continued to believe in their existence.

It did not take long for new claims for death rays to make their appearance. The first was attributed indirectly to Adolf Hitler upon the conclusion of the rapid conquest of Poland. Speaking in Danzig on 25 September 1939, he warned the British and French that he had a new secret weapon. According to the *Dallas Morning News*, the speculation was that it concerned a death ray.[49] In October a story appeared in the *New York Herald*, as well as in other newspapers, about a former engineer with the U.S. Department of the Interior, Otto H. Mohr, who had notified the War Department that he had a ray capable of remote detonation of explosives.[50] Like previous announcements, nothing more was heard, probably convincing some that it must be real, as the military would want to guard any secrets about such a device. The following January, the *New York Times* published an article about a decision by the British and French to share scientific information so as not to fall behind the Germans. The Allies believed that Hitler had for some time had his scientists working on powerful, secret weapons, and therefore precious time could not be lost in bureaucratic red tape. The British announced that they had already organized at the beginning of the war teams of scientists and their assistants to work on secret projects in diverse fields. They also set up a research department within the Ministry of Supply to evaluate the practicality of the many suggestions it received from inventors and others. Receiving about three hundred a week, the *New York Times* stated that the department "is doing a wholesale business in death rays these days. They come in on the average of two a week."[51]

In February 1940 *Forum Magazine* had an article entitled "Has Germany a 'Death Ray?'" by Albert Brandt. The opening paragraph expressed surprise that the fearsome weapons foretold ever since the end of the Great War had not been used: "What about the threatened 'war by science,' which was to hurl Europe into chaos overnight and destroy cities and annihilate civilian populations? Certain commentators were even moved to suggest that, if things didn't start happening, this would be a 'dull' war."[52] The answer, according to Brandt, was that maybe this "war of science" had begun after all. Referring to Germany's use of contact mines against British shipping, he went on to raise the specter of more weapons being deployed, specifically the death ray. He also made it clear to his readers that the controversy over such a weapon had not ended. Brandt cited a recent dispute between two leading French scientists, one of them Professor Langevin of the Collège de France, who maintained that the death ray was only theoretically possible but not within the reach of present-day science. His colleague, Professor Mangin, however, disagreed and stressed that the Germans might have made it a reality or, at least, were on the verge of transforming it into a viable weapon.[53]

A rebuttal to the death-ray advocates appeared the following August in *Science Digest* (originally in *Discovery*) in an article written by Douglas W. F. Mayer. In "The Truth About Death Rays," he conceded that some of the various types of rays reported over the years did have the properties to kill or to stop gasoline motors but only within distances completely insufficient for a military weapon. Mayer told his readers the same thing that other skeptics had said. No known means of generating the energy required to make the rays effective over great distances had been discovered. The only exception was the possibility of discharging electricity through powerful jets of water such as used by firemen. The problem, of course, according to Mayer, was that the means of storing and transporting the water and the electrical components would be so cumbersome as to make it impractical for the modern battlefield.[54]

Throughout the course of the Second World War, reports of death rays continued periodically to appear in the popular media. In describing the German march into Belgium in 1940, for example, the *New York Times* mentioned rumors of a German "secret weapon" used to secure the fort at Liége. Although serious speculation was that it might be a new type of gas or some other conventional device, the term "super-radium death rays" also surfaced but was dismissed by military authorities.[55] In October 1944 newspapers carried a story emanating from Brussels that the Germans had been working on a death ray for the past seven years. According to the account, the first demonstration took place in 1937 at the Tempelhof Airport in Berlin. There, representatives of A.E.G. and Siemens saw an electrically produced ray stop an internal combustion engine at five hundred yards. In a later experiment, guinea pigs were placed in a cage about two hundred yards in front of a small structure which housed the device. Onlookers heard a zooming noise and after ten minutes the little animals were dead. The most ambitious experiment, according to the article, involved the research facilities at Peenemünde, more famous later for the development of the V-rockets. Researchers placed guinea pigs, a horse, and a pig in front of the death-ray machine and turned it on for just three seconds. All of the unfortunate creatures were killed, the horse reportedly suffering great agony before it succumbed to the rays. Afterward, a doctor concluded that death resulted from an "interference with the white blood corpuscles."[56] Another claim for a German death ray appeared in February

1945. As reported in *The Press and Journal* of Aberdeen, Scotland, a story out of Stockholm contained the news that the German V-bomb could release "sound waves of a very high frequency which can decompose living tissue."[57] And in January 1945, Radio Singapore announced that Japan had a death ray strong enough to destroy an entire American city.[58] Allied military spokesmen were therefore kept busy refuting these claims and reassuring their people that such weapons were not to be taken seriously. At least they did so publicly.

To underscore this point, the governments of Great Britain and the United States did consider death rays a serious matter, as attested by revelations after the Second World War. Harry E. Wimperis, who had witnessed Grindell Matthews's tests with his death ray back in 1924, was in 1935 Director of Scientific Research in the British Air Ministry. Britain's weak air defenses, revealed in the RAF exercise of 1934, caused Wimperis grave concern. He therefore helped organize the Air Defence Committee and placed at its head Henry Tizard, a respected scientist and rector of the Imperial College in London who had also been a member of the group to examine death-ray claims after the First World War. One of the tasks of Tizard and this new committee was to evaluate these in order to be on the safe side regarding national security. Although most could easily be dismissed as bogus, some death-ray claims had to be taken seriously. One such was the report mentioned above of a German inventor having supposedly used a ray of some type to kill animals at the Tempelhof Airport in Berlin. After having arranged a meeting with the man, the committee concluded that he was a fraud.[59] Wimperis also contacted Robert A. Watson-Watt, superintendent of the Radio Research Station at Slough and a descendant of James Watt, and asked him to investigate the possibility of developing some type of radiation that could be directed against an incoming enemy airplane and destroy it. Wimperis conceived of a strong beam of electromagnetic waves that could damage the aircraft and heat up the body temperature of the pilot.[60] Watson-Watt and his assistant, Arnold "Skip" Wilkins, went to work in their laboratory. After a few tests performed by Wilkins, they reached the same conclusion that a number of other researchers had previously in the 1920s and early 1930s: it was technologically impossible to generate enough energy to make the ray effective at the distances required for military use. In the process, however, Watson-Watt speculated that radio beams might be reflected back from aircraft. As a result, he and other British scientists went on to develop a means of detecting enemy airplanes before they could cross the Channel and attack Britain. This later came to be called "radar."[61]

During the Second World War, American leaders did not allow their skepticism about death rays to risk falling behind the Axis Powers in the development of new weapons. The National Defense Research Committee created in September 1940 a section designed to utilize radio communications to aid in defending the country. By late 1942 this organization had become known as Division 13. After the war, Dr. A. F. Murray revealed this information in an article that appeared in the 2 December 1946 issue of *Time*. Murray was the Technical Aide in Division 13 until 1944. According to him, he was assigned the task of investigating the death-ray claims made by inventors to see if any yielded practical results. He and his team undertook twelve projects and concluded that such a weapon was beyond the capability of the existing technology. Some of the claims made by inventors turned out to be hoaxes while a few were valid. But these, like all the others that had enjoyed successful publicity earlier were effective at short distances only. Murray did, however, say that atomic radiation offered the possibility of realizing this goal.[62]

As things turned out, the Germans initiated a number of exotic weapons projects during the war,[63] including death rays. Shortly after Germany surrendered in 1945, U.S. forces came across a secret laboratory installation at Hillersleben where scientists had been working on a type of death ray of true science fictional proportions. Labeled the *Sonnengewehr*, or "sun gun," the plan was to construct a space platform mounted with a large reflector three square kilometers that could harness the sun's rays. The "gun" could then concentrate the energy like a giant magnifying glass and direct it to targets on earth. Although most American scientists reacted with extreme skepticism, Lieutenant Colonel John A. Keck, who headed the enemy technical intelligence branch of the U.S. Army's Ordnance Service, did not consider the work at Hillersleben so fantastic. An engineer in civilian life, Keck said in a press conference that these men were among the top rocket scientists in Germany and that they had been diligently carrying on this work in a methodical, highly structured manner. The Germans did tell their interrogators they realized that such a project might take fifty years or more to complete and would therefore have no effect on the outcome of the war.[64]

Another revelation of a secret German plan to develop a death ray comes from physicist Pedro Waloschek, whose book *Todesstrahlen als Lebensretter* (Death Rays as a Life Savior), focuses on the work of Ernst Schiebold. According to Waloschek, in April 1943 Schiebold offered to Field Marshal Erhard Milch, the General Inspector of the Luftwaffe, a proposal to develop a death ray capable of stopping an airplane motor and killing the pilot and other crew members. His ray would also be effective against ground troops. Schiebold's background and expertise was in the use of X-rays, which he believed could be intensified and harnessed as a weapon. He told Milch that he could set up ray generators, "death ray cannons," around cities to protect them from air raids. Given the increased Allied bombing of German cities as well as the slow progress with the secret V-weapons, Milch decided to fund the project. After about a year of work, however, it was canceled.[65] In his memoirs, Nazi Minister of Armaments Albert Speer mentioned an incident in which Dr. Robert Ley, head of the German Labor Front, informed him excitedly that "Death rays have been invented! A simple apparatus that we can produce in large quantities. I've studied the documentation; there's no doubt about it. This will be the decisive weapon!"[66] Speer did not share his enthusiasm and jokingly told Ley that he could have the title "Commissioner for Death Rays." Speer did not name the inventor of the alleged apparatus.

Germany's Axis partner Japan also tried to create some type of death ray. Although the announcement by Singapore Radio mentioned above was a hollow boast for its propaganda effect, the Japanese were indeed working on such a device, confirmed shortly after their surrender. According to a press release from General Douglas MacArthur's headquarters in Tokyo, the project had been going on for five and a half years, and the Japanese government had continued to fund it even in 1945. By concentrating short radio waves, the Japanese had had some limited success in producing adverse physiological effects on rabbits up to forty yards away.[67] Studies later showed that both the Japanese army and navy had become interested in the possibility of developing a death ray as far back as 1930.[68] Researchers at the Army Institute of Scientific Research, however, did not proceed with actual laboratory work until 1936 because they realized, as had their American and European counterparts, the limitations on producing sufficient power to make the death ray a feasible weapon. The question was taken up again because of improvements in generating microwave energy, primarily with the development of the magnetron; and in 1939 a team of scientists and technicians began work in earnest. Naval researchers also worked on a magnetron and became interested in radar. Efforts to develop a death ray continued off and on during the Second World War, with both services receiving renewed funding for their projects in 1944 and 1945. The fruits of their labors, however, were no more successful than those of others. The Japanese managed to injure and kill small animals using microwave energy, but only at short distances. Their goal of creating a death ray that would cause airplane engines to stop and to harm enemy pilots remained elusive.[69]

Often dismissed simply as the product of con artists, quacks, overzealous journalists, and science fiction writers, the death ray was a much more complex phenomenon than usually depicted. It was indeed a gold mine for newspapers and magazines, but the sensationalist nature of the mysterious ray alone could not have sustained it as a news item for more than five decades. This was accomplished to a large extent by the contradictory messages that continually appeared in the popular media. For almost every scientist and military official who regarded it as fantasy, there were those who either endorsed it openly or gave tacit support to its possibility. The revelations after the Second World War concerning efforts by governments either to ascertain the viability of such a weapon or to construct one further attest to the death ray's significance during this period.

Part II

The Death Ray in Fiction and Popular Culture

5

Early Death-Ray Novels and Short Stories

Beginning with the last few years of the nineteenth century and continuing on into the twentieth, authors of adventure tales and imaginary war scenarios turned increasingly to storylines requiring advanced technology that included some type of directed energy weapon. The earliest published did not follow a common pattern with these devices, as one encounters a variety of energy sources and properties employed, often defined vaguely. A common thread, however, was their overall connection to current scientific developments and newspaper accounts of claims for what one may categorize as death rays. As these increased, so did the number of fictional works employing such a weapon. By the time the First World War broke out in 1914, the death ray was a well-established feature in fiction.

Late Nineteenth Century through the First World War

Forerunners of this type of literature predate the period of intense research into electricity but had little effect on the later connection between fiction and science. An early example is Washington Irving's description of an invasion of Earth by people from the Moon, for the "Lunatics" are equipped with "concentrated sunbeams."[1] Edward Bulwer Lytton's novel *The Coming Race* published in 1871, however, appeared just as electricity had become something more than a curiosity and reflected a stronger relationship to scientific research. In a letter to his close friend John Forster in March 1870 when the manuscript was completed, Lytton indicated he had selected electricity simply as a force that a superior race of beings would understand and be able to control.[2] The story is about an American who discovers an advanced civilization deep within the earth and populated by an ancient race of beings who survived the Great Flood. They call themselves the Vril-ya, a name connected to their word for a powerful force, "vril." Lytton describes it as something essentially electricity but comprising several other manifestations of energy as well. It can be used to kill or to heal. As a weapon, its power is formidable and can be contained in a staff. In one scene, the American adventurer is saved from a fierce reptilian creature by a boy wielding the weapon. With a flash of lightning the beast is reduced to ashes.[3]

Commentary on Lytton's book and how it might presage real developments with future weapons surfaced a number of years later. In 1887 the *Belfast News-Letter* in Ireland had a brief article about a Professor Henry Robinson speaking at the annual dinner of the Society of Engineers, in which he described a test conducted in Antwerp of an advanced type of artillery gun. The purpose of his address was to inform his audience of the rapid changes in warfare and of what could be expected in the future. He added that it reminded him of Lytton's book and, in particular, the scene involving the power of the "vril wands." The newspaper commentary indicated this reference as showing Robinson "clearly anticipating the deadly and rapid action of electric currents, whereby one army of subterranean inhabitants destroyed an opposing army by a single discharge of their electrical weapons, leaving as a residuum a small amount of carbonaceous matter."[4] In 1905 Charles Lester Leonard, president of the American Roentgen Society, delivered an address in which he quoted several passages about "vril," praising the perspicacity of the author: "The quotations are from Lord Lytton's book, 'The Coming Race,' and sound almost prophetic when viewed with our present knowledge."[5] His statement reflected the assumption prevailing in some scientific circles that the concept of an energy beam weapon would be a plausible result of continued scientific progress.

Despite the success of Lytton's novel, wireless energy and its use as a weapon did not become an important subject of fiction until later, beginning with H. G. Wells's *The War of the Worlds*, after which writers featured it increasingly on up to the First World War. Much of the death-ray fiction written during this time reflected a direct relationship to research with electricity by Heinrich Hertz, Henri Becquerel, Thomas Edison, Nikola Tesla, Guglielmo Marconi, and others. It was also influenced by news reports and claims that wireless electricity could be harnessed as a weapon. Although not indicating its energy source, H. G. Wells in *The*

War of the Worlds, serialized first in *Pearson's Magazine* and *Cosmopolitan* in 1897 before being published in book form in 1898, described just such a force, in this case the Martian heat ray: "However it is done, it is certain that a beam of heat is the essence of the matter. Heat, and invisible, instead of visible light. Whatever is combustible flashes into flame at its touch, lead runs like water, it softens iron, cracks and melts glass, and when it falls upon water, incontinently that explodes into steam."[6] Wells told a reporter for *The Daily News* of London that he got the idea of the heat ray from Archimedes,[7] but he was most certainly familiar with the current scientific advances in electricity and probably with some of the news reports concerning wireless energy and its application to warfare.

Clement Shorter, who reviewed Wells's novel for *The Bookman*, moreover, did not consider such a weapon all that surprising. He began with a quotation from the *Westminster Gazette* regarding the American named John Hartman, mentioned in Chapter 1, who had supposedly developed a gun that discharged electricity by using the beam of a searchlight as a conductor. The article repeated the information about its killing properties, including the experiment with a rabbit. Shorter then linked this report to *The War of the Worlds*: "It set me thinking that if the Martians did not war on the world some human enemy armed with those heat-rays might, and instead of killing rabbits might kill men, until London became the silent, empty city that Mr. Wells's imagination has pictured with so much force."[8]

Shortly after the appearance of *The War of the Worlds* in *Cosmopolitan*, Garrett P. Serviss serialized in 1897 in the *New York Evening Journal* an unauthorized version entitled *Fighters from Mars* and another one in 1898 in the *Boston Evening Post*, in which the action is moved to those two cities. He followed this up with *Edison's Conquest of Mars*, which ran in installments in the *New York Journal* in 1898.[9] Billed as a sequel to *The War of the Worlds*, it had the endorsement of Edison but not that of Wells. In the story Serviss utilized two types of weapons. To the Martians, whom he changed from Wells's creatures resembling octopi into humanlike giants, he gave devices that were electrical in nature and discharged something akin to a lightning bolt. The second was a type of sound weapon referred to as a "disintegrator," developed by the fictional Edison, for it was based on harmonic vibrations which disrupted the atoms of whatever was struck by the waves. As described by Serviss, this weapon concentrated "its energy upon a given object in order that the atoms composing that object should be set into violent undulation, sufficient to burst it asunder and to scatter its molecules broadcast. This the inventor effected by the simplest means in the world—simply a parabolic reflector by which the destructive waves could be sent like a beam of light, but invisible, in any direction and focused upon any desired point."[10] It is not clear whether these devices were entirely the products of his creative imagination or were inspired by newspaper accounts. The electrical weapon bears resemblance to claims for such inventions dating back to 1890. It is less clear about the disintegrator, but Serviss, an amateur scientist greatly interested in astronomy, would probably have been aware of stories circulating in the press about fantastic powers attributed to electricity. As Park Benjamin said in his 1896 article, previously mentioned, referring to some of these popular notions, "we cannot shake ships to pieces by induced vibrations in the cosmic ether, and that we cannot send disintegrating currents to them."

Another fictional work involving wireless energy came out the same year, but the weapon described was not a heat ray and therefore, like the disintegrator in *Edison's Conquest of Mars*, not an imitation of Wells. Instead, it appears to have been based on reports about the possibility of exploding gunpowder and ammunition without directly harming living things. In *The Warstock: A Tale of To-morrow*, Wirt Gerrare (pseudonym of William L. Greener) depicted a utopian community called Cristallia located on the coast of Morocco. Established under the guidance of a wealthy American inventor named Robert Sterry and his close friend and fellow scientist Willie Redhead, it is a communistic society for inventors and like-minded savants, many of whom belong to a group called the Isocrats, founded in London. Women share equality with men and enjoy considerable influence. Dedicated to common ideals of right and wrong, the inhabitants focus their energies on creating marvelous inventions and selling products derived from them to sustain the community. Although recognized by several countries, including Norway, the Great Powers still regard Cristallia as an irritating anomaly, more so as its superior products begin to cause economic disturbances in Europe and the United States. Ultimately, the little country is attacked and has to defend itself. The greatest threat comes from Germany, as the neighboring colony of "Pieterlanders" assisted by a German naval task force storms Cristallia. At first overwhelmed by the onslaught, Sterry and his followers eventually regroup and triumph. At this stage late in the novel, the "Warstock," as it is called, makes its appearance. Before he dies, Willie manages to set in motion this secret invention. The author does not provide much detail about its properties and its energy source; the machine vibrates and shakes as it sends out energy waves that locate and destroy gunpowder in magazines of ships and arsenals. A rash of mysterious explosions erupts across Continental

Europe and ultimately Britain. This device quickly brings about an end to war, and Sterry and his remaining followers rebuild Cristallia in all its glory and become the arbiters of the world in this new age.[11]

The following year, naval writer Frederick Thomas Jane employed an energy beam weapon in *The Violet Flame: A Story of Armageddon and After*. In this story set in London, an eccentric Anglo-French scientist, Professor Mirzarbeau, concocts a theory that all matter in the universe is composed of hydrogen atoms and that planets and stars are living, sentient entities. He has also developed a weapon dubbed the "annihilating machine," which can project some type of ray, violet in color, into the atmosphere, whereupon it is reflected down to its target, reducing it to hydrogen atoms while leaving only a slight trace. The ray can destroy anything, including people, and operate over great distances. Mirzarbeau performs a demonstration early on by causing Waterloo Station to disappear, with only a flat, smooth surface resembling cement remaining. But the weapon does more than strike quickly, for it can create a radius of death lasting for quite some time. A number of people, including policemen, who venture too closely to examine the vacant spot where Waterloo Station stood, suddenly disappear as well. In the end Mirzarbeau is killed by his own invention, but ironically his foes unwittingly destroy his machines that are actually preventing a comet from striking the earth. Only two people survive the catastrophe, an American woman who happened to be staying in London when the adventure began and the Englishman seeking to marry her.[12] Like Wells and Gerrare, Jane did not provide much information about the properties of his fictional machine.

In his 1902 work *The World Masters*, however, fellow British author George Griffith[13] was more specific about the killing agent, as he described a device capable of controlling the world's electrical energy and also functioning as a weapon. The story is about a private business enterprise, the International Electrical Power and Storage Trust headed by an American and an Englishman, that benefits from this invention and creates a giant complex in northeastern Canada near the Magnetic Pole to provide electricity to millions of customers. Russia and France form an alliance to obtain this power and at the same time conquer Germany. Much of the novel involves cloak-and-dagger subplots but reaches a climax when the Trust issues an ultimatum to the Continental powers of Europe to stop their preparations for war. French and Russian armies threaten to invade Germany from the west and the east, naval squadrons have taken up positions in the North and Baltic seas, and Germany has called upon its Austrian and Italian allies to mobilize in support. With the expiration of the ultimatum's deadline, the Trust uses its powerful machines to garner the electrical energy in Europe and elsewhere to immobilize the belligerents. Britain and America are only moderately inconvenienced. The effect of this process wreaks havoc on anything made of iron or steel and all things using electricity. It also affects the human body, rendering a person somewhat listless. The antagonists, nevertheless, do not believe that the Trust can stop them from fighting and action begins. The French fleet off the coast at the North Sea entrance to the Kiel Canal, however, experiences engine problems, and when the ships try to engage a German fort, the big guns blow up—their steel barrels shattering as if made of glass. The Germans fare no better, as the great Krupp shore guns experience the same fate.[14] The leaders of the warring nations finally agree to peace terms, with King Edward VII of England acting as mediator. A joint Franco-Russian naval force under the guise of polar exploration has been out of communication with the respective governments—and in a zone not affected by the Trust's power—and continues on its mission to capture or destroy the great storage facility.

In depicting the battle scene which ensues, Griffith was possibly the first author to apply the term "death ray" to a weapon in literature. Whether or not he was influenced by the newspaper article regarding John Hartman mentioned in Chapter 1 remains to be seen. As Griffith describes: "Then it stopped. Every gun was silent, for not a man dared go near it. Every officer and man who had shown himself in the open had been reduced to a heap of bones before he could get back under shelter. Then those who were out of reach of the terrible death-rays saw six long guns rise from the masked batteries beside the two towers and over the central gate." After a pounding from these massive weapons, the ray is employed once more against the ships: "The death-ray played continuously over their decks and every man who showed himself fell dead with the flesh withered from his face and skull."[15]

Griffith also wrote a novel in 1906, published posthumously in 1911, about a world war breaking out in 1909,[16] in which he described two advanced weapons, including a variant of those possessing the capability of remote detonation so frequently reported in newspapers. Entitled *The Lord of Labour*, the story begins with a young Englishman discovering a radium-based mineral from which he develops an extremely powerful explosive. He harnesses this energy and fashions a radium rifle as well as radium shells for artillery guns. In the meantime a German scientist has produced for Kaiser Wilhelm II a "demagnetizer" device, which convinces the monarch to go to war against Britain. This invention sends out rays that weaken the molecular integrity of iron and steel, causing these metals to crumble into fine dust particles when hit by explosive projectiles. The demagnetizer can also transmit impulses that wreak havoc on electrical systems of naval vessels, including the capability of causing the shells to explode inside the big guns when fired. In the course of the war, the Germans use their demagnetizer to destroy several British and French naval squadrons before invading Britain. Although coming close to victory, the Germans are finally stopped primarily by the "Craftsmen," English union workers armed with radium rifles and formed in units in the spirit of the yeomen archers at the Battle of Crécy during the Hundred Years' War.[17]

Griffith wrote another novel, entitled *The World Peril of 1910* and published in 1907, in which a major war engulfs Europe and a comet hurtling toward Earth threatens to destroy all life on the planet. In this scenario, he has Britain confronted by an alliance of several countries, including Germany, Russia, France, Spain, and Austria. The chief weapons in this war are special explosives, highly advanced airships, and submarines. There is, however, one anomaly. In the first chapter, a scientist of Irish and Spanish lineage named Castellan is demonstrating for the Kaiser and two of his ministers a model of his "flying fish," which combines the capabilities of an aircraft and a submarine. He has an apparatus that controls it by wireless means. With the "flying fish"—and his new type of explosive—he destroys a model fleet floating in an experimental tank. Castellan then wants to show them another capability and asks the chancellor and the field marshal to come at him with their swords. As Griffith describes the scene:

> The sword points advanced towards him; the keys of the machine clicked faster and faster. The atmosphere of the room became tenser and tenser; the Kaiser leaned back against the door with his arms folded. When the points were within three feet of Castellan's head, the steel began to gleam with a bluish green light. The Chancellor and the Field Marshal stopped; they saw sparkles of blue flame running along the sword blades. Then came paralysis! the swords dropped from their hands, and they staggered back.[18]

Before using his apparatus for this demonstration, Castellan also tells the Kaiser for safety reasons to remove his pistol from his pocket. When asked why, he responds that the cartridges will explode. In this scene Griffith has his character employing some type of wireless waves capable of remote detonation. The anomaly is that it does not play a role in the war. The conflict is fought along conventional lines, with the more advanced weapons mentioned above dominating the action. Britain ultimately triumphs, and the comet is destroyed by a huge gun built just for that purpose.

Griffith was one of several authors to use this power in novels and short stories, as wireless remote detonation emerged as a dominant capability of the death ray in fiction prior to the First World War. Many of the works involve a single individual who has developed a force, usually electrical but occasionally of some other type, to destroy battleships and other engines of war. In 1906, for example, "The Wireless Death" by C. S. Raymond appeared in the February issue of *Technical World Magazine*. It concerns an impending war between the United States and Germany, with the Americans at a great disadvantage because of a vastly superior German fleet of airships. While the nation waits anxiously as Congress debates whether or not to declare war, a young electrician named Atsins gains admittance to General Montrus, the commander of U.S. forces. He shows him his design for a "concentrator" that will channel as much as two million volts of electricity into a lethal beam capable of traveling thousands of miles and annihilating any target. Montrus gives him the authority to head up the project to develop this weapon. In the meantime, the Americans have a "televue," which permits wireless transmissions from a scout plane to be viewed at the general's headquarters. This allows Montrus to keep an eye on the German airship fleet stationed at Kiel, as everyone waits for news from Congress. When the declaration of war is announced, the general and his staff see the German fleet beginning to make its move. Atsins is ready, however, and "in the twinkling of an eye," the airships are destroyed.[19]

A different type of energy source for a wireless device appeared in Jack London's 1908 tale *Goliah*. This was "energon," a force composed of cosmic energy found in solar rays and used as a weapon or for peaceful purposes. In the story, set in 1924, a scientist identified simply as "Goliah" has developed a means to explode at a distance the shells and gunpowder of warships as well as submarine mines and the magazines of coast defenses. He uses it to dispatch an entire American fleet sent to capture his island headquarters and to destroy a Japanese force trying to take advantage of America's sudden weakness. This invisible energy can also kill individuals. Goliah's objective is to put an end to war and create a new world order based on socialist principles, and in this he succeeds.[20]

One novel in 1908 utilized a form of atomic energy as the force powering a ray weapon. Hollis Godfrey's *The Man Who Ended War* also had the theme of the good scientist trying to put a stop to armed conflict. The most dramatic scene is the annihilation of the entire British and German battle fleets by a "radioactive wave beam." As the character Dorothy Haldane speculates, the weapon must be some kind of radioactive wave generator that breaks down the electrons, causing them to fly apart as gas.[21] Although the shock of the wave can stun or kill a person in close proximity, the wave itself acts only on metal. After sending an ultimatum to all the major powers to disarm, the unknown scientist demonstrates his weapon by destroying one battleship each of the United States, Great Britain, and France, and two of Germany. The Kaiser, however, believes that the English are responsible and declares war. Just as the two mighty battle fleets numbering more than eighty vessels engage one another in the Channel, radioactive waves begin their deadly work. As described by the author, each ship disappears "like a bursting soap bubble."[22] In the end, the scientist achieves his purpose, for disarmament takes place and nations pledge to abandon war, but he destroys his machine and takes his own life. One writer who reviewed this novel was not only favorable to the work but did not seem to consider such a weapon unusual.[23]

Another ray tale involving the power of wireless energy came out in 1908 as part of a collection of stories describing wars between the United States and Japan.[24] In "Sorakichi,—Prometheus," writer Rowan Stevens featured an American scientist named Adams who lived in Japan for a number of years before returning to the United States. While overseas, he secretly develops a device that can harness electrical energy and convert it into a weapon. When war breaks out between the United States and Japan—initiated by a sudden and swift Japanese capture of Honolulu and Pearl Harbor, an American warship finds itself at the mercy of three airships launched from an enemy vessel, the cruiser *Fujiyama*. At the last minute, an unconventional ship, the *Franklin*, designed, built, and commanded by the wayward scientist, suddenly appears and saves the day with this new weapon. Stevens does not go into any detail describing the appearance of the apparatus or how it utilizes energy to fire. He simply depicts a tube on the ship sending a "blinding blue glare" that completely annihilates two of the airships, resulting in the surrender of the *Fujiyama*.[25]

F. D'A. C. De L'Isle, however, was more specific and described a weapon employing wireless electricity in "The Strange Adventures of Bailey Catford, Scientist and Inventor." First appearing as a serial in *The Queenslander* of Brisbane in June and July 1910, it tells the story of a young English scientific genius who first makes a name for himself by inventing compressed air cells, enabling submarine crews to navigate their craft for longer periods of time without surfacing for fresh oxygen. Pilots can stay at high altitudes longer as well because of this discovery. Having acquired widespread fame and the attention of high society in London, Catford's world crashes when he is falsely accused of being responsible for the death of a young woman to whom he is engaged. Sentenced to several years in prison, he escapes and sails away in his highly advanced submarine, the *Ravager*. He catches up with his accuser, who is frightened into signing a full confession and conveniently drops dead. Returning to London, Catford is exonerated and restored to prominence, especially since he is now rumored to have developed a new weapon using Hertzian waves. The press has labeled it the "Catford Death Wave" and describes it as being capable of destroying cities and electrocuting entire armies.[26]

He next finds himself going to the aid of a young woman swindled out of her fortune by a man who threatened Catford, trying to acquire the *Ravager* to foment a revolution in a fictitious country somewhere in Latin America. The woman, named Jeannie, is an American and former actress in Vaudeville; she also happens to be the widow of Catford's accuser. Reaching the capital of the little republic, Catford gets the government to pay Jeannie a hefty sum after he successfully thwarts the attempt to overthrow the regime. He does so by using his Hertzian rays to cause the shells fired from the rebel gunboat to fall harmlessly into the water. Meanwhile, Jeannie and Catford are developing strong feelings toward one another that do not openly manifest themselves until after he rescues her from pirates. In doing so, he uses his inventions, including a "Death Tube," to eradicate the parasitical scoundrels. Catford and Jeannie marry and return to London in triumph, as they become the center of attention for high society as well as for the British government, foreign ambassadors, and their military attachés.

After describing several other adventures, including one with a new submarine developed by Catford, De L'Isle finishes the story with a chapter entitled "The Asiatic Revolt," in which Japan and China acting together lead a war of various yellow and brown peoples of Asia, Africa, and the Americas against the White race. Most of the countries are caught off guard by this sudden and well-orchestrated assault and give ground in several areas. Japanese forces invade and take control over part of Australia and New Zealand, while Mongolians march west, overrunning much of Russia east of the Urals. Britain, however, was forewarned and able to salvage India, as many of the Sikh and Gurkha troops remain loyal. Catford begins to equip British warships with his inventions and provides some to allies. One of the greatest engagements is between the Russians and the Mongolians along the line of the Urals. After several days of intensive fighting and horrific casualties on both sides, the Russians receive and deploy two hundred of Catford's Death Wave units. When the Mongolians resume their attack, they are annihilated:

For ten miles north and south of the centre of the battle ground the air suddenly became surcharged with electricity. Horrid and awful crackling sounds, deafening reports, followed by terrific explosions of blue flames, and forks of serried lightning played over and along the earth. As though the last trumpet had sounded—as though the Angel of Death were sweeping over the land those howling hordes were hurled to the ground, black, charred indistinguishable corpses.[27]

This is followed by a great naval engagement between the British navy and the Japanese squadrons off the coast of Australia. Although the big guns do their work efficiently, Catford's two submarines are present as well. The *Ravager* uses its Hertzian rays to explode some Japanese mines floating in the water. Catford's powerful weapons force the Asian-led war to collapse as quickly as it began. "Stability" has once again returned to the world, although this time, it is believed by many in Europe, war has become impossible.

C. J. Cutcliffe Hyne, better known for *The Lost Continent: The Story of Atlantis* (1900), published *Empire of the World* in 1910. It tells the story of another man, this one an Englishman named John Bryn-Scarlet, who wants to end war and does so through the power of what the press calls "The New Force" (similar to the label given to the weapon utilized by James Wingard mentioned in Chapter 1). A member of Parliament, and hopeless in managing his personal finances, he appears an unlikely character to develop a weapon that ultimately bends the great nations to his will and establishes him as the "emperor of the world." Unlike the rays that explode ships, his in less dramatic fashion reduce iron and steel to a yellow sludge. Periodically giving warnings to the leaders of the nations, he sinks ships, wrecks railroads, newspaper offices, and cable services. He singles out Germany, in particular, as a main stumbling block to peace, for the first victims of his ray are two of its vessels, including the great battleship *Kaiser Charlemagne*.[28]

One tale during this time utilizing wireless energy should be mentioned because it contributed to the discussion in the 1930s of using invisible rays as a means of air defense. Unlike most of those previously treated, the weapon in this story did not involve remote detonation or incineration. Stewart Edward White's *The Sign at Six*, published in 1912, is a story about an angry old man out for revenge against the political boss of New York City, threatening to wreak havoc on the metropolis unless he leaves. Monsieur X, as he is called, has developed a means—a formula of some sort using conventional wireless devices—whereby he can manipulate light and darkness, sound, and heat and cold. Most of the action in the novel concerns the efforts to find him and determine how he manages periodically to affect sections of the city. The hero, Percy Darrow, is a scientist himself and ultimately saves the day and captures the villain before he can execute his deadliest scheme. Among other things, Monsieur X can create an area of absolute darkness in which the flame of a match or the glow of an incandescent light bulb is neutralized even though both still produce heat. The mad scientist can also eliminate sound completely in a given radius, causing major disorientation and confusion among the people within it. Near the end of the story, he plans to kill by producing a freezing zone that will turn people into lumps of ice. He first demonstrates this power on the mayor and several others at city hall.[29] Afterward, one of the characters speculates on Monsieur X's abilities: "It is at last evident that this man's power over ethereal vibrations extends to those forming heat-rays. If this is so, it follows that he can cut off all life by stopping all heat. If his threat is carried out, we can but look forward to a repetition on a large scale of the City Hall affair."[30]

In 1935 an article in the *San Antonio Light* connected *The Sign at Six* to the issue of death rays and the "next war." The article covered much of the history surrounding directed energy weapons, mentioning Grindell Matthews, Erich Graichen, and R.C. Chadfield among others. The author presented an overview of the different sources for a proposed military ray, including electricity, X-rays, and gamma rays as well as some of the scientific reasons for skepticism. In the end, however, he considered some type of energy weapon plausible and commented on White's 1912 novel, providing a synopsis and speculating on Monsieur X's ability to create a freezing zone: "It is not unthinkable that cities and even frontiers of future countries at war may be guarded by invisible walls of absolute zero temperature, miles high, through which neither bird, insect, nor aviator can pass without being frozen in an instant. No scientist would know how to go about erecting such a wall today. But then no scientist knew how to go about building a submarine or flying machine when Jules Verne's imagination foretold them."[31]

Arthur B. Reeve, one of America's most prolific detective story writers and creator of the character Craig Kennedy, hailed as an "American Sherlock Holmes," utilized well-known wireless energy research for some of his tales. In 1910 he published a volume of stories entitled *The Silent Bullet: The Adventures of Craig Kennedy, Scientific Detective*, in which he capitalized on the work of Tesla. In Chapter IX, "The Terror in the Air," Kennedy and his "Dr. Watson" sidekick, Walter, try to unravel a mysterious cause of airplane crashes. It turns out that a rival to a popular pilot who has just invented a new gyroscope has been sending a burst of electrical energy to burn out the wires of the dynamo connected to that apparatus, causing loss of power and control. Kennedy has figured this out in time to save the pilot from certain death and has had a sheet of lead covering placed around the dynamo and battery, which shields against the rays. After capturing the scoundrel, Kennedy explains that the weapon is based on Tesla's theory about wireless transmission of electrical energy using the atmosphere as a conductor.[32]

Reeve was also probably the first writer to profit from the publicity surrounding Giulio Ulivi. In *The Exploits of Elaine* in 1914, Reeve describes the evil villain, the Clutching Hand, as employing an inventor who has developed a lethal weapon. In a passage from the chapter entitled "The Death Ray," sleuth Craig Kennedy points to a detection device and exclaims: "There *is* something queer going on Walter, ... This thing registers some kind of wireless rays—infra-red, I think,—something like those that they say that Italian scientist, Ulivi, claims he has discovered and called the 'F-rays.'"[33] Unlike the wireless energy for remote detonation of explosives claimed by Ulivi, Reeve gave his F-rays the ability to kill people and has one of the villains simply expanding the work done by the Italian to create a lethal ray. In a scene in which the inventor LeCroix has just dispatched two unfortunate victims, the reader also gets a description of the weapon: "Apparently it was a combination of powerful electric arcs, the rays of which were shot through a funnel-like arrangement into a converter or, rather, a sort of concentration apparatus from which the dread power could be released through a tube-like affair at one end. It was his infra-red heat wave, F-ray, engine."[34] In the movie serial *The Exploits of Elaine*, the death ray is represented by a device that looks more like a small searchlight with a conical cover designed to concentrate the beam.[35] Reeve tapped into Ulivi again with "The Sixth Sense," which came out in *Cosmopolitan* magazine in May 1915. Detective Kennedy comments "somewhere around here there is a generator of infra-red rays and a projector of those rays. It reminds me of those so-called F rays of Ulivi—or, at least, of a very powerful wireless."[36]

Ulivi's influence also appeared in *La Machine à finir la guerre* (*The Machine to End War*), published in 1917 by French authors Roland Dorgelès, a veteran of the Western Front, and Régis Gignoux. In this satire on war, the character Antoine Toutlevent in 1917 accidentally discovers an ad in an old newspaper dated January 1913, in which an unnamed inventor identified only as "R. C." claims to have a machine capable of making war impossible. Intrigued by the prospect of ending the terrible conflict with Germany, Toutlevent sets out to ascertain the identity of this person, locate him, and help him develop this marvelous device. He quickly makes the acquaintance of Clairette Bravo, an actress and former lover of the young engineer whom she remembers only as Raymond. After numerous twists and turns faintly reminiscent of Candide in Voltaire's great satire, Toutlevent, with the aid of Clairette and her new benefactor, Monsieur Vingtdoix, finds Raymond "Chartier" serving in an infantry regiment at the front. With their help, he constructs a small prototype and demonstrates it successfully. Later, although opposed by powerful business interests who thrive on war, Chartier gains the support of the French army and government to build several machines. Just before setting them into operation at the front, the Germans surrender, having apparently heard of the weapon and deciding that discretion was the better part of valor.

Chartier's machine utilizes rays which set off explosives at great distances. He describes them as the result of a process in which ultraviolet rays are transformed into ultra-blue rays.[37] Although he tells Clairette and Toutlevent that he was influenced by the work of Crookes[38] and his cathode tubes, the device's capabilities portrayed in the story for the most part—except for their lethality—correspond to the F-rays of Ulivi. Upon completing his prototype, Chartier demonstrates it by killing a finch sitting on a tree limb. Then he shows how he can use the ray against a German soldier:

> In the back of the shed ten meters from the machine was a wicker mannequin, dressed in a feldgrau uniform and equipped for combat with bullets and a rifle.... He started up his motor again ... and slowly directed his stream of invisible rays toward the dummy. By the time one can count to ten, the dummy moved. A flame flashed from its ammunition belts, while another flame came out of its rifle with a muffled explosion.

After exploding a small amount of melinite placed on the ground a short distance away, Chartier boasts:

> At one hundred kilometers, all the bullets of the soldiers, all the belts of the machine guns, all the shells loaded in the cannons, all the bombs, all the grenades, ... all will explode. The blue rays will leave nothing, not even a gram of explosive.... A ship armed with a Chartier projector on its bow will explode submarine mines without even seeing them; it will sink submarines and dreadnoughts the same way; it will sweep the seas. I will go further. A projection of powerful blue rays directed in the air will explode projectiles in mid-course; but even this will be needless since we will be able to disarm the enemy out to a distance of eighty to one hundred kilometers....[39]

Several other types of rays came out in stories leading up to the First World War. One employing an incinerating weapon using electricity appeared as a serial in *The Wireless World*, running from May 1913 to March 1914. Bernard C. White's "A Pawn in the Game" is a tale about a brief war between Britain and Germany in which a young English inventor named Charles Summers develops a weapon that gives his country the victory. He constructs a remote-controlled airship equipped with a death ray which destroys airplanes in a flash. After warding off two waves of German attacks, Summers is incapacitated by a mild stroke, and the only person who can operate the controlling apparatus is his girlfriend, Gwen Thrale. Despite some of the refinements and additions to the new machine, Gwen's basic understanding of its operations enables her to handle it. As the author describes: "All her learning had come back to her, and in a few moments the three vessels [aircraft], one after another, had sunk beneath the searching death ray."[40] The power of this new weapon ends the conflict quickly. It should be noted that author White also described a type of detecting device resembling radar that enabled the operator of the machine to locate and destroy the targets.[41]

Two stories about other ray weapons actually came out before news reports announcing the corresponding inventions and discoveries. As mentioned in Chapter 2, *Le Matin* stated that a Lieutenant Peyvel had invented an electric rifle in 1917; but such a weapon appeared in the popular "Tom Swift" series of books for boys created by Edward Stratemeyer and written under the general pseudonym Victor Appleton. In the 1911 novel *Tom Swift and His Electric Rifle or Daring Adventures in Elephant Land*, the hero is asked by a friend how it works. Tom replies: "By means of a concentrated charge of electricity which is shot from the barrel with great force. You can't see it, yet it is there. It's just as if you concentrated a charge of electricity of five thousand volts into a small globule the size of a bullet. That flies through space, strikes the object aimed at and—well, we'll see what it does in a minute."[42] Two years later, "The Isolated Continent: A Romance of the Future" preceded by several months American "scientist" Bernays Johnson's announcement about having discovered a Z-ray capable of being used as a weapon. Written by Guido Horvath and Dean Hoard and appearing in numerous American newspapers, the story featured two energy devices: a Z-ray, which projects a force field impenetrable to solid objects, and a type of death ray, called artificial lightning, used to destroy enemy aircraft and warships. The latter resembles Ulivi's F-rays as well as earlier devices allegedly capable of remote detonation. As the authors describe, "lightning after lightning darted toward the two boats, the powder magazines exploded and the dreaded giants were wrecks, sinking. A few minutes later, the boats were gone, leaving a mass of floating debris and dead men."⁴³ As time went on, the Z-ray acquired different properties in both fiction and in the realm of press reports, for example, the one described in 1935 in reference to Germany, mentioned in Chapter 4.

Another type of ray appeared in M. P. Shiel's *The Dragon*, which came out in 1913 and was re-issued in 1929 as *The Yellow Peril*. In this story Shiel has the Prince of Wales as the leading character, who warns his countrymen of the threat from the East and then uses the weapon to defeat the evil Li Ku Yu and his Asian forces trying to conquer Britain. Labeled the "Redlike Ray," it functions somewhat as a laser, with its chief effect causing blindness. An early experiment by the inventor, the character Richard Chinnery, results in rendering a dog sightless in five seconds. As he explains later in the story: "There are still more X-rays than known rays in nature, I think—still half of even the solar spectrum unknown. I got a ray with only 397 millions of vibrations a second—almost hot with Herschellian rays—resembling the two lines of rubidium, but quite faint, and paralyzing to the optic nerve-ends."⁴⁴

In addition to the works by Reeve and Dorgelès and Gignoux, a number of other ray stories appeared during the First World War. One utilizing atomic energy as the source for a powerful beam weapon was *The Man Who Rocked the Earth*, written by Arthur Train and Robert Williams Wood and published in 1915. As the World War is raging, a man identified only as "PAX" announces that he is going to stop the conflict and performs a demonstration of his power by lengthening the day by five minutes. He later uses his atomic disintegrator, referred to as the "Lavender Ray," to rip open the Atlas Mountains, causing the Mediterranean to flood into the Sahara. A conference in Washington leads to an agreement among the belligerents to observe an armistice as a first step toward world peace. A German commander not far from Paris, however, disobeys orders to stand down and launches an attack on the French capital by means of a powerful type of explosive developed by German scientists. No sooner do the projectiles hit their targets than PAX in his aircraft, the Flying Ring, uses his Lavender Ray to obliterate the French village where the German force is located. He then announces that he will shift the earth's axis, making all but Central and South America and South Africa uninhabitable. Unwilling to concede defeat, the German high command authorizes a secret expedition to Labrador, pinpointed as the location of the mysterious PAX, in order to capture the scientist and his weapon. The mission fails, as PAX uses his ray to dry up a river leaving the German barges loaded with equipment stuck in mud. All but one of the soldiers die from thirst. In the meantime, Cambridge scientist Bennie Hooker, who has also been working on developing a means to unleash and control atomic power, embarks on his own to find PAX. In the end, Hooker locates PAX's installation but witnesses an accidental explosion that kills the mystery man, whose true identity is never revealed. With the help of the only surviving assistant and the arrival of a colleague, Hooker secures the Flying Ring and returns home. PAX's death is not in vain, as the nations of the world dismantle their armed forces and universal peace prevails.[45]

Instead of using a death ray in a tale about war or espionage, one author employed this weapon in a detective story as an incidental means for a scoundrel attempting to kill in order to obtain a large inheritance. Harold MacGrath, a leading American writer during the early twentieth century, wrote the screenplay for a serial film entitled *Zudora* in 1914, adapted from his movie serial *The Million Dollar Mystery*. In 1915 the story of *Zudora* appeared in installments in many newspapers throughout the United States, and *The Million Dollar Mystery* was published in book form as a novel. Both included photo stills from the film versions. The story is about a young woman named Zudora who is the heir to a fortune entrusted to her guardian uncle. Desiring the money for himself, he decides to have her killed. Among the various plots to accomplish this is the employment of an inventor of a recently developed heat ray. He has already blown up a submarine and two commercial ships by sending electric waves through the water. Zudora manages to escape this attempt on her life, and the heat ray is subsequently destroyed. It therefore plays only a minor role in the story. The newspaper version includes a photo still of the inventor working his heat ray, depicted as a bulky apparatus.[46]

Several ray stories during the First World War were produced by prolific British writer and Germanophobe William Le Queux. One in 1915 was entitled *The Mystery of the Green Ray*, a weapon possessing several capabilities, including that of creating an atmosphere powerful enough to suffocate a person and to repel all known poisonous gases.[47] He followed this up in 1916 with *The Zeppelin Destroyer: Being Some Chapters of Secret History*. The Great War is raging, and Britain has begun to come under attack by German zeppelins, but anti-aircraft guns and airplanes offer little defense against them. Two civilian pilots, Claude Munro and Teddy Ashton, along with two assistants, are secretly working on an apparatus that will produce electric sparks and direct them in concentrated form up to three thousand yards away. Munro's girlfriend and expert pilot, Roseye Lethmere, is also involved in the project. Much of the story revolves around a German spy ring led by the "Invisible Hand," who turns out to be a fellow Englishman and an acquaintance trying to sabotage their work. After several attempts on their lives and the abduction of Roseye, Munro and Ashton succeed in perfecting their device and destroying a zeppelin. The novel ends with the anticipation that Britain will completely eliminate the menace in the skies and safeguard the nation from further threats from the air.

The novel employs a weapon based on the principles proposed by several scientists but takes them to a new level of development. It also reflects a connection to Ulivi, and the effect is similar to that suspected by some people at the time to have been the cause of the destruction of the French battleship *Iéna* in 1907, with wireless electric rays creating sparks that exploded the gunpowder and shells in the ship's magazine. As described by the character Munro: "I have found out the means by which to create and to direct a flash of intense electrical current, a kind of false lightning. And that current, sparking over the interstices between the aluminum lattice-work and envelope of a Zeppelin, must certainly ignite the inflammable gas with which the ballonets are filled and which is so constantly escaping."[48]

Le Queux also had a one-page short story about a German death ray that appeared in a newspaper in January 1918 while the First World War was still raging. A young German inventor by the name of Otto Schultz has produced an astounding weapon that will make Germany invincible. Although successfully tested in front of high-ranking officials, including the Kaiser himself, it is rejected and ordered to be destroyed. The reason is that the Kaiser has already proclaimed Ferdinand Zeppelin the greatest aeronautical genius of his time and wants to preserve his reputation as the one who will enable Germany to triumph. Meanwhile, the Crown Prince wants to replace the Kaiser with himself as ruler and therefore decides to use this as an opportunity to expose to the nation that His Majesty is willing to sacrifice the interests of the Fatherland because of Zeppelin. He meets with the young inventor, who tells him about his audience with Professor von Deimling, the director of the Department of Aeronautics: "At first the Herr Director was most enthusiastic, for I demonstrated that an airship fitted with my electrical invention for the dissemination of what I have called the Death-Rays would be invincible. Both speed and lifting power would be increased, while any hostile aircraft coming within a certain zone would be destroyed instantly. Germany would by its adoption become master of the air, as well as of underseas."[49] Asked to build another device, Schultz later turns up dead, electrocuted by his own death ray. The verdict of the police is that someone tampered with the mechanism and its wiring to produce the fatal shock. The culprit is his wife, who turns out not to be German but a Russian loyal to her country and taking this action to prevent Germany from gaining an advantage.

Postwar

Death-ray fiction began to experience a thematic shift during the First World War, but this would become more pronounced in the next decade, as writers increasingly turned to a wider variety of subjects for use with directed energy weapons. In the developing genre of what came to be called "science fiction," some writers focused on tales about strange alien worlds and futuristic societies on Earth, but many chose more realistic topics dealing with the contemporary world of the 1920s and 1930s. Despite this shift, several authors continued to utilize pre-war "science," featuring devices capable of wireless remote detonation and often bearing some resemblance to Ulivi's F-rays and to those of his predecessors.

One of the first was *The Golden Scorpion* by Sax Rohmer (real name Arthur Henry Ward), the creator of the Fu Manchu stories. This 1920 "yellow peril" tale has Fo-Hi, the villainous "Scorpion," employing several advanced weapons, including a variety of poisons and a disintegrating ray. In the chapter entitled "The Blue Ray," Rohmer's description of the weapon's effect resembles that of a modern laser. In one scene the hero, Dr. Stuart, who is in his study, just barely avoids being struck by the lethal beam and then examines the result: "His dictionary was smoldering slowly. It had a neat round hole some three inches in diameter, bored completely through, cover to cover!"[50] Later in the story, Stuart encounters the Scorpion, who describes to him a larger weapon that has a range of more than seven miles and can detonate ammunition.[51]

Several French works of the early 1920s also had Ulivi-type rays capable of remote detonation or weapons resembling Maclay's "burning glasses."[52] In 1925 André Falcoz published *Le Semeur de feu* (The Sower of Fire), in which he tells the story of a mad scientist whose death ray can set off explosives at a distance, and José Moselli's *Le Maître de la Foudre* (The Lightning Master, 1922) has a Japanese inventor with a ray capable of remote detonation as well. In *Le Rayon phi* (The Phi Ray, 1921), however, Moselli utilizes a device reminiscent of Maclay's, for the weapon consists of prisms and lenses to harness the heat of sunlight and direct it to selected targets.

Ulivi-type weapons appeared in death-ray novels by German authors during the early Weimar period. This literature, however, took on a special character of its own, reflecting the anger, disillusionment, and confusion following defeat in the First World War. Some authors who pursued the *Zukunftsroman* (novel about the future) enjoyed varying degrees of popularity with the masses, especially with works depicting a revived Germany or involving German individuals who possessed advanced weapons. Although German writers of this genre had various messages—both aggressive and pacifist—a dominant theme was that of revenge.[53]

One work reflecting this motif popular among many Germans was *1934 Deutschlands Auferstehung* (1934 Germany's Resurrection) by Ferdinand Eugen Solf, a retired German artillery officer, published in 1922. The setting is 1934, fifteen years after the start of the occupation of the Rhineland by Allied forces, during which a group of German army officers has been secretly planning to end the conditions imposed by Versailles.[54] These men do not want to restore the old empire as it was but to establish a constitutional monarchy. They also believe that Germany should expel all people of foreign blood and gather back those native Germans living in Poland, Czechoslovakia, and other neighboring lands. Operating under the cover of the sports "Club of the Harmless," they employ specialists of all kinds to develop new weapons, including three types of death-ray devices, to ensure victory. All emit powerful wireless rays that explode ammunition and gunpowder in the style of Ulivi but are not harmful to living tissue. One fits the role of artillery in that it has the greatest range and destructive power. It is described as similar to a searchlight and can set off explosions up to forty kilometers away. Another is a small rectangular box with a mid-range beam of four to five kilometers that can be used to detonate ammunition in rifles and in cartridge belts. The third device looks more like a flashlight and is effective for only a few hundred meters. The liberation of Germany begins when these weapons are used to destroy several British and French naval vessels anchored at Kiel. This is followed by attacks on French forces garrisoned in Berlin, with the rays exploding the ammunition in the guns of the French soldiers. After a general uprising throughout Germany, the story ends with the successful expulsion of foreign troops from the Rhineland and the dawning of a new day of pride and hope for the German people. The book cover has two men dressed in civilian clothing on the shore, one observing through binoculars while the other discharges a death ray at a ship on the horizon. The apparatus is depicted as a rectangular box emitting a lightning bolt which has caused an explosion on the vessel now engulfed in flames.[55]

The most popular author of this type of literature with the theme of

5. Early Death-Ray Novels and Short Stories

the scientifically superior Aryan, however, was Hans Dominik, who in 1922 published *Die Macht der Drei* (*The Power of the Three*). The story is that of three men who employ a death ray to stop a war between the British Empire and the United States, the latter at this time under a dictatorship. The three are Silvester Bursfeld, a German, Erik Truwor, a Swede, and Soma Atma, a Hindu from India. The story, which takes place in 1955, features a machine referred to as a *Strahler*, or "ray-sender," that garners energy and then releases it in the form of a powerful wireless ray. It appears to be based on the ideas of several scientists, especially those of Nikola Tesla. In the novel two devices are constructed, a small *Strahler* carried as a sidearm and a larger one with far greater range and destructive power. Some of its capabilities include exploding ammunition at a distance à la Guilio Ulivi and his F-rays, knocking out the magnetos of airplane engines, and incinerating objects and human beings. Dominik, however, gives his large *Strahler* an added feature. The beam reflects back to the sending apparatus and produces an optical image of the target, making it a more precise weapon.[56] The power of the *Strahler* is portrayed several times throughout the novel, including one scene in which Truwor activates the optical reflector to pinpoint his target one thousand miles away. He disables the engines of two American aircraft before destroying them completely along with their crews. The commanding officer meets his doom, as Dominik describes: he "fell into the scorching ray of the concentrated wireless energy. Instantly the clothing on his body burst into flames. He tried to escape it but, even before he could comprehend the danger, was burned to death, reduced to glowing embers and ash."[57] Then Truwor continues to kill the villains: "With raised hands the crew burst outside through the opening. One lit up like a spark and fizzled out the moment he jumped. A second man was struck by the ray in the tenth of a second that he was in the air. Some white ash fell on the grass."[58] Dominik's weapon was as lethal as any other death ray portrayed by later fiction writers.

Use of the *Strahler* in this novel, however, invites scrutiny. Dominik had been trained in electronics and had worked briefly for the Siemens Company as an engineer. During the First World War, he tried to construct a ray device, but his intention was not to produce a weapon; rather, he and a colleague sought to develop a beam to detect ships at night or in a fog. Referred to as a *Strahlenzieler* (ray aimer), it was an attempt at an early form of radar. Considerable time and effort went into the project, and Dominik managed to put together a carefully worked-out design and present it to the *Reichsmarineamt* (Reich naval office) in the spring of 1916. According to Dominik, he was turned down because he said it would take six months to construct a fully operational device. The response indicated that the naval authorities believed the war would be over before it could be ready.[59] His own work on this project therefore served as an inspiration for his novel. After publication of *Die Macht der Drei*, furthermore, a book review carried in several newspapers in the United States connected the novel to the recent incident involving the wireless station at Nauen and indirectly to the mystery of the French airplanes flying over Bavaria, mentioned in Chapter 2, suggesting that Dominik's *Strahler* may have fueled the continuing rumors of a German ray capable of halting airplane and automobile motors.[60]

Three other German works with Ulivi-type rays capable of remote detonation deserve mention. One was Werner Grassegger's *Die rächende Stünde. Englands Schicksalstag: Ein Zukunftsbild* (The Hour of Revenge. England's Fateful Day: A Picture of the Future), published in 1922. In this tale set in 1927, Germany has been occupied by forces from Britain, France, Belgium, Italy, and Poland because it cannot make its reparations payments. The hero, a German exile named Wilhelm Gering, teams up with a former war buddy who happens to know an Austrian inventor with a ray device that can set off explosives from a distance. Having commandeered a German warship taken over by the British after the Armistice, Gering and his colleagues outfit the vessel with the ray weapon and proceed to destroy the Royal Navy. After having forced Britain to surrender, German forces armed with ray weapons ultimately defeat all their enemies and reclaim their lost lands in Europe as well as obtain much of what had been the Austro-Hungarian empire.[61] Also published in 1922, Fritz Skowronnek's *Dies Irae* utilized the principle of remote wireless detonation, and the following year Adolf Saager's *Menschlichkeit* (Humanity), depicted the German army equipped with similar ray weapons neutralizing all the armies, navies, and air forces in the world. As quoted by Dina Brandt: It has "devices which by means of electrical rays directed to great distances can render harmless all types of explosives. With them all warships, fortresses, munitions dumps, artillery, and aircraft with bombs are destroyed in short order."[62]

One German novel of this period utilized weapons bearing resemblance to Ulivi's F-rays and to some extent Maclay's "burning glasses." Although expressing the theme of the superior Aryan, Joseph Delmont's 1925 *Die Stadt unter dem Meere* (The City under the Sea) differs somewhat from many of the other Weimar-era works in that romance plays a major role. The story begins in 1916 with German submarine commander Eugen Mader and his crew discovering an immense cave inside an island mountain just off the Italian coast in the Gulf of Genoa. The only entrance is underwater and has just been opened up by an earthquake. Mader and his men set up a base to repair submarines in order to get them back into operation in Mediterranean waters more quickly. When they receive word that the war is over, they split up. One group, led by Captain Zirbenthal, decides to return home to Germany, and the rest remain with Mader at the "City under the Sea," as they call it. He plans to continue working, train his men, and develop new technology with the ultimate goal of returning to help his homeland. Throughout this time he maintains contact with Zirbental, who later informs him that he and some of the others have decided to leave the Fatherland for Ecuador. The government there has granted them permission to set up on the coast a colony, which they intend to call "Nuova Germanica."

At this point the story introduces a romance component and intertwines it with the activities of the Germans. Some of Mader's men go ashore to procure supplies in the little town on the coast but bring back to the "City" several Italian women as well. One of them, Emilia, falls in love with the captain. Because she is already promised to a young man, Mader sends her back to her home whereupon she undergoes considerable hardship since she will reveal nothing about her disappearance to the Italian authorities.

In the meantime, Mader and his crew continue their work. They construct a super submarine, equip it with a revolutionary fuel-efficient propulsion system, and outfit two smaller craft with the same capability. Two of the most important inventions—discovered by accident—are powerful ray devices. One is a quartz-lens reflector that can neutralize all modern weapons, causing shells in guns big and small not to discharge and aerial bombs and torpedoes not to explode. The other can detonate the shells and bombs in the fashion of Ulivi. As expected, they come in handy.

Rumors of strangers and the unsolved mystery regarding the disappearance of the women have led Italian authorities to suspect that there must be some hidden base nearby, and a naval squadron is sent to the area. Convinced that Germans are somehow involved, France and Britain go on alert and agree to cooperate with the Italians. Having learned of Emilia's distress and that she is virtually under house arrest, Mader successfully rescues the girl and then engages the Italian naval squadron off the coast, for he knows that he and his men can no longer stay in the City under the Sea. The admiral in command is astonished when he sees that neither the shore batteries nor the naval guns will fire and the aerial bombs and torpedoes do not explode. Believing that some kind of mysterious ray is the obstacle and that it has a limited range, the admiral withdraws his ships to a distance of ten kilometers from the Germans and tries again. This time the shells roar from the big guns but when they reach a certain point, they explode. Mader has initiated electromagnetic rays which detonate all explosive materials they touch.

Escaping the Italians, Mader and his men must also get by a British naval squadron on the lookout for them at Gibraltar. Hostilities ensue—with the same result. Mader's ray weapons completely neutralize the British guns and torpedoes. By now the world is in panic, for people everywhere are anxious about these mysterious German devices that so easily defeated the Italian and British naval forces. France and Britain threaten to declare war on Germany, believing that it has been secretly rearming with the intention of overturning Versailles. Panic turns into chaos, revolutions break out, and stock markets crash, threatening the entire economic system of the world. In the end, everything turns out favorably for the Germans. Mader and all the expatriate German naval personnel return and are received as heroes, with Mader becoming the man of destiny to reunite the Fatherland.[63]

Two works involving Ulivi belong in a class of their own. They are most remarkable pieces of fiction—remarkable because they were passed off as true stories. The first was by H. Ashton-Wolfe in his collection published in 1928 as *Warped in the Making: Crimes of Love and Hate*. Equally remarkable is that a number of reviewers, including one for the *New York Times*,[64] accepted its veracity. The author, who worked for some time with the French Sûreté, claimed that these tales were based on his own experiences as well as on police files, although acknowledging that he had made a few changes. In the case entitled "Allivi: The Bogus Death Ray," Ashton-Wolfe did much more than take a few liberties with the facts, for he turned part of the story about Giulio Ulivi into an outlandish concoction of half-truths and sheer fabrications. Mario Allivi (Giulio Ulivi) is a handsome young Italian inventor trying to sell his invention to three different parties, two of which send their agents to see a demonstration before purchasing it. One is an American, the other a Frenchman. They are joined by the third potential buyer, an Italian admiral named Giuseppe Ricci-Ferroni (alias Pietro Fornari), who also has a beautiful young daughter, Giuseppina (alias Maria Fornari). As in the real story of Ulivi, Ashton-Wolfe's "fictional" character explodes mines in water by using a device that sends out an electronic beam—or so it seems. He always performs the demonstrations at night, has an assistant to signal him when the mines have been placed in the water, and then is seen manipulating his apparatus. Suspecting some fakery, especially since Allivi supplied his own mines, the agents secretly discover that he has used "doctored" explosives. When he is found out, the Italian hoaxer flees the country with the admiral's daughter and marries her on board a ship bound for America. Allivi arrived at the beginning of the story with another girlfriend, however, who becomes furious when she learns of his betrayal of her affections and reveals how Allivi pulled off his trick. It is almost identical to the story in the *New York Times*. She says that he bored a hole into each mine and inserted sodium and then covered up the opening with a material that would let water soak through to ignite the sodium. Aside from having the wrong names and distorting the information about Ulivi's activities in Florence, Ashton-Wolfe omitted altogether the Italian inventor's dealings with the French and the British. The author failed even to mention the single most important buzzword attached to Ulivi: the "F-ray."[65]

A variation of this tale appeared in the *San Antonio Express* in 1930, with significant and equally outlandish changes, especially since it was also peddled as a true story. Entitled "Almost Perfect Crimes, No. V.—The F-Ray,"[66] it was the last in a series featured by the newspaper. At the beginning of the story, a handsome young man accosts Admiral Fornari on the street in front of the entrance to the Italian Navy Department in Rome and boldly asserts that he has created a marvelous new invention and invites him to witness a demonstration. Several nights later, the admiral accompanies Ulivi to the coast near Rome and watches as a mine is set off by the young man's apparatus. After a later demonstration with seven mines, Fornari is convinced and offers his support. Ulivi excitedly responds that he will call his ray the "F-ray" in honor of the admiral. Things move rapidly and Ulivi and the Admiral's daughter, Eleanor, fall in love and become engaged. Fornari then tries to gain the support of the scientist Guido Alfani, who is at first skeptical. To convince him, the admiral relates the story involving the Japanese battleship *Mikasa* (Chapter 1) with the men seen on the shore manipulating some type of device shortly before the vessel exploded. The scientist decides to witness a demonstration and is convinced that the young man has succeeded in perfecting wireless remote detonation. He contacts a British colleague for his opinion and receives a disturbing reply. According to the letter, a young Brazilian named "Alonzo" and bearing a remarkable resemblance to Ulivi had tried unsuccessfully to get the British government to purchase his "Red Ray." A demonstration went awry, as British officers discovered that the detonation occurred apparently without his intervention. In a fit of rage, "Alonzo" destroyed his machine and left. Alfani then learns that the man showed up in France in the guise of a Chilean named "Bolido." His attempt to sell his device to the French government likewise failed. With this information, Alfani demands that Ulivi detonate a mine prepared by the scientist himself, to which the latter agrees. Alfani brings along some police who hide in order to watch the cottage where the inventor operates his F-ray. Ulivi, however, does not appear, and the police find inside several bombs doctored with sodium. The charlatan's whereabouts are unknown for about a year when he turns up in Chile trying the same stunt. The Italian government has spread the word and this time Ulivi is arrested and thrown in jail. As a parting note, the newspaper article added that Fornari's daughter, "Eleanor," did not pine away for her lost lover and quickly got over him.

Scientific research with various energy sources and the attendant news reports about the invention of some type of death ray greatly influenced authors of mystery and imaginary war fiction beginning in the late nineteenth and early twentieth centuries. Some tales utilized radium and the power of the atom, but electricity emerged as the favorite among writers, with wireless remote detonation the dominant capability of this fictional weapon. Although the "science" of Giulio Ulivi and others of his time period continued to appear, death-ray novels and short stories after the First World War increasingly reflected the influence of other claims for directed energy weapons reported in newspapers and magazines. In addition, authors frequently turned to new developments in science, such as sound vibrations and cathode ray research to power their devices. As the next chapter will show, the publicity surrounding Harry Grindell Matthews and the French airplanes over Bavaria had a significant impact on mystery tales in general as well as on the emerging genre of science fiction.

6

Death-Ray Novels and Short Stories of the Interwar Years

As stated in the previous chapter, a thematic shift in death-ray fiction occurred during the First World War and became more pronounced in the years following. While some writers utilized directed energy weapons in stories involving alien beings and strange worlds, others chose to place them in tales dealing with more contmeporary situations. Although imaginary wars remained an important topic, authors tended more and more to fashion them into conflicts based on the real fears of another world war as predicted by experts and laymen alike and sensationalized in newspapers and magazines. These stories also incorporated the most likely belligerents based on the prevailing dynamics of world power, with Germany and France the most prominent. Some combinations included the Soviet Union, Japan, China, Britain, and occasionally, the United States. One writer chose as his subject the contemporary Italian invasion of Ethiopia and provided Africans with ray weapons to achieve victory. Death rays involving espionage also became a popular theme during this time, with many of the tales pitting. German spies against British secret servicce agents and even amateur detectives. Some authors, including Agatha Christie, chose crime as a topic and gave death rays to their villians. Several stories, such as Edmund Snell's *The Sound Machine* and Austin J. Small's *The Avenging Ray*, continued with the traditional theme of the mad scientist. An additional aspect of the death ray in fiction was the frequent reference to it by publishers and reviewers as a real weapon or at least one that was plausible. In many cases this was probably the result of a marketing strategy to increase book sales and box office receipts.

Novels and short stories reflecting the direct influence of Harry

Grindell Matthews began to appear not long after he had become a celebrity and continued for quite some time. A few of these also combined the alleged capabilities of his invention with those of Ulivi's F-rays. The first was *The Story Without a Name* by Arthur Stringer and Russell Holman, published in 1924, but it is treated in Chapter 7 because of its connection to the movie based on the original manuscript. Another early novel connected to the work of the English inventor was *Voyage de cinq Américains dans les planètes: roman astronomique* (Voyage of Five Americans to the Planets: An Astronomical Novel) by Frenchman Henry de Graffigny. In a revealing passage, three of the Americans encounter two Martians, one of whom is armed with an apparatus resembling some type of light projector. But it emits invisible heat rays that ignite one man's fur cap and singe his hair. While escaping from the Martians, the character "Daniel Fairchild reflected for an instant on the famous *green ray* of Wells in the novel *The War of the Worlds*, a ray recently made reality by the English engineer Grindell Matthews."[1] One work with a weapon bearing the unmistakable influence of his invention appeared in the *Oakland Tribune* in May 1926. A one-page short story entitled "Jezzard of the Mill" and written by Gordon Sussex is about an old scientist living in the English countryside who has both a death ray and a protective ray that neutralizes its effect. After a series of strange incidents, including the inexplicable death of a German traveler, a retired constable and a young woman secretly observe the old man kill some rabbits and stop a motorcycle engine with his ray. Shortly after, the local police pay a visit to his house. As they are about to arrest the old man on suspicion of murder, a general and three other army officers arrive and inform the police that they have come to witness a demonstration of this marvelous new weapon. The scientist proceeds to dispatch a rabbit with the death ray and shields others with the protective antidote but then tries to take his own life and the secret formula with him. He is prevented from doing so by a young constable, however, and the story ends with the preservation of the ray machines for Britain.[2] In early January of the same year, Francis Beeding published a novel entitled *The Little White Hag* that became serialized afterward in numerous newspapers. The story of an American banker who teams up with the U.S. Secret Service to foil an international gang of drug traffickers, it also has an indirect reference to Grindell Matthews. As one character says: "In fact you haven't the least idea how up-to-date we are. They call it the death ray in the English newspapers. That's like English newspapers—so wonderfully picturesque, don't you think? Of course it isn't really a death ray at all. It is only a small device for jamming a magneto."[3] A brief reference to both Grindell Matthews and the stories about French airplanes over Bavaria appeared in the 1929 novel *L'Éther-Alpha: grand roman d'aventures* by Albert Bailly. In one scene, a crew member of an airplane expresses concern about the possibility of being attacked and destroyed by electric rays. The response is that all the necessary precautions have been made to protect the engine: "No known ray could paralyze the magnetos or short circuit the spark plugs."[4]

One story reflecting the influence of Grindell Matthews and Ulivi appeared in a German novel in 1924, another Weimar-era tale of revenge against France and the Treaty of Versailles. In *Der Kampf ums Gold* (The Struggle for Gold), Reinhold Eichacker depicted Germany with a super weapon that combined the capabilities of Grindell Matthews's death rays and Ulivi's F-rays with some imaginative creations of his own. At the beginning of the story, the German cabinet is deliberating on how to respond to a new French ultimatum, one that demands French control over the entire German chemical industry. A scientist named Walter Werndt provides the answer, as he informs government leaders of several new inventions that will enable Germany to settle its reparations burden, throw off the shackles of Versailles, and make Germany a strong nation once more. One of his new discoveries is a process by which he can transmute lead into pure gold. When Germany pays off in one lump sum the debts owed to France and Britain, it leads to a glut on the world gold market and wreaks havoc with the international financial system. This act upsets the plans of the French president, Grandmaire, portrayed by Eichacker as irrational and seething with hatred toward Germany. He has hoped that German default on reparations, combined with a German refusal to surrender control over its chemical industry, will give France an excuse for a war to destroy the Teutonic foe once and for all. Consumed with anger, he secretly begins to mobilize the armed forces for a surprise attack. In the meantime, Werndt has become the new finance minister and has calmed the fears of the other cabinet members about the falling gold prices and their effect on the German economy by revealing that he has through a similar process created a substantial amount of platinum. The German government, aware of hostile French intentions, sends Grandmaire an ultimatum to withdraw all his forces from the Rhineland. Unknown to the French, Werndt has developed an elaborate system of interconnected poles and a "dynamo motor" that harnesses solar power and generates virtually unlimited electrical energy. From this he has developed the means to detonate explosives from a distance with his "W-rays," create local vortexes (*Luftwirbeln*) of great intensity, and disrupt the electrical system over an entire region or country. He first demonstrates this latter capability by sending an electrical surge throughout the French telephone system, giving President Grandmaire a nasty shock that partially paralyzes him.[5] When the French do attack, their airplanes first encounter the vortexes and are tossed around until they crash. Others are struck by electronic rays and burst into flames. French artillery guns fare no better, as their shells explode inside the breeches, causing the German defense minister watching to exclaim "Electrical remote detonation—Werndt's W-rays—munitions exploded—dreadful—."[6] Later, when the French reject an ultimatum to cease hostilities and attend a peace conference in Berlin, Werndt launches a horrific thirty-minute attack on Paris by means of his ability to create storms. France then accepts the terms and Germany triumphs.

A French novel, Eugène Thébault's *Radio-terreur, grand roman de mystère* (Radio Terror, A Great Mystery Novel), published in 1927, also had a weapon with properties similar to those of Grindell Matthews as well as Ulivi. Set in Paris in 1952, the story is that of a mad scientist, in this case a marquis named Saint-Imier, threatening to destroy the world with electric waves that can disrupt the atoms of both animate and inanimate matter. The opening scene has a large crowd gathered at the Place de l'Opéra listening to a program broadcast over a loudspeaker when suddenly it is interrupted by a voice threatening to annihilate the world: "I am the master of unknown rays and waves that have unlimited destructive power."[7] This is followed by a demonstration, with darkness suddenly blotting out the sunlight on a clear October day and a "polar chill" descending on the city. Throughout the novel, Saint-Imier uses his weapon to kill selected individuals, including children. An engineer working at the Ministry of Scientific Research and his mentor, the most prominent scientist in France, however, manage to foil the villain's plans with their own ray device and in the end kill this self-proclaimed misanthropist. Both weapons have similar properties, including the capability to affect the human body in different ways, but they can also detonate explosives at a distance and cause motors to stop functioning.

A direct reference to Grindell Matthews showed up in what is regarded as one of the earliest Soviet science fiction novels. In *Engineer Garin and His Death Ray* in 1925, Alexei Tolstoy tells the story of an inventor who develops a powerful beam weapon.[8] His overall aim is to create his own society on an island from which he can dominate the world. A Soviet police detective is on his trail, and an American who runs a huge chemical company wants to purchase his death ray. In this novel full of cloak-and-dagger, Garin eludes his pursuers, cuts deals, destroys an entire town, builds his colony on an island below which is a large subterranean layer of gold, wipes out squadrons of U.S. warships, gains mastery over the world only to be overthrown by a revolution, and finally ends up with a woman companion on an isolated speck of land in the ocean, powerless and a failure.

Many of the situations in the novel reflect a close connection to real death-ray claims in the news. One reference is to both Ulivi and Grindell Matthews, whose name Tolstoy actually uses—with a slight alteration. In this scene, the character Khlinov tells Russian Inspector Shelga:

> That's exactly the way Garin uses his genius. I know that he has made an important discovery concerning the transmission of infra-red rays over a distance. You've heard, of course, of the Rindel-Matthews Death Ray? That death ray proved to be a fake although he had the right principles. Heat waves at a temperature of a thousand degrees centigrade transmitted parallel to each other constitute a monstrous weapon of destruction and defence in time of war. The whole secret lies in the transmission of a ray that does not disperse.[9]

Garin himself describes what his weapon can do: "There is nothing in the whole world that can stand up against the power of the ray.... Buildings, fortresses, dreadnoughts, airships, rocks, mountains, the earth's crust ... my ray will pierce, and cut through and destroy everything."[10] As portrayed in the novel, the weapon acts more like a laser, for in one scene Garin uses a smaller model to cut a man in half, neatly and quickly. One of the most dramatic demonstrations of its power is when Garin trains his weapon on the Aniline Chemical Works in Germany, destroying the facility completely and killing much of the neighboring town's population.[11]

One German author did not simply allude to Grindell Matthews or mention him and his death ray in passing but unabashedly named the weapon in his story the "Rindell Matthews ray." In *Elektropolis: Die Stadt der technischen Wunder* (*Electropolis: The City of Technical Wonder*), a *Zukunftsroman* published in 1928, Otfrid von Hanstein described an attempt by Germans to establish a utopian colony in an uninhabited region of Australia. A man named Schmidt discovers a large deposit of radium inside a mountain and secretly mines and sells it. Now provided with considerable wealth, he purchases from the Australian government the mountain containing the radium as well as a large tract of wasteland surrounding it. He plans to use highly advanced technology to reclaim the barren region and turn it into a paradise for future colonization by Germans. With the help of a small number of colleagues, Schmidt completes the initial stages of developing "Desert City" inside a huge cavern. To continue with the project, however, he needs to recruit technicians and others with special skills. One of those is a young man from Berlin named Fritz, who upon arrival learns that Schmidt is his long lost uncle. As the facility, now renamed "Electropolis," reaches its final stage of completion, the Australian government decides that it has made a mistake in selling the land and now wants to annul the contract. Schmidt refuses and a brief war ensues. Australian forces are helpless against the super weapons employed against them. There is a ray-generated, impenetrable shield enveloping most of the city and its environs, and individual death-ray units are deployed where needed. After successfully defending his land, Schmidt then faces a revolt by a handful of disgruntled employees. He puts it down but dies in the struggle, leaving his nephew as sole heir to his property.

In 1933 French author Tancrède Vallerey published a translation entitled *Radiopolis*, in which he adapted Hanstein's work to a French audience. Although keeping to the story, he changed the main characters, Schmidt and his nephew Fritz, into Monsieur Henri Fournier and Frédéric Fournier. Vallerey also altered the purpose of the colony somewhat by making it clear that it would be open to selected individuals from different countries, not just to Germans.

For his weaponry in the novel, Hanstein borrowed almost exclusively from Grindell Matthews, giving his device the same lethal and non-lethal capabilities as the one described in newspaper accounts in 1924. As depicted in the *Radiopolis* version, it serves as the main defense system for the domain of Desert City: a ring of stations outfitted with "the famous Rindell-Matthews rays."[12] In one scene, a unit mounted on an airplane piloted by Fournier is used to disrupt the magneto of a small motorboat carrying a man who has stolen some important papers belonging to him. It is referred to as an "appareil émetteur des rayons de Rindell-Matthews" (an apparatus emitting the Rindell-Matthews rays).[13] Later, when Australian forces attack, their airplanes encounter both capabilities of the weapon. Some are stopped by the "cascades de rayons" which put the magnetos out of action while a lone pilot tries to force his craft through the invisible wall generated by the rays. His plane is destroyed.[14]

A French novel of 1935 bore remarkable similarity to Hanstein's work, for the story is that of a scientist who uses his marvelous electrical inventions to build an island paradise which will help serve as a base—and a model—to ennoble humanity. He also possesses ray weapons for defense that exhibit some of the same capabilities as those of Grindell Matthews's alleged invention. *Les rayons ensorcelés* (The Bewitched Rays) by Henri Allorge begins with concern in France about a series of unexplained explosions at chemical and munitions plants. This is followed by news that an anonymous donor has given a large sum of money to help the surviving victims and families. Jérémie Durand-Galmier, a war veteran and currently a journalist for a Parisian newspaper, takes on the job of trying to find out the identity of the mystery philanthropist. He is joined by Major Jolly, an American with whom he served on the Western Front. They eventually make contact with and gain the confidence of the mystery man, known only as "Dr. Kryptos," who turns out to be an acquaintance of Jolly, a fellow American and scientist named John Johnson. Somewhat older than the two war buddies, Johnson agrees to make a public appearance and brings along his beautiful daughter, Viviane. By now the talk of Parisian society, he tells his audience that he wishes to use all of his resources, including his new inventions, to bring humanity into a new era of happiness and moral improvement. Shortly afterward, however, false accusations force Johnson to flee the city and head for "Deep Island," an uncharted piece of volcanic rock in the Pacific Ocean. Viviane and Jérémie accompany him, while Major Jolly remains behind to keep them informed of developments in the French capital.

By this time, a group calling itself the *"Néantistes"* (anarchists) have made their presence known and taken credit for the mysterious bombings, fires, thefts, and assassinations in different countries. Their goal is to acquire as much money and power as possible in order to destroy the world system and create their own. They see in John Johnson and his wealth and inventions a means to achieve their ends. Having unsuccessfully tried to steal his secrets in Paris, they now plot to learn the location of his island paradise.

From this point on, events move quickly, as the *Néantistes* succeed in locating the island. A brief period of relative peace and quiet is broken when a spy manages to spread a disease germ by means of what Johnson calls the "N-ray." Its effects, however, are only temporary. Johnson and his team then learn of an impending attack. The women and children on the island are evacuated, and the remaining workers prepare to fight. Two airplanes try to penetrate the island's defenses but are shot down by the rays, and a submarine aborts its assault when the element of surprise is lost. One of the leaders on board is taken prisoner but manages to escape and release another deadly microbe before being killed. Johnson and his physician neutralize the germ, but Johnson has also been affected and his condition is too advanced for the antidote. To make matters worse, another saboteur has destroyed the ray generators, rendering the island almost defenseless. Weakened by the microbe, Johnson dies, leaving Viviane and Jérémie—now engaged to be married—as his heirs. The climax is a whirlwind of complications, as *Néantistes* arrive, and American and Japanese warships show up with claims to the island as well. In the end Jérémie, Viviane, and Jolly leave with the Americans, but before doing so plant explosive charges to remove all traces of Johnson's inventions. The blast destroys not only these and the *Néantistes* but triggers a volcanic eruption that completely obliterates the island.

The sigma ray weapon employed in the story by author Allorge affects living things and machines differently. On people the rays cause a disturbance to the nervous system, producing loss of memory, disorientation, and even temporary paralysis. As for machines using electricity, Allorge follows the pattern set by Grindell Matthews and Ulivi. The rays can disrupt the functioning of engines and cause explosions. The author adds another capability by giving them the power to rend to shreds the outer skin of an airplane. During the attack by the *Néantistes*, one of their scout planes is struck by the rays, which stop the engine and send the craft into a nosedive and crash. The other, a bomber, is destroyed when the rays explode its complement of torpedoes and bombs.[15]

Previously mentioned British scientist and inventor A. M. Low also described in a novel several types of rays reflecting the influence of Grindell Matthews and Ulivi. This was "The Great Murchison Mystery," which appeared first as a newspaper serial in 1936. Although the framework of the story involves a fugitive alien from Mars who comes to Earth seeking to use this planet's resources to attack his home world, most of the novel really deals with the contemporary issues of the "next war" and the possibility of exotic weapons such as death rays. Concerned that the world is rushing headlong toward another devastating conflict, scientist Dr. Julian Verity has been working on a type of atom disintegrator that will make war impossible. He also practices hypnosis and treats a few individuals who suffer from various anxieties. Arriving one evening is Calvin Murchison, regarded as the world's richest man, who has had difficulty sleeping. Placing Murchison in a hypnotic trance for his therapy, the scientist leaves him for a while and goes to his laboratory. Working with forces that he does not quite comprehend, Verity receives a telepathic communication from a Martian who calls himself "Zendra." This alien convinces Verity to open a space portal allowing him to come to the scientist's laboratory, promising that his people know all about Earth's history and that he can prevent the war feared by Verity. As soon as he gets through, however, his sinister nature reveals itself. He takes possession of the body of the sleeping Murchison and exerts a mind control over Verity. After a series of strange events, "Murchison" holds a press conference and announces that he owns controlling stock in the armaments industries of the major military powers and that he will have the factories switch over to other types of manufacturing as the best means of eliminating the scourge of war. He and Dr. Verity then go to Geneva to meet with representatives of the League of Nations where he has the scientist demonstrate some of the new inventions that will make war impossible. These include a means to neutralize a new death ray recently created and other wondrous discoveries. "Murchison" then drops a bombshell—these are the result of Dr. Verity receiving communications from Mars. He asks that the nations of the world pool their resources with him and set up huge communications towers so that Earth can begin to develop formal contact with the inhabitants of the red planet. His secret agenda, however, is to use these as platforms for powerful weapons to strike Mars and avenge himself for having fallen from power there. In the end Zendra is foiled when authorities from Mars manage to come through the portal and apprehend him.

Technology in the novel reflected author Low's own research as well as press reports regarding Grindell Matthews and others, including Ulivi. At the meeting in Geneva, for example, Murchison announces that Dr. Verity has developed a ray capable of neutralizing all the modern weapons of war: "The bombing menace, for one. The antidote for such shock terrorism from the air is a certain beam-ray which not only can stop aeroplane engines from functioning over a radius of 300 miles from its source, but also has the power to explode the cargo of bombs. This ray can also be directed at munition factories, dumps, underground mines, and battleships, exploding all gun-powder and dynamite in its path."[16] He also explains that Verity has developed an antidote to all known poison gases as well as any that might be created in the near future. Another invention can wreak havoc on armored vehicles such as tanks by causing the metal to crumble. Murchison has Verity demonstrate how he has an apparatus that can protect against the Dumas Death Ray recently developed. First, the ray is used to kill a horse; then a set of wooden boxes with wires connecting one another are set up in front of a man and another horse. The Dumas Death Ray is switched on, but nothing happens, for Dr. Verity's device has set up an invisible shield to block it. Shortly afterward, Verity performs a Ulivi-type maneuver by using another ray to detonate a small pile of explosives wirelessly.[17]

Two "next war" stories utilizing rays designed to stop airplane engines as well as kill were written by generals, one a Frenchman and the other a German. *La Guerre de 1924* by General Gaston de St. Quentin, Director of the Service of Aeronautical Fabrications in the First World War, was designed to alert the French people and government to the danger of a German war of revenge and to take steps to be prepared. The following summary is taken from a lengthy review in the *New York Times*. Most of the story is told by means of a notebook found on the body of the character Monsieur Florent Girodin, the French air minister, who dies while visiting troops at the front. A series of events leads to growing tensions between the two countries, capped off by a German ultimatum for France to evacuate the Ruhr, which it refuses to do. All during this time, the French government has not taken seriously reports of the threat, believing Germany militarily weak and therefore bluffing. When war begins, the French discover to their dismay that the Germans have huge numbers of modern bombers, larger and more powerful than their own. Most of these have been secretly constructed in Minsk (a reference to Rapallo and the German-Soviet collaboration). Although France possesses a superior army, it can do little as wave after wave of German air squadrons ravage Paris and other cities, killing men, women, and children by the hundreds of thousands. Just when all seems lost, however, a young French scientist invents a ray that can stop airplane motors in flight. He is able to expand the range of his device and completely eliminate the German air threat. The French army then launches an all-out drive and wins the war.[18]

Not long after appeared *Der Krieg im Jahre 1930* (*The War of 1930*) by Freiherr Paul von Schoenaich. A retired artillery general and veteran of the Great War, von Schoenaich later became a pacifist and included this brief story (thirty-one pages) as a chapter in his 1924 book *Vom vorigen zum nächsten Krieg* (From the Last War to the Next). Although written in May 1924, this chapter was subsequently published separately in 1925. A warning of what would occur in the event of another major war, it begins with several crises underway, including a clash of interests in the Far East between Japan and the Anglo-American powers, which ends with a conference after a brief war scare. In Europe an improvement in relations between France and Germany collapses as a threatening situation in Poland precipitates a chain reaction that leads to war. A mutiny in the Polish army sends the government fleeing into exile, with Communists taking control. Although Russia promises to prevent the revolution from spilling over the frontiers when it intervenes, Berlin dispatches troops to occupy those parts of Poland adjacent to Germany and inhabited by mostly ethnic Germans, at the same time assuring the French that this is not a violation of the Treaty of Versailles. The French government, now in the hands of the nationalists, however, decides to send an unacceptable ultimatum to Germany, thereby giving it an excuse to launch a war. The plan

6. Death-Ray Novels and Short Stories of the Interwar Years

is to attack primarily Berlin and Munich with bombs outfitted with a new gas that can penetrate all known masks. The French also have death rays—but only four of them are as yet operational. In the meantime, the Fatherland Party in Germany has placed government leaders under house arrest and announced to them that it has been quietly preparing for a war of revenge for several years. Along their frontiers with France and Belgium the Germans have secretly placed a series of death-ray machines. When the ultimatum expires, the French launch several air squadrons toward their predetermined targets. Although the German ray weapons destroy large numbers of airplanes, some of the French bombers get through and kill 100,000 civilians in Berlin and wreak havoc elsewhere in the country. The Germans then go on the offensive and utilize a highly toxic poison to contaminate the water supply in sections of France, resulting in horrendous casualties among civilians. The war lasts only twelve hours, for the United States intercedes to bring about a peace conference. Of particular importance is the reaction of the *Chicago Tribune* writer who reviewed the book, for he described it as being based on real military capabilities.[19]

Von Schoenaich's brief tale reflected the influence of several sources prominent in the news and, especially, in other literary works. When, for example, the deputy of the Fatherland Party announces to the Reich council of ministers that the army has ray weapons, the Reichswehr minister scoffs that he has been reading Dominik's *Die Macht der Drei*. The deputy replies that Dominik has in fact been at work in his laboratory and has helped produce them. The author describes these as being capable of heating a section of the atmosphere up to twenty kilometers and quickly killing the crew of an airplane passing through it. This heat beam will also explode the aircraft's fuel.[20] As for the French rays, von Schoenaich tells the reader in a footnote that the concept for these had appeared first in Claude Farrère's *Die Todgeweihten* (*Les condamnés à mort*), described below. The French rays in Schoenaich's novel are called *Vibrationsstrahler* and utilize sound that not only kills but reduces the dead body to a gaseous state.[21]

One "next war" work, another *Zukunftsroman*, alluded to the stories of mystery rays and French commercial airplanes flying over Bavaria in 1923. German Paul Thieme's *Der Flug zur Sonne* (The Flight to the Sun) in 1926 includes a war between Germany and France, but the Germans win without harming their enemy, for they want to establish a "United States of Europe" under their aegis. They deploy rays that force the French airplanes to land because of mechanical failure, and their gas bombs merely induce sleep, thereby rendering French ground forces helpless.[22]

Somewhat related to these stories was a novel by a writer who capitalized on the reports about German and French efforts to develop a death ray but wove them into a tale warning about the possibility of world destruction. Pierrepont B. Noyes, an American diplomat who served as a member of the Inter-Allied Rhineland Commission during the early years following the First World War, published *The Pallid Giant: A Tale of Yesterday and Tomorrow* in 1927. It tells the story of several men in the aftermath of the Great War who discover that an ancient race of beings living on Earth destroyed their world in the distant past with a type of death ray. The weapon is called the "Klepton-Holorif" based on a type of atomic energy that did not release explosive power through a chain reaction. It functioned, rather, by dissolving the cohesive force holding together the matter in all living tissue. It killed by reducing people to dust. As for what is happening in Europe at the same time that the investigators learn of this prehistoric culture, Noyes tells the reader about the frantic efforts by European powers to develop a death ray, especially France and Germany. At the end of the novel, the men receive word that the French have just perfected one, suggesting that modern man is about to repeat the disaster of their ancient forebears.[23]

Instead of a future war, George S. Schuyler, an African American writer who worked some time for the *Pittsburgh Courier*, utilized death rays in two of his works dealing with the Italian invasion of Ethiopia. In *Black Empire* the author described an ambitious plan by blacks to drive all the European colonial powers out of Africa. A force assembled by a Dr. Belsidus succeeds in destroying the armed forces of Italy, France, and Britain by means of two super energy beam weapons developed by Brazilian Dr. Portabla. One is an "infernal radio machine" that sends out an electric ray to shut off electricity (whether dynamos, batteries, or magnetos) to airplanes, ships, vehicles, and weapon systems, the other a "proton ray" that causes explosions. The former's capabilities resemble to a degree those of Grindell Matthews's apparatus. As Schuyler describes in the final battle with Mussolini's air force: "On came the Italian air fleet. But now an amazing thing happened. On plane after plane, the propellers suddenly went dead and the machines glided to the earth. Several crashed out of control. Again and again this happened, until the earth was covered with grounded ships."[24] Belsidus employs the proton ray to dispatch the combined naval squadrons of Britain and France off the coast at Monrovia, Liberia.[25] In "The Ethiopian Murder Mystery, A Story of Love and International Intrigue," Schuyler introduced a non-descript death ray at the end of the short story, announcing only that a Dr. Tankkard has developed one for use in Ethiopia against the Italians.[26]

6. Death-Ray Novels and Short Stories of the Interwar Years   161

In reference to Italy, one novel serialized in a Swiss newspaper in 1937 had a death ray based on the work of Guglielmo Marconi. "Tu mourras le ..." (You will die on ...) by Édouard Adenis is a murder mystery set in French Indochina. A Professor Germain-Paulin delivering an address to a scholarly institute in Saigon suddenly drops dead. The medical examiner concludes heart attack, but an associate tells police that the famed archaeologist had recently received a death warning not to proceed with his plans to excavate a site of the ancient Khmer empire. The rest of the story is about the sleuthing work to uncover the means, the motive, and the culprits. A native prince, outwardly professing his loyalty to France, has engaged several Europeans to help him secretly amass weapons for an uprising to overthrow colonial rule. These are being stored in an ancient archeological site, the one Professor Germain-Paulin intended to excavate. One of these Europeans is a German named Schwartz, who has developed a death-ray device that is placed inside a wall clock, the mechanism of which triggers the lethal, invisible beam.

Adenis utilized Marconi by having the character Daverne refer to a newspaper article in 1933 about the inventor's experiments on board his yacht *Elettra*. According to it, the Italian radio wizard succeeded in sending microwaves in a straight line rather than in concentric circles. Daverne then concludes that someone must have hit upon this prior to Marconi and fashioned a weapon, for the archaeologist Germain-Paulin was murdered in 1932.[27] As noted in Chapter 4, however, Marconi announced in 1931 that he might consider looking into the possibility of a death ray. Newspapers in August 1933 did indeed report on Marconi's experiments with microwaves on his yacht *Elettra*, but these concerned primarily his efforts to find a means of perfecting television. Interviewed by *Pearson's Weekly* of London, Marconi was also asked about the military application of his work, in particular toward constructing a death ray to render war impossible. Reluctant to deny or confirm that he was doing so, he nevertheless observed that such a weapon might be possible but that no one had yet succeeded in developing one.[28]

Agatha Christie employed a death ray in one of her works featuring her brilliant detective Hercule Poirot. In *The Big Four*, published in 1927, the famed mystery novelist tells the story of a group of four people planning to create anarchy in the world in order to take power. One is a scientist named Madame Olivier, who, in addition to succeeding in releasing and controlling atomic energy, has developed a death ray, as suggested by Poirot: "she has also experimented in the concentration of wireless energy, so that a beam of great intensity can be focused upon some given spot.

Exactly how far she has progressed, nobody knows, but it is certain that it is much farther than has ever been given out."[29] Most of the story involves the detective work to identify, find, and foil the Big Four; but mention of a wireless energy weapon occurs in several other instances. One is a report in connection with the destruction of some warships off the west coast of the United States. Papers obtained by the authorities "gave an incomplete description of some powerful wireless installation— a concentration of wireless energy far beyond anything so far attempted, and capable of focusing a beam of great intensity upon some given spot."[30] This is followed by a report of a scientist having read a paper on his research with wireless energy to his peers at a convention. Although this is a somewhat vague description which could be based on any number of claims in the press, another reference to rays clearly shows the influence of the stories about the French airplane mystery in 1923. Christie has Poirot mentioning "a series of aeroplane accidents and forced landings."[31]

Some of the death rays employed in stories lacked specific definition or were described as simply the result of harnessing electrical energy. One such work was *Drake's Mantle* by Norman K. Bentley, published in 1928, and another *The Rebel Passion* by Katharine Burdekin in 1929. The former is a story about a Communist uprising in Britain, coinciding with a Soviet invasion, that is stopped by a death ray invented by former Admiral Wroxley of the Royal Navy. With this apparatus the British defeat the enemy in two weeks. What is significant about this novel is that one of the reviewers did not consider such a weapon fantastic. According to *The Courier and Advertiser* of Dundee, Scotland: "victory is decided by 'death rays' of a power happily unachieved in actual practice, but—bearing in mind the innovations of the last war—still within the realms of possibility."[32]

In Burdekin's novel the story is told by a monk named Giraldus living at Glastonbury Abbey in medieval England during the reign of King Stephen. His soul in torment, the monk one night receives a visitor whom he refers to as "the Child," a spirit in the form of a boy about ten years of age. Over the course of many evenings, this emissary of God shows Giraldus visions of the development of humanity from the beginning of time to the distant future. When the story reaches the aftermath of the First World War, Burdekin introduces a heat ray. Shortly after that conflict, a German invents such a weapon and manufactures two thousand devices for future use, taking care to hide them because of the restrictions placed on German armaments by the Treaty of Versailles. Fifty years later Europe is threatened by Mongolians, and the League of Nations, made aware of the secret weapons, authorizes their deployment to save civilization. These "death engines," as Giraldus calls them, are mounted on "powerful flying boats" and loosed against the enemy. The monk then describes the battle scene: "And in the vision I saw how they flew high over the air fleet and ground army of the Yellow Men, and destroyed them with sheets of flame. In every one of these appalling death-engines was a ray of heat which spread out to an enormous extent, and everything that was beneath it melted away, even if it were the hardest metal."[33]

In 1932 well-known Melbourne journalist Arthur Russell contributed "The Ether King" as a serial to the *Central Queensland Herald* (Rockhampton). The story is that of an English scientist named Hinkelston, who creates several devices utilizing wireless energy and employing them to commit crimes. He is challenged throughout by Harrington Graves, a detective from Scotland Yard and a wireless radio enthusiast himself. His knowledge of radio and electricity enables him early on to realize who is behind several mysterious crimes and to come up with ways of thwarting the "professor." The plot is one continuous confrontation between the two men, with one or the other always managing to escape a dangerous situation. Among the weapons developed by Hinkelston is an apparatus that sends a wireless signal for thousands of miles to detonate bombs that he has secretly placed in ships. He uses this on one occasion as a warning to try to get a shipping company to pay him a large sum of money. He later develops the capability to transmit electrical energy wirelessly to a target, causing it to heat up and burn or explode depending on its composition. Hinkelston also has what he calls "death rockets" and almost succeeds in killing Graves with them. When set loose, these small devices form a circle around the target and destroy it by burning through it similar to a modern laser. Graves develops a short-range death ray himself, but Hinkelston has improved upon his earlier work and his ray is more powerful. At the end of the story, Hinkelston is killed, and Graves is rescued by Eve, the professor's niece with whom he is in love.[34]

Fellow Australian journalist and writer Erle Cox wrote a serial entitled "Out of the Silence," which appeared first in *The Argus* (Melbourne) in 1919. After being published as a book, it was serialized again in 1934 in numerous Australian newspapers, this time in cartoon form. Alan Dundas, a onetime lawyer, and bachelor, accidentally discovers in his vineyards a large underground structure built by an ancient race of humans extinct for millions of years. A beautiful young woman named Earani is awakened from suspended animation by Dundas and his doctor friend, Richard Barry, and proceeds to tell them about her people and the reason for her presence in the chamber. Faced with imminent destruction of their world, the leaders chose three people to be placed in deep sleep together with a vast storehouse of knowledge in separate locations. Earani and the others, when awakened, will bring this advanced science of their lost civilization to improve the lot of modern humans—with or without their permission. She quickly ascertains that one of them has not survived and that the other's chamber lies deep under the Himalayas. Before she and Dundas can embark on the journey to awaken him, another woman kills Earani out of jealousy, thus causing the original mission to fail. Before her death, however, the woman of the lost world has shown Dundas how to destroy the underground structure with all its advanced science. Having fallen in love with her, Dundas does so, preferring to join Earani in death.

Among the machines developed by her people are a death ray and a device that can be used for constructive purposes as well as a weapon. The death ray was used by its inventor to exterminate the inferior race of people inhabiting the earth at that time.[35] As for the other, Earani calls it a "devastator" and tells Dundas that it can destroy anything within a radius of one hundred miles.[36] The 1919 serial version did not have illustrations, but in one frame of that of 1934 one sees a type of cylinder mounted on a base containing various controls. The next frame shows two ancient warriors operating the "devastator."[37] Cox did not supply any description of the power source for either of the devices other than implying an advanced knowledge of electricity.

Another newspaper serial story with a non-descript death ray was L. Bamberg's "Septimus March Again," appearing in the *Sunday Times* of Perth in December 1929. Each installment dealt with a mystery to be solved by the British secret service agent with Scotland Yard, Septimus March, and one episode is entitled "The Secret Cypher." A young man is found dead in his apartment, but there is no detectable cause of death or evidence of foul play. After a brief investigation, March exposes the culprit, a Polish inventor who used his death ray to murder the victim. No specific information about the apparatus is provided by the author other than the fact that its killing agent is electricity.[38]

In a similar fashion John Kirke contributed a serialized short novel to *The Argus* of Melbourne, which ran from late 1935 to spring 1936. Written as a boys' story, "Captain Midnight" appeared in *The Junior Argus* supplement. In contrast to philanthropists who wanted to create utopian societies protected by death rays, Kirke's tale was about a group of misfits and scoundrels of several different nationalities led by a sinister character named "Captain Midnight" that sought to take control of Australia and then the world. Having created a secret base called Conquest City located in a remote area on the island of Tasmania, they aim to carry out their plans by means of a powerful death ray created by a German scientist named Krauss. Two young men, one of whose brother is a naval officer and member of the secret service, thwart their plans and save the day. Kirke does not provide much information about this death ray other than it exudes a violet glow and completely annihilates what it strikes, leaving nothing at all. The weapon is used only twice in the story, once when it dispatches four birds and a small animal, and at the end when it destroys the base.[39]

Two other such examples were Gregory Baxter's *Blue Lightning* in 1926 and Maryse Rutledge's *The Silver Peril* in 1931. *Blue Lightning* is a detective novel with a "yellow peril" theme, as an English lord, with the aid of a death ray, secretly plots to foment a general uprising of non-white peoples to overthrow Western civilization. Sir Cosmo Domval, a Eurasian by birth, is immensely wealthy and exerts considerable influence over business and political leaders in several countries, including Britain, where the action takes place, mostly in London. Similar to other novels of this type involving love and intrigue, the usual cast of characters includes a former member of the secret service, Frank Manvers, and a young, robust country gentleman named Keith Stanfield, as well as two beautiful women, Nora Partridge and Lady Ena Greenway. Domval is coordinating a worldwide uprising that consists primarily of a Japanese attack on the United States simultaneously with uprisings of blacks in America, a Mexican invasion across its southern border, and rebellions in India, Egypt, and other areas under European domination. To ensure victory, Domval has employed a Russian inventor named Klivinsky who has developed a death ray. Most of the novel deals with the efforts of the villain to bring his plans to fruition and those of Stanfield and Manvers to stop him. In the end, Domval dies and the death ray is destroyed before it can be employed on a large scale. It is first described as the Televisual Light, for the apparatus is connected to a screen that shows a live picture of the intended victim and guides the lethal ray to its quarry. The weapon is used to kill two people, including the Under-Secretary of State for Foreign Affairs, but an attempt on the prime minister's life fails only because of the last minute intervention by Manvers, who manages to smash the infernal machine to bits. Baxter clearly demonstrates his indebtedness to newspaper stories current at the time, for he refers to the German "heliotaueb" mentioned in Chapter 3 and E. R. Scott's "death stroke" in 1924. When told about such a weapon in the hands of Domval, Sir Handley Clough, the Under-Secretary of State for Foreign Affairs, expresses his skepticism:

> You remember the German "Heliotraub" [sic], which was to be capable of clearing the air of hostile aeroplanes to the altitude of forty-five thousand feet, and at the same time of paralysing all life within a radius of forty miles? What happened to that? And the American "death stroke" which was said to be capable of the destruction of all life on land, sea, or in the air within a radius of twenty miles? We have heard no more of that. So with numerous other claims.[40]

Rutledge's *The Silver Peril* focuses on a Russian misanthropist named de Raskoff who has developed both a magnificent helicopter and a weapon which he calls the To-Ray. Once the leader of an international crime syndicate, de Raskoff now goes by the name of Torad and decides to destroy the world because of its evil ways. In his first demonstration of power, Torad uses bombs to kill and injure many people in a crowd in Bucharest in broad daylight, after which the European press labels his mysterious helicopter the "Silver Peril." Although this occurs early in the story, most of the novel is really a detective mystery. A British secret service officer infiltrates the syndicate in an attempt to learn more about Torad, who is now an enemy of his former associates. A beautiful and wealthy American woman completes the usual cast of characters, and Paris is the setting for much of the action. In the climax to the story, Torad and his chief rival from the syndicate die in a struggle aboard the helicopter when the ray blows up the craft. The weapon itself is described as a ray that quickly incinerates people, leaving virtually no trace. It can also destroy buildings, whole cities, and almost anything else. Rutledge does not provide specific information about the weapon's killing agent, only indirect references suggesting electricity.[41]

One of the most prolific writers of mystery stories of the early twentieth century, E. Phillips Oppenheim, also utilized a type of death ray in his 1937 novel, *The Dumb Gods Speak*. This is significant, for the author was dubbed "The Prince of Storytellers" in his own time, having published more than one hundred and fifty novels and short stories, some of which were adapted as movies; and *Time* magazine featured his picture on its cover in 1927. As an aside, the exiled Kaiser Wilhelm II proclaimed that Oppenheim was his favorite author and read many of his novels. In the story, set in the year 1947, American Mark Humberstone, Jr., the son of the greatest scientist in history, and Prince Cheng, a descendant of an ancient and noble Chinese family, team up together to end war forever. Mark's father had created a number of inventions, including a weapon of immeasurable power that could neutralize—even destroy—all conventional armies, navies, and air forces; and before he died he had bequeathed them to a Council of Seven to use for peace. As a member of this secretive circle, Mark, Jr., continues his father's work. At Harvard, he has met Cheng, and the two have come to a meeting of the minds, whereby they seek to apply these devices to make war impossible. Their plan is to assemble a great Chinese army to oppose the Communist regime in Russia, which they believe has poisoned the soul of a once great people, and then demonstrate their weapon as an invincible force that no conventional army can resist. Cheng intends, furthermore, to put back on the throne of Russia a member of the tsarist family in order to rebuild the country. He also plans to marry a young princess descended from the last empress of China and rejuvenate his country to its former position of greatness. Almost all of the novel is concerned with their plans and their use of spies to achieve the final victory which ushers in a new age. The action itself is centered primarily in Nice and the activities of the International Bureau of Espionage created by Mark and Cheng. One of their chief assistants is Catherine Oronoff, a Russian princess who ends up marrying Mark. The most dramatic use of the death ray takes place before the beginning of the story, as Mark's father destroyed the entire Japanese fleet when the Mikado foolishly tried to attack the Philippines. Japan's disastrous defeat then gave China its opportunity to emerge out from under the shadow of its chief antagonist in the Far East. The death ray's power also appears near the end of the novel, as a demonstration to the Russians and again when Mark explains to the French premier, Monsieur Châtelain, and the minister of police, General Levissier, how he would use the improved wireless electrical weapon to stop a German army if France's old enemy in the meantime should attack the Republic: "Supposing that happened this week, or next, I could guarantee to throw the German army into utter disorder within a radius of a hundred miles anywhere, and if it were necessary I could destroy the whole electrical equipment throughout Germany at the same time, so that commercially as well as from a military point of view she would become inert."[42] He goes on, however, to explain that he will soon be able to send this devastating electrical energy and hit a target within a radius of just one mile. In a favorable review of the novel appearing in the *Albany Advertiser* (Western Australia), attention is drawn to Oppenheim's death ray as "the dream of all inventors."[43]

One mystery novel utilized an electric ray weapon whose range was considerably less than most. Serialized in 1938 in the Swiss newspaper *Feuille d'Avis de Lausanne*, "Le masque de feu" by Maurice Boué and Édouard Aujay was a story involving a cult inspired by ancient Egypt. Its leader's overall objective is to exact revenge on those who have despoiled the tombs of pharaohs and other antiquities and also to free Egypt from British control.[44] He has developed a portable death ray contained in a box resembling a camera which he uses to strike down his victims. The authors capitalized on the publicity surrounding the famous discovery of the burial site of Tutankhamun in November 1922 by Howard Carter and Lord Carnarvon, especially the famous "curse." They included a warning inscription on the entrance to the tomb similar to one claimed to be real: "Death will come on swift wings to whoever touches the tombs of the pharaohs."[45] After dispatching several people, including a Lord Westbury (a real participant with the Carter expedition who was an early victim of the "curse"), the villain meets his own doom by electrocution from another of his devices—the mask of fire. The only description of the death ray is that it is wireless electricity that can kill at an unspecified, but short, distance.

"Alphabet" rays with varying capabilities also became fashionable during the interwar period. Eichacker's "W-ray" in *Der Kampf ums Gold* has already been described, but others emerged as well. A "Q-ray" showed up in Peter Cheyney's "The Gold Kimono, A Great Mystery Story," which appeared first as a serial in *The Sunday Times* of Perth in 1930. Captain Josiah Peabody of the British army invents this weapon and provides the information to the British government but receives no word as to whether or not Whitehall considers the device useful. For the time being he keeps it in a secret location. Peabody then becomes part of the force sent to Russia when Britain intervenes in the civil war between the Reds and the Whites, whereupon he meets a beautiful young woman fleeing the Bolsheviks, marries her, and brings her back to England. After having told her about his invention, she disappears and the intrigue begins. As the plot moves along, it turns out that Soviet agents have taken possession of his Q-ray and plan to destroy a British torpedo flotilla that will be sailing past the secret location about three to four miles out to sea. In the end Peabody, with two of his friends and the British secret service, foils the villains and is happily reunited with his wife, who turns out to be innocent of any wrongdoing. Cheyney does not provide the reader with information about the death ray's properties—its energy source or destructive agent—only that it is powerful enough to annihilate any target it strikes.[46]

French writer and journalist Léon Groc presented another variant with the "J-ray" in his novel *L'impossible rançon* (The Impossible Ransom), which started as a serial in *Le Petit Parisien* in 1937. It is the story of a film actress, Jacqueline Bligny, who tries to protect her career and her young daughter from scandal, as she had divorced her husband because of his treatment of her and because of the fact that he was a crook, leaving him in French Guiana and hoping that he never returned to France. In the meantime, she meets and falls in love with the brilliant and well-respected Henri-Maximilien de Roche-Tonnerre, a descendant of a distinguished family of the old nobility. He also happens to be a leading scientist. As their relationship develops, he lets her in on his great secret invention: a weapon that will end war—a device that utilizes "J-rays." A group of local gangsters then kidnaps her daughter and holds the child as ransom in exchange for the plans and mathematical formulas of the death ray. Her ex-husband turns up working for them, but his paternal instincts prove too strong and he gives his life to protect his daughter. In the end, the villains are foiled and Jacqueline and Max plan to marry.

The weapon is described as consisting of two parts, one a parabolic mirror and the other a quadrangular prism, with all the necessary wires, dials, and gadgets that were standard fare. Max first explains to Jacqueline that this is a device to make war impossible and stresses its defensive capabilities: "in case of invasion, I would be able to stop the airplanes, the autos, and the tanks of the enemy, and protect our cities or armies by an invisible, impassable barrier."[47] He then demonstrates in dramatic fashion the devastating "offensive" power of his invention by using it to reduce a group of lab mice in their cage to a pile of ashes.

The most popular type of alphabet ray, however, was the previously mentioned "Z-ray," and it came in a number of varieties depending on the authors' preferences. A one-page short story by the prolific British writer Warwick Deeping appeared in *The Queenslander* of Brisbane in 1921. Entitled "Trelawney's Z-Rays," it describes Britain under some type of Communist dictatorship opposed by an underground movement calling itself the "Knights of the Imperial Secret Council." An aristocrat named Trelawney invents a Z-ray that kills and, together with agents of the underground, succeeds in defeating the Communists and making war obsolete.[48]

One novel published in 1925 bore some similarity to "The Isolated Continent: A Romance of the Future" mentioned in the previous chapter in that it featured a Z-ray and a separate death ray. In *Ruled by Radio*, by Robert L. Hadfield and Frank E. Farncombe, a British scientist has produced a radio emitted Z-ray, which can stop all other radio transmissions in a selected area. This translates into tremendous power since the future world of 1930 runs almost entirely on wireless (radio) energy for all means of transportation, industry, and communication. Even most household appliances depend on it. The scientist, Professor Calos, has also perfected a wireless death ray capable of killing anyone, anywhere, regardless of the distance involved. Unknown to Calos, his financial backer, a German named Karl Lunt, is an international crook who intends to use these devices to make himself master of the world. Having taken control of them and kidnapping Calos, he puts on a few demonstrations of shutting down all radio transmissions in Britain and killing the chief of Newer Scotland Yard with the death ray. Lunt then begins a series of broadcasts in which he demands a huge ransom of gold as well as submission to his will. Failure to comply will mean the death of the premier and other selected individuals. In the meantime, another scientist, Richard "Dick" Holmes, tries to find a way to neutralize the Z-ray and the death ray but comes up empty-handed. At the last minute, he finds the solution created by Professor Calos, who took the precaution of developing a means of controlling these powerful weapons, and defeats the villain and his accomplices.[49] The world of radio power described in the story is based on the principles advocated by Tesla, in which wireless energy could be transmitted through the ether.

Apparently not content with just one Z-ray, popular writer of stories for boys Percy F. Westerman employed two in his 1923 novel *The War of the Wireless Waves*. A few years after the First World War, British scientists have revolutionized naval warfare by developing two types of radio-electric energy weapons referred to as the ZZ ray and the –Z ray. The former seems to be based on the claims made by Ulivi, for it has the capability of exploding the magazines of ships. Somewhat less powerful, the latter provides a good air defense by causing gasoline motors to stop functioning. In sole possession of these rays, Britain is once again undisputed mistress of the seas, having placed them aboard all ships of the Royal Navy. A rival appears in the form of the Ultra-K Ray developed by Austrian Professor Bohmer, but his turns out to be unwieldy and therefore impractical. Just when the British breathe a sigh of relief that they still have a monopoly on ray weapons, a new menace threatens. Georgeos Kosmosoli, a scientist from a small region called Mpiki under the nominal rule of the king of Albania, has succeeded in developing something more powerful. Employing an agent who steals the schematics to the British radio-electric devices, he uses them to complete his own invention that operates along similar lines. His Kosmosoli Rays, however, are stronger. The Second Degree beams can completely shut down all electrical impulses over a broad area, and Kosmosoli demonstrates this on several occasions, causing widespread fear and panic throughout Europe and elsewhere. All communications, transportation, anything running on electricity comes to a halt. The First Degree weapon, although more limited in range, wreaks havoc on all metals by heating them to high temperatures. Its rays destroy ships by exploding the gunpowder and shells, cause metal frames and fastenings to crumple, and electrocute anyone in close proximity to metal. Soldiers are killed by their own cartridge belts. Kosmosoli seeks to rule the world and uses both of these weapons in the story, threatening to destroy any country that does not meet his demands. Most of the novel involves the sleuthing work to determine the exact identity of this villain and his location. Since modern warships and airplanes are vulnerable, the British ultimately foil Kosmosoli by constructing wooden ships and dispatching a force of sailors armed with non-metallic weapons, including bows with stone-tipped arrows and clubs. Having come to rely entirely on the electrical rays, the dictator's men have destroyed their guns and ammunition lest they become victims of his weapons and are therefore ill-equipped to deal with the invasion. Time and again throughout the story, Westerman's description of the Kosmosoli rays doing their mischief seems to imitate the F-rays of Ulivi and the magneto-stopping beams involved in the French airplane mystery over Germany in 1923.[50]

Another "Z-ray" novel was one simply entitled *The Z Ray* and published by Edmund Snell in 1932. It also bore some connection, albeit tenuously, with Grindell Matthews. Unlike the Z-ray described in the foregoing work, this beam is lethal. In the story a British secret service officer and his best friend investigate a report about a Z-ray operation set up in a country house near the Channel coast in Britain. The plot involves two Dutch brothers, Arnst and Karel Dorpmann, who have developed an apparatus producing an invisible ray that hits its target with high voltage electricity similar to that claimed by Grindell Matthews. They are not connected with any foreign power, however, and do not have sinister motives. The Dorpmann brothers are simply planning to make money by selling their invention once it is perfected. For their experiments, they have chosen a remote location that also gives them easy access to major electric power lines. A secret cable connection allows them to tap into electricity generated from the power station in Brighton, providing their Z-ray with a virtually unlimited energy supply. Unfortunately for the Dutchmen, an unscrupulous, international former spy of the Great War concocts a plan to gain control of the Z-ray and reap the profits for himself. One of his accomplices is a character named "Maurice Matthews." As usual, the heroes triumph in the end and the ray is destroyed—but not before a number of people, including the Dorpmans, have been fried to death by the diabolical contraption.[51]

The plot of one "Z-ray" novel places the book in a category of its own. *The Black Satchel* by Harry Stephen Keeler, published in 1931, is a detective tale in which most of the action involves sleuthing work to unmask a murderer. Set in Chicago, a young man by the name of Jerry Evans receives an unexpected visit from his aunt, who is carrying in a sealed black satchel what she believes is a "Z-ray" weapon invented by one of her new boarders, a man named Michaux. Fearful that something has happened to him, she faithfully obeys his previous instructions to take the satchel to a safe place. After listening to her tale for a while, Evans leaves his room to answer the telephone but on his return he finds the old woman dead. Believing that she may have accidently triggered the lethal device, he contacts the police. This sets into motion a bizarre case of murder, robbery, and perceived insurance fraud, in which Evans finds himself a chief suspect. Aided by the brilliance of "criminological scientist" Tuddleton Trotter, the young man is ultimately cleared of all charges and the mystery is unraveled.

Keeler gave his tale two unusual twists. Early in the novel, the reader encounters a newspaper clipping entitled "Has a New Military Weapon Been Discovered?" It was an interview by Evans's cousin of a well-known British scientist named Cyril Burthrick and head of a commission overseeing the coordination of scientific experiments to aid in the defense of the country. When asked about any recent improvements, Burthrick strongly implies that "a ray-projecting weapon utilizing the energy of the atom"[52] has either been developed, or will soon become reality. This provides part of the basis for the logical deduction that the character Michaux may have succeeded in inventing a "Z-ray." The other is the news about a Frenchman living in England who claimed to have constructed one as well and later disappeared. Evans and Trotter operate under the false assumption that he is the same man who showed up in the aunt's boarding house. Near the end of the story, however, it turns out that Michaux, who dies mysteriously, has fabricated such a tale in order to cover up a theft, and the deaths attributed to this weapon the result of other causes. In other words, a death ray serves only as part of the framework for Keeler's detective mystery and is not actually used. This reference to the possibility of a real wireless ray to defend Britain and the false belief of one as a murder weapon leads to another category of death-ray fiction.

Several authors employed ray weapons simply as props, some of which served no real purpose in the stories. One such was the novel *Scissors Cut Paper* written by Gerard Fairlie[53] and published in 1928, for its death ray plays such a minor part that it seems like an obligatory feature. The author weaves together a mystery involving an international gang of crooks counterfeiting huge sums of money in different currencies, a beautiful woman, and two upper class Englishmen taking on the role of detectives. For about two hundred and fifty pages, the story follows conventional

6. Death-Ray Novels and Short Stories of the Interwar Years

crime detective plots. As a favor, a young man escorts his best friend's wife for a night out on the town, but upon their return they hear a gunshot upstairs. Entering the home, Bill Wilson discovers a body he believes to be that of Derek Sinclaire. Exiting the building, he finds the taxi and Anne Sinclaire gone and the driver lying dead in the street. Wilson then awakes in jail, with his old friend and lawyer Victor Caryll bailing him out and filling in a most remarkable tale, essentially that Wilson in a drunken stupor had told the police about what had happened but that their investigation revealed no bodies, no mysterious disappearances, and that he had been arrested for public drunkenness. Unable to accept this, Wilson convinces his friend to help him solve the mystery. Their detective work and encounters with some of the crooks in London take up nearly half the book, followed by a shift in the action to France, ultimately to Biarritz, where the gang has its headquarters in a villa just outside the city. It turns out that its "Chief," alias "Brain," is none other than Derek Sinclaire, who managed to fake his own death. He has developed a sophisticated printing press for counterfeiting money and in the process has accumulated a fortune. Although Anne does not condone his crime when she learns the truth, she still loves him and remains loyal. After a few more encounters between Wilson and Caryll with Derek's henchmen, a force of police attempts to storm the villa and apprehend the crooks. This is the moment when author Fairlie suddenly has Derek's men turn loose a death ray on the unfortunate gendarmes. As the character Wilson describes the scene:

> And then a thing occurred which I shall remember with horror to my dying day. The yellowish white rays of the searchlight turned to a pale green, and as they did so the effect on the men below was instantaneous. They seemed to be doubled backwards in agony, and fall writhing to the ground, to become motionless almost at once, and lie in grotesque positions. The searchlight had been turned into a death-ray![54]

After about a dozen are killed, Caryll manages to shoot the machine's operator. That is the extent of the presence of the death ray in the story, with only a few subsequent references to it. There is neither a warning to the reader that such a device has been developed by one of the characters nor any description of its properties, except that it might be based on electricity. Afterward, the plot reaches its inevitable conclusion without any real discussion of the death ray. Fairlie does not have his main characters, Bill and Victor, express any curiosity as to its existence or its origin, as if such a weapon were commonplace.

In a similar fashion, Mark Channing waited until near the end of his novel *King Cobra* before suddenly introducing a death ray. First appearing in serialized form in newspapers in 1933, it is a story of high adventure in a fictitious little independent kingdom called Yanistan nestled between modern-day Pakistan and Afghanistan. A mysterious character referred to as the "Veiled Man" is plotting to overthrow British rule in the region and mete out punishment to India's Hindus. His chief lieutenant is a ruthless leader called the "Cobra," who starts the action by killing the British representative in Yanistan and kidnapping his beautiful daughter, Diana, and taking her back to his mountain stronghold. Most of the novel is taken up with events there and the efforts of a dashing British major named Gray, who ultimately kills the Cobra and rescues Diana, with whom he is in love. Throughout, a mysterious Hindu Brahmin, the Swastika Sadhu, capable of projecting himself outside his body, periodically guides and encourages the actions of the two lovers. Near the end of the novel, he shows up in the nick of time and kills the Veiled Man with a death ray invented by one of his followers. Afterward, he offers it to the British as a means of preserving their empire. The appearance of this weapon is abrupt and totally unexpected, especially since the entire story deals with conventional issues of unrest among native peoples under colonial rule and traditional tales of the mysteries of the East.[55]

Although entertaining his readers with a conventional murder and detective mystery for two hundred and eighty-seven pages before introducing his death ray, Charman Edwards made his device logically connect the clues that have baffled the police and his brilliant sleuth, Percy Aloysius Huff. Published in 1936, *Fear Haunts the Roses* is a story about several prominent people in Britain committing suicide and the efforts of a semi-retired detective and a few Scotland Yard investigators attempting to determine if they were actually murdered. Before their deaths, some of these individuals had been given a green rose as a warning, leading Huff and his associates to believe that some criminal organization, for reasons yet unknown, was responsible. Near the end, it is revealed that the "gang" is made up of idealistic individuals, among them war veterans, on the trail of an evil inventor working on a death ray and the wealthy investors who have helped finance his research in order to reap substantial profits. Before that happens, however, the author tips off the reader that something greater than simple murder is afoot. Huff is informed by a British intelligence official that the country of "Balkania" is threatening war against its neighbor. This is baffling to them since that country's extremely limited military capabilities are well known. The reason is that Balkania is anticipating delivery of the death ray, described by Edwards as "something that could wipe out life from horizon to horizon."[56] The plan fails, as the inventor blows up his laboratory, killing himself and destroying the weapon. Like other stories in this category, the death ray appears to have been selected by the author because of its ongoing popularity. A new explosive, an advanced type of airplane, or a more potent poison gas could have easily served the purpose of the plot. In fact, Edwards first mentions the death-ray inventor as a chemist, suggesting to the reader that chemical warfare might be involved.

Another work with a death ray as an incidental prop was Canadian writer Madge Macbeth's *Wings in the West*, published in 1937. It is a mystery story involving Chicago gangsters who have hired an unemployed university professor, a Russian named Kalunin, with a device that turns various metals into gold. Accompanied by his beautiful daughter, he is provided a home and laboratory in a remote area in the Canadian wilderness to conduct experiments to improve the process. After the strange disappearance of several prospectors in that vicinity, a commercial pilot planning to investigate is threatened by the gangster leader to stay away. Jack McCaffrey decides to take a look anyway, especially since the local Indians believe that malevolent spirits inhabit the area near a mysterious lake where the prospectors had gone. With a young woman as a traveling companion, McCaffrey encounters a snowstorm and damages his airplane in a forced landing. From this point on, the story deals with how the hero unravels the mystery and foils the villains. At the end of the story, he learns that Professor Kalunin's gold-making machine can also be used as a lethal ray and has been responsible for a number of bizarre deaths. It is another one of those vaguely defined death rays, described simply as based on electricity.[57]

Several authors, like Edwards above, did not even put death rays to use in their novels, apparently content with simply mentioning them. In his 1936 work *Bread and Wine*, Italian writer Ignazio Silone tells the story of a revolutionary named Pietro Spina, who returns from exile to an Italy under fascist dictatorship. The death ray appears shortly after the call for mobilization in the Abyssinian Crisis. In the first scene, two gentlemen discuss how Italy will win: "'With the new invention at our army's disposal, it will be over in a few weeks,' one of them said. 'The death-ray will pulverize the enemy.' 'The bishop is going to bless the Avezzano conscripts today,' said the other. 'The death-ray will open the way for the Pope's missionaries.'"[58] Shortly afterward, one of the characters addresses a crowd and tells them about this marvelous invention. Silone's description of its capabilities, however, is full of sarcasm: "The death ray can stop engines, bring trains running over the earth and ships furrowing the sea to a standstill, deflate bicycle tires, dry up women's breasts, stop clocks and watches, make the birds of the air lose their plumage, the clappers of bells fall to earth, and turn the enemy soldiers into salt!"[59] This "new invention" reflects the contemporary newspaper reports regarding Marconi's alleged "death ray."

Three other examples of a death ray as a perfunctory weapon in fiction were in novels appearing as newspaper serials. The first was "Interrupted Romance" in 1937 by Julie Anne Moore, who contributed detective stories to several local newspapers in the United States. The main character, Polly Markey, takes a job as a secretary and file clerk for an inventor who has worked out plans for new weapons to be offered to the U.S. War Department, including a death ray and an incendiary gas bomb. After he is murdered, Polly and a young army officer with whom she becomes romantically involved then proceed to unravel the mystery. There is little discussion of the weapon's properties or how it works; it is simply an incidental prop for the mystery.[60]

The second was Arthur Gask's "The Fall of the Dictator," serialized in *The Advertiser* of Adelaide starting in December 1938. In this novel, a young Englishman named Ashleigh Brendon joins the secret service and is sent to Cyrania to learn about a new torpedo being developed that would be undetectable before it detonated against a ship. This fictitious country is headed by a ruthless dictator, General Bratz, who is arming his country and planning to conquer Europe. Full of harrowing adventures, this spy story includes a brief mention of a death ray that does not serve any purpose other than to underscore the danger posed by the Cyranian engineer working on the torpedo at a highly restricted armaments plant. Author Gask describes it as something resembling newspaper accounts in the mid–1930s of a capability attributed to the Germans. Referencing the Cyranian engineer, Gask writes: "Jahn was pretty certain that he had at last discovered the secret of a death ray that would kill at a distance of a mile, and if he were right, then all Cyranian aeroplanes would be equipped with it within six months."[61] This threat is averted when Brendon blows up the factory, killing Jahn.

The other serial novel was "The Silver Assassin," written by William J. Makin and appearing in *The Northern Star* of Lismore, New South Wales, Australia, in 1937. It is a detective story involving a series of mysterious murders of prominent astronomers. After the death of the first one, there is much speculation in the press as to who was responsible. In one scene, the author has the Scotland Yard detective assigned to the case reading *Le Matin*: "Inspector Graves sighed and turned to 'Le Matin,' which in a special article rumoured that the great Frenchman, Pierre Kessel had discovered the secret of the Death Ray, and had been lured to England by secret service agents there to be foully murdered by Nazis to whom he had refused to divulge his great discovery."[62] This is the only mention of a death ray in the novel.

Other types of rays also appeared in fiction during the interwar period, several by French writers. Jean d'Agraives, for example, published an adventure novel entitled *La Cité des sables* (*The City of the Sands*) in 1924 that featured paralyzing rays. It is the story of a French war veteran named Conan de Kérilis, who embarks on a quest to find the legendary city of the Sheik of the Mountain, whose successors continue to exert influence and power. Having learned that his crusader ancestor had married the daughter of the first Sheik and forged an alliance, Kérilis persuades some of his old comrades to help him locate the city, which he believes still exists. His goal is to renew the bond between his country and the Muslim world as a means of furthering French influence in the Middle East. His first task, however, serves both the need for transportation and French national security. Kérilis and his men travel to an island in the Baltic and steal a highly advanced aircraft secretly developed by the Germans and with which they plan to launch a surprise attack on France by unleashing deadly germs. After a relatively short but perilous journey, the Frenchmen reach the entrance to the City of the Sands and encounter a guard of mounted knights who escort them to the Sheik. In the end, a new alliance is formed.

In the story Agraives described two similar types of weapons. One is a pistol that fires cartridges which, upon striking a solid object, release a "stupefying gas." It has been created by a friend of Kérilis and first tried out successfully on a neighboring farmer's flock of sheep, rendering the animals immobile for about an hour. The other is a ray with the same effect but lasting for only a few moments. According to the story, a Belgian inventor developed the basic idea but was killed by Germans who stole the secret and improved upon it. They also outfitted their new airplane with several of these "appareils inhibiteurs." As Kérilis explains to one of his assistants: "These waves are electric in nature and analogous to hertzian waves."[63] While escaping with the stolen aircraft, Kérilis and his companions are attacked by German planes but use this weapon to their advantage, as the German pilots are paralyzed enough to lose control of their machines and crash. Later, both the paralyzing rays and the stupefying gas enable Kérilis to complete his mission.

Other works by Agraives include *Le Rayon Svastika* (*The Swastika*

Ray) in 1925 and *Le Sorcier de la mer* (The Sorcerer of the Sea) the following year. The first one, a "yellow peril" novel, involves a mysterious land called Khokkim, just beyond Nepal, where evil forces plot the destruction of the white race by means of a powerful ray endowed with both healing and killing properties. Diamonds serve as an important component for the device to operate,[64] and a race of apelike men controlled by the inhabitants of Khokkim provides the labor force to mine the precious energy source. The cover of the book depicts one of these primitive creatures in a tattered robe being struck by a ray emitted from a weapon that looks more like a light saber from *Star Wars*. The figure wielding it bears a faint resemblance to a Chinese or Mongol warrior of the thirteenth century.[65] In *Le Sorcier de la mer*, Agraives created a ray capable of attracting fish—any and all. It could be used to empty the seas of marine life. In the story the Japanese steal the secret of this diabolical weapon.[66]

Edmond Romazières (Édouard de Keyser), a prolific writer of adventure and detective stories, contributed a serial entitled "Le sommeil qui tue" (The Sleep that Kills). Appearing in *L'Aventure* magazine in 1928, the plot revolves around an inventor who develops a device that he hopes will prevent war. This is an apparatus using electronic waves that cause immediate sleep, but too much exposure to them can be lethal. When thieves steal the ray projector, the inventor develops a machine that neutralizes the waves and in the end foils his adversaries.[67]

Another type of ray appeared in 1931 in a British novel entitled *Armoured Doves: A Peace Book*, written by Bernard Newman. The main character, scientist Paul de Montigny, decides to put a stop to war altogether after a terrible Russo-Polish conflict in 1942. The son of German and French parents, he has a special interest in doing so and organizes a league of scientists to develop new weapons to impose peace on the world. In 1962 another European war breaks out, and this league announces its Peace Ray, which "disintegrates all copper that lies in its path."[68] Since battleships and other weapon systems utilize electricity and copper is the chief conductor, this ray effectively neutralizes the means to wage modern war. As an aside, the book review in the *Sydney Morning Herald* had this to say about one of the characters Newman put in his novel: "Nor was it well-advised in a story of this type to portray Mr. Winston Churchill as Prime Minister of Britain in the year 1942, chatting affably at Downing-street with his alleged predecessor, Sir Oswald Mosley. It is difficult to imagine the buoyant Mr. Churchill as one of England's elder statesmen, and Mr. Newman's conception of him as such is unconvincing, if not quite ridiculous."[69]

Michael Arlen, an Armenian writer living in Britain, employed three different types of ray weapons in his 1933 novel *Man's Mortality*. It is a story about the future in which the world of 1987 is under the Pax Aeronautica, a conglomeration of industries called International Aircraft and Airways, Inc., or I. A. & A., with its own air police to maintain order. Its two main weapons are the Knoxray, named after its inventor, and the ectrogen ray. The former does not kill, merely stunning a person for twenty-four hours, while the latter destroys any matter coming within range. After many years of peace, a revolt against I. A. & A. breaks out that turns into a nationalistic world war fought in the air and involving most of the major nations. The leader of the revolt utilizes a new weapon referred to simply as an "unknown ray," for it causes the metal body of the air police craft to turn soft as butter. The rebel planes, which have been strengthened by another process, then cut through them easily with their propellers.[70] The *New York Times* pointed out that the book had received favorable reviews in Britain, had become a bestseller, and was strongly endorsed by the English Book Society. It added that H. G. Wells had praised the work as "a big and worthwhile gesture of the imagination."[71]

One novel serialized in an Australian newspaper in 1937 capitalized on the publicity surrounding British government announcements about a ray to protect against air attacks. In "The Ghost Counts Ten," Ralph Trevor described an attempt by foreign agents to acquire the formula to a death ray invented by a young Englishman named Conrad Quest. Most of the action takes place in an old manor house recently purchased by the villains and converted into a private club. In the end British secret service agent Dick Ferring, with the aid of Quest and others, manages to foil the scoundrels and preserve the secret of the death ray for England. Near the beginning of the story, author Trevor describes a conversation between Agent Ferring and his superior, Sir Mark Freeland, which could have been pieced together from reading British newspaper accounts in 1936 and 1937. Freeland tells Ferring that, after having met with the Air Minister, he is convinced of the weapon's primary importance to national defense. Acknowledging his inability to comprehend the science involved, Freeland adds: "What I do know is that this invisible ray, or death ray, whichever you care to name it, means that Britain is safe from aerial invasion so long as the secret of the ray's composition remains in the hands of the Government."[72]

Several death-ray novels appeared in which the lethal force is not electricity. A 1920 French work, Claude Farrère's *Les condamnés à mort* (Those Condemned to Death, but entitled *Useless Hands* in English), referenced above in connection with Schoenaich's *Der Krieg im Jahre 1930*, employed a type of weapon based on sound. The author describes a future in which a man named James Fergus Mac Head Vohr, called the Man of Wheat (*l'Homme du Blé*), has monopolized this commodity and its products worldwide. A strong believer in the Darwinian principle of Natural Selection, he sees manual labor destined to be replaced by machines, with the poor, uneducated workers not adapting to change and therefore becoming extinct. A plot, however, hatches among a handful of the thousands of laborers housed on the vast tract of land that also contains the factory as well as Vohr's palatial residence. The conspiracy to overthrow the Man of Wheat and free the workers from their humdrum existence is led by one of his chief supervisors and Vohr's own daughter. The climax of the story is their assault on Vohr's estate. In the meantime, his scientist, Georges Torral, has developed a ray weapon that will kill any living thing by decomposing matter, with the added benefit of not leaving any trace. The device utilizes sound vibration, as described by Torral: "You are perhaps familiar with the postulate of synchronized vibrations? ... and the theorem of visual cones? These explain everything. It is simply a generator of N rays at differentiated vibrations, with a reflector and lenses."[73] Torral then unleashes his weapon on the workers, killing all of them, including Vohr's daughter.

Another novel employing a death ray composed of powerful sound waves was by Sax Rohmer. *The Day the World Ended* first made its appearance in serialized installments in *Collier's* from May to July 1929. A villain named Anubis plans to destroy the world so that he and his followers can rule what remains. He has set up his operations at a castle in Baden, Germany, which is protected by lethal zones of sound waves generated by the device he created. In one scene Anubis explains to one of the heroes how it operates and that it is superior to an (electrical) "energy" weapon: "Energy has a limited range.... One station is insufficient. Unlike *sound*. Sound can be transmitted from this laboratory all round the world. *And sound can kill*." And, as the hero relates to a companion, "From the spot he calls 'the control tower,' those death waves may be sent in uniting circles! There is a great model of the terrestrial globe.... Anubis can cover all its surface with his waves of sound. He can focus them—or deflect them. It is for him a matter of choice, only. Where he wishes to spare—he spares!"[74] In the end, Anubis is foiled and his castle destroyed when a powerful artillery shell from one of the giant Krupp guns of the World War manages to penetrate the sonic force field.

Edmund Snell, the author of *The Z Ray* mentioned above, also wrote a novel about a weapon based on sound vibration entitled *The Sound*

Machine. Like many other stories during this period it is a mystery involving well-to-do Englishmen doing battle with a mad scientist who has perfected a device against which there does not appear to be any defense. Peter Enright owns a major electrical company called Power House in London and incurs the wrath of Professor Antonio Gerardo, an Italian inventor who tries to interest him in his sound machine. Considering him mad, Enright rejects his device as useless, whereupon the professor vows to get even. In the meantime Michael Rodd, a big game hunter and guide who recently saved Enright from a charging rhino when the young entrepreneur was on safari in Africa, shows up for a visit. He learns a little of the developing feud from Marian Granger, the niece of Gerardo, who has been trying unsuccessfully to meet with Enright and prevent the situation from becoming more serious. Later, when Rodd is staying with Enright and his sister, a new wing of the house collapses, demonstrating the power of Gerardo's invention. This is followed shortly by the destruction of Power House itself and the loss of many lives. The rest of the novel is taken up with the chase to find the mad professor and his niece, with whom Rodd is now in love. Most of the action is in London, but the final scenes are on board a ship bound for the Italian Riviera and the climax at Gerardo's villa. In the end, the mad scientist dies and his invention is destroyed, but Rodd rescues Marian and all is well.

Snell's sound machine incorporates some of the features of other energy weapons appearing in fiction but differs from almost all of them in one respect. Instead of an apparatus that transmits its power over a great distance, Gerardo's has a limited range and must be placed inside the building destined for destruction, therefore requiring him to make several machines, for each can be used only once. But, similar to the demagnetizer in Griffith's *The Lord of Labour*, the vibrations affect the molecular integrity of the target, causing weakness and collapse. When Enright picks up a brick from his destroyed house wing, it crumbles into dust. Shortly afterward, he and Rodd hear a pathetic howl from Gerardo's dog locked up in its master's shed. When they manage to get in, they find the poor beast dead in a most bizarre condition, described by Snell: "As Enright gazed, the collar appeared to slip away through solid dog, decapitating it—and the whole structure of the thing crumbled into an unrecognizable mass!"[75] Enright and Rodd have discovered another effect of the device, for it can also be attuned to the vibrations of living creatures and cause extreme physiological discomfort before bringing on death. The two men begin to feel this power but leave the shed before serious exposure. The dog was not so fortunate.

A different type of powerful weapon appeared in *El Camino de los Dioses (novela de la próxima guerra)* (The Road of the Gods, a Story of the Next War), a 1926 novel published by Argentine writer Manuel Ugarte. Another "yellow peril" story, this one is about a secret plan by the Japanese and Chinese to conquer the Western Hemisphere. They have sent agents ahead to Costa Rica to prepare the way for the use of a weapon far deadlier than anything yet seen by humankind. Ugarte emphasizes that it is not a death ray ("Ya no es el rayo muerte ... ni las ondas eléctricas"), a significant point in itself; rather, it is a machine capable of creating powerful storms.[76] In the end a young American woman upsets the enemy's plans, and the deadly apparatus becomes the property of the U.S. government. The *New York Times* reviewer of Ugarte's novel, nevertheless, had this to say in endorsing its scientific qualities: "The novel is up to date in its references to the latest more or less attested scientific discoveries and inventions in the realm of the transmission of 'death rays,' etc."[77]

Two other variants on the death ray appeared in 1929 and 1930. In Sir Arthur Conan Doyle's short story "The Disintegration Machine," an evil British scientist has developed a device that can disassemble and reassemble solid objects, including people. Having already made arrangements to sell it to a foreign government for use as a weapon, the villain is foiled when the hero tricks him into entering the disintegration chamber and kills him with his own diabolical machine. As was often the case in other tales, the weapon is described as a prototype, with the inventor predicting that with a larger instrument he can cause destruction on a far greater scale. As Doyle's evil scientist gleefully explains: "'Conceive a quarter of London in which such machines have been erected. Imagine the effect of such a current upon the scale which could easily be adopted. Why,' he burst into laughter, 'I could imagine the whole Thames valley being swept clean, and not one man, woman, or child left of all those teeming millions!'"[78] The other novel, Austin J. Small's *The Avenging Ray*, is a story about a British misanthropist named Carlo Damian who wants to destroy the world with a weapon that upsets gravity and breaks down the cohesion of molecules in all matter—animate and inanimate. His "disintegrator ray" will travel through the vast network of wires in the country and utterly annihilate the entire planet. The plans go awry at the last minute and, predictably, he meets his own doom.[79]

A rather strange but satirical story with a death ray was "Broadcasting the Tea Race," written by "Junius" (pseudonym of Fred Rhodes) and appearing in installments in the *Central Queensland Herald* of Rockhampton, Australia, in late 1934 and early 1935.[80] Set in 1866, the tale is about a race involving ships carrying tea from China to London but has, anachronistically, wireless radio as a common means of communication. An annoying obstacle to the competitors comes in the form of a demon ray, which can reproduce any human sound by capturing it from the ether as well as jam any radio signal, override it, and take control. Several installations with the demon ray are located in different parts of the world. A group of unnamed scoundrels operating a master station in the Gobi Desert are in charge of this device and protect the locations with a death ray capable of melting all metals. Bored with simply causing wireless interference, these "lunatics" drink too much liquor and decide to unleash their death ray on people they do not like, especially politicians, bookies, and bank managers. They also target broadcasting corporations. Much of this is accomplished by locating the wireless receiving sets found in most homes and businesses. After having killed many victims and wreaking havoc on the world, the Gobi crew members accidentally blow up their master station and their rays. Before doing so, they attempt an even more grandiose but comedic undertaking, as described by the author: "Then the sozzled Gobi crew mixed the station gears and the dread death-ray swept the untidy earth which stood in such need of sweeping. Fortunately for humanity, the ray was focused on the North Polar regions where it melted the earth's night cap and threw all the polar bears to the seals."[81]

Although death-ray fiction flourished in novels and short stories during the interwar years, other media also capitalized on this type of weapon. As the next chapter will show, energy devices became a popular subject of film, the stage, comics, and other means of expression as well. These likewise often reflected a connection with real claims about death rays and similar devices.

7

Death Rays in Other Media: Movies, Theater, Pulps, Radio and Humor

The popularity of death-ray fiction expanded to other media, especially after the First World War, and included the newer forms of entertainment such as motion pictures and pulp magazines. Even the traditional theatrical play was not immune to the growing interest in tales involving such a weapon, as several stage productions featured it prominently. Death rays also appeared in comic strips, including those with subjects other than space heroes such as Buck Rogers and Flash Gordon, and made their way occasionally into radio programs. Such was the pervasiveness of the death ray in the popular culture that one could often find it in general humor, political commentary, and even in advertising. As was the case with novels and short stories discussed in the previous chapters, the devices employed in these other media forms often reflected the influence of news reports.

Film

One of the most popular forms of entertainment for mysterious rays was the budding industry of motion pictures. Producers of single films and serials quickly latched on to these powerful devices and often featured them not as futuristic fantasy but as plausible science fact, both out of genuine belief and for commercial value. Many of the stories involved mad scientists and traditional villains employing these weapons, usually in the contemporary world or within the near future. In addition to *The Exploits of Elaine* mentioned in Chapter 5, some of the early ray movies reflected the influence of Giulio Ulivi.

Two appeared while the First World War was raging in Europe. Released in 1915 by Vitagraph, an American film company, *Pawns of Mars* depicted a war between two imaginary countries named Mapadonia and Cosmotania. A Mapadonian chemist, Dr. Lefone, has just developed and manufactured some powerful bombs, but Rizo Turbal, a Cosmotanian spy, manages to steal them, giving his country the advantage. A young inventor in love with Lefone's daughter discovers a means to project wireless rays through the air and detonate explosives from a distance. When the war begins, he employs this weapon to explode the Lefone bombs stolen by the enemy. He also destroys an enemy airplane with his wireless apparatus.[1] Another ray movie with a similar theme appeared the following year. This was *The Intrigue*, a 1916 film about an American inventor named Guy Longstreet who has developed an X-ray gun capable of hitting targets up to twenty-five miles away. After offering it to the U.S. War Department and being turned down, he demonstrates it to leaders of an unnamed European country, who decide to do business with him. Returning to the United States to make some final adjustments to his machine, he awaits the arrival of Baron Rogniat, the agent who will make the arrangements to purchase the X-ray gun. Another unnamed country learns of this plan and sends one of its spies, Countess Sonia, to thwart the baron. She gains employment in his service as a maid and quickly realizes that Rogniat also plans to kill Longstreet once the gun or its design is in his possession. The countess manages to warn the young American inventor that his life is in danger, and together they stop the baron. Longstreet then destroys his apparatus, and the two make plans to be married.[2]

Other early films with some type of wireless energy device include three released in 1924. Although these did not have any particular connection to Ulivi or other inventors, they nevertheless reflected the growing popularity of mysterious rays. *The Perils of Paris*, the last performance of serial star Pearl White, was about criminals stealing a ray apparatus. The famed actress of *The Perils of Pauline* and *The Exploits of Elaine* also wrote the story herself.[3] René Clair's *Paris qui dort* (Paris Which Sleeps, but entitled *The Crazy Ray* in English) was a lighthearted tale about a mad— or simply eccentric—scientist who invents a ray which causes people to remain motionless and unaware while under its influence.[4] *La Cité Foudroyée* (The City Struck by Lightning, but also referred to as "The Destroyed City") depicted the destruction of Paris and received favorable reviews in newspapers and magazines for its cinematographic effects.

Set in 1930, *La Cité Foudroyée* is a story about a young engineer, Richard Gallée, who has conducted extensive research into electrical energy that exists in nature, believing that its power can be harnessed. Derided as a fool by others, he leaves Paris and goes to live in the country with his Uncle Vrécourt and his beautiful cousin, Huguette, with whom he is already in love. But there are three other suitors, and his hope of marrying her appears unlikely because of a recent tragedy. Uncle Vrécourt has been wiped out financially and is in dire straits. To save her father, Huguette calls all the suitors together, including Richard, and announces that she will marry the one who in three month's time can come up with the greatest fortune. Lacking funds sufficient to compete for her hand, Richard meets a mysterious new neighbor who has recently arrived in the country. The nearby villagers fear him and have labeled the stranger "le mauvais homme" (the bad man). After learning of Richard's research into controlling electricity as a weapon, "le mauvais homme" buys the rights to all of the young engineer's papers and constructs a laboratory in which they produce a powerful machine capable of generating storms and directing lightning bolts to selected targets. When the three months have expired, only one of the suitors has come up with the money, but it turns out that he was responsible for ruining Uncle Vrécourt. Angered at this revelation, Richard promises to produce many times over the amount of money presented by the other man. He decides to use his powerful new weapon as a means of blackmail and sends a message to the Paris city government demanding fifty million francs. If the officials do not comply with his request, he threatens to incinerate the capital. He first sets fire to a forest and then, after another warning goes unheeded, scorches a section of Paris. The final blow descends on a city in panic. Thick clouds roll in and his machine creates lightning strikes that cause massive conflagrations and destroy great monuments, including La Madeleine and the Eiffel Tower. Afterward, however, the audience learns that this obliteration of Paris is only an illusion, for the young scientist has simply been writing a novel and fantasizing about such events. Having realized that his studies have no practical application, he decided to use his science to write fiction. "Le mauvais homme" turns out to be a Strasburg publisher, who has bought his new novel entitled *La Cité foudroyée*. In the end, all is well; the Eiffel Tower still stands, Uncle Vrécourt is saved, and Richard marries Huguette.[5]

Many of the movies with ray weapons, however, did reflect the influence directly or indirectly of Grindell Matthews and his claims. In October 1924, for example, the *New York Times* ran a brief description of a new movie to be released even before a real title had been selected. It was called *The Story Without a Name* and starred Antonio Moreno and Agnes Ayres. The film was based on Arthur Stringer's serial with that title, which had first appeared in *Photoplay*. The public was told that it could participate in a contest sponsored by the magazine, with a $5,000 reward for coming up with the best title. The film, according to the *New York Times*, "deals with the most recent invention of modern warfare, the much-talked-of death ray."[6] In addition to *Photoplay*'s offer, local newspapers throughout the United States participated in a campaign to promote the film with their own contests. Those entries selected would then be sent on to *Photoplay*. When the movie came to Terre Haute, Indiana, later that month, a local newspaper offered a $25 reward for naming it. More than one hundred and fifty entries were submitted along with the names of the persons and their street addresses, including "The Death Ray" by Joseph Tallon of 1834 North Eighth; "A Modern Fairy Tale" by Hans Fischer of 809 Maple Avenue; and "Radio Romance" by Robert Ferguson of 2116 South Eighth.[7] The winning title ultimately selected by *Photoplay* was *Without Warning*. Sometime after the filming of the movie, the story was published by Grosset and Dunlap, for the book features stills from the screen version by Paramount.[8] The following description of the story is taken from the novel.

The hero, Alan Holt (Moreno), is a naval veteran of the World War but now lives with his mother in a small town in Virginia not far from Washington. Employed at a local garage, he is an avid radio enthusiast who has developed a death ray that he refers to as a "triangulator." When he meets a beautiful young woman, Mary Walsworth (Ayres), and her father, Admiral Walsworth, he tells them about his invention. The admiral, a chief member of the navy's Consulting Board, agrees to let Alan send him a letter describing his apparatus, but several weeks go by without word from Washington. Holt's close friend, a Marine sergeant named Don Powell, has a reporter write a story about his death ray to get the navy's attention. It does, but not before unscrupulous characters enter the picture. Mark Drakma, one of the chief villains in the story, seeks to acquire Holt's new device, or at least the plans, so that he can sell it to a foreign power. One of his henchmen steals the triangulator, but as a precaution Holt has already removed an important component without which the weapon is useless. The Consulting Board then signs on Holt to build another device and conduct experiments at a facility near the capital. In the meantime, the young inventor and the admiral's daughter fall in love. The rest of the plot involves typical intrigue, with Holt ultimately rescuing Mary from the clutches of Drakma's henchmen and foiling their leader. There is also the presence of a femme fatale in the employ of Drakma, who manages for a while to deceive the widowed admiral and gain information about the death ray.

The connection to Grindell Matthews in the story is unmistakable. At the beginning when Alan is first telling Mary and her father about his invention, he refers to the press reports about the man in Europe who has just invented a death ray. Later, Holt emphasizes that he has no desire to sell his weapon to the highest bidder, as that chap is doing. As a good patriot, he wants his country alone to have the device, for he believes that an invincible America will use it to make war impossible. The properties of the triangulator are different from the description of Grindell Matthews's death ray, but its capabilities are similar. The triangulator focuses radio waves into a single destructive beam, rather than the flow of electricity inside a path of ionized air. Holt's triangulator can stop battleships at a great distance, take out submarines, annihilate armies on the battlefield, and set fire to cities.

In the story, the weapon is employed on several occasions, including experiments with it at the naval facility. Working with Powell, Holt kills a chicken hawk about to pester a farmer's hens and then melts ice cream in a vendor's truck some distance away. He also tells Don about a somewhat humorous experiment involving a rather large golfer playing on the nearby course. Over several days, Holt subjected the man to gradual doses of his death ray, causing him to become irritably hot and uncomfortable, even to the point of bringing his doctor along to determine why. Holt considers this a remarkable discovery, as he tells Powell: "And this time that big red-faced hulk of a man took two drinks from his pocket-flask, although I'd only given him a fraction of one per cent. of my wave-power. With five per cent. I could have stopped his heart-action inside of three seconds. And with my full power I could have struck him cold, fifteen miles away!"[9] Near the end of the story, Holt uses his triangulator to disrupt the engine of a small airplane piloted by one of the crooks.

Other films influenced by the work of Grindell Matthews also came out in 1924 and 1925. One was *Laughing at Danger*, involving a stolen death ray and advertised as based on a genuine invention. Released by Carlos Productions, it starred Richard Talmadge as the hero Alan Remington and Eva Novak as the heroine Carolyn Hollister. Having been dumped by a girl with whom he is in love, Remington sinks into a depression. A doctor tells Alan's father that what he needs is some excitement to take his mind off his sorrows. The father's attempts prove fruitless, but in the process young Remington uncovers a real plot by a gang of crooks to steal a death ray invented by Carolyn Hollister's father. Believing it is all part of the fun and excitement generated for him, Remington throws himself into the fray. As one reviewer wrote: "It makes a laughable story to see Richard 'Laughing at Danger.'"[10] In the end, he and Carolyn foil the crooks and save an American naval squadron from certain destruction. Another 1924 movie reflecting the popular interest in news about death rays was *Lone Wolf's Last Adventure*, produced by Ideal Film Company and based on the novel series created by Louis Joseph Vance. It tells the by now familiar story of death-ray plans stolen by crooks and the ultimate triumph of the hero.[11] A Western also bearing an unmistakable reflection of Grindell Matthews's work was *The Mystery of Lost Ranch* in 1925. In the story a scientist and his daughter are living on a ranch near the Grand Canyon, where he experiments with his death ray on animals. Foreign agents try to steal the weapon but are thwarted with the aid of a young man who ends up falling in love with the scientist's daughter.[12] A poster for the movie shows several people watching the scientist as he uses the death ray to shoot down an eagle. The apparatus shown appears shaped somewhat like a small searchlight with a "gun barrel" in front projecting the ray at the unfortunate bird. It rests on a circular plate supported by several metallic canisters and connected by wires.

Although Russian Lev Kuleshov's *Luch Smerti* (*The Death Ray*) in 1925 focused on political propaganda, the weapon described in the movie also reflected to a degree the influence of Grindell Matthews. This is a somewhat difficult film to follow, for the setting is in a country referred to simply as "the West," where fascism prevails; but the action takes place in Moscow as well, which does not seem far away. The first part of the film is missing, and it begins with the scene of dead bodies, as a workers' uprising at the Gelium factory has just been ruthlessly crushed. One of the leaders, Thomas Lann, has been caught, is sentenced to death, but escapes and goes to Moscow. Later, when the factory owner demands mass production of ammunition for Venezuela, the lingering anger of the workers intensifies and the threat of a strike increases. If that happens, the local fascist boss, Major Hart, plans to help the owner by destroying the workers' housing area near the factory. In the meantime, a Russian scientist in Moscow, Podobed, has developed a death ray and shows it to Lann, but fascist agents steal it and kidnap the scientist. Near the end of the movie, one sees the workers and their families fleeing, as three airplanes—with white swastikas on their tails—are in pursuit.[13] By now, the scientist has been rescued, and Lann has managed to retrieve the death ray. Mounting it on a truck, Lann and others arrive just in time to protect the workers and their families, presumably by using the weapon against the fascist aircraft. Unfortunately, the surviving reel of film breaks off at this point, the remainder considered irretrievably lost. Aside from its probable employment at the end, Kuleshov depicts the death ray in action in only one other scene, in which Podobed and his assistants are shown using it to ignite fuel in a glass container from about fifteen feet away. This resembles the demonstrations performed by Grindell Matthews with small amounts of gunpowder.[14]

"Anti-aircraft ray" movies suggesting the influence of news stories about French airplanes being forced down over Bavaria (as well as Grindell Matthews) began to appear toward the end of the 1920s and continued on into the next decade. Among the first was *Code of the Air* in 1928, a Samuel Bischoff Productions film starring Kenneth Harlan, June Marlowe (the beautiful young teacher, "Miss Crabtree," from the *Our Gang* series), and William V. Mong, as the crazed scientist with a death ray. It is the story of a gang of crooks led by Mong's character who uses this device, emitting "Kappa Rays," to bring down mail planes and rob them of their valuables. With no substantial leads, the government calls in a former army pilot to solve the mystery.[15]

In one of his earliest roles, actor Ralph Bellamy appeared in a similar type of movie, entitled *Air Hawks* and released in 1935, a story about two airlines competing for a government contract to deliver mail. One, however, resorts to the services of a mad scientist whose death ray can explode airplanes. The man in question is a German named Shulter, suspected of being responsible for a number of mysterious airplane crashes in Europe. He was known to have carried out experiments with a type of ray machine in Germany and Russia before disappearing. In a scene early in the film, he demonstrates his device to an executive of Consolidated Industries, who has failed to buy out the airline owned by Bellamy's character, Barry Eldon. This death ray resembles a searchlight and has probably the most equipment and gadgetry accompanying it of any depicted in other movies. One sees all kinds of dynamos, electrical gizmos, and other machinery filling up the laboratory. After causing a model airplane to explode, Shulter exclaims that with a larger machine he can destroy "barracks, battleships, airplanes, anything!" He then tells the airline executive, Drewen, that it works by emitting a beam of light which acts as a path of conductivity for a surge of electricity to follow to the target. This description is almost identical to the one given by Grindell Matthews—as well as that of John Hartmann, mentioned in Chapter 1. An impressed Drewen decides to utilize Shulter's services in order to drive Eldon's Independent Transcontinental Lines out of business and agrees to finance the construction of a much larger and more powerful weapon. When completed, this is mounted inside a truck equipped with all the necessary paraphernalia to power it. Shulter and his assistant then go to work targeting Eldon's aircraft as they fly their routes. The electric ray causes the engines to sputter before the planes burst into flames and explode. At a loss for an explanation, Eldon is contacted by government agents who tell him about Shulter. In the end Bellamy's character solves the mystery and foils the villains. One added feature is the cameo appearance of famed pilot Wiley Post, who died in an airplane crash in Alaska a few months after the release of the picture. Popular humorist Will Rogers was also killed in the accident.[16] In a review of *Air Hawks* an Australian newspaper suggested that the story depicted a degree of reality: "While the ray in the film is not actually the type with which scientists and military experts have been experimenting for many years, it shows conclusively the manner in which the beam may be used in the future."[17] The reviewer apparently failed to notice the similarity to the death ray of Grindell Matthews.

Other films dealing with rays to bring down aircraft followed. In 1936, Tim McCoy starred in *The Ghost Patrol*, a story about a series of incidents in which planes experience sudden mechanical difficulties and crash. A gang of thieves utilizes a ray weapon to target mail planes, especially one carrying a shipment of gold. In the opening scene, one sees an apparatus with the flashes of a Tesla coil and a radium tube that affects all electrical impulses within a certain range. McCoy is flying over the area to try to unravel the mystery when his plane's engine suddenly begins to sputter and finally conks out, forcing him to parachute to safety.[18] A remake of *The Ghost Patrol* appeared the following year as *Sky Racket*. There was also *Flight to Fame* in 1938, starring Charles Farrell, in which a former pilot in the World War tries unsuccessfully to get the U.S. Army Air Force interested in his invention—an electronic ray weapon. Another one-time pilot of the war, played by Jason Robards, then secretly uses it to bring down air force planes in an attempt to settle old scores with former members of his squadron. Farrell's character, an army captain, is instrumental in solving the mystery. It should be noted that an anti-aircraft ray figures prominently on a poster advertising this movie, and one newspaper review of the film informed readers that the device was "patterned after designs on which several scientists are now at work."[19] Even the two budding stars, Laurence Olivier and Ralph Richardson, appeared in this type of film. In *Q Planes*, a light comedy released in early1939, their characters try to find out who is behind the crash landings of several British airplanes equipped with new, supercharged engines. Olivier, playing an expert civilian pilot, and Richardson, who works with Scotland Yard and the secret service, find and foil a group of unnamed, but obviously German, saboteurs who operate a ray gun mounted on a ship in the English Channel.[20]

Blake of Scotland Yard (1937), a single film version of the earlier serial, combined a little bit of Grindell Matthews and Ulivi with the pacifist desire for a means to abolish war. In the story, Blake, a retired member of Scotland Yard, has assisted two others who have created a ray which he believes will make war impossible. Having contacted the League of Nations, he wants to make the device available to all countries, thereby ensuring that no one will have an advantage. (Article 8 of the League Covenant required full disclosure to the League of any new armament or military invention.)[21] In the story the League helps arrange a demonstration in England with the cooperation of the British government. Several people are present, among them representatives of the British military and an agent of the League. The complex apparatus shown in the film includes a television screen and a magnetic-beam target locator. Once the target has been found and its coordinates locked in, a powerful ray is sent via the magnetic beam. This resembles the device utilized by Giulio Ulivi and the description he gave to the newspapers about waves from a generator locating the mines and bombs and bouncing back to his telephonic headgear. In the demonstration in the movie, an obsolete battleship is guided by remote control from an airplane overhead. In just a matter of seconds, the ray completely destroys the vessel from a distance of 190 miles.[22]

It should be noted that one movie in 1932 originally called *Murder at Dawn* was subsequently released in Britain under the somewhat misleading title *The Death Ray*. It featured an apparatus that harnessed solar power and was called the "VXO Accumulator." Instead of a tale involving mad scientists threatening the world or enemy agents of an unnamed military power, however, the story is that of a typical murder mystery, with sinister characters trying to obtain the device for monetary gain. The purpose of the "accumulator" was not to function as a weapon but instead, as its creator says, provide unlimited energy for peaceful purposes, "setting millions of wage-earners free." In the wrong hands, of course, it could be used with lethal effect. Near the end of the movie, the chief villain ties up the inventor and his daughter in a room with the accumulator directed at them. He turns on the machine and leaves, for the complex device cannot build up energy until dawn when struck by the rays of the sun. As usual, the heroes triumph and the crook is killed.[23]

One of the most popular types of death-ray movies during this era was the serial, which had appeared before and during the First World War, the previously mentioned *The Exploits of Elaine* being a prime example. In 1920 audiences were entertained by *The Invisible Ray*, a story revolving around a mineralogist who discovers a ray of incredible power and a group of sinister scientists who plan to steal it from him. In a review before its release, the *New York Times* linked the concept of *The Invisible Ray*'s power to British scientist Sir Oliver Lodge, thereby bestowing upon it a degree of plausibility. Lodge had asserted that the earth possessed an energy force far greater than anything known, adding that the recent war had demonstrated mankind's propensity to bring about its own demise by unlocking such power.[24] The same year *The Flaming Disk* served up a modernized magnifying glass that could concentrate the rays of the sun strongly enough to be a weapon, reminiscent of Maclay's "burning glasses." According to a description of the flaming disk in one newspaper, it "consists of a composite lens in two parts, which, when focused upon iron, steel or other metals, emits a blinding ray of light and reduces the metal to the consistency of putty."[25] The story involves a Professor Wade who invents such a death ray, attracting the interest of the U.S. government as well as of a gang of crooks. Before the apparatus can be handed over to the agents sent to acquire it, the criminals murder the scientist and steal his death ray, although one of its components is snatched from them by a mystery man on a motorcycle. Predictably, the villains are foiled in the end. Most of the story involves typical crime detective action, with the government agents on the trail of the gang members and their leader. Another early death-ray serial was *The Scarlet Streak*, which came out in 1925 and ran in many local movie theaters on into 1927. Advertised as being inspired by news reports that such a weapon had actually been developed, the movie is about a reporter foiling a group of spies who have stolen a death ray created by an inventor hoping to use it to end war forever. It is referred to as the "Scarlet Ray." According to the *Sheboygan Press*, it was "the finest serial ever filmed."[26]

Serials during the next decade continued to employ death-ray devices with properties corresponding directly to news reports. In *The Fighting Marines* in 1935, a bandit leader called the "Tiger Shark" gathers stolen treasure on Halfway Island in the South Pacific.[27] Conflict arises when the United States Marines plan to construct a landing base there. The Tiger Shark has inside a mountain on the island a complex apparatus that powers a ray gun, also referred to as a "gravity gun," because it operates as an antiaircraft weapon by causing engine failure. In the end he is no match for the Marines and dies trying to escape when a container of nitroglycerin explodes inside his treasure cave.[28] Another serial involving the Marines defeating a villain came out in 1938. Entitled *The Fighting Devil Dogs*, a masked antagonist called "Lightning" possesses aerial torpedoes that when exploded set off electrical fireworks, electrocuting anyone within range. He also wields a ray gun pistol. Like the Tiger Shark, he and his henchmen cannot prevail against the Leathernecks and meet their deaths when the heroes employ a powerful ray device of their own to destroy his aircraft.[29]

Arrest Bulldog Drummond, which came out in 1939 and was based on Sapper's novel *The Final Count*,[30] was another film incorporating some of the principles of Ulivi, in this case a weapon that disrupts atoms. According to the *New York Times* review, "It's a bifocal gadget guaranteed to detonate any explosives within range of half a mile. Just press the switch, synchronize the rays on the combustibles and bang!"[31] The story is about two crooks, a man and a woman, who have murdered the scientist who developed the ray and plan to sell it but are stopped by Drummond. In one scene, an agent for prospective buyers is shown the machine and comments that it looks like another one of those "impractical" death rays that were supposed to stop airplane engines. The seller tells him that it is really an atomic disintegrator and demonstrates by aiming it at a man sitting outside holding a rifle. Two rays that look like flashlight beams converge on the gun, causing the cartridges to fire. In another scene the ray is directed at a store window display with a mannequin dressed for hunting. Again the beams converge on a gun and set off the cartridges.[32]

Some serials had rays resembling the more generic descriptions in newspapers and magazines, with devices utilizing electricity in a variety of ways to do mischief. In 1933 Bela Lugosi starred in *The Whispering Shadow*, playing one of the good guys helping to defeat the evil genius who operates a wireless, radio-transmitted death ray. The "Shadow" poses as a somewhat clumsy dispatcher while secretly controlling a gang of criminals to help him acquire wealth and power. His death ray is concealed inside a normal radio broadcasting unit at a storage and transfer company and functions by sending a wireless transmission to set off a specially designed explosive disk planted on the intended victim.[33] In the 1934 serial, *The Vanishing Shadow*, two types of ray devices appear. One enables the wearer of a special apparatus to become invisible while the other is a ray gun. As the scientist tells the hero, he has developed it to help defend the United States against potential enemies. One significant difference between his ray and others, however, is that it affects only living tissue. In this scene, he demonstrates it on a flower, causing the plant to wilt in a matter of seconds.[34] Two years later, cowboy legend Gene Autry got his first starring role in a bizarre Western-science-fiction serial entitled *The Phantom Empire*. The story revolves around the subterranean civilization of Murania created by survivors of the legendary continent of Mu destroyed eons ago. It is located beneath Autry's ranch, and a clash erupts between surface-dwellers and the Muranians. The ruthless queen of the subterranean society has at her disposal a "lightning chamber" for executions and a "disintegrator ray."[35]

Another serial that came out in 1935 was *The Lost City*. At the beginning of the story, the world is being buffeted by a series of unexplained weather disturbances of great intensity. A young scientist is shown using a type of ray generator to try to locate the source of the problem. Having done so, he and a team head to Africa. There, they find an underground facility with a mad scientist who is the last of a people that fled the destruction of their continent thousands of years before. He has developed a death ray as well as a device that is responsible for the weather disturbances. One scene is quite similar to the one in the 1964 James Bond thriller *Goldfinger*, in which Bond is placed on a gold table as a laser beam slowly makes its way toward him, burning right through the metal. In *The Lost City*, the hero is strapped to a chair adjacent to a rectangular metal plate as the "destroying ray" inches its way toward him only to stop when someone manages to shut off the power.[36]

Other serials followed suit. *Undersea Kingdom* appeared in 1936, starring Ray "Crash" Corrigan as a U.S. naval officer fresh out of Annapolis. In this film the fabled civilization of Atlantis turns out not to be a legend after all. A civil war between two factions there has led to the seizure of power by an evil warlord who seeks to conquer and rule the surface world. Before he is stopped by the hero and the U.S. Navy, the warlord uses a disintegrator ray, a force shield, and hand-held ray guns.[37] Another serial from 1936 was *Ace Drummond*. Not to be confused with "Bulldog Drummond," this character was based on a comic-strip series created by America's great combat pilot of the First World War, Eddie Rickenbacker. "Ace" is in Mongolia battling a villain called "The Dragon," who uses a radio-transmitted ray to bring down airplanes. It works by sending a wireless burst of electricity to the earphones of pilots and co-pilots, causing instant death.[38] In the 1939 serial, *The Phantom Creeps*, Bela Lugosi played the role of ruthless scientist Dr. Zorka wreaking havoc with a ray gun, a robot, and a machine to make himself invisible. He also has a powerful explosive made from a meteorite that he discovered. One other weapon has two components: a disk and a small mechanical spider. After placing the disk on his intended victim—in the clothing, purse, or anything else in close proximity—Zorka releases the spider, which automatically seeks it out and, when contact is made, detonates.[39]

Probably one of the most spectacular of the science fiction films was *The Invisible Ray*, which appeared in theaters in 1936. Starring the two icons of the horror flick, Boris Karloff and Bela Lugosi, its death ray uses radium as its energy source. In the story a scientist named Janos Rukh (Karloff) has developed an apparatus that can receive light images from Earth's distant past traveling to the far reaches of space and then project them on to the ceiling of his laboratory. Rukh demonstrates his invention to a group of people, focusing on the Andromeda nebula 750,000 light years away. What they see is a meteor heading to Earth millions of years ago and striking Africa. Rukh tells them that the meteorite contains "Radium X," an element which he believes possesses virtually unlimited power. Somewhat skeptical, Dr. Benet (Lugosi), along with the others, decides to help him find it. After discovering the meteorite with its priceless space cargo, Rukh loads some of the radium into a large ray gun, which he demonstrates to his terrified native laborers by melting a huge boulder. Later, Dr. Benet learns that "Radium X" has the capability to heal as well and uses it to cure all sorts of maladies at his clinic in Paris. Rukh develops radiation poisoning while in Africa, but it also gives him the ability to kill by touch. His wife leaves him for another man, and he believes the other members of the expedition have taken credit for finding "Radium X." Consumed by madness and revenge, he goes on a killing spree before he dies by bursting into flames.

A number of commentaries about *The Invisible Ray* focused on the plausibility of such a weapon. One was a review from the magazine *The Catholic World*, which cited the film as depicting something close to reality, or at least within the realm of possibility. After a brief description of the plot, the editorial comment continues: "Take it as a flight of imagination, or as a nightmare. But we have no certainty that something almost equally terrible is not now being prepared in chemical or physical laboratories at the service of the War Departments. Sooner or later the chemists and physicians will invent or discover something that can blow us all to atoms, or make us evaporate like steam."[40] When the movie was about to open in Perth, Australia, a local newspaper article about it included brief references to Marconi allegedly stopping car engines and Tesla's claims of a new type of energy weapon in order to show that the idea of a death ray was not far-fetched. The paper also mentioned the recent story about Victor Penny, adding that he had disappeared and was believed to be in contact with the British Admiralty.[41]

Other films featuring some variety of death ray in the 1930s deserve mention as evidence of the increased popularity of this type of movie.

Bela Lugosi played the madman Roxor threatening the world in *Chandu the Magician* (1932). In one scene, the viewer is treated to visions of London and Paris being destroyed by a death ray, as the villain imagines what he will do with this power to make himself master of all.[42] In a review of this film, which appeared in several newspapers, the writer acknowledged the real possibility of science developing such a weapon utilizing electricity and added: "The gun used in the picture was constructed by Fox studio technicians and it is in every way the embodiment of all scientists know of projecting through the air electrical waves of sufficient force to kill at a distance."[43] Boris Karloff and Myrna Loy appeared as an evil father-daughter duo in the 1932 movie, *The Mask of Fu Manchu*, which also employed a death ray.[44] A German film released in 1934 was entitled *Der Herr der Welt* (also called *Master of the World* and *Ruler of the World*) and included robots equipped with death rays.[45]

Even Sir Arthur Conan Doyle's great sleuth got into the act, as Fox Film came out with a ray movie in 1932 entitled *Sherlock Holmes*. In this early version, Holmes's character is played by Clive Brook rather than Basil Rathbone, who would later become synonymous with the part. What is peculiar is that in one scene early in the film Holmes is demonstrating what he calls a "motor-wrecking ray" on a model car, causing the ignition coil to overheat and burn out, reminiscent of reports about French and German experiments in 1923. This device, however, plays no part in the film other than as an example of Holmes's contention that modern science is the best way to combat crime. He simply tells his fiancé that he plans to give it to Scotland Yard as a means to stop and apprehend criminals fleeing by automobile. The story itself is all about Holmes trying to prevent Professor Moriarty from carrying out his usual diabolical plans.[46] The reason for the ray is probably the result of director William K. Howard's aim of making this version of Holmes more up-to-date, as the review in the *Times* criticized the film as barely resembling the stories created by Conan Doyle.[47]

A 1937 film entitled *The Girl From Scotland Yard* provoked a response from the news media that seemed to substantiate the reality of death rays. The story is about an English inventor named Franz Borg who goes to France after having been exiled for trying to sell his death ray to a foreign power. Seeking revenge, Borg, now the leader of a spy ring, plans to cripple Britain's defenses and uses his weapon to destroy several warships and airplanes. This prompts the British secret service to put one of its agents, Linda Beech (played by actress Karen Morley), on his trail. She teams up with an American newspaperman on his way to London to cover the coronation of the new king (Edward VIII), and together they discover the identity of the villain. Borg takes off in his airplane mounted with the death ray and plans to target RAF squadrons participating in the ceremonies. Beech and the American pursue in their aircraft and ultimately shoot down Borg with machine guns but not until he has destroyed two bombers with his death ray. As described in several American newspapers, the write-ups suggested that the death ray was in fact real and that its appearance in the film was by no means simply an artistic feature.[48] According to the *Gastonia Daily Gazette* (North Carolina), "Since the World War the secret laboratories of many nations have been busy developing the death ray and while these devices have been surrounded by the greatest secrecy it is known in military circles that such rays have been developed and are ready for use."[49] A similar view was expressed in the *Winnipeg Free Press*: "The picture, 'The Girl from Scotland Yard,' concerns the mysterious 'death ray,' science's latest contribution to the art of warfare, a death-dealing device which promises to lay whole cities waste in future wars."[50]

Similar to the previously mentioned novels by Claude Farrère and Sax Rohmer, Hollywood also came out with a movie utilizing sound as a weapon. In the 1937 serial film entitled *Dick Tracy* and starring Ralph Byrd, the fictional sleuth has to contend with a villain known as the Spider, who possesses a sound-wave disintegrator which can disrupt matter. He first demonstrates a small device by shattering a vase, but he has a much more powerful one on his flying craft, "the Wing." The Spider's gang then sets out to destroy the [Oakland] Bay Bridge, but Tracy has discovered the mathematical calculations on the sound cycles required for this operation and manages to lessen the impact of the attack. Later, the famous detective wrecks the apparatus, and the Spider dies as he attempts to escape.[51]

The Theater

In addition to movies, mysterious rays showed up on the stage. Probably the first theatrical production with such a weapon appeared shortly after the publication of *The War of the Worlds* and dealt with the Cuban revolution that led to the Spanish-American War. It was first performed on 18 April 1898, just five days before Spain declared war on the United States. Written by Charles Whitlock and entitled *The God of War*, this four-act play is more about love and intrigue than about the revolution, with various characters vying for one another's affections as well as for power. The lead players, furthermore, are mostly Spanish aristocrats and government officials. Whitlock seems to have borrowed the idea for a weapon from Wells and introduces it in the fourth act. In the review carried in the London newspaper *The Era*, the device is briefly mentioned without any detailed description: the murdered "Governor's will ... is destroyed by the heat rays (a wonderful invention)...."[52]

Death rays in the theater, however, appeared more frequently after the First World War and reflected the influence of news coverage regarding claims by inventors. Noted writer Cicely Hamilton's *The Old Adam* was first performed in November 1924 at the Birmingham Repertory Theatre. Billed as a "fantastic comedy," the story is that of two fictitious countries going to war, but the use of the "Negative Ray" by both sides at the outset neutralizes all machines that depend on electricity as well as all other conventional weapons, forcing them to resort to cavalry, swords, pikes, and sailing vessels. Having received an ultimatum from Ruritania to accede to its demands, Paphlagonia employs the services of a scientist who has just invented an immobilizing ray. The audience is told that experiments have already been conducted in which the device has stopped engines of various types, including trains, airplanes, a ship, and a motorcar—like that of the Nauen incident in Chapter 2. When the ultimatum expires, the Paphlagonian scientist, accompanied by the prime minister and other high-ranking dignitaries, presses the button that sends the immobilizing current on its way. Before they can rejoice, however, the lights go out all over the city. They then realize that a Ruritanian scientist must have developed a similar device. The play ends with an old fashioned war in full swing, underscoring author Hamilton's point that the lust for war still dominates the human spirit. Instead of looking upon the ray devices as a means to end the scourge of war completely, the belligerents merely resort to whatever is available to help them fight. That the ray was based on a real claim, one that was most certainly that of Grindell Matthews, is provided by a note from the publisher: "The 'Motif' of the plot is not a figment of the author's brain. As a scientific discovery in embryo it has been rumoured in the press and ascribed both to British and foreign inventors."[53]

Charles Bennett, one of the most prolific stage writers of the twentieth century and who later collaborated with Alfred Hitchcock, wrote *The Last Hour*, which debuted on 20 December 1928 at the Comedy Theatre in London. This highly successful melodrama tells the story of a secret agent who is foiled in his efforts to steal a powerful death ray from the British government. According to Bennett, it was a big hit "mainly because I burned two of my main characters to charred embers before the thrilled eyes of my audience...."[54] *The Last Hour* received praise for this technical feat from reviewer Charles Morgan in the *New York Times*: "The prince turns his death ray on to an intruder, there is a blinding flash, and when you look again there is the charred body of a man rolling on the floor. This was an extraordinarily successful piece of wizardry."[55] Although later made into a film that reduced the role of the death ray to one demonstration, Bennett credited this play with ensuring his career as a writer of melodrama.

Other death-ray plays with a comedic air include *Khaki* in 1925 and *The Council of Seven* in 1930. The former was advertised as a burlesque by the local newspaper when it opened in Nottingham, England. In this story set in the Great War, the lead comedian played several roles, one of which was a British soldier made prisoner by the Germans and subjected to a "wonderful" death ray.[56] Full of thrills and chills, the latter play by Sax Rohmer is a story of a man greatly interested in learning about the mysteries of Buddhism only to find himself the target of a sinister band known as the "Council of Seven," whose members are ruthless in the pursuit of their victims. Their main weapon, however, is a death ray which causes the "smiling death," so-called because of the grin left on the faces of those killed by it. According to *The Argus*, special guests attended performances of this play when it opened at the Bijou Theatre in Melbourne and appeared quite pleased with the entertainment provided. Members of the Friendly Union of Sailor's and Soldiers' Wives and Mothers, along with Major General W. A. Coxen, Inspector-General of the Commonwealth Military Forces, saw the matinee, while the Geelong football team watched the evening rendition.[57]

Ray weapons were also featured in other theatrical productions. One was a blue ray in *Before Midnight* by Irish playwright Gerald Brosnan. A one-act tragedy, it is a story about a mad professor who kidnaps people and uses his diabolical invention to turn them into "living corpses for the purpose of his gruesome experiments, which, he imagines, will ultimately benefit mankind."[58] First performed at the Abbey Theatre in Dublin in 1928, it also played at the Little Theatre in London, after which it received a bad rating by the *Times*.[59] Two other productions were J. W. Elliott's *Death Ray* in 1931 in New York and Mary Pakington's *Pirate Mallory*, which hit the London stage in October of 1935. The story of an inventor who builds a death ray but then tries to destroy the apparatus, *Pirate Mallory* received good reviews from the critics.[60] Frenchman Émile Lartaud came out with a one-act play entitled *Le rayon de la mort* in 1938, and Langdon McCormick wrote *The Rogues March* in late 1939 after the start of the war in Europe to entertain audiences by showing a death ray destroying New York on stage.[61]

One play featuring another one of those death rays with the letter "Z" was *Nineteen-Sixty-Four* by H.E.M. Flinn. A central theme is the belief that it is better to fight for humanity than to fight for one's country. First performed in Perth in 1932 and reviewed by the local newspaper *The Western Australian*, the play tells the story of a world war breaking out in 1964 and the development of a "Z-ray" by a British officer, Captain Peter O'Brien. It is a true death ray, for, according to the review, it "can kill silently and invisibly any living thing within focus, and no barrier is proof against it."[62] A spy, who turns out to be O'Brien's new love, is caught trying to steal the weapon and is sentenced to be shot. Unable to bear such a loss, he uses the Z-ray to free the girl and escape to Ireland. There he gives the weapon to an American millionaire who wants to force peace on the world. The play ends with the assumption that this will happen.

Pulp Fiction

Another important literary medium for the death ray was that of the pulp magazine. Publications specializing in science fiction such as *Amazing Stories*, *Air Wonder Stories*, *Wonder Stories*, and others began to appear in the latter part of the 1920s and acquired a considerable readership. Their pages are filled with stories of mysterious rays of all sorts, often corresponding to the descriptions in news reports. The prime mover behind the development of this format was Hugo Gernsback, regarded as the "father of science fiction," who established *Amazing Stories* in 1926. A precursor to these publications was his technological magazine *The Electrical Experimenter*, founded in 1913.[63] In addition to articles about news involving electricity, Gernsback in this publication featured what later came to be called science fiction stories. His success with this type of literature rested primarily on attracting authors who also had some knowledge of science and could therefore write stories involving plausible technology. One, of course, was the concept of wireless energy weapons utilizing electricity or radium, which had been a news item and the subject of numerous novels and short stories for quite some time.

One of the first ray stories to appear in *The Electrical Experimenter* was George F. Stratton's "The Poniatowski Ray" in 1916, part of a series involving the character Ned Cawthorne. In this brief tale the United States defeats the invasion force of the Japanese-Chinese alliance with which it is at war. The secret to its success is the Poniatowski Ray created by a Polish inventor who shares the plans and diagrams of the weapon with

Cawthorne. Stratton describes the ray in action as the enemy airplanes attack:

> Instantly a tiny ray of light, so nearly as blue as the sky as to be barely discernible, shot from the tube, and from the aero fleet, a mile away and nearly a mile above the earth, came lightning flashes of flame with terrific crashes, drowning out the continuous rattle of the rapid-fire gun. Cawthorne swung the tube across the sky with some little deviation in the elevation and that ray ... fired every bomb, every gun and every holster revolver among them. The gasoline tanks went as instantly, wrecking the aeroplanes.[64]

The ray in the story exhibits the same general capabilities as those in some of the fiction described in the preceding chapter, in particular, the "blinding blue glare" fired from a tube on the *Franklin* in Rowan Stevens's "Sorakichi,—Prometheus," and resembles the F-rays of Giulio Ulivi. The Poniatowski Ray can, for example, also detonate submarine mines, as described in a conversation between Cawthorne and an army lieutenant: "if they put that projector in action it will explode every mine and every submarine within reach of the ray, and we've tested that up to six miles." The lieutenant responds almost incredulously: "What! That marvelous ray can operate under water? Can find and explode the hidden mines?"[65] As an aside, Gernsback inserted an editorial comment suggesting that something like the energy weapon in the story was not that far-fetched: "The Poniatowski Ray ... is believed by many to be a future scientific possibility and one that may become a practical device for military uses within a shorter time than one may suspect."[66]

A story appearing in installments in *The Argosy-Allstory Weekly* in 1922 had a "light ray" that could incinerate airplanes, people, and whole towns. In "The Fire People," author Ray Cummings described an exploratory invasion by a rebel faction from Mercury that wants to learn if Earth can be conquered. Although most of the action takes place on the closest planet to the sun as two Earthmen with the aid of a native woman foil the renegades, the first part of the story describes the initial invasion, which occurs in the western part of the United States. Cummings imitates Wells's *The War of the Worlds* to an extent, as newspaper reports of meteors striking the ground are followed by the realization that they are spaceships from which aliens emerge to set up fortified bases. The invaders then set about destroying surrounding towns as well as the American military forces sent against them. As described by one of the characters, the light ray is based on generating tremendous molecular vibration, causing anything it strikes to heat up to the point of bursting into flames.[67] Two separate devices are wielded by the Mercutians, a large one and a smaller one carried as a sidearm. In one scene the latter is described in a manner resembling a laser: "Mercer's body was examined that same afternoon. It was found to have been drilled completely through the chest by a hole about the diameter of a lead pencil. This hole did not seem to have been made by the passage of any foreign object, but had more the aspect of a burn."[68] The appearance of the larger weapon resembles a camera projector or a floodlight. On the cover of the magazine one sees three of these light rays mounted on tall supports firing their beams at a city on Mercury while a young woman watches. She is the character Miela, the Mercutian who helps the Earthmen stop the rebels in their attempt to gain support for a return to Earth to conquer the planet.

A weapon bearing the influence of the death ray of Grindell Matthews appeared in Philip Francis Nowlan's *Armageddon 2419 A.D.* in the August 1928 issue of *Amazing Stories*. This novella introduced the character "Anthony Rogers" that became better known as "Buck Rogers." Nowlan's description of a disintegrator ray in the tale resembles both the destructive properties and images of the one developed by Grindell Matthews: "These rays were projected from a machine not unlike a searchlight in appearance, the reflector of which, however, was not material substance, but a complicated balance of interacting electronic forces."[69] As mentioned in Chapter 2, the *New York Times* and other print media had carried photographs and artistic representations of the English inventor's death ray beginning in 1924. One was the image resembling a searchlight.

Other pulp stories also borrowed from news reports. Nikola Tesla's experiments with electricity inspired Hugo Gernsback's "The Magnetic Storm," which appeared in the July 1926 issue of *Amazing Stories*. In an inset the author states: "This story was written during the world war, long before the death ray was ever 'invented.'"[70] Gernsbach's comment is somewhat strange, for such an astute observer of scientific developments as he would have known about death-ray claims, including that of Ulivi. Furthermore, he would have been familiar with the numerous ray tales already published, including Griffith's *World Masters*, in which the term "death ray" appeared. He also writes that "Nikola Tesla, who read the original proofs of this story, endorses the idea [of the possibility of a death ray]."[71] Incorporating the famous electrical wizard himself into the story, Gernsbach describes an apprentice of Tesla, called "Sparks," developing a ray capable of disabling airplane magnetos. This comes in handy in the World War when German air squadrons attack American positions in France. Sparks also extends the power of the ray to disrupt communications throughout the enemy's lines as well as in the German homeland, leading to Allied victory.

Several tales based on newspaper articles in 1923 and 1924 about rays developed to short-circuit airplane motors also made their way into pulp magazines. One entitled "Clouds of Death" and written by Louis Buswell was published in the June 1929 issue of *Amazing Stories*. After a second world war in which the United States did not participate, a third world war breaks out, and America is attacked by an unnamed enemy using a "directional death ray" that knocks out gasoline engines. In a short time the invaders occupy part of the country, making Boise their Pacific headquarters. Just as the people are asking the government to make peace, a young man by the name of Icarus Wright Langley shows up at the headquarters of the American commanding general with a new invention to save the nation. Known as an outstanding math and science student in college but also as a dreamer seeking to revolutionize air travel, Langley has developed a new type of small airplane with human-powered flapping wings. He then tells the general his story. While working on the flying machine in a secluded part of Nevada, he and his fellow pilots also discovered a large deposit of sodium carbonate and processed the mineral, making bombs with powder and some with thermite. Leading a force of two hundred planes, Langley and his companions dropped the bombs on the enemy at Boise and at Chicago. When the sodium broke open, nothing happened. The thermite caused fires, however, eliciting a response from the enemy fire fighters, who turned on the water hoses. Upon contact with sodium powder, a powerful conflagration erupted. Calling his unconventional airplane the *Jeanne d'Arc*, the young genius proposes to the general that a thousand such machines armed with the new bombs can lead America to victory just as the Maid of Orleans had done for her country centuries before. The commander agrees to place the resources of the nation at Langley's disposal, and the swarms of blue and white "birds" defeat the enemy and restore peace.[72]

Another work utilizing rays to disable aircraft appeared in 1931 in *Wonder Stories*. Morrison F. Colladay, who had already introduced "The Cosmic Gun" in the May issue, followed up with "The Return of the Cosmic Gun" in October. In the earlier tale, the author described the invention of a powerful weapon that harnessed cosmic rays from space and converted them into an energy beam. Although the second story utilizes the cosmic gun invented by the scientist Hartridge in the first one, "The Return of the Cosmic Gun" is not really a sequel. It describes a plot by a sinister organization to overthrow the government of the United States and take control of the country. The IBPA, the International Business Protective Association headquartered in Chicago, is run by gangsters who want to expand

7. Death Rays in Other Media   205

beyond the boundaries of simple criminal activity. In addition to the usual thugs and bribed police and political officials, they now have an army of scientists at their disposal who develop several types of ray weapons. In the end they are thwarted by the cosmic gun and an ether wave generator invented by a professor at the University of Chicago.

Colladay borrowed heavily from news reports about rays to knock out the magnetos of gasoline engines as well as others frequently publicized. At the beginning of the story, a three-motored airplane is forced to make an emergency crash landing because of unexplained engine failure. Afterward, two of the characters, one of them Professor Henry Carey and his companion Bill Adams, discuss the incident. Adams says that the IBPA was trying to kill them with an arrestor ray that "paralyzes the ignition systems of all internal combustion engines." In response, Carey says "I remember there were newspaper reports a few years ago about the trial of some such ray by the German army. I seem to remember the German government denied the whole thing." Adams replies: "Suppose when the next war starts, France sends a fleet of airplanes to bombard the German cities. The Germans raise a barrage of the rays and the planes fall to the ground."[73] Following up on this, Colladay introduces an autogiro (helicopter) with a diesel engine which does not operate on ignition and is therefore unaffected by these rays. The author also gives the IBPA an Ulivi-type "detonating ray machine" that can set off explosives, including cartridges in the belts of soldiers, up to a distance of ten miles. Another weapon in its arsenal is the "devil feeder," a ray that incinerates anything it strikes.

A short novel also about ray weapons designed to paralyze airplane motors and to incinerate appeared in 1935 in a type of paperback series for juvenile readers. *Le rayon infernal* by Félix Celval described an attempt by an unscrupulous French arms manufacturer named Fulgur (flash) to procure a "rayon de mort" from Maurice Cardan, a young engineer. Fulgur is head of a large company that has produced a powerful explosive called Fulgurite. Pretending to be an ardent patriot, he is secretly working with an unnamed foreign syndicate seeking to destroy France and therefore has taken a great interest in Cardan's ray. After a round of intrigue, Cardan and his mechanic assistant, Zanzi, launch an air attack on Fulgur's secluded factory. Not only do they employ the green ray which immobilizes gasoline engines but also reveal a new and more powerful weapon: the *"radiardant,"* an incinerating red beam. In the end, Fulgur and his installation are destroyed and the syndicate is exposed. Celval does not say that the foreigners are Germans, but most readers would infer such a connection. Like so many other fictional works influenced by news reports, this one, too, seems to borrow from Grindell Matthews. The engine-paralyzing ray is described by Cardan as follows: "I can, in a manner, halt airplanes flying at full speed, electric trains, cars, submarines and tanks. In other words, I can make war materially impossible by destroying all the matériel of an army without running the least risk to myself."[74]

Instead of disrupting internal combustion engines or incinerating objects, the "blue ray" created by Lowell Howard Morrow kills crews without directly causing damage to their aircraft. In "The Blue Demon," published in *Air Wonder Stories* in December 1929, an unseen enemy destroys most of the American air fleet before being stopped. The weapon mounted on its planes shoots a ray that projects a blue poison at its target up to two thousand yards away. The men inside die almost immediately upon contact with the lethal beam, and their aircraft then spins out of control and crashes. Their bodies even exude a bluish sheen. As with commentary on some of the movies previously mentioned, an editorial inset suggests that a death ray is a possibility: "Incidentally, Mr. Morrow has evolved a number of brand new ideas which, sooner or later, will be used for warfare. It is becoming recognized that it may be much easier in combat to cripple the engine of the enemy's plane than to attempt to puncture it with bullets."[75]

Whether by intent or by chance, R. V. Happel's "The Triple Ray," appearing in the fall 1930 *Amazing Stories Quarterly*, described a device seemingly influenced by Ulivi and Grindell Matthews. At the beginning of the story, the narrator reminds the readers that his friend, Professor Lucius Raymond, had developed a weapon that convinced the Germans and Austrians to make peace just as the German army was poised to take Paris. A demonstration of the Twin Ray to the Teutonic representatives at a secret conference held in a neutral country showed them the futility of continuing the World War. The ray reduced to dust whatever it struck. As described by the narrator: "It was, in fact, nothing more than the combination, in a single beam, of ultra-violet and infra-red rays. One acted merely as the carrier of the other, the violet ray insinuating itself within the atomic structure of the object to be destroyed, while the infra-red was carried 'on its back.'"[76] The rest of the story is about a further development of this into the Triple Ray, which when released is destined to traverse the curved universe and ultimately return to destroy the earth.

Another type of death ray appeared in the series of stories featuring the British crime fighter Simon Templar, known as The Saint, created by Leslie Charteris. "The Creeping Death," published in the 13 July 1929 issue of *The Thriller* magazine later formed the core of a novel entitled both

The Last Hero and, subsequently, *The Saint Closes the Case*. This and other stories in the series were adapted to radio in the 1940s and 1950s, with Vincent Price as one of the readers, and presented on NBC. In the story taken from the radio version, a villain named Dr. Vargon has invented a powerful weapon he hopes to sell to a foreign power in order to become rich. It operates by releasing a cloud, violet in color, that completely destroys living organisms. Like many other death-ray tales of the period, this one, too, focuses on the detective aspects and limits the action involving the weapon. Much of the story is taken up with various characters and their motives for involvement, such as the wealthy and ruthless financier Rayt Marius, who hopes to profit from wars. In the end, The Saint defeats the sinister agents and Vargon is killed. One scene early on depicts the "electron cloud" in action, as related by one of the characters. A goat is tethered at one end of a room reinforced by thick concrete walls while the violet cloud accompanied by sparks moves toward it. Upon contact, the unfortunate animal turns black and then crumbles into a type of dust which gives off bluish smoke.[77]

One story, appearing in the April 1930 issue of *Wonder Stories*, has a weapon resembling Maclay's "burning glasses" and bears some similarity to the real-life account of Kurt Schimkus a year later as described in Chapter 3. "The Heat Ray" by O.L. Beckwith features an inventor who develops a powerful heat ray but is killed by gangsters, who then replicate several copies of the weapon and mount them on aircraft. In the end, the inventor's son saves the day and ultimately destroys the diagrams of the ray. The apparatus is described as consisting of prisms and mirrors to concentrate the rays of the sun similar to that described by Maclay.[78]

Several stories capitalized on the research of W.D. Coolidge of the General Electric Company. As mentioned in Chapter 3, his cathode tube was often portrayed in the press erroneously as a "death ray." Jack Barnette's "The Purple Death" appeared in the July 1929 issue of *Amazing Stories*, with an inset on the first page referencing the well-known scientist: "Quite recently, Dr. Coolidge of the Great Electric Company, experimented with a new ray by means of which startling experiments were made. These rays changed the color of a rabbit's hair."[79] The story is about two scientists, Bernard Grey and George Le Brun, who try to develop a ray that can kill disease germs without harming the host body. Grey develops an ultraviolet beam that has some effect on microbes but is powerless against more lethal forms of bacilli. Le Brun designs an apparatus resembling "an X-ray tube that had suffered from convulsions," and the two men employ it to achieve their objective. All proceeds well on the great day of their first experiments with the "El Ray" as it was dubbed, but soon they make a fascinating discovery. Grey turns on his ultraviolet ray projector and notices that some objects and a mouse are destroyed, a result of having already been exposed to the El Ray. The two men experiment further and kill numerous mice and guinea pigs. In addition to its use as a tool for medical science, Grey exclaims to Le Brun: "Imagine it in warfare—a beam of the El-rays from your tube and a beam of ultra-violet rays sending an army into eternity. An invisible knife that would cut airplanes or battleships in twain as if they were made of cheese."[80] Afterward, they are accidentally killed by their own invention, which also gradually consumes the house and laboratory where they were working.

Three other pulp tales also referenced Coolidge with their cathode weapons. In "Dust of Destruction" in 1931, P. Schuyler Miller created a tale in which beings on the Moon attack Earth with a powerful cathode ray. After the annihilation of the town of Norfolk, Nebraska, several men take off in a rocket ship to locate the source of the weapon and destroy it. Miller directly names the famous inventor in a conversation between two of his characters: "You, Hank, have seen Coolidge's cathode ray at work. Remember how it makes rock salt turn violet, and how acetylene gas falls in a dense yellow powder? There is your clue. This is a ray, a cathode ray generated on the Moon, of such a frequency as will pump energy into the nitrogen of our atmosphere and cause it to fall in the fluffy green powder that you saw."[81] John W. Campbell, Jr., in "When the Atoms Failed" appearing in the January 1930 issue of *Amazing Stories*, described an invasion from Mars in which an American inventor battles against aliens who employ cathode ray projectors and heat rays. He manages almost single-handedly to defeat them by using heat rays, atomic disintegrators, and other technology.[82] In "The Mole-Men of Mercury," published in the December 1933 issue of *Amazing Stories*, writer Arthur K. Barnes had cathode rays as the only weapon that can kill these creatures.[83]

Although incorporating a type of cathode device, Eando Binder produced a work for *Thrilling Wonder Stories* that combined it with the killing properties corresponding to generic descriptions of death rays in newspapers and magazines, especially those of Ulivi and Grindell Matthews. He also followed the pattern frequently found in novels and movies in which crooks try to steal a scientist's death ray for nefarious purposes, in this case to conquer the world. Appearing in the December 1936 issue, "Static" depicts a brief encounter between a Professor Hobson and two armed masked men in his laboratory. One of them, also a scientist, describes the capabilities of the weapon:

Think once, Professor Hobson, of that beam centered on an airplane high up. Think of those thousands of watts curling into a vortex around the pilot, searing him to a crisp in three seconds. Think of it as a death ray sweeping across an advancing army's front—picture each gun sparkling like a super-static machine, charring each soldier's hand and arm. Imagine this beam centered on an arsenal, changing metal containers to hot bolts of electricity![84]

Hobson manages to kill the two intruders with his death ray and then destroys it.

Included in the same issue was "The Island of Doctor X" by Allan K. Echols, another work referencing W. D. Coolidge. The story is about a mad scientist named Dupree who plans to rule the world by first destroying the value of gold, upon which the entire economic system of the planet is based. Having concluded that every existing thing is fundamentally electrical energy, he has spent years of research learning how to reduce something to this state and reverse the process as well. The fruit of his labors is a machine that can manufacture gold. His plan is to distribute as much of the precious metal as possible, thereby making it valueless. The resulting world economic crash and chaos will enable him and his small army to take control, as he has also developed a type of force field causing paralysis to anyone trapped inside. His nemesis, the hero in the story, is a young and athletic scientist named Lowell Best. He and a government agent team up to stop Dupree and thwart his plan to conquer the world. Lowell uses a type of death ray rifle he has invented to destroy the gold-making machine and then kill the mad scientist and his henchmen. As described to the government agent, Gregory: "'That's a disintegrator gun,' Best said, leading the way out of the room. 'I haven't time to explain the details now, but it is a variation of the Coolidge tube.'"[85] Anything struck by the ray is reduced to a thin layer of gray dust.

Radio

Another medium that occasionally featured death-ray stories during the interwar period was that of radio. In 1928 the BBC broadcast a dramatization of a play entitled *The Greater Power* by Francis J. Mott. It was another story of a misanthropist wanting to destroy the world, this one set in the year 1978. As described in the *Nottingham Evening Post* announcing its upcoming presentation, the play provided "'death rays' and other 'easy aids to easy dying.'"[86]

The *Phyl Coe Mysteries* sponsored by Philco Radio Tubes was a quite popular program in the mid–1930s, for it invited the radio audience to participate, with a cash reward for determining how the heroine solved the mystery. One particular episode in 1936 utilized a device resembling descriptions of both Coolidge's instrument and Grindell Matthews's death ray. Entitled "The Mystery of the Death Ray Tube," this fifteen-minute program begins with private detective Phyl (Phyllis) Coe and her sidekick Tom Taylor arriving at the lodge of Dr. Joseph Crowfoot in the mountains of Colorado. An old friend of her father, Dr. Crowfoot and his two assistants have been working on an astounding invention, which he wants to show to Phyl and Taylor. At that moment a Major William Osborne of the U.S. War Department joins their discussion. He has arrived from Washington at the invitation of Dr. Crowfoot, who is anxious to give his new "death ray" to the government. Crowfoot escorts them to a shed where the apparatus is kept and uses it to kill a guinea pig in just seconds. He claims that a larger and more powerful device would enable him to annihilate whole armies. Impressed, they retire for the evening only to be awakened later by a fire in the shed. Discovering that the death ray has been stolen, Phyl asks everyone to return to the lodge while she tries to solve the case. She quickly realizes that the culprit is "Major Osborne," actually a foreign agent who has assumed the major's identity. When Phyl exposes him as the thief, he pulls out the death ray and kills Crowfoot before being overpowered by one of the professor's assistants. The weapon crashes to the floor and is destroyed. Dr. Crowfoot had never written down the exact nature of the device and its properties, keeping all of that information in his head. Consequently, the secret of the death ray dies with him.[87]

The Death Ray and Humor

Publicity surrounding the death ray even found its way into the realm of everyday humor. Much of this resulted from the notoriety given to Grindell Matthews. In a satirical piece for *Le Figaro* in April 1924, author Régis Gignoux scolded him for having stolen the idea of the death ray from the one described in *La Machine à finir la guerre* (discussed in Chapter 5). Gignoux reminded his readers that he and Roland Dorgelès had created such a device for their novel published in 1917.[88] There was also a short comedy skit entitled "Olympic=City" that appeared in the Parisian magazine *Les Annales* in early July. In one scene the character Arsène Rupin enters brandishing an apparatus that renders a woman and a man motionless. He then says: "There! You see. It was as easy as that. What did I do to you? ... I have just simply 'matthewsed' you!" (Je viens simplement de vous matthewser). When the woman responds quizzically, he answers, "Of course! Don't you know who M. Grindell Matthews is, the inventor of the diabolical ray?" He then goes on to identify himself as an agent for the English inventor and his company, describing to them and to the audience the power of the *rayon diabolique* and its incredibly diverse capabilities, suggesting in comic fashion that only gullible people would believe such nonsense. Having piqued their interest, Rupin breaks into a song about Grindell Matthews and his ray. Afterward, he continues: "Yes, ladies and gentlemen, the *rayon ardent* is the last word in scientific progress. With it, there is no longer any need to be tormented in life. You have a creditor? Poof! You burn up his bills.... There is a woman you love? Poof! You capture her heart.... You have an annoying mother-in-law? Poof! You pulverize her.... You find a scene too long? Poof! You cut it in half.... You have spectators who do not find you a genius? Poof! They will applaud you without letup."[89] Facing the audience, Rupin then makes a sales pitch to the man and woman, offering the ray for the modest, even ridiculously low, sum of 432,827,472,149 francs, plus 5 centimes for postage. When the gentleman sighs that he does not have 432 billion francs, Rupin informs the pair that he has other wonderful items for sale.[90] In another setting, this time in the French fashion magazine *Les Modes de la Femme de France*, author Georges-Armand Masson asked his female readers if they were up on the latest creation by men, referencing a death ray in Britain. It was "an apparatus ... to mow down an army, to blow up towns, and to sink entire fleets in less time than it takes me to dip my pen in ink and draw your portrait on my blotter."[91] A cartoon in *Le Journal amusant* shows a mother mouse with two of her little ones on what appears to be a tabletop, telling them that "a pig has once again discovered a diabolical ray with which he can kill at a distance of ten kilometers from the jar of jam that you are going to nibble."[92] The same magazine had another reference to Grindell Matthews in its 3 January 1925 issue. A cartoon of a man with a portable death ray shooting at another man has the following caption: "The diabolical ray (which kills at a distance) has been an enormous success. We will be counting on it considerably in the next war, the last one."[93]

This type of humor appeared in Britain and other parts of the English-speaking world as well. In 1924 the popular London magazine *Punch* featured a political cartoon with former Prime Minister Herbert Asquith carrying a death ray under his arm labeled "Liberal Vote" and shaking his finger at a robin sitting in a tree. The title of the cartoon was "Robin Red

Flag," referring to the demonstrations of Socialists and their Labour Party allies who often sang "The Red Flag," on one occasion interrupting Asquith during a political speech.[94] The caption reads as follows: "'Who'll kill Cock Robin?' 'I,' said Mr. A., 'With my death ray (some other day) I'll kill Cock Robin.'"[95] This particular cartoon could be referencing both Grindell Matthews and fellow Englishman William Prior, who claimed to have invented a death ray even more powerful than his. Prior's apparatus was described as being "easily carried under the arm."[96] The same issue of *Punch* also made sport of Grindell Matthews's invention with a story about three magicians who came before a king offering him their gifts, one of which was called "Perpetual Death." According to its creator, "It is very useful against the King's enemies. I have a Secret Ray that can wither everything that lives. It can also stop a motor-car twenty yards away."[97] The magazine contained another cartoon, entitled "The 'Death-Ray' in Antiquity," showing a king sitting on a raised platform with two of his advisors watching a funny-looking chap directing his evil eye stare at a terrified soldier. Behind him is another of his type with a blindfold, to be kept on until it was time for his evil eye to swing into action. In the lower left of the picture, a dog slinks away, apparently wanting nothing to do with the affair. The caption reads: "A king and his war council testing the efficacy of the evil eye as a weapon."[98]

And according to a story making the rounds in newspapers, the notoriety regarding Grindell Matthews gave rise to a new expression. As reported by *The West Australian* of Perth, "The climax to a long and intimate tale of feminine friction, overheard recently in a London tube, was this: '— and then, my dear, she just looked death rays at me!'"[99] This expression caught on and lasted for some time, as evidenced by a story in the *Oakland Tribune* in March 1936. Reporter Henry McLemore, in "Death Ray Glances Gone From Gals' Golf Tourneys," noted that a change had taken place in the realm of women's golf, one in which the female competitors had become friendlier to one another. According to him, it used to be quite different: "And the looks these combatants exchanged during a round. They were the original death rays."[100]

A humorous poem by an anonymous author appeared in April 1924 a month before Grindell Matthews performed his demonstrations for the British government representatives. Entitled "Motor Tragedy," it is taken from the newspaper *The Advocate* of Burnie, Tasmania. The speaker is a young fellow out for a walk with his girlfriend, as they come across a man trying to get his car started. When his first suggestions to fix the problem are met with swearing, the young fellow continues:

> In spite of rudeness, still polite
> I asked: "Is your magneto right?
> Perchance, in some new manner
> This Grindell Matthews is to-day
> Trying that brand new thermic ray—"
> He slew me with his spanner.[101]

Humor surrounding the death ray was not restricted to commentary related to Grindell Matthews. Novelist John Galsworthy included a snipe at this diabolical weapon in *A Modern Comedy* published in 1929. An admiral responds to a question, saying "Foggartism! What's that—new kind of death ray? I saw a fellow yesterday, Mrs. Mont—give you my word!—who's got a ray that goes through three bullocks, a nine-inch brick wall, and gives a shock to a donkey on the other side; and only at quarter strength."[102] One story reported in *The Mercury* of Hobart, Tasmania, in 1931 concerned an incident outside the Lewisham Hotel in West Bromwich, England. A policeman on his routine beat suddenly went into strange gyrations, spinning and jumping as if he were demented. While this bizarre performance was going on, a crowd gathered and people expressed their comments. One young woman thought it must be a new dance, "the policeman's tango or something." A man of the cloth then stepped forward and chided the constable for his undignified behavior; but he, too, suddenly did strange things, including jumping at the policeman and hugging him. Many in the crowd by now believed the whole spectacle was a stunt staged for their benefit. At that moment a pair of young lovers happened along and, when stepping onto the same spot in front of the hotel, likewise suddenly manifested strange behavior. Later, the official explanation was that an electric wire in a supply box had fused, sending an electric current along the wet pavement to that exact location. The last comment from the crowd in reference to the young couple, however, was "It's a death ray."[103] In 1935 an issue of the French magazine *L'Aéro* depicted the continuing popularity of the death ray as a news item. A cartoon shows a scruffy-looking father in what looks to be a type of smock worn by physicians and scientists. Behind him is a beaker with boiling liquid as well as machinery, giving the appearance of a laboratory. He is scolding his young son, who has something smeared all over his face. The father says "You touched my black ray again!" The little boy replies "No, Dad, just a ray of jam!"[104] The following year, an Australian newspaper utilized this diabolical weapon in a commentary on the harm created by the chain store phenomenon: "Wollongong is the latest country town to be invaded by the chain store, which by the irony of fate, has acquired a church property from which to launch its death-rays upon the struggling businessmen of that locality."[105] This was not the only connection to the world of commercialism, as one business enterprise in Dunedin, New Zealand, bore the name "Death Ray Co." and specialized in a new type of poison labeled "Death Ray." One can of the substance was advertised as capable of killing five hundred rabbits.[106]

In August and September 1939, another example of humor connected to the death ray was a short story designed for young readers that appeared in the Children's Corner section of the *Townsville Daily Bulletin* of Queensland. Frank Reid's "Invisible Ray" described some activities of a group of Australian schoolboys led by two brothers, Phillip and Roy Blake. One of the features of the story is the mysterious death of a local farmer's cows and an investigation by a detective who knows Phillip and Roy. He tells them that a "mad inventor" escaped from a lunatic asylum in Melbourne and that he was rumored to have developed a short-range death ray. Phillip scoffs somewhat, saying "Scores of inventors are working on the same idea, but they get nowhere. Suppose they did strike on a ray that worked, once they let it go they would not be able to limit the distance in which it would operate. Let loose it would go on and on, perhaps round the world, and catch those using it in the rear."[107] Later, the two brothers encounter the "mad inventor" and his assistant temporarily living in a house on the edge of town. It turns out that he did not escape from an asylum and is in fact an acquaintance of their father, currently in India. The man, identified simply as a Mr. Chartres, came to this small town in order to work in relative peace and quiet on his latest invention and has already visited with Detective West, who was satisfied that no skullduggery was afoot. Chartres then demonstrates his device to the boys. It is television—not a death ray.

And in August 1937, probably the most flippant commentary on the death ray appeared in a regular feature of the *Kossuth County Advance* of Algona, Iowa. The COLYUM, Let's Not Be Too D___d Serious ran "Suggestion for Movie Bedtime Story," in which the sleuth "Detective Defective" begins his investigation of a murder mystery. He has found a man and a woman lying dead "drilled through their heads by some mysterious ray gun." Among the villainous suspects is a nine-year-old boy. Telling readers to catch the next episode to find out the answer, the narrator says: "Good night, children. This is Tom Yawk speaking for Eenie Meenies Itsy Bitsy breakfast food."[108]

Another medium for death-ray related humor was the newspaper comic strip, in this case not the science fiction tales but the more common type reflecting what was happening in society and in the world. A good example is the long-running "Our Boarding House" by Gene Ahern, one of whose main characters was the retired "Major Hoople," a blustering old windbag. In the 2 September 1933 episode, Hoople is seen sitting alongside a stranger at the end of a pier as the two men fish. The Major begins to expound on how to end wars and quickly tells his companion that he is developing several marvelous weapons to do just that. One of those happens to be the "Hoople-ray," which is a Z-ray projected out to ten miles. The reader then sees the Major's daydream of himself in uniform directing his weapon at approaching aircraft that are in various stages of losing power and plummeting to earth. Hoople says: "For instance—take an attack by an enemy squadron of planes—my Z-ray is sent up, and it stalls the airplane motors by arresting the function of their magnetos and generators!" After listening to descriptions of other bizarre weapons, the gentleman leaves and tells a man working at his boat that Hoople is crazy.[109] Other examples include a non-descript death ray wielded by a misanthropist in a series of 1930 episodes of "Jane Arden," a Z-ray that acts as a mind control in several 1938 installments of "Li'l Abner" by Al Capp, and a Z-ray business operation appearing in 1932 in "The Bungle Family" by Harry J. Tuthill.[110] In one episode entitled "More Z-Ray Products," George Bungle says "Ho Hum, another big day! Those Z-Ray devices are selling like battleships at a peace conference." His wife is upset because the Z-ray appears to be playing havoc with the clocks and the doorbell. Bungle tells her he will check with his associate, Professor Diogenes.[111] The comic strip "Sappo" by E. C. Segar, the creator of "Popeye," featured a quack scientist named O. G. Wottasnozzle, who was continually developing some kind of ray to serve different needs. In a March 1934 episode, he has just invented a device that can render anything invisible by combining Z-Rays, J-Rays, and X-Rays. To restore visibility, he uses his Q-63-R: 71 Ray.[112]

One cartoon series entitled "Inspector Post and His Junior Detective Aides," was sponsored by General Foods and featured Post Toasties in each episode. Inspector Post resembles the character Dick Tracy somewhat and is assisted by a boy and girl named Tom and Nancy. In an installment about a Q-ray, a Dr. Bell tells an army general that he plans to give his invention to the United States government. Tom and Nancy have been posted to watch the building where Bell has his laboratory, and they notice a suspicious stranger coming and going from a candy store across the street. They telephone Inspector Post, and when he arrives, they discover a tunnel leading from the candy store to the laboratory. While waiting to see if the stranger will try to use the tunnel to get into Bell's building, Tom and Nancy take a break and eat some delicious Post Toasties. The crook then saws through the floor and Inspector Post captures him.[113]

Along with novels and short stories, the expansion of the death ray into other media forms indicates its importance to the culture of the period, especially after the First World War. The motion picture became one of the most popular forms of entertainment, as moviegoers increasingly turned out to see the latest productions. Pulp magazines and radio provided new platforms for this weapon, while traditional media such as the stage and comic strips embraced the death ray as well. Its appearance in political commentary, advertising, and general humor also attest to its significance in the 1920s and 1930s.

Conclusion

As this study has demonstrated, the death ray in all its manifestations became an important news item in America, Europe, and elsewhere during the late nineteenth century and continued as such on up to the Second World War. It also became a prominent feature of fiction, first attracting the attention of writers of novels and short stories then expanding to the stage, screen, radio, and other media. In the years prior to 1914, the possibility of wireless energy weapons using electricity or some other power source received favorable support from well-known inventors and some mainstream scientists. During this age of faith in science, accompanied by periodic announcements of new technological wonders, many people regarded such an invention plausible and even a natural outcome of continued progress. After the tremendous devastation of the First World War, fears associated with the aero-chemical threat to large metropolitan areas led many to hope for a means to escape the horrors predicted for the inevitable "next war." For some people, a "new and improved" death ray provided just such a solution. Despite skeptics who dismissed it as a fantasy, claims for such a device persisted throughout the 1920s and 1930s, its heyday of popularity.

Research into electricity, radium, and X-rays in the latter part of the nineteenth and the early twentieth centuries led to the concept of a directed energy weapon. Although no one actually produced a working example during this time and some claims were proved to be frauds, few questioned that such a device would sooner or later make its appearance. This was buttressed by reports from time to time, whether true or not, that various governments had expressed an interest in these energy weapons. The most famous episode prior to the First World War was that of Giulio Ulivi and his dealings with the French, British, and Italian military establishments. Despite the fact that his claims were considered inconclusive at best and a downright hoax at worst, the idea of the death ray emerged unscathed and enjoyed considerable attention during the First World War and after.

From 1919 to the German attack on Poland in 1939, stories of death rays or commentary on them appeared almost on a daily basis and could be found not only in major newspapers like the *New York Times*, the London *Times*, and the myriad publications in Paris but in Bradford, Pennsylvania, Brownwood, Texas, and hundreds of other small towns on several continents. Stories about French airplanes forced down over Bavaria by a German ray and the incredible saga of Grindell Matthews opened up whole new possibilities for warfare both chilling and hopeful, as death rays were seen as possessing offensive and defensive capabilities. What sustained the death ray as a news item for so long were the constant reports of new claims, periodic support from governments and their military representatives, and the documented cases of some actually working. Although many mainstream scientists argued that an effective energy weapon was technologically impossible, they weakened their own arguments by ignoring statements by other credible experts. Revelations after the Second World War confirmed that some governments, including those of Great Britain, Germany, and Japan, had taken the death ray quite seriously.

This study has also shown that a considerable body of death-ray fiction during the same period reflected the influence of real claims reported in the press. Writers continually drew upon the wealth of information regarding various types of directed energy weapons and utilized them for their storylines. The practice of doing so also led to some authors inserting them into their plots for apparently no other reason than that death rays had become fashionable. In many works such a device seemed to be more of an obligatory feature and served no real purpose. Prior to 1914 most authors employing some form of directed energy weapon placed it in the hands of philanthropists desiring to bring about an end to conflict or gave it to one or more belligerents in imaginary war tales. During the First World War, a shift occurred that expanded to include a wider variety of storylines and different media, including the stage and screen. Although some of this fiction involved the use of death rays in war, many of the tales focused on mad scientists and other villains using them for various evil purposes: threatening to destroy the world, a nation, or some other entity; or simply to aid them in regular criminal activities. Espionage was also the backdrop for a number of ray stories, with secret agents of a foreign power trying to steal death-ray machines or their plans. And as pointed out, the setting for much of this fiction was the contemporary world of the 1920s and 1930s.

Finally, the death ray also became part of popular culture. Established comic strips incorporated it into their routine commentaries on life and society, while political cartoonists found it a valuable source for their trade. It also showed up in the world of business and entered into general public discourse.

Chapter Notes

Introduction

1. R. Ernest Dupuy and George Fielding Eliot, *If War Comes* (New York: Macmillan, 1937), 46–47.
2. "The Death of the Death Ray," *Scientific American*, December 1934, 287.
3. For a more in-depth treatment of imaginary war during this period, see I. F. Clarke, *Voices Prophesying War 1763–1984* (London: Oxford University Press, 1966) and Brian Stableford, *Scientific Romance in Britain 1890–1950* (New York: St. Martin's Press, 1985).
4. Will Irwin, *"The Next War": An Appeal to Common Sense* (New York: E. P. Dutton,1921), 1. Irwin's book included an analysis of how the next war would be fought based on what prominent military leaders were saying.
5. Charles A. Selden, "World Destruction," *The Ladies Home Journal*, September 1923, 6.
6. "Airplanes and General Slaughter in the Next War," *The Literary Digest*, 17 November 1923, 60.
7. "Allenby, at 70, Warns Next War Means 'End of Civilization,'" *NYT*, 24 April 1931, p. 1; "Man Doomed by Arms, General Smuts Warns," *NYT*, 9 October 1931, p. 2.
8. "Whole Cities Will Wear Gas Masks," *Dallas Morning News*, 10 April 1921, p. 11.
9. Irwin, *"The Next War*," 47.
10. Richard Barry, "Vast U.S. Poison Gas Plant Was Working at Full Blast for 1919 Campaign," *NYT*, 8 December 1918, 4: 1.
11. "Martin Hussingtree" was the pen name of Oliver Ridsdale Baldwin, son of Prime Minister Stanley Baldwin.
12. Probably the most well-known and prominent British prophet of doom regarding chemical warfare was the Earl of Halsbury. During the First World War, he served as an assistant in the Ministry of Munitions and took part in the planning for massive aerial bombardments to be directed against Germany in the later stages of the conflict. Although regarded by many experts as an alarmist, his experience and position in the government made him a credible spokesman in the eyes of the public.
13. Helders's real name was Robert Knauss, an officer in the German air corps, clandestinely until it officially became the Luftwaffe under the Nazis.
14. *The War of the Worlds* appeared first in *Pearson's Magazine* in Britain and in *Cosmopolitan* magazine in the United States in 1897 before being published in 1898 by William Heinemann (London).
15. "Mystery Tales More Numerous," *NYT*, 1 April 1928, 9: 22.
16. G. K. Chesterton, "The End of the Armistice," in *The Collected Works of G. K. Chesterton*, vol. 5 (San Francisco: Ignatius Press, 1987), 644.

Chapter 1

1. Some inventors believed that electricity could do more than just cause machines to run, as they envisaged it as a

means of supercharging weapons. Reports appeared in 1893 about a "war engine" attributed to Frenchman Eugène Turpin, the inventor of the explosive called "melinite," or "turpinite." Billed by newspapers as a device that would make war impossible, it was designed to discharge a "shot" consisting of 25,000 projectiles at a range up to 3,500 meters or more and covering approximately 22,000 square meters. Turpin claimed that the firepower from such a weapon would be capable of destroying all known types of fortifications, therefore rendering such fixed defensive positions obsolete. But his "angel of death," as it was sometimes called, did not come to fruition. It was only on paper; a drawing, in fact, appeared in newspapers in 1894, and it looked more like a multiple-barreled cannon. See "Une invention effrayante," *La Presse*, 18 June 1893, p. 3; "Nouvelles Diverses," *Journal des Débats politiques et littéraires*, 16 June 1893, p. 2, Gallica; "An Electric War Machine in France," *NYT*, 1 July 1893, p. 3; "Turpin's Wonderful Invention," *NYT*, 1 July 1894, p. 3; and "Turpin's 'Angel of Death' Not Tried," *NYT*, 27 August 1924, p. 3.

2. A New Orleans riverboat pilot by trade, he had also dabbled in spiritualism and become a medium prior to 1861. With the outbreak of the Civil War, he decided to try his hand at being an inventor and came up with the idea of a type of machine gun. For more on this and Wingard's demonstrations at New Orleans and Boston, see Mike Dash, "The Amazing (If True) Story of the Submarine Mechanic Who Blew Himself Up Then Resurfaced as a Secret Agent for Queen Victoria," 30 June 2014, Smithsonian.com. Accessed 6 January 2014. Although Wingard did not actually build such a weapon, newspapers later referred to him as the "original inventor of the Gatling gun." See From the Capital, "Is It Dynamite or What?," *Boston Daily Globe*, 7 February 1876, p. 1, NA.

3. "The Nameless Force," *St. Louis Daily Globe-Democrat*, 15 May 1876, p. 2, Nineteenth Century U.S. Newspapers Database.

4. "The Nameless Force," *Burlington Daily Hawk-Eye* (Iowa), 8 June 1876, p. 2, NA.

5. Untitled, *Galveston Daily News*, 6 June 1876, p. 1, NA.

6. There was some confusion as to whether or not McClintock died in the accident. See Dash, "The Amazing (If True) Story of the Submarine Mechanic...." See also "The Torpedo Mystery," *Indiana State Sentinel* (Indianapolis), 29 October 1879, p. 1, NA.

7. "Some Scientific Hoaxes," *Chambers's Journal of Popular Literature, Science and Arts*, 12 June 1880, 378, GB. See also "Wireless and War," *The Advertiser* (Adelaide), 13 January 1927, p. 15, Trove.

8. "A New Agent in Warfare," *Clarence and Richmond Examiner and New England Advertiser* (Grafton, New South Wales), 15 January 1878, p. 4, Trove.

9. "A Novel Mode of Warfare," *San Antonio Daily Light*, 23 January 1890, p. 11, (from the *Western Electrician*), NA. See also "Cuttings from the Society Papers," *The Isle of Wight Observer*, 8 March 1890, p. 6, BNA.

10. "Artificial Lightning in War," *The Daily Independent* (Monroe, Wisconsin), 6 February 1890, p. 3, NA.

11. Field of Science. "For Offensive and Defensive Warfare," *The Daily Review* (Decatur, Illinois), 3 October 1894, p. 7, NA.

12. "Latest in Warfare," *Progress Review* (La Porte City, Iowa), 28 September 1895, p. 9, NA.

13. "Mr. Edison's New Weapons," *Manchester Evening News*, 24 December 1895, p. 3, BNA.

See also "Electricity in War," *The Daily Northwestern* (Oshkosh), 11 February 1896, p. 7, NA.

14. "Electricity in War." Park Benjamin, "A Network of Deadly Forces," *Galveston Daily News*, 12 January 1896, p. 19, NA.

15. "Edison Out-Edisoned," *Lightning*, 6 February 1896, 111. Quoted in Carolyn Marvin, *When Old Technologies Were New: Thinking About Electric Communication in the Late Nineteenth Century* (New York: Oxford University Press, 1988), 146.

16. "Says He Can Destroy Ships by Lightning," *Estherville Democrat* (Iowa), 23 June 1897, p. 3, NA. See also "Artificial Lightning," *Hutchinson News* (Kansas), 16 June 1897, p. 8, NA.

17. "Oh Dear! Another War Terror," *Answers* (London), 30 July 1897, 182. Quoted in Marvin, *When Old Technologies Were New*, 146.

18. "Electricity in Warfare, and Telegraphing Without Wires," *Chambers's*

Journal of Popular Literature, Science and Arts, 9 October 1897, 655–656, GB.

19. "A Gun Which Shoots Electricity," *The World* (New York), 9 January 1898, p. 37 [33], NA.

20. "An Alleged Electric Gun," *The Literary Digest* (from *Electricity*), 5 February 1898, 167. See also "Annihilating Armies by Electricity," *Clarence and Richmond Examiner* (Grafton, New South Wales), 5 April 1898, p. 3, Trove.

21. Gossip of the Day, "The 'Death Ray,'" *The Northern Daily Mail and South Durham Herald* (Durham), 28 January 1898, p. 1, BNA.

22. "Electrical Engines of War," *The Literary Digest* (from *Electricity*), 7 May 1898, 554. See also "A Wonderful Invention," *The Evening Telegraph* (Angus, Scotland), 28 April 1898, p. 3, BNA.

23. "New Weapons," *The Advertiser* (Adelaide), 1 June 1898, p. 4, Trove.

24. "A Dog Drama," *The West Australian Sunday Times* (Perth), 31 July 1898, p. 6, Trove.

25. "Fight with Lightning," *The West Gipsland Gazette* (Warragul, Victoria), 9 August 1898, p. 6, Trove.

26. "To Transmit Electric Power," *NYT*, 27 October 1898, p. 12. See also "An Ocean 'Current,'" *The Weekly Wisconsin* (Milwaukee), 19 November 1898, p. 8, NA.

27. "Oscillator's Use in War," *NYT*, 27 April 1898, p. 5. See also British and Foreign News, *Albury Banner and Wodonga Express* (New South Wales), 19 August 1898, p. 33, Trove, as well as "Army and Navy," *The Daily News* (Perth), 3 December 1898, p. 6, Trove.

28. Notes from All Quarters, *The Western Gazette* (Somerset, England), 18 November 1898, p. 8, BNA.

29. "From Day to Day," *West Australian Sunday Times* (Perth), 7 August 1898, p. 2, Trove.

30. "Army and Navy," *The Daily News* (Perth), 3 December 1898, p. 6, Trove.

31. "Electrical Wonders," *The Western Champion* (Barcaldine, Queensland), 26 June 1905, p. 2, Trove. Tesla's 1898 experiment at Colorado Springs, resulting in a massive power surge and blackout, however, had confirmed that tremendous electrical energy could be generated artificially.

32. Untitled, *Warren Review* (Williamsport, Indiana), 2 June 1898, p. 2, NA.

33. Untitled, *The National Democrat* (Jeffersonville, Indiana), 8 July 1898, p. 2, NA.

34. Notes from all Quarters, *The Western Gazette* (Somerset), 18 November 1898, p. 8, BNA. "Dagonet" was George Robert Sims (1847–1922), an English novelist, dramatist, poet, and journalist noted for his humor as well as his interest in social reform. The name "Dagonet" comes from the Arthurian tales and refers to the great king's jester and comical knight.

35. H. Winfield Secor, "The Tesla High Frequency Oscillator," *The Electrical Experimenter*, March 1916, 614. Partially constructed in 1902, the tower was demolished in 1917.

36. "The Use of 'Wireless' in War," *The North Western Advocate and the Emu Bay Times* (Tasmania), 18 November 1905, p. 5, Trove.

37. "The Modern Science of Slaughter," *The Freeman's Journal and National Press* (Dublin), 29 July 1899, p. 4, BNA.

38. "Wireless Telegraphy as a Weapon of War," *The North Western Advocate and the Emu Bay Times* (Tasmania), 28 July 1899, p. 2, Trove. J. N. Maskelyne was a well-known illusionist and entertainer who teamed with a man named Cooke to put on variety shows featuring performers with magic talents. His son, Nevil, followed in his footsteps.

39. "New Weapons," *The Argus* (Melbourne), 8 July 1899, p. 14, Trove.

40. "Wireless Telegraphy as a Weapon of War," *The North Western Advocate and the Emu Bay Times* (Tasmania), 28 July 1899, p. 2, Trove.

41. News from All Sources, *Broadford Courier and Reedy Creek Times* (Broadford, Victoria), 6 December 1901, p. 5, Trove.

42. "A Remarkable Experiment," *Liverpool Herald* (Liverpool, New South Wales), 19 September 1903, p. 12, Trove.

43. Ibid.

44. Interesting Items, "The Use of 'Wireless' in War," *Lincolnshire Chronicle and General Advertiser* (Lincoln, England), 8 December 1903, p. 9, BNA.

45. "The Submarine Searchlight," *The Advertiser* (Adelaide), 4 November 1903, p. 6, Trove.

46. "The Future of the Fleet," *The Daily News* (Perth), 5 February 1907, p. 3, Trove.

47. "The Submarine Searchlight," *The Advertiser* (Adelaide), 4 November 1903, p. 6, Trove.
48. "The Future of the Fleet," *The Daily News* (Perth), 5 February 1907, p. 3, Trove.
49. Spencer R. Weart, *Nuclear Fear: A History of Images* (Cambridge, Massachusetts: Harvard University Press, 1988), 46.
50. "What Radium May Do," *Oamaru Mail* (New Zealand), 8 September 1909, p. 2, Papers Past.
51. "Radium to End Warfare, Amazing Discovery," *The Register* (Adelaide), 5 November 1909, p. 9, Trove. The Metropolitan Life Building was the tallest structure in New York at the time, rising fifty stories.
52. "Possibilities of Radium," *NYT*, 28 January 1904, p. 6. There seems to be little information in English about Prince Tarkhanoff, but a death notice appeared in *Nature* magazine in 1908, briefly listing his credentials. See Notes, *Nature* 78 (24 September 1908): 513.
53. "Some Recent Inventions," *The Evening Post* (Wellington, New Zealand), 19 October 1901, p. 2, Papers Past.
54. "Rays that Can Blow Up Battleships," *Current Opinion*, January 1914, 36. Harry Cox was an electrical engineer who became interested in X-rays and created a company to manufacture and sell X-ray machines. Long exposure to the rays, however, made him one of the early victims of this discovery.
55. Georges Bourdon, "La Catastrophe de l'*Iéna*," *Le Figaro*, 15 March 1907, p. 2, Gallica.
56. "Wireless Caused *Iéna* Disaster?," *NYT*, 19 March 1907, p. 1. An official inquiry resulted in no definitive conclusions, and, consequently, the causes to date remain a mystery. See Philippe Caresse, "The *Iéna* Disaster," *Warship* 2007, 121–137, GB.
57. "Ought Britain to Sell Her Fleet?," *Albury Banner and Wodonga Express* (New South Wales), 17 July 1908, p. 45, Trove. These and several other ships in addition to the *Iéna* experienced similar fates during this time. Most experts attributed the cause to chemical decomposition of the powder for the guns, wherein it became susceptible to premature explosion.
58. Renseignements Divers, *Revue d'Artillerie* 71 (December 1907): 184, Gallica.
59. "The German Menace to England on the Sea," *NYT*, 4 April 1909, 5: 5.
60. "Our Domestic Circle," *Manchester Courier*, 2 April 1909, Supplement, p. 3, BNA.
61. "Metropolitan Mems.," *Albury Banner and Wodonga Express* (New South Wales), 12 November 1909, p. 29, Trove.
62. "Making War Impossible," *Albany Advertiser* (Western Australia), 27 April 1910, p. 4, Trove.
63. "The Death Ray," *Waiwarapa Daily Tribune* (Greytown, New Zealand), 21 April 1910, p. 3, Papers Past.
64. "Coming Wonders of Wireless," *Taranaki Daily News* (New Zealand), 8 June 1912, Supplement, p. 2, Papers Past.
65. Helen Zimmern, *Italy of the Italians*, new and rev. ed. (New York: Charles Scribner's Sons, 1914), 206–07, GB. Zimmern says that the owner was a Frenchman, but *L'Éclair* and other contemporary sources identify him as English.
66. "Explosive Feats of Giulio Ulivi," *NYT*, 7 September 1913, 3: 5. See also "Exploding Mines by Wireless," *Dallas Morning News*, 7 September 1913, p. 5, as well as "Rays that Can Blow Up Battleships," *Current Opinion*, January 1914, 36–37. Other print sources carrying the story included Late Inventions and Technical News, "Ulivi's Experiments in Exploding Bombs with Infra-Red Rays," *The Labor Digest*, July 1914, 31–32, GB; "Bombs Exploded from a Distance by F-Rays," *Popular Mechanics*, August 1914, 204; and "New Scientific Discovery," *The Ohio Architect, Engineer and Builder*, October 1913, 60, GB.
67. "Explosive Feats of Giulio Ulivi," *NYT*, 7 September 1913, 3: 5.
68. From the *Indianapolis News*, "New Engines of War," *Anaconda Standard* (Anaconda, Montana), 19 November 1913, p. 5 [9], NA.
69. "Explosive Feats of Giulio Ulivi," *NYT*, 7 September 1913, 3: 5. See also "Find 'F' Rays A Hoax," *NYT*, 5 October 1913, 4: 3. The author of an article in one French colonial newspaper expressed skepticism about Ulivi, suggesting that his "F-rays" would turn out to be like the "N-rays" of a few years before. A number of prominent scientists examined the claims made in 1903 by the Frenchman René Blondlot and found that the so-called "N-

rays" simply did not exist. See A. B. C., "Les Rayons F. de M. Ulivi," *Le Courrier de Tlemecen* (Algeria), 10 October 1913, pp. 1–2, Gallica. Blondlot nevertheless received acclaim at the time from the French Academy of Sciences, being awarded the Leconte Prize of 50,000 francs in 1904. The article in *Le Temps* describing the ceremony added that "M. Blondlot is the scientist who discovered the N rays, which are the object of study by all in the scientific world." See Dernières Nouvelles, "À l'Académie des sciences," *Le Temps*, 20 December 1904, p. 4, Gallica.

70. There was some confusion about the sequence of events regarding Ulivi's dealings with both the French and the British. The 1913 *New York Times* article "Explosive Feats of Giulio Ulivi" provides a brief background sketch of the Italian inventor before describing his demonstrations for General Joffre at Le Havre. There is no mention of Ulivi's involvement with the British. In its 21 June 1914 article, "Invention of an Italian May Put an End to War" (5: 2), the *New York Times* writer states that Ulivi had tried unsuccessfully to interest the British admiralty in his device *before* approaching Joffre. Several other newspaper articles, however, confirm that Ulivi traveled to Britain *after* his demonstrations for the French. The *Manitoba Free Press* on 11 October 1913 stated that Ulivi had arrived in Portsmouth the previous week to detonate explosives from a distance of fifty miles. See "To Destroy at Great Distance," 11 October 1913, p. 12, NA. (This must be accessed as *Winnipeg Free Press*.) The next day, the *Galveston Daily News* carried a brief story about Ulivi's experiments near Le Havre, with the French deciding that the Italian's invention might not be genuine after all since it broke down conveniently when he was asked to conduct further tests under their supervision. The paper added that Ulivi was currently in Britain negotiating with the naval authorities there. See "Wonder of the Century Is Found to Be a Hoax," 12 October 1913, p. 32, NA; see also "United Service, Important Experiment Is Made by Admiralty," *The Daily Gleaner* (Kingston, Jamaica), 22 November 1913, p. 13 [29], NA.

71. See, for example, News of World Told in Brief, "Use Ulivi's F-Rays," *Syracuse Herald*, 10 October 1913, p. 24 [48], NA, as well as "To Destroy at Great Distance," *Manitoba Free Press* (Winnipeg), 11 October 1913, p. 12, NA.

72. Zimmern, *Italy of the Italians*, 207.

73. "F-Ray Experiments Witnessed by Naval Officer, Disguised as Second Mate," *The Evening Telegraph and Post* (Dundee, Scotland), 29 October 1913, p. 2, BNA.

74. "Die Strahlen der Zerstörung," *Die Neue Zeitung* (Vienna), 28 October 1913, p. 3, ANNO.

75. "Submarine Mine Experiments," *Times*, 28 October 1913, p. 7.

76. Henri Murat, "Les Explosions provoquées à distance et sans fil," *Le Journal Général de l'Algérie, de la Tunisie et du Maroc* (Algiers), 6 November 1913, pp. 1–2, Gallica. A similar view appeared in *The Argus* of Melbourne although the writer labeled the means used as resembling Ulivi's F-Rays. See "War of the Future," 28 October 1913, p. 9, Trove.

77. "Battleship Blown Up," *The Register* (Adelaide), 2 December 1913, p. 10, Trove.

78. "Mine Fired by Wireless," *NYT*, 27 October 1913, p. 4.

79. "New Discovery for Exploding Shells," *Galveston Daily News*, 22 November 1914, p. 10, NA.

80. "Navy and 'F' Rays," *The Western Gazette* (Somerset, England), 31 October 1913, p. 10, BNA. One newspaper put the distance between the ship and the source of the rays at eight miles. See "An Achievement of Science," *Barrier Miner* (Broken Hill, New South Wales), 28 October 1913, p. 2, Trove.

81. "Nation Duped by Death Ray Inventor," *Albany Banner and Wodonga Express* (New South Wales), 30 October 1936, p. 26, Trove. A similar story about the British imposing conditions on him had already appeared in 1925. See "Death Ray Secrets Revealed," *The Register* (Adelaide), 15 December 1925, p. 19, Trove.

82. Many newspapers carried this story. See, for example, "Radioballistik," *Vorarlberger Volksblatt* (Bregenz, Austria), 21 May 1914, pp. 1–2, ANNO.

83. "Inventor Elopes on Eve of Tests," *NYT*, 18 July 1914, p. 1.

84. "Calls Ulivi Bomb a Chemical Fake," *NYT*, 20 July 1914, p. 1. See also "The 'War Eliminator' that Proved to be Only a Love Hoax," *Indianapolis Sunday Star*, 4 Octo-

ber 1914, Magazine Section, p. 6 [62], NA. (It must be accessed under *Indianapolis Star*.)

85. "Calls Ulivi Bomb a Chemical Fake," *NYT*, 20 July 1914, p. 1. See also "Contemporary Thought, The 'Death Ray,'" *Dallas Morning News*, 3 June 1924, p. 14. Charles Nordmann claims that Commandant Ferrié of the French wireless service was the one who discovered how Ulivi pulled off his hoax. See Charles Nordmann, "Le rayon de la mort paraît bien mort," *Le Matin*, 7 August 1924, p. 2, Gallica. Yet a newspaper article in July 1914 indicates that Italian police looking for Ulivi after he eloped with Maria found a large quantity of metal sodium in his workshop. See "Claim Chemist in Flight Is a Fakir," *Trenton Evening Times*, 21 July 1914, p. 2 [10], NA.

86. "Invention of an Italian May Put an End to War," *NYT*, 21 June 1914, 5: 2.

87. Late Inventions and Technical News, "Ulivi's Experiments in Exploding Bombs with Infra-Red Rays," *The Labor Digest*, July 1914, 31, GB. The *Richwood Gazette* (Ohio) stated that Ulivi had exploded gunpowder carefully wrapped in waterproof packages and sunk in the Arno. See "More About 'F' Rays," *Richwood Gazette* (Ohio), 18 June 1914, p. 4, NA. This year for the newspaper is no longer available on the website, but the author printed out a copy when it was accessed.

88. "The 'F' Rays," *North China Herald* (Shanghai), 3 October 1914, p. 2 [4], NA.

89. "Rays Explode Sea Mines," *Tamworth Daily Observer* (New South Wales), 1 July 1914, p. 4, Trove.

90. "Rückblicke," *Tages-Post* (Linz), 2 January 1915, p. 1, ANNO.

91. "Die Rätselhaften M-Strahlen," *Illustriertes Österreichisches Journal* (Vienna), 1 August 1914, p. 4, ANNO.

92. Frank Crane, "The World Set Free," *Manitoba Free Press* (Winnipeg), 30 May 1914, Special Section, p. 1 [39], NA.

93. "Italian's Rays May Change Warfare; Explodes Bombs 12 Miles Away," *Washington Post*, 21 June 1914, p. 13.

94. Rudolf Hensingmuller, "New Invisible Perils That Menace the Airmen," *Washington Post*, 19 July 1914, p. 3 [49]. See also Summary of the War News, "The Last Gunpowder War," *Wellsboro Gazette* (Pennsylvania), 10 December 1914, [7], NA. The pages are in disarray, with the one for the article placed between pages 7 and 8, but the number is illegible.

95. H. Jartraux, "Une dangereuse invention," *Le Journal Général de l'Algérie, de la Tunisie et du Maroc* (Algiers), 14 August 1913, p. 1, Gallica.

96. "Blown Up By Wireless," *The Dominion* (Auckland), 3 June 1915, p. 5, Papers Past.

97. "Italy's Terrible Secret," *Raleigh Register* (Beckley, West Virginia), 29 July 1915, [12], NA. Few page numbers are visible.

98. Carried in "Blasts Kaiser's Hope of Victory," *Adams County Union-Republic* (Corning, Iowa), 10 July 1918, p. [8], NA. Page numbers are not visible. This is incorrectly listed under *Adams County Free Press*.

99. "Frightful Arc Ray New Weapon of War," *Indianapolis Sunday Star*, 12 May 1918, Magazine Section, p. 2 [49], NA.

100. José Marva, *The Sciences and War, Memorial de Ingenieros* (Madrid) 15 November 1915, (The inaugural discourse of the 5th Congress of the Spanish Association for the Progress of the Sciences, in Valladolid, 17–22 October 1915), "XI.—Intervention of Science to Diminish the Evils of War," in Cornélis De Witt Willcox, *The International Military Digest Annual: A Review of the Current Literature of Military Science for 1916*. New York: Cumulative Digest Corporation, 1917, GB.

101. B. F. Miessner, *Radiodynamics: The Wireless Control of Torpedoes and Other Mechanisms* (New York: D. Van Nostrand Company, 1916), 194, GB. See also Zimmern, *Italy of the Italians*, 206–07.

102. "Invisible Death Waves for War," *The Daily News* (Perth), 26 September 1916, p. 6, Trove.

103. "Searching for Secrets That May End War," *Malvern Standard* (Malvern, Victoria), 23 June 1917, p. 6, Trove.

104. *The American Library Annual 1914–1915* (New York: R. R. Bowker Co., 1915), 53, GB.

105. "New Searchlight Is Invented," *Logansport Chronicle* (Indiana), 25 November 1916, [3], NA. Page numbers are not present.

106. Charles R. Anderson, *Giulio Ulivi:*

Notes—Chapter 1

The Inventor Who Might Have Ended Wars (ebook, Charles R. Anderson, 2013). The author is indebted to Anderson for valuable suggestions and recommendations regarding details of Ulivi's life and work. He also graciously provided a translation of the Hilzinger and Ulivi reports published in Mario La Stella's *Il Raggio della Morte* (Rome: Istituto per L'Enciclopedia de Carlo, 1942), 65–76.

107. "Ulivi's Marvellous Discovery," *The World's News* (Sydney), 5 November 1921, pp. 12–13, Trove. See also Arthur Bennington, "A World Destroying Ray," *Syracuse Herald*, 18 September 1921, Magazine Section, p. 1 [44], NA.

108. "News in Sunday's Papers," *Indiana Evening Gazette* (Pennsylvania), 21 July 1913, p. 2, NA.

109. "Death Via Wireless Plan of Blackmailer," *Indianapolis Star*, 20 July 1913, p. 7 [39], NA.

110. "Danish Inventor First," *The Western Gazette* (Somerset, England), 31 October 1913, p. 10, BNA. See also "Truth About F-Rays," *Townsville Daily Bulletin* (Queensland), 22 December 1913, p. 5, Trove.

111. "Fires Buried Dynamite," *NYT*, 2 March 1914, p. 1.

112. "New Z-Ray May Put End to Wars," *The Daily Review* (Decatur, Illinois), 1 August 1914, p. 4, NA.

113. "Vision of What May Be Great Cataclysm of Land, Sea, and Sky By Which Destructive Wars as They Are Waged Today May End," *Washington Post*, 23 August 1914, p. 11.

114. "The New French Explosive," *Stratford Sentinel and Briagolong Express* (Stratford, Victoria), 23 October 1914, p. 3, Trove.

115. "Wireless Death Dealer Used by German Armies?," *Beatrice Daily Sun* (Nebraska), 2 September 1915, p. 1, NA.

116. Frank O'Callaghan, "New Ray Destroys Zeppelins," *Popular Mechanics*, May 1917, 679–680.

117. "Deadly Heat Ray Being Developed: Radio Activity May Figure in War," *Oakland Tribune*, 11 June 1917, p. 14, NA.

118. Summary of the War News, "The Last Gunpowder War," *Wellsboro Gazette* (Pennsylvania), 10 December 1914, [7], NA.

119. Donald G. French, "Unlimited Power from the Sun," *Illustrated World*, December 1917, 511–512, Hathi.

120. "The War of the Future," *Warwick Examiner* (St. Lucia, Queensland), 7 September 1914, p. 6, Trove. A similar view was expressed in a newspaper article in August 1915. See "Wars of the Future," *Wodonga and Towong Sentinel* (Victoria), 13 August 1915, p. 6, Trove.

121. "Warfare of the Future: The Radium Destroyer," *The Electrical Experimenter*, November 1915, 315.

122. "Wars of the Future," *The Western Champion* (Barcaldine, Queensland), 21 August 1915, p. 3, Trove.

123. "Edison and Future Wars," *The Western Champion* (Barcaldine, Queensland), 27 November 1915, p. 3, Trove.

124. "Invisible Death Waves for War," *The Daily News* (Perth), 26 September 1916, p. 6, Trove. His novel, *Edison's Conquest of Mars*, is described in Chapter 5.

125. Some are addressed in Chapter 2 because of their association with Harry Grindell Matthews.

126. Ferdinand Tuohy, "World's Next War Will Be Scientific Horror of Unbelievable Slaughter," *Syracuse Herald*, 5 September 1921, p. 2, NA.

127. "Soldier's Bluff," *The Mercury* (Hobart, Tasmania), 31 January 1936, p. 6, Trove.

128. "Corporal's 'Invention,'" *Times*, 14 October 1937, p. 14.

129. Ronald W. Clark, *Tizard* (Cambridge, Massachusetts: The M.I.T. Press, 1965), 62.

130. "The 'Death Ray' Melodrama," *Manchester Guardian*, 30 May 1924, p. 423.

131. Harold T. Wilkins, "War Secrets Revealed," *Popular Mechanics*, June 1927, 982.

132. "Power from the Invisible World," *Popular Mechanics*, June 1933, 891.

133. See "Vagaries of Inventive Minds," *New York Times Current History: The European War*, vol. 17 (New York: New York Times Company, 1919), 145, GB.

134. It should be noted that the same story had appeared one day before in another newspaper but did not list an author although it had to be Maclay. See "Huns Saved by Mercy from Most Deadly Secret of Destruction," *Cedar Rapids Evening Gazette* (Iowa), 19 July 1919, p. 5, NA.

135. Edgar Stanton Maclay, "'Burning-Glasses,' Dundonald's Destroyer?," *The North American Review*, March 1915, 434–438. In his article, Maclay refers to an editorial comment entitled "Dundonald's Destroyer" that appeared in the November 1914 issue of this magazine. Although describing the same general information about a powerful weapon invented by the admiral and the British government's decision not to use it, the editor acknowledges that the nature of the device remains a mystery. He speculates that it could be electrical, mechanical, or chemical; furthermore, he makes no mention of the newspaper articles appearing at the time of the Crimean War which suggested some type of noxious fumes or poisoned air. See "Dundonald's Destroyer," *The North American Review*, November 1914, 656–660.

136. Edgar Stanton Maclay, "Burning Glasses," *NYT*, 20 July 1919, 7:11.

137. Thomas Cochrane, later the Tenth Earl of Dundonald, did ask government leaders in 1812 permission to use a new, powerful weapon against fortresses and ships of the enemy, but it was a primitive form of chemical warfare—not a super ray. The idea was to burn a mixture of sulfur and wood, with the noxious fumes drifting over to the enemy and rendering them incapable of resistance. A committee of five high-ranking officials—the Duke of York (the future King William IV), Lord Keith and Lord Exmouth of the Admiralty, and the two Congreve brothers—admitted its efficacy but decided not to employ it since it appeared to them beyond the bounds of civilized warfare. They then ordered the plans to be kept secret. In the early stages of the First World War, the Twelfth Earl of Dundonald proposed that British authorities, among them First Lord of the Admiralty Winston Churchill, reopen the matter and consider using his grandfather's weapon. He thought it would be effective against German trenches. Although receiving some support, the proposal failed to win over British leaders, many of whom worried about the moral and legal questions regarding the Hague Conventions banning chemical weapons. After the German introduction of poison gas at Ypres in 1915, Dundonald's sulfur fumes appeared obsolete, superseded by newer gases and modes of delivery. See Winston S. Churchill, *The Dardanelles Campaign and the Fall of the Cabinet*, vol. 2 of *The World Crisis* (New York: Charles Scribner's Sons, 1923), 72–75.

138. "Gas in War Old Secret," *Washington Post*, 23 May 1915, 3: 4 [38], NA.

139. "Poisonous Gases," *North China Herald* (Shanghai), 19 June 1915, p. 823 [17], NA.

140. See Imperial Parliament. House of Commons, "Lord Dundonald's Plan for Destroying Fortifications," *Illustrated Times* (London), 14 July 1855, p. 10 [90], NA.

141. "Lord Dundonald's Plan," *The Patriot* (London), 27 August 1855, p. 4 [102], NA.

142 "The Way to Get Blown Up," *Harper's New Monthly Magazine*, January 1856, 208, NA.

143. Sir George Douglas and Sir George Dalhousie, eds., *The Panmure Papers*, vol. 1 (London: Hodder and Stoughton, 1908), 340–342. See also Charles Stephenson's study *The Admiral's Secret Weapon: Lord Dundonald and the Origins of Chemical Warfare* (Woodbridge, UK: The Boydell Press, 2006). Stephenson does not mention the articles by Maclay and others who asserted that Dundonald's weapon was a heat-ray device.

144. Mary Boyle O'Reilly, "Dundonald Plan to Give Victory at a Single Blow," *Laurel Leader* (Mississippi), 12 June 1916, p. 2, NA. The former prison commissioner of Massachusetts, O'Reilly slipped into Belgium disguised as a peasant to report on the war but was taken prisoner by the Germans along with several other journalists, including Will Irwin. After their release, she later returned to Belgium to continue her reporting activities. She was also in London when the first zeppelin raids occurred.

145. "Will England, If Beaten to Her Knees, Unseal Dundonald's 'Inhuman Destroyer' To Wipe Teuton Millions from Earth?," *Muskogee Times Democrat* (Oklahoma), 15 December 1912, p. 1, NA. This particular day's issue is now missing from the website.

146. Edgar Stanton Maclay, "Most Frightful of War's Devices Suppressed by British Admiralty," *Manitoba Free Press* (Winnipeg), 27 September 1919, p. 18 [48], NA.

147. The Odd Measure, "Did the British Admiralty Decline to Use Burning-Glasses?" and "Lord Cochrane's 'Horrible' War Device," *Munsey's Magazine*, October 1919, 126. Internet Archive.
148. "Playing With Fire," *San Antonio Express*, 28 May 1924, p. 8, NA.

Chapter 2

1. "Science Will Win Next War," *The Agitator* (Wellsboro, Pennsylvania), 4 August 1920, p. 6, NA.
2. "Death Rays in the Air," *La Crosse Tribune and Leader-Press* (Wisconsin), 29 March 1935, p. 3, NA.
3. Cuthbert Hicks, "A World Ruled From the Air," *NYT*, 3 October 1920, 3: 7.
4. "Science Will Win Next War," *The Agitator* (Wellsboro, Pennsylvania), 4 August 1920, p. 6, NA.
5. Will Irwin, *The "Next War": An Appeal to Common Sense* (New York: E. P. Dutton, 1921), 49.
6. Joseph K. Hart, "The Next War," *The Survey*, 21 May 1921, 234; "Aerial Navies and Armies of Chemists," *The Literary Digest*, 12 November 1921, 28; Ibid., "'Viper' Weapons," 24 December, 9; and Victor LeFebure, *The Riddle of the Rhine: Chemical Strategy in Peace and War* (London: W. Collins Sons and Company, Limited, 1921), 230.
7. "Civilization Must Abolish War or War Will Destroy Civilization," *Popular Science Monthly*, December 1921, 27.
8. Wythe Williams, "Next War to be Electric, Says French Officer," from the *Public Ledger* (Philadelphia) in *The Daily Gleaner*, Kingston (Jamaica), 25 January 1924, p. 15 [39], NA.
9. Eugène Debeney, "The War of Tomorrow," *NYT*, 25 September 1921, 7: 1.
10. General Bernard Serrigny, "L'organisation de la nation pour le temps de guerre," *Revue des Deux Mondes*, 1 December 1923, 591, Gallica.
11. "Making Weapons Innocuous," *The Sunday Times* (Perth), 13 November 1921, p. 3, Trove.
12. "Horrors of Next War," *Joplin Globe*, 2 June 1922, p. 7, NA.
13. A. M. Low, "How We Shall Fight in A. D. 2023," *The Nineteenth Century and After*, September 1923, 357.

14. "New War Horror," *The Argus* (Melbourne), 30 August 1923, p. 9, and "New War Horror," 31 August 1923, p. 9, Trove.
15. "May Use Lightning in Our Future Wars," *NYT*, 7 October 1923, Sec. 1, Pt 2: 5. The *Ogden Standard-Examiner* added that Ryan believed 3,000,000 volts would be sufficient to throw a bolt of electrical energy to a distance of eighteen miles. "To Make the Next War More Horrible Than the Last," *Ogden Standard-Examiner*, 16 December 1923, Sunday Feature Section, p. 2 [18], NA. See also "Lightning as a Weapon," *Popular Science Monthly*, January 1924, 61.
16. "War Engines of Future to Be Electric," *Popular Mechanics*, November 1923, 757.
17. "To Make the Next War More Horrible Than the Last," *Ogden Standard-Examiner*, 16 December 1923, Sunday Feature Section, p. 2 [18], NA.
18. "The Next War: Electric Aeroplanes," *The Daily Herald* (Adelaide), 30 December 1921, p. 6, Trove.
19. Carl D. Groat, "German Science Seeks the ?-Ray," *Stevens Point Daily Journal* (Wisconsin), 30 June 1922, p. 4, NA.
20. "Un avion commercial français ayant atterri en Bavière est saisi par les Allemands," *Le Matin*, 20 May 1923, p. 1, Gallica. The story in the *New York Times* said that the pilot was arrested. See "Seize French Plane Landing in Germany," 20 May 1923, p. 17.
21. "Death-Dealing Ray," *Queensland Times* (Ipswich), 25 June 1923, p. 5, Trove.
22. While attending the Genoa Conference in 1922, in which more than thirty countries sent representatives to discuss economic issues, German and Russian delegates quietly met during a recess in nearby Rapallo and on 16 April suddenly announced an agreement between their respective nations. By the terms of the treaty, the two countries renounced all territorial and financial claims left over from the war and agreed to establish normal diplomatic relations and economic ties. From the beginning, however, many observers believed that the rapprochement between the two "pariahs" signaled a military alliance, a combination that boded ill for the future. Within days, stories began to appear in the press about secret military collaboration, followed

later by rumors of German companies setting up plants in Russia to manufacture weapons, including aircraft and poison gas. The British and French governments, however, did not seem to take these reports seriously. When the issue came up in the House of Commons on 30 May 1922, for example, Prime Minister Lloyd George indicated that the British government was looking into the allegations but so far no proof of such an agreement had been found. See Parliament, House of Commons, "Russo-German Military Pact," *Times*, 30 May 1922, p. 19.

23. Cyril Brown, "Wireless Wrecking of Airplane A Myth," *NYT*, 3 July 1923, p. 4.

24. Charles Nordmann, "Est-il possible d'arrêter les moteurs à distance?," *Le Matin*, 6 August 1923, p. 1, Gallica.

25. E. Nicolet, "L'arrête à distance des moteurs d'avions," *L'Écho de Paris*, 5 December 1923, p. 4, Gallica.

26. F. Honoré, "L'arrêt des avions par ondes hertziennes," *L'Illustration*, 29 December 1923, 689. Much later, in April 1924, *Le Matin* quoted a Commandant Mesny as saying that none of the aircraft had experienced any problems with the magnetos. "À qui la paternité du rayon diabolique?," *Le Matin*, 18 April 1924, p. 2, Gallica.

27. "The Invisible Ray," *Dundee Courier* (Scotland), 12 September 1923, p. 4, BNA.

28. "War Without Armies or Ships," *The Advertiser* (Adelaide), 20 October 1923, p. 15, Trove.

29. "The Mystery Ray That Is Wrecking Airplanes," *Mansfield News* (Ohio), 28 November 1923, p. 17 [6], NA. The same article also mentioned Ulivi, now crediting him with having increased the capabilities of his ray device.

30. "Invention Stops Motors at Will From Afar, Says a Paris Editor Who Saw the Tests," *NYT*, 22 November 1923, p. 1.

31. "Hope to Halt Airplanes by Wireless Device," *NYT*, 23 November 1923, p. 19. See also "Wireless Waves in War," *Moberly Weekly Monitor* (Moberly, Missouri), 13 December 1923, p. 2, NA, as well as "Can Aero Engines Be Stopt By A Mysterious Ray?," *Literary Digest*, February 1924, 67. In his 1932 book *Guerre qui revient fraîche et gazeuse!*, Victor Méric mentioned a naval officer named Ullmo experimenting with invisible rays at Toulon in 1923. The French government supposedly kept this secret, but the British government's lack of interest in Grindell Matthews's ray suggested that it already had something superior. See Victor Méric, *Guerre qui revient fraîche et gazeuse!* (Paris: Éditions Sirius, 1932), 48–49, Gallica.

32. "A War Invention," *The Register* (Sandusky, Ohio), 6 December 1923, p. 4, NA.

33. "To Make the Next War More Horrible Than the Last," *Ogden Standard-Examiner*, 16 December 1923, Sunday Feature Section, p. 2 [18], NA.

34. "Secret Ray to Stop Planes Is Seen in Accidents," *Popular Mechanics*, December 1923, 931.

35. "Radio Wave Halts Autos," *The Gazette* (Sumner, Iowa), 20 December 1923, p. 11, NA. See also Samuel J. McCoy, "Diabolic Ray Makes Scientists Wonder," *NYT*, 1 June 1924, 8: 3.

36. "Radio Wave Halts Autos," *Woodland Daily Democrat* (California), 9 May 1924, p. 8 [15], NA.

37. "Ray to Disable Planes," *The Advertiser* (Adelaide), 23 November 1923, p. 10, Trove. This article was written about the French airplanes over Bavaria, but the author used the incident at Nauen to support the idea of the Germans having such a ray that could interfere with the magnetos of engines.

38. "The Mystery Ray That Is Wrecking Airplanes," *Mansfield News* (Ohio), 28 November 1923, p. 17 [6], NA.

39. Ibid.

40. "Can Aero Engines Be Stopt By A Mysterious Ray?," *Literary Digest*, 23 February 1924, 69–70.

41. Ibid., 70. In 1927 the writer of a newspaper article suggested that the cause of the forced landings was none other than the radio sending station at Nauen. See "Germany's New War Secret," *New Castle News* (Pennsylvania), 5 August 1927, p. 4 [8], NA. Years later, an article in the *Lowell Sun* (Massachusetts) in 1943, however, stated that the answer was a French engineer's attempt to try out an adjustment to the airplane motors made at the plant. He then sent all of these modified engines to the French airline that flew the Bavarian route in order to test the changes. According to the paper, his failed experiment thus proved to be the mechanical cause. See

"Major Al Williams," *Lowell Sun*, 2 November 1943, p. 14, NA. The article mentioned only the one airline route over Bavaria and said nothing about the other one.

42. Court Circular, *Times*, 5 July 1912, p. 11. Grindell Matthews also demonstrated his wireless telephone in August for David Lloyd George, then Chancellor of the Exchequer, and J. E. B. Seely, then Secretary of State for War. See From the World's Press, "Wireless Telephone," *The West Australian* (Perth), 24 August 1912, p. 12, Trove.

43. Edmund Edward Fournier D'Albe was a scientist who dabbled in numerous fields of study, including spiritualism. One of his inventions was the optophone, which converted sound into light. He later broke with Grindell Matthews and became a critic of the death ray.

44. Balfour had replaced Churchill as First Lord in May 1915 as a result of a shakeup in the Asquith cabinet due in part to the setbacks in the ongoing Dardenelles Campaign against the Turks. He would later serve as Britain's Foreign Secretary and sponsor the famous 1917 declaration bearing his name that called for the creation of a Jewish homeland in Palestine.

45. E. E. Fournier D'Albe, *The Moon-Element: An Introduction to the Wonders of Selenium* (New York: D. Appleton and Company, 1924), 68–73, Hathi. See also "Young Inventor's Great Secret Revealed," *Evening Telegraph and Post* (Dundee), 2 April 1924, p. 1, BNA. One puzzling aspect to this story remains. D'Albe stated there was no reported use during the war of a selenium type mine device as described above. Yet in September 1916 an article entitled "Light Rays New Aid in Warfare" appeared in newspapers detailing an invention of a Mr. Grindell Matthews which was called the "light-o-mine" and being used in combat by British, French, and Russian soldiers. According to the article, he had developed a device measuring a yard in length with a lens at one end and containing on the inside a dry battery and other components. At the other end were wires for connections to trench bombs. These were fashioned by placing TNT and shrapnel inside long sections of iron pipes. The paper described a typical operation. Attacking troops would capture a forward position, kill all the enemy soldiers, place the bombs throughout the trench, and connect them to the wires of the light-o-mine, leaving only the lens at a slight angle sticking out from the dirt. The attackers would then leave and allow the Germans to reoccupy the trench. Later, a star shell would be fired and its intensely bright light would, upon striking the lens, detonate the bombs. The article added that this was about the only feasible way to set off the explosion, for a wireless device posed problems: it would require aerials visible to the enemy and therefore give away the plan, and constant radio traffic enveloping the battlefield would likely jam the signals. See "Light Rays New Aid in Warfare," *Monticello Express* (Iowa), 28 September 1916, p. 9, NA.

46. The idea of wireless transmission of electricity was, of course, based on Tesla's work and continued to be a topic of discussion. In a March 1920 article in the magazine *Electrical Experimenter*, Thomas Benson discussed the possibility of transmitting radio energy waves along paths of conductivity created by ionizing air with ultraviolet light. See Thomas Benson, "Wireless Transmission of Power Now Possible," 1118–1119.

47. "The Electric Ray and War," *Times*, 16 April 1924, p. 12.

48. "Invisible Death," *Time*, 21 April 1924, 19. See also "The Ray That Stops Motors," *Manchester Guardian*, 11 April 1924, p. 287.

49. "L'invisible 'Rayon Thermique' détruit la vie à de grandes distances," *Mercure Africain* (Algiers), 30 April 1924, pp. 579, 581, Gallica. See also "War Impossible," *Brisbane Courier*, 17 April 1924, p. 7, Trove. Jonathan Foster in his biography of Grindell Matthews says the inventor never claimed that his device could kill people, but many newspapers in addition to the *Brisbane Courier* quoted Grindell Matthews as stating that it could. See Jonathan Foster, *The Death Ray: The Secret Life of Harry Grindell Matthews* (Gloucester, UK: Inventive Publishing, 2009), 140.

50. Martin Gilbert, *The Prophet of Truth: 1922–1939*, vol. 5 of *Winston S. Churchill* (Boston: Houghton Mifflin Company, 1977), 50.

51. For more on this, see International Relations Section, Winston S. Churchill,

"Shall We Commit Suicide?," *The Nation*, 3 December 1924, 608, 610. For review and commentary, see Leading Articles of the Month, "Shall We Commit Suicide?" in *The American Review of Reviews*, November 1924, 537–538.

52. "Eine angebliche englische Erfindung zur Verhinderung von Luftangriffen," *Neue Freie Presse* (Vienna), 10 April 1924, pp. 8–9. See also Captain Emo Tescovich, "Eine neue Strahlenart?," *Neue Freie Presse*, 10 April 1924, p. 9, ANNO.

53. From the *Daily News* (London], "On nous écrit de Paris...," *L'Intransigeant*, 21 May 1924, p. 1, Gallica.

54. "M. Grindell Matthews l'inventeur du 'rayon ardent' est à Paris," *Le Matin*, 20 May 1924, p. 1, Gallica.

55. "Tells Death Power of 'Diabolical Rays,'" *NYT*, 21 May 1924, p. 1. See also Paul Roche, "Les rayons diaboliques," *Le Gaulois*, 25 May 1924, p. 1, Gallica, and "Frankreich kauft die 'Teufelsstrahlen,'" *Prager Tagblatt* (Prague), 28 May 1924, p. 4, ANNO.

56. "Tells Death Power of 'Diabolical Rays,'" *NYT*, 21 May 1924, p. 1. See also "Claims Ray Will Wreck Planes," *Dallas Morning News*, 25 May 1924, p. 10.

57. "Tells Death Power of 'Diabolical Rays,'" *NYT*, 21 May 1924, p. 1.

58. "The Death Ray," *Times*, 23 May 1924, p. 9. A humorous question put forward by a Mr. Greene drew laughter: "Does the hon. gentleman admit that this invention would, in all probability, be more effectual in repelling hostile aircraft than babbling beatitudes and high moral gestures?," Ibid.

59. "The 'Death Ray,'" *Times*, 28 May 1924, p. 14.

60. "'Death Ray' Test To-Morrow," *Sunday Times*, 25 May 1924, p. 13. See also "The 'Death Ray,'" *Times*, 26 May 1924, p. 16.

61. "The Death Ray," *Times*, 28 May 1924, p. 14.

62. "'Death Ray,' Expert Stands in the Way Deliberately," *Aberdeen Press and Journal*, 6 June 1924, p. 7, BNA. See also "The 'Death Ray,'" *Times*, 6 June 1924, p. 11. An American army pilot named Walter Sutter volunteered to fly a plane and test Grindell Matthews's ray, an offer the inventor declined. See "A Death Ray Challenge," *Dundee Courier*, 31 May 1924, p. 4, BNA.

63. "The 'Death Ray,'" *Manchester Guardian*, 30 May 1924, p. 425.

64. "Las des tergiversations des 'officiels' anglais M. Matthews va reprendre ses expériences en France," *Le Matin*, 27 May 1924, p. 3, Gallica.

65. "The Death Ray," *Times*, 28 May 1924, p. 14.

66. "Death Ray Surprise," *Aberdeen Press and Journal*, 28 May 1924, p. 7, BNA.

67. "Second British Inventor Reveals a Death Ray; Patents Device to Send It in Any Direction," *NYT*, 25 May 1924, p. 1. See also "England," *The Independent*, 7 June 1924, 323.

68. "The 'Death Ray,'" *Times*, 29 May 1924, p. 8. A newspaper article in July, however, suggested that the Air Ministry was indeed developing a ray to destroy aircraft, in particular, airships. As reported in *The Morning Bulletin* of Rockhampton, Australia, a group of naval personnel was on its way to Sydney on a secret mission in connection with experiments with a death ray, authorized by British Air Minister Lord Thomson. See "Interstate News," 25 July 1924, p. 8, Trove.

69. "The Versatile Ray. From Mechanics to Medicine, Lord Birkenhead's Comments," *Times*, 28 May 1924, p. 15. Suzanne Lenglen of France was the dominant women's tennis player at the time, winning Wimbledon and other major tournaments on numerous occasions.

70. "The 'Death Ray.' Sir Richard Gregory's Criticism," *Times*, 29 May 1924, p. 13.

71. "Doubts 'Diabolical Rays,'" *NYT*, 22 May 1924, p. 3. "For Test of Death Ray," *NYT*, 7 August 1924, p. 5.

72. Simon Arbellot, "Le Rayon porte-foudre de M. Grindell Matthews," *Le Figaro*, 9 April 1924, p. 1, Gallica.

73. Georges Urbain, La vie scientifique. "Considérations sur le Verre et l'État Vitreux; Le 'Rayon Invisible' de M. Grindell Matthews," *Les Annales politiques et littéraires*, 20 April 1924, 458, Gallica.

74. Edwin L. James, "Matthews Shuns 'Death Ray' Tests," *NYT*, 29 May 1924, p. 5.

75. F. Honoré, "Le rayon invisible et son inventeur," *L'Illustration*, 24 May 1924, 512.

76. E. E. Fournier D'Albe, "The Myth of the Death Ray," *The New Republic*, 16 July 1924, 208.

77. Science, "Invisible Death," *Time*, 21 April 1924, 19.
78. "An Answer to the Attacking Airplane," *The Outlook*, 30 April 1924, 720.
79. Kapitän Emo Tescovich, "Eine neue Strahlenart?," *Neue Freie Presse* (Vienna), 10 April 1924, p. 9, ANNO.
80. "A Violet Ray That Kills," *Current Opinion*, June 1924, 829.
81. "'Death Ray' Is Carried by Shafts of Light," *Popular Mechanics*, August 1924, 189–192.
82. Frederic Mortimer Delano, "Man's Most Terrible Invention," *Popular Science Monthly*, August 1924, 33–34.
83. Samuel J. McCoy, "Diabolic Ray Makes Scientists Wonder," *NYT*, 1 June 1924, 8: 3. See also "Thunderbolts Made to Order," *Current Opinion*, August 1923, 169.
84. McCoy, "Diabolic Ray...," *NYT*, 1 June 1924, 8.
85. "The 'Death Ray' Tests," *Times*, 3 June 1924, p. 11.
86. "No U.S. Navy Department Offer," *NYT*, 29 May 1924, p. 5. See also "Deny U.S. Negotiates 'Death Ray' Purchase," *Dallas Morning News*, 30 May 1924, p. 1.
87. Frank F. Mason, "America Far Ahead with Death Ray Experiments," *The Coshocton Tribune* (Ohio), 28 May 1924, p. 12, NA. This is located erroneously on the website as 29 May 1924, p. 2.
88. "Les États-Unis et l'Allemagne font des offres à M. Grindell Matthews," *Le Matin*, 2 June 1924, p. 3, Gallica.
89. "Says His 'Death Ray' Could Stun Armies," *NYT*, 20 July 1924, p. 1.
90. "Russian Inventor Tells of Death Ray Fatal at 25 Miles," *Daily Kennebec Journal* (Augusta, Maine), 8 February 1926, p. 1, NA.
91. "The 'Death Ray,'" *Times*, 20 September 1924, p. 10.
92. "'Death Ray' Shown Vividly in a Movie," *NYT*, 3 November 1924, p. 21. See also "Pictures Based on Researches in Death Ray," *Oakland Tribune*, 7 December 1924, W: 1 [29], NA. Since Grindell Matthews said that his was an invisible ray, a "visible" beam had to be generated for the film. See "Le rayon mortel," *Les Spectacles*, 20 June 1924, 16, Gallica.
93. "He's Stealing Jove's Thunderbolts," *Iowa City Press-Citizen*, 8 November 1924, p. 1, NA.

94. "Will 'Death Rays' Destroy Armies and Make Aircraft Useless," *San Antonio Express*, 16 November 1924, p. 20, NA.
95. "Says He Sold 'Death Ray,'" *NYT*, 2 March 1925, p. 4.
96. It has been suggested that this was the inspiration for the "Bat Signal" created for the fictional character "Batman."
97. From the *Chicago Tribune*, quoted in the *NYT*, 25 May 1924, p. 1. See also Frederic Mortimer Delano, "Man's Most Terrible Invention," *Popular Science Monthly*, August 1924, 33.
98. "Death Rays a New Terror," *Sioux City Sunday Journal*, 25 May 1924, p. 1, NA. This is found under the heading of the *Sioux City Journal* on the website.
99. "Suggests Russia Has a 'Ray,'" *NYT*, 28 May 1924, p. 25.
100. "Les armaments et l'industrie lourde en U. R. S. S.," *Le Temps*, 21 November 1932, p. 4, Gallica.
101. "An Epidemic of Death Rays," *The Advertiser* (Adelaide), 30 August 1924, p. 21, Trove.
102. "A Death Ray Challenge," *The Dundee Courier* (Dundee, Scotland), 31 May 1924, p. 4, BNA.
103. See "'Death Ray' Test To-Morrow," *Sunday Times*, 25 May 1924, p. 13; "Second British Inventor Reveals a Death Ray; Patents Device to Send It in Any Direction," *NYT*, 25 May 1924, p. 1; "The 'Death Ray,'" *Times*, 26 May 1924, p. 16; and "The 'Death Ray,'" *Manchester Guardian*, 30 May 1924, p. 425.
104. Milton Bronner, "Britain Has New War Terrors," *The Bee* (Danville, Virginia), 1 August 1924, p. 5, NA.
105. "Breaking Up Atom Now Seems Likely," *Olean Evening Times* (New York), 27 October 1924, p. 5, NA. See also "Shattering the Atom," *The Literary Digest*, 31 January 1925, 23.
106. "Death-Dealing and Labor-Saving Rays," *Scientific Monthly*, January 1925, 109.
107. "More Death Ray Inventors," *Dundee Courier*, 2 June 1924, p. 5, BNA.
108. "Another Invisible Ray," *Western Daily Press* (Bristol), 5 June 1924, p. 12, BNA.
109. "Tries to Sell Us A Deadly War Ray," *NYT*, 29 May 1924, p. 5. See also "Les inventeurs de rayons diaboliques surgissent de toutes parts," *Le Matin*, 30 May 1924, p. 3, Gallica.

110. "'Heat Ray' to Melt Battleship," *Evening Telegraph and Post* (Dundee), 29 July 1924, p. 1, BNA.
111. Things Scientific, "Sh! That Mysterious Ray of Light," *The Pathfinder*, 3 May 1924, 12. See also "A New Death-Dealing Ray," *Literary Digest*, 7 June 1924, 27–28.
112. "The Death Ray," *Northern Times* (Carnarvon, Western Australia), 4 July 1924, p. 6, Trove.
113. "À qui la paternité du rayon diabolique?," *Le Matin*, 18 April 1924, pp. 1–2, Gallica.
114. "Le rayon ardent," *Le Phare de Majunga* (Tananarive), 9 August 1924, p. 2, Gallica.
115. "M. Charbonneau, père du rayon rouge explique le 'rayon diabolique,'" *Le Matin*, 15 April 1924, p. 1, Gallica.
116. "Un autre ingénieur anglais revendique la paternité du 'rayon ardent,'" *Le Matin*, 1 June 1924, p. 3, Gallica.
117. "The Ray of Death," *Nottingham Evening Post*, 16 April 1924, p. 1, BNA.
118. W. R. Bennett, "War and the Inventor," from *Reynolds's*, in the *Sunday Times* (Perth), 26 December 1915, p. 12, Trove. See also "War Impossible," *Brisbane Courier*, 17 April 1924, p. 7, Trove.

Chapter 3

1. "Radio Death Ray to Abolish Wars," *Nevada State Journal* (Reno), 14 November 1926, p. 6 [11], NA.
2. "Hears German Device Prevents Air Attacks," *NYT*, 30 November 1928, p. 2.
3. "Un nouveau 'rayon de la mort' est découvert," *L'Action française*, 4 March 1929, p. 2, Gallica. See also "La renaissance industrielle à Damas," *Les Échos* (Damascus), 31 March 1931, p. 1, Gallica.
4. "Destructive-Ray Machine Invented on Coast Is Claim," *Charleston Daily Mail* (West Virginia), 24 April 1929, p. 1, NA. On the same page, the newspaper added the contradiction that a J. B. Martin was the inventor, confusing this with the company president, John T. Martin.
5. "Tells of a 'Death Ray,'" *NYT*, 24 April 1929, p. 34. The *NYT* also confused the name of the inventor with that of the company president.
6. "New Death Ray Device," *Lowell Sun* (Massachusetts), 24 April 1929, p. 13 [35], NA.
7. "To End War," *The World's News* (Sydney), 14 August 1929, p. 7, Trove.
8. "Local Man Invents Death Ray Which He Says Will Extinguish Lives of an Army of One Million Soldiers," *Charleroi Mail* (Pennsylvania), 28 September 1929, p. 1, NA.
9. "The Death Ray," *Burra Record* (South Australia), 13 November 1929, p. 2, Trove.
10. "Death Ray: To Foil Burglars," *Auckland Star*, 3 May 1930, p. 3, Papers Past.
11. "A Mystery Ray," *Horsham Times* (Victoria), 10 June 1930, p. 9, Trove.
12. "Amazing Death Ray Experiment," *The Evening Telegraph* (Angus, Scotland), 27 July 1932, p. 10, BNA.
13. "Trails 'Life or Death' Ray," *Dallas Morning News*, 7 July 1935, p. 15.
14. "Irish Death Ray Claim," *Nottingham Evening Post*, 28 December 1935, p. 3, BNA.
15. "Encore un rayon de la mort," *La Tribune de Madagascar et Dépendances* (Tananarive) 10 November 1938, p. 2, Gallica. See also "Death Ray: Small Animals Killed," *Auckland Star*, 29 October 1938, p. 18, Papers Past.
16. Untitled, *Ogden Standard-Examiner*, 20 May 1936, p. 2, NA. This could be related to the "Hungarian Suicide Song" phenomenon that appeared in Europe and elsewhere in the mid–1930s. In Vienna in 1933, Lazlo Javor wrote a song called "Gloomy Sunday," which depicts suicide after his girlfriend leaves him. After a rash of suicides in several countries, radio stations refused to play it. When the count reached eighteen in Austria, the government officially banned it. For an example of the song's impact, see "Eleven Persons Will Commit Suicide Here!," *Lancaster Eagle-Gazette* (Ohio), 10 April 1936, p. 5, NA. And along these lines, a strange story appeared in an Australian newspaper about a certain Margaret Ramsey, described as a recluse, who was found dead in her home. Known for her eccentricities, neighbors told investigators she was terrified of the "secret ray." See "Hoards of Hermits," *Singleton Argus* (Singleton, New South Wales), 6 June 1930, p. 9, Trove.
17. "Death-Ray Search Causes Boy's

Notes—Chapter 3

Breakdown," *The Daily News* (Perth), 1 August 1936, p. 2, Trove. (The discrepancy in dates between this note and the next one is due to the *Daily News* carrying the earlier story while the *Canberra Times* already had the newest version.)
18. "Mystery Ray," *Canberra Times*, 29 July 1936, p. 3, Trove.
19. Jeff Davis, Around the Plaza, *San Antonio Light*, 11 April 1939, B:1 [11], NA.
20. "New Death Ray, Work of German, Said to Be Most Destructive," *Dallas Morning News*, 10 May 1925, p. 1.
21. Les Échos, *Le Gaulois*, 11 May 1925, p. 1, Gallica.
22. "Mystery-Ray Makes Planes Red Hot," *The Examiner* (Launceston, Tasmania), 30 June 1925, p. 7, Trove.
23. Truman Stevens, "Manless Monsters to Decide Future War," *Popular Science Monthly*, August 1925, 24.
24. "War-Mad Scientists," *Nottingham Evening Post*, 1 April 1926, p. 6, BNA.
25. "Five Minutes' War," *The Evening Post* (Wellington), 6 July 1926, p. 8, Papers Past.
26. "Russian Magic," *Bradford Era* (Pennsylvania), 11 February 1926, p. 4, NA.
27. "A Mysterious Ray," *Brisbane Courier*, 6 March 1929, p. 14, Trove.
28. "Death Ray 'Inventor,' Story of Plan Against Jews of Berlin," *The Western Morning News and Mercury* (Plymouth and Exeter), 5 July 1929, p. 9, BNA.
29. JTA, "Wie Berlin 'judenrein' gemacht werden sollte," *La Tribune Juive* (Strasbourg), 12 July 1929, p. 432, Gallica. See also "'Death Ray' Frauds," *Nottingham Evening Post*, 6 July 1929, p. 6, BNA.
30. "'Anti-War' Ray Reported," *NYT*, 29 November 1931, p. 31.
31. "'Anti-War Rays' Shine," *The Pathfinder*, 26 December 1931, 14.
32. "Another Death Ray," *Middleton Times Herald* (New York), 19 October 1934, p. 4, NA.
33. "Cobden Engineer's Discovery," *Camperdown Chronicle* (Victoria), 23 November 1935, p. 2; and "Melbourne Man's 'Heat Ray,'" *The Mail* (Adelaide), 29 February 1936, p. 13, Trove.
34. Entre les lignes, "Rayons mortels," *Le Madécasse* (Tananarive), 18 September 1936, p. 3, Gallica. Although Italian troops marched into Addis Ababa in May 1936, effectively ending the war, the regent appointed by Haile Selassie did not surrender until December.
35. See "Mystery Solved," *New Zealand Herald* (Auckland), 20 March 1936, p. 10, Papers Past; "Secret Ray to Stop 'Planes," *Courier-Mail* (Brisbane), 20 March 1936, p. 15; and "Invisible Ray," *Northern Star* (Lismore, New South Wales), 21 March 1936, p. 9, Trove. A radio program in 2009 added some other details to the Penny story, including the claim that documents pertaining to it are still classified and that the British War Ministry was involved in some capacity—the particulars of which are also still classified. The program included interviews with some of the family members who provided interesting and amusing anecdotes. See "Sounds Historical Hour One–30 August 2009, Radio New Zealand National, www.radionz.co.nz/national/programmes/soundshistorical/audio/2050197/sounds-historical-hour-one-30-august-2009. Accessed 11 June 2014. The Penny section begins at 21:10.
36. "Boy Invents New Warfare Ray," *Morning Bulletin* (Rockhampton, Queensland), 15 July 1938, p. 6, Trove.
37. "Death Ray Brought Down Franco 'Planes," *The Northern Star* (Lismore, New South Wales), 6 December 1937, p. 11, Trove.
38. "Why Woman Ended Friendship," *Western Daily Press and Bristol Mirror* (Bristol, England), 10 November 1937, p. 11, BNA.
39. Ici, Là et Ailleurs, *Journal des Mutilés et Combattants*, 14 November 1937, p. 2, Gallica.
40. "A Storm Raised over Dover," *Dover Express and East Kent News* (Kent), 16 December 1938, p. 13, BNA. David Zimmerman says that a newspaper article about Coxhead's "heat ray" had appeared in 1933 and that the Englishman had met with officers of the Royal Engineers to discuss his invention but failed to satisfy their requirements for proof. Unfortunately, the document file from British records used by Zimmerman does not provide the name of the newspaper, and searches in several digitized collections, including British Newspaper Archive, did not produce anything other than the article of 1938. See Zimmerman, *Britain's Shield: Radar and the Defeat of the Luftwaffe* (The

Hill, Stroud, Gloucestershire, United Kingdom: Amberley Publishing, 2001, electronic edition 2012).

41. "Quartz 'Death Ray' May Revolutionize Methods of Warfare," *San Antonio Light*, 11 May 1927, p. 7, NA.

42. "Electro-Tank Shoots Lightning Rays," *Modern Mechanix and Inventions*, August 1935, 81.

43. John Bakeless, "The Weapons of the Next War," *The Reader's Digest*, April 1926, 814.

44. F. Canonge, "L'art de la guerre, Époque contemporain," Livre II, *Revue militaire française* 24 (April-June 1927): 46, Gallica.

45. "Sultan's Skull Riddle," *Kalgoorlie Miner* (Western Australia), 30 January 1931, p. 1, Trove.

46. Jay Earle Miller, "New Weapons for the Next War," *Modern Mechanix and Inventions*, November 1931, 47, http://blog.modernmechanix.com/?s=new+weapons+for.

47. "Valley's Boom in Case of War Seen," *Charleston Daily Mail* (West Virginia), 19 April 1932, p. 13, NA.

48. "X-Ray May Wreck Planes," *NYT*, 30 January 1933, p. 15.

49. "The Latest Menace," *The Worker* (Brisbane), 26 February 1935, p. 22, Trove.

50. "Death by Wireless," *Riverine Herald* (Echuca, Victoria, Moama, New South Wales), 31 January 1935, p. 1, Trove.

51. Howard Berry, "'Death Ray' Fatal, Sans Pain, at Thirty Yards," *Indiana Evening Gazette* (Indiana, Pennsylvania), 7 March 1935, p. 1, NA.

52. "Practical Perfection of Death Rays Denied," *Blytheville Courier News* (Arkansas), 28 November 1936, p. 4, NA.

53. Charles Reber, "Montagnes blindées," *L'Intransigeant*, 25 September 1936, p. 5, Gallica. The story was also carried in *The Western Morning News and Daily Gazette* (Devon, England). See "Rays to Stop 'Planes?," 25 September 1936, p. 7, BNA. In reply to a request for information about Guber de Saentis and his experiments, a spokesperson for the Swiss Defense Ministry stated that no one by that name is listed in its records for that time period. Anna Weitert, Forschungsdienst, Sekretariat BiG, email to author, 2 April 2014.

54. "Dicing with Death; Attempt to Sell the Death Ray," *Auckland Star*, 17 November 1934, Supplement, p. 4, Papers Past. His book was entitled *Memoirs of a Royal Detective* (London: Hurst and Blackett, Limited, 1936).

55. "Making War More Deadly Than Ever," *Hutchinson News* (Kansas), 11 November 1921, p. 7, NA. The Brethren Historical Library and Archives at Bethany Theological Seminary has Kurtz becoming president of McPherson in 1924. Newspapers from 1921, however, clearly address him as "president." See "Representatives From Kansas Colleges Meet in Student Volunteer Convention," *The Ottawa Campus* (Ottawa, Kansas), 15 February 1921, p. 1, NA.

56. "Death Rays Hit Kiwanians," *Indiana Evening Gazette* (Pennsylvania), 31 August 1937, p. 1, NA.

57. "Mystery of the Death Ray," *The Daily Mail* (Hull, England), 28 September 1935, p. 5, BNA.

58. Hanson Baldwin, "The Terror That Rides the Air," *NYT*, 5 January 1936, 7: 4.

59. "Evil Inventions," *The Chronicle Telegram* (Elyria, Ohio), 17 August 1938, p. 12, NA.

60. "Finds a 'Death Ray' Fatal to Humans," *NYT*, 4 June 1928, p. 1.

61. William Hillman, "Scientist Sees Cities Burned by Death Rays," *The Davenport Democrat and Leader* (Iowa), 28 October 1928, p. 26, NA.

62. "Tests of Death Ray Aim at Saving Lives," *NYT*, Sunday, 2 February 1936, 2: 2.

63. Ibid. For more on the machine, an eighty-five ton cyclotron, see "Neutrons, Tool of Physics, Deadly Biological Menace," *Science News Letter*, 14 March 1936, 163.

64. "The 'Death Ray' and the Next War," *San Antonio Light*, 15 December 1935, p. 14 [92] NA.

65. Watson Davis, "Cathode Ray a New Tool of Science," *Current History*, December 1926, 392–393; Watson Davis, "Momentous Discovery in the Science of Radiation," *Current History*, January 1926, 553–554; and "New Ray Makes Cold Stones Glow," *Popular Mechanics*, January 1927, 1–2.

66. "May Be Daddy of Death Ray," *Waterloo Evening Courier*, 23 October 1926, p. 1, NA.

Notes—Chapter 3

67. "Killing by Radio," *The Advertiser* (Adelaide), 27 February 1929, p. 15, Trove.
68. "Death Ray," *Canberra Times*, 14 May 1929, p. 4, Trove.
69. Frank Thone, "A New Magic," *Century Magazine*, February 1927, 451. Loomis later became involved with the American radar program in collaboration with the British.
70. "High-Frequency Sound Waves Destroy Life," *Popular Mechanics*, February 1927, 241.
71. "Sound That Will Set Fire to Wood," *NYT*, 25 March 1928, 10: 2. See also Waldemar Kaempffert, "Year's Review of the Sciences Reveals Much New Knowledge," *NYT*, 3 January 1932, 9: 5.
72. "Radio Death Force," *Science News Letter*, 8 January 1927, 17.
73. "Perfecting a New Death Ray," *Dallas Morning News*, 7 March 1927, p. 6.
74. "Can Inaudible Sounds Kill?," *Popular Mechanics*, May 1927, 705.
75. "Kills Animals with Noises," *Science News Letter*, 5 May 1926, 9. One newspaper labeled it the "voice of death." See "Death Dealing Sound Waves Harnessed by Scientists," *Port Arthur News* (Texas), 6 May 1927, p. 19, NA.
76. "What's New?," *The Chillicothe Daily Tribune* (Missouri), 22 November 1927, p. 3, NA.
77. H. A. Y., "The Silent Noise," *Auckland Star*, 12 January 1929, p. 8, Papers Past.
78. "Death Rays from Silent Sounds," *Modern Mechanix and Inventions*, May 1932, 67, http://blog.modernmechanix.com/death-rays-from-silent-sounds/.
79. Cuthbert Hicks, "A World Ruled From the Air," *NYT*, 3 October 1920, 3: 7.
80. "Claims to Know Secret of Death Ray," *Evening Telegraph and Post* (Dundee), 28 May 1924, p. 1, BNA.
81. "Scientist Ridicules 'Ray,'" *NYT*, 28 May 1924, p. 25.
82. "Matthew's [sic] Death Rays Not Deadly," *Tyrone Daily Herald* (Pennsylvania), 9 August 1924, p. 1, NA.
83. "Predicts Sound Waves From Buildings Will Be Used to Extinguish Fires," *NYT*, 13 November 1925, p. 6.
84. "Après le 'rayon de la mort' voici l'onde sonore qui tue... ," *Le Matin*, 15 August 1926, p. 3, Gallica.
85. "Trenches Destroyed by New French Device," *NYT*, 14 February 1927, p. 4. See also "War!—Man's Greatest Industry," *NYT*, 13 March 1927, 4: 1.
86. "Can Inaudible Sounds Kill?," *Popular Mechanics*, May 1927, 706.
87. "Waves to End Armies," *San Antonio Light*, 1 September 1929, 4:1 [35], NA.
88. Thomas E. Stimson, "The Wonders of High Frequency," *Popular Mechanics*, December 1935, 862.
89. Frank Thone, "Death Rays? No!," *Science News Letter*, 23 March 1935, 186.
90. Hiram Percy Maxim, "The Next War on the Land," Part II, *Popular Mechanics*, February 1936, 136A. Maxim's opinion carried some weight with the general public, for he was a well- known engineer and inventor who was also the founder of the American Radio Relay League, an organization supported mostly by ham radio operators. One of his inventions was the Maxim gun silencer. He also had an impressive pedigree. His father was Sir Hiram Stevens Maxim, the inventor of the Maxim machine gun, and his uncle, Hudson Maxim, had developed some high explosives.
91. Douglas W. F. Mayer, "The Truth About Death Rays," *Science Digest* (from *Discovery*), August 1940, 45.
92. "Powerful Light Rays Looked Upon as Coming War Weapon, Both Offensive and Defensive," *Blockton News* (Iowa), 7 March 1935, p. 3, NA. See also Arthur Brisbane, Today, *Harrison Times* (Arkansas), 11 October 1934, p. 1, NA.
93. "A Mercy Gun," *The Morning Bulletin* (Rockhampton, Queensland), 22 February 1935, p. 6, Trove.
94. "'Death Ray' Turned on Dancers," *The Advertiser* (Adelaide), 5 October 1934, p. 24, Trove.
95. "Mystery of the Death Ray," *The Daily Mail* (Hull, England), 28 September 1935, p. 5, BNA.
96. "Tesla at 75," *Time*, 20 July 1931, 27.
97. "Death Ray Again," *The Pathfinder*, 28 July 1934, 14.
98. "Tesla: Inventor Has Scheme for Dealing Out Death Wholesale," *News-Week*, 21 July 1934, 25.
99. "Tesla, at 78, Bares New 'Death-Beam,'" *NYT*, 11 July 1934, p. 18.
100. "Le rayon de la mort, capable d'anéantir à distance armées terrestres et

avions, nous déclare M. d'Arsonval, est une chose réalisable, mais qui n'a pas encore été realisée," *Le Matin*, 16 July 1934, p. 1, Gallica.

101. "Death Ray, of What?," *The Pathfinder*, 11 August 1934, 14.

102. "'Invisible Dust' Curtain to Halt War Planes," *Popular Mechanics*, November 1934, 693.

103. "Demonstration of Death Ray Device Acquits Inventor," *Fort Worth Star Telegram*, 14 May 1936, p. 1. The story in the *San Antonio Light* on 17 May featured a photograph of Fleur showing his death ray to Judge Steiger and members of the jury. See "Inventor Is Freed by Test," 17 May 1936, p. 9, NA.

104. Albert Brandt, "Has Germany a 'Death Ray?,'" *Forum*, February 1940, 66. See also "Inventor Plans Long-Distance 'Death Ray,'" *Portsmouth Herald and Times* (New Hampshire), 28 May 1936, p. 8, NA.

105. "How Science's New Death Ray Can Save or Destroy Humanity," *Hamilton Evening Journal* (Ohio), 25 October 1930, 2: 3 [18], NA.

106. Ibid.

107. "'Death Ray' Expert Scoffs at War Use," *NYT*, 2 May 1935, p. 22.

108. "'Death Ray' Something That Isn't," *The Daily Northwestern*, 12 October 1925, p. 2, NA. According to a story thirteen years later, R. W. Wood of Johns Hopkins was the one who exposed this hoax. See "Who's News This Week," *Elma New Era* (Elma, Iowa), 24 November 1938, p. 7, NA.

109. "Death Ray Kills Bull at 2 ½ Miles," *Wisconsin State Journal* (Madison), 10 July 1940, p. 20, NA.

110. "'Ray Inventor' Gaoled," *Auckland Star*, 18 May 1933, p. 4, Papers Past.

111. "New Death Ray," *Cheltenham Chronicle and Gloucestershire Graphic*, 6 March 1926, p. 4, BNA.

112. "Wireless Death Ray Discovered," *Burra Record* (Burra, South Australia), 18 April 1934, p. 1; "New Death Ray Reported," *The Daily News* (Perth), 26 December 1933, p. 1, Trove.

113. Un bourgeois de Paris, Chronique Parisienne, *La Tribune de Madagascar et Dépendences* (Tananarive), 4 November 1937, p. 1, Gallica. This newspaper referred to him simply as "Professeur Anthony."

114. Ibid. See also "Inventions of Death, Grim and Fantastic," *The Argus* (Melbourne), 10 August 1937, p. 8, Trove.

115. "Spy Drama in Paris," *The Advertiser* (Adelaide), 25 March 1929, p. 10, Trove.

116. See "Mystérieuse agression au Bois de Boulogne," *Le Gaulois*, 1 February 1929, p. 2; Faits Divers, "On arrête l'un des agresseurs du mythomane Delattre," *Le Gaulois*, 2 February 1929, p. 6; as well as "Le juge d'instruction voulait entendre le Belge Delattre," *Le Matin*, 3 February 1929, p. 2, Gallica.

117. "'Gold-Finder' Sentenced," *Times*, 9 January 1933, p. 11; Georges Martin, "Le 'faiseur d'or' Zbiniew Dunikowski est condamné à deux ans de prison," *Le Petit Journal*, 8 January 1933, p. 2, Gallica.

118. "À San Remo chez Dunikowski, une nouvelle révélation: le 'rayon de la mort,'" *Le Matin*, 19 February 1935, pp. 1, 5, Gallica. See also "L' 'alchimiste' Dunikowski en veine de découvertes," *Le Figaro*, 20 February 1935, p. 1, Gallica; "Frenchmen Fear Curse in Cheaply Produced Gold," *Adair County Democrat* (Stillwater, Oklahoma), 27 June 1935, p. 5, NA; and Max Seydewitz and Kurt Doberer, *Todesstrahlen und andere neue Kriegswaffen* (London: Malik-Verlag, 1936), 67–68. Much of the story involving Dunikowski also appeared in a novel serialized in a Swiss newspaper. See Lucien Prioly, "L'île des hommes de fer," *Feuille d'avis de Lausanne*, 14 June 1937, p. 7, Scriptorium.

119. John L. Coontz, "New War Terrors May Assure Peace," *Galveston Daily News*, 8 November 1934, p. 10, NA.

120. "German Death Ray Pistol Stuns Animals at Mile Range," *Modern Mechanix and Inventions*, January 1935, 18, http://blog.modernmechanix.com/?s=German+death+ray.

121. "Ray of Death Kills at 6 Miles," *Modern Mechanix and Inventions*, August 1935, 31. See also "Au fil des jours," *La Dépêche de Madagascar* (Tananarive), 13 July 1935, p. 1, Gallica.

122. "'Death Ray' May Outlaw War," *Modern Mechanix and Inventions*, October 1936, 5, http://blog.modernmechanix.com/?s=Death+Ray+May+Outlaw+war.

123. "Official Guide Souvenir Program, California Pacific International Exposi-

tion, San Diego," 1936, Hathi. An added feature was May's "Alpha the Robot."
124. N. A. Rynin, *Radiant Energy: Science Fiction and Scientific Projects*. Translated by IPST Staff. First published in Leningrad, 1931), 13; Vol. I, No. 3 of *Interplanetary Flight and Communication* (Jerusalem: Published for the National Aeronautics and Space Administration and the National Science Foundation, Washington, D.C., by the Israel Program for Scientific Translations, 1971), 13.
125. "War Plans Forever Secret," *Ada Evening News* (Oklahoma), 8 May 1906, p. 8, NA.
126. Max Seydewitz and Kurt Doberer, *Todesstrahlen und andere neue Kriegswaffen* (London: Malik-Verlag, 1936), 70.
127. Kurt Doberer, *On the Way to Electro War* (London: John Gifford Ltd., 1943), 45.
128. Ibid., 41.
129. Ibid., 123–124.
130. Ibid., 142.
131. Ibid., 124.
132. "Air Death Ray Claim," *Nottingham Evening Post*, 18 May 1935, p. 7, and "Thieves Want Death Ray Secret," *The Daily Mail* (East Riding of Yorkshire, England), p. 3, BNA. See also "Seek 'Death Ray,'" *The Star* (Marion, Ohio), 4 December 1935, 9: 3 [36], NA.
133. Phil's Old Radios, http://www.antiqueradio.org/rn28061.htm. Accessed 26 June 2014.
134. "How the Radio Gun Will Broadcast Death Waves with Speed of Light," *Sandusky Register* (Ohio), 24 June 1928, 3: 5 [23], NA.
135. "Making War 'Too Horrible,'" *The Mail* (Adelaide), 7 May 1932, p. 17, Trove.
136. "Roasted by Radio," *The Advocate* (Burnie, Tasmania), 13 October 1931, p. 5, Trove.
137. "Making War 'Too Horrible,'" *The Mail* (Adelaide), 7 May 1932, p. 17, Trove.
138. "Science's New 'Remote Control' Death Mystery—to Stop War," *Ogden Standard Examiner*, 3 April 1932, 2: 10 [24], NA. See also Nouvelles Diverses, "Un nouveau 'rayon de la mort,'" *Le Figaro*, 8 April 1932, p. 4, Gallica.
139. "Science's New 'Remote Control' Death Mystery—to Stop War," *Ogden Standard Examiner*, 3 April 1932, 2: 10 [24], NA.

140. Bonita Witt, "Pacifist Is Inventor of Death Ray Powerful Enough to Wipe Out Army," *Montana Standard* (Butte), 5 July 1934, p. 2, NA.
141. Science, "Tesla's Ray," *Time*, 23 July 1934, 49.
142. Features of the Day, "Death Ray Banned," *The Advocate* (Burnie, Tasmania), 31 July 1934, p. 2, Trove.
143. Science, "Welder at Work," *Time*, 10 August 1936, 29.
144. Albert Brandt, "Has Germany a 'Death Ray?,'" *Forum*, February 1940, 66.
145. "Inventor Hides Secret of 'Death Ray,'" *Popular Science Monthly*, February 1940, 117.
146. "Army Gets Death Ray that Cuts Steel and Withers Human Bodies," *Lowell Sun* (Massachusetts), 1 August 1938, p. 18, NA.

Chapter 4

1. "More Air Strength Sought by Britain," *NYT*, 20 March 1935, p. 3.
2. "Defence Against Air Attack," *Times*, 5 March 1936, p. 7.
3. Fred Bells, Syracuse, *Syracuse Herald*, 3 April 1936, p. 23 [19], NA.
4. Entre les lignes, "Le mur invisible," *Le Madécasse* (Tananarive) 5–6 June 1936, p. 3, Gallica.
5. "'Death Ray' Barrier to Protect Britain from Enemy Planes," *Hammond Times* (Ohio), 9 November 1936, 2: 2, (22), NA. See also "The Death Ray," *The Republican-Courier* (Findlay, Ohio), 23 November 1936, p. 4, as well as "Britain Plans New Defense," *Escanaba Daily Press* (Michigan), 1 December 1936, p. 2, NA.
6. "Secret Ray," *Longreach Leader* (Queensland), 5 December 1936, p. 6, Trove.
7. "Scientists Working on New Death Ray to Protect Britain from Air Invasion," *The Daily Gleaner* (Kingston, Jamaica), 18 August 1937, p. 1, NA. See also "General Items of Interest," *The Scrutineer and Berrima District Press* (Moss Vale, New South Wales), 4 August 1937, p. 4. Trove.
8. News of the World, "Is There a Death Ray?," *Albury Banner and Wodonga Express* (New South Wales), 4 February 1938, p. 26, Trove.

9. "My Invention May Prevent War," *The Mirror* (Perth), 14 September 1935, p. 9, Trove.

10. "Secret Ray," *Cairns Post* (Queensland), 11 February 1937, p. 5, Trove. A serialized novel about such a ray to protect Britain from aerial attacks appeared in an Australian newspaper not long afterward. See Chapter 6 for the story.

11. An article carried in *The Courier-Mail* of Brisbane confirmed that much of the general public believed that a death ray would protect it from aerial attacks. See "Old Stager," "Death Ray Talk; What Is the Truth?," 28 August 1937, p. 12, Trove. As for the announcement by the British government using death rays as a cover, see "Scientists Sought for Death Ray, Found Radar," *The Press and Journal* (Aberdeen, Scotland), 15 August 1945, p. 3, BNA.

12. Brian Bond, *Liddell Hart: A Study of His Military Thought* (London: Cassell, 1977), 110.

13. Correspondent, A Letter From London, "Science to the Rescue?," *Devon and Exeter Gazette* (Devon), 6 August 1937, p. 11, BNA.

14. Number 5, "Making Poison Gas," *Chronicle-Telegram* (Elyria, Ohio), 21 January 1938, pp. 1–2, NA.

15. "Une invention anglaise: la 'barrière de la mort,'" *Le Matin*, 4 November 1938, p. 1. Gallica.

16. "The 'Death Ray' Again," *Auckland Star*, 26 August 1939, 16, Papers Past.

17. "Magnetische Fernstrahlen," *Die Neue Freie Presse* (Vienna), 25 October 1930, p. 9, ANNO. See also "Le rayon qui arrête," *Le Figaro*, 25 October 1930, p. 3, Gallica; as well as "Un essai en Saxe d'immobilisation des autos," *Le Matin*, 25 October 1930, p. 3 Gallica.

18. "Doubts Ray Stops Motor," *NYT*, 27 October 1930, p. 15.

19. "Deny Using Invisible Ray," *NYT*, 25 October 1930, p. 3. See also "Invisible Ray Stalls Autos," *Reno Evening Gazette*, 25 October 1930, p. 2, NA. In a 1935 article from *The Daily Gleaner* of Kingston, Jamaica, in reference to a new German ray in the news, an odd item was included. According to the story, there was a certain area near Waynesboro, Virginia, where certain mineral deposits emitted a magnetic ray that caused car engines to stop. See "Diesel Motor Planes Would Thwart Wireless Death Rays," *The Daily Gleaner* (Kingston, Jamaica), 19 March 1935, p. 8 (34), NA.

20. "New Ray Capable of Stopping Motors," *The Examiner* (Launceston, Tasmania), 1 June 1935, p. 5S (15), Trove.

21. Ibid.

22. Frederick T. Birchall "Reich Burns Oil in Planes; Would Foil Radio Beams," *NYT*, 15 March 1935, p. 1.

23. "Experts Doubt Ray Can Stop Airplane," *NYT*, 16 March 1935, p. 32. See also "Autogyros, Diesels, and 'Secret Rays,'" *The Literary Digest*, 30 March 1935, 17.

24. "Le réarmament de l'Allemagne," *La Croix*, 9 April 1935, p. 2, Gallica. Another story about German Z-rays appeared in American newspapers in early 1936. See "This War-Mad World," *Centralia Daily Chronicle* (Washington), 1 February 1936, 2: 6 (12), NA. In 1960 the *Dallas Morning News* had an article about a contemporary death-ray project discussed in Britain but made reference to this 1935 story regarding German experiments, which it said were carried out in Westphalia. According to the article, the Wehrmacht had supposedly managed to knock out airplane engines at a distance of two thousand feet. See "Death Ray Project Pressed in Britain," *Dallas Morning News*, 7 June 1960, p. 3.

25. "New Wireless Ray," *The Mercury* (Hobart, Tasmania), 17 July 1935, p. 11, Trove.

26. Ibid. The person most likely referred to here is Ernst Udet, Germany's second greatest ace during the First World War and a member of the famous Flying Circus commanded by Baron Manfred von Richthofen. He was an old friend and comrade of Herman Göring, who appointed him to the post of Director-General of Equipment in the new Luftwaffe. The stresses of the war and criticism that he had failed in his job drove him to suicide in 1941.

27. "Death Ray Rumours Denied," *Nottingham Evening Post*, 17 August 1933, p. 3, BNA.

28. "Old Jack," "Talks on European Affairs," *Muswellbrook Chronicle* (New South Wales), 28 November 1933, p. 3, Trove.

29. "Mysteries of the War," The *Argus* (Melbourne), 5 October 1935, p. 10, Trove.

30. H. R. Knickerbocker, "Bacteria-Spread Disease New War Consideration," *Indiana Evening Gazette* (Indiana, Pennsylvania), 23 July 1935, p. 14, NA.
31. "Death Ray Here?," *Sheboygan Press*, 8 August 1936, 2: 4 (20), NA.
32. "Nazi Working on Death Ray," *Logansport Pharos-Tribune* (Indiana), 12 January 1937, p. 4, NA.
33. "Nazis Equip Planes with 'Death Rays,'" *Charleston Gazette* (West Virginia), 15 June 1938, p. 1, NA.
34. "Germany Using 'Death Ray,'" *The Western Morning News and Daily Gazette* (Bristol, England), 15 June 1938, p. 7, BNA. The rumor about Heinkels equipped with some type of death ray re-emerged in 1939 a few days before the German attack on Poland. See "The 'Death Ray' Again," *Auckland Star*, 26 August 1939, 16, Papers Past.
35. "Hitler's Secret," *The Evening Telegraph* (Angus, Scotland), 12 March 1937, p. 5, BNA.
36. "Possibility of Discovery of Long Sought Death Ray," *Van Wert Daily Bulletin* (Ohio), 12 December 1931, p. 1, NA.
37. "Americans Think They Could Armor Planes Against Radio 'Death Ray,'" *NYT*, 1 September 1935, 9: 7.
38. Hiram Percy Maxim, "The Next War in the Air," Part I, *Popular Mechanics*, January 1936, 124A.
39. "Marconi Invention Would Halt All War Machines," *The Times and Daily News Leader* (San Mateo, California), 28 August 1935, p. 3, NA; see also "Marconi's Tests May Alter Wars," *Ames Daily Tribune Times* (Iowa), 29 August 1935, p. 4, NA.
40. "Marconi Ready to Take Micro-Wave to War; Said to Have Tested Halting Planes in Air," *NYT*, 18 October 1935, p. 17.
41. Nicholas Pirolo, *Babylon: Political and Ecclesiastical, showing characteristics of Anti-Christ and False Prophet considering Mussolini and the Pope with their respective "VV Il Duce" and Vicarius Filii Dei" 666* (Milwaukee: Word Publishing Company, 1937), 27, Hathi.
42. Ibid.
43. Lisa Sergio, "Le rayon de la mort, menace ou légende?," *Le Petit Parisien*, 5 June 1937, p. 4, Gallica. In his biography of Mussolini, Denis Mack Smith refers to a statement by Il Duce that Marconi had indeed developed a death ray but had carried its secret to the grave. See Denis Mack Smith, *Mussolini* (New York: Vintage Books, A Division of Random House, 1983), 316.
44. "Rayons de la mort et Rayons de la vie," *Le Progrès de Sidi-Bel-Abbès*, 27 August 1935, p. 2, Gallica.
45. "New British Ray to Stop All Wars," *The Barrier Miner* (Broken Hill, New South Wales), 22 November 1935, p. 4, Trove.
46. A Letter From London, "That Ray?," *Devon and Exeter Gazette* (Devon), 25 March 1937, p. 11, BNA.
47. "Army Ray that Will Stop Cars," *Bath Weekly Chronicle and Herald*, 26 August 1939, p. 7, BNA.
48. "Excited Over New Ray," *Rivers Gazette* (Rivers, Manitoba), 6 April 1939, p. 6, NA.
49. "Hitler Threat of New Killer Taken Lightly," *Dallas Morning News*, 25 September 1939, p. 10.
50. "Un nouveau rayon de la mort," *Le Matin*, 29 October 1939, p. 3, Gallica.
51. "Allies Pool Brains to Devise Defenses," *NYT*, 23 January 1940, p. 8.
52. Brandt, "Has Germany a 'Death Ray?,'" *Forum*, February 1940, 65.
53. Ibid.
54. Douglas W. F. Mayer, "The Truth About Death Rays," *Science Digest* (from *Discovery*), August 1940, 47.
55. "Nazis Claim Liege," *NYT*, 14 May 1940, p. 8. Yet, in February 1941, *Le Matin* carried a story about American inventors forming the Association of Death Ray Inventors to help the U.S. War Department evaluate claims of such a weapon. See "L'Association des Inventeurs du rayon de la mort!," *Le Matin*, 6 February 1941, p. 1, Gallica.
56. "Nazi Search for Death Ray," *The Citizen* (Gloucestershire, England), 27 October 1944, p. 6, BNA.
57. "The Voice of the Nazi Now," *The Press and Journal* (Aberdeen, Scotland), 26 February 1945, p. 1, BNA.
58. "Japs Claim New Death Ray," *The Courier and Advertiser* (Dundee, Scotland), 11 January 1945, p. 3, BNA.
59. Ronald Clark, *Tizard* (Cambridge, Massachusetts: The M. I. T. Press, 1965), 132.
60. Ibid., 110.

61. William B. Breuer, *Secret Weapons of World War II*, 35. See also Brown, *Radar History*, 50.

62. "Death Rays Deferred," *Time*, 2 December 1946, 99. See also *Applied Physics. Science in World War II*. C. G. Suits, George R. Harrison, and Louis Jordan, eds. (Boston: Little, Brown and Company, 1948), 125.

63. One project was that of a "sound gun," in which the waves generated could penetrate the human body and kill a person in thirty seconds up to one hundred yards. It was dropped because the machine was too large to be practical. Another failed project was that of the vortex gun to disable aircraft. "Weird Weapons—The Axis," Modern Marvels, *The History Channel*, Season 12, Episode 8.

64. "Nazis' Scientists Planned Sun 'Gun' 5,100 Miles Up," *NYT*, 29 June 1945, p. 1. See also "Sun Gun," *Time*, 9 July 1945, 58–60.

65. See Pedro Waloschek, *Todesstrahlen als Lebensretter* (Norderstedt: Books on Demand, GmbH, 2004), GB. See also Mario Beck, "Schiebolds braune Sciencefiction," *Leipziger Volkszeitung Magazin*, 16/17 April 2005, p. M2. www.waloschek.de/pedro/lvz-rezension-beck-A4.pdf.

66. Albert Speer, *Inside the Third Reich: Memoirs by Albert Speer*, trans. Richard and Clara Winston (New York: The Macmillan Company, 1970), 464. See also Tom Schachtman, *Terrors and Marvels: How Science and Technology Changed the Character and Outcome of World War II* (New York: William Morrow, An Imprint of HarperCollins-Publishers, 2002), 304–305.

67. "Japanese Had 'Death Ray' in Stage of Development," *NYT*, 7 October 1945, p. 32.

68. Walter E. Grunden, *Secret Weapons and World War II: Japan in the Shadow of Big Science* (Lawrence, Kansas: University Press of Kansas, 2005), 110.

69. Ibid., 115–116. Two puzzles concerning a Japanese death ray remain. One has to do with the experiments on small animals. The American Army report utilizing captured Japanese records as well as interrogations of Japanese scientists involved in the project indicate no real work was done until 1939, but Seydewitz and Doberer mentioned in their 1936 book Japanese death-ray experiments with rabbits. See Seydewitz and Doberer, *Todesstrahlen*, 73, as well as Doberer, *Electro War*, 46. Albert Brandt cited this fact in his 1940 article but added that the original source was a story in *Neues Tagebuch* of 23 June 1934. (Brandt, "Has Germany a 'Death Ray?,'" 66). Another oddity is that the U.S. Army report stated the Japanese became interested in trying to develop a death ray after the appearance of one newspaper article claiming that the Germans had such a weapon during the First World War. This seems unlikely since there were so many stories in the news about death rays. Japanese military attachés in London and other major capitals would have certainly been following the news about Grindell Matthews, the French airplanes over Bavaria, and the occasional claim in newspapers about death-ray inventors being in contact with Japanese authorities—whether true or not. They may have also been reporting back to Tokyo on what mainstream scientists had to say about the technological limitations to such a weapon. As an aside, there was also a curious story about a Japanese man named Takoyi Miyoshi, who won a prize for an essay depicting a near war between Japan and the United States. It was averted at the last moment by the development of a death ray in Japan. This news item appeared in *The Advocate* (Burnie, Tasmania) in January 1927. See "War Grouping," 22 January 1927, p. 1, Trove.

Chapter 5

1. Washington Irving, *Knickerbocker's History of New York*, Author's Autograph Edition, vol. 1 (New York: G. P. Putnam's Sons, 1895), 103, GB. One writer has suggested that Irving gave his imaginary invaders "the superweapon sought by the major powers of the late twentieth century, directed-energy beams." H. Bruce Franklin, *Future Perfect: American Science Fiction of the Nineteenth Century—An Anthology* (New York: Oxford University Press, 1968), 250.

2. Earl of Lytton, *The Life of Edward Bulwer First Lord Lytton*, vol. 1 (London: Macmillan and Company, 1913), 465, GB.

3. Edward Bulwer Lytton, *The Coming*

Race (Edinburgh: William Blackwood and Sons, 1871), 181, Hathi.

4. Untitled, *Belfast News-Letter* (Ireland), 17 December 1887, p. 5, BNA.

5. Charles Lester Leonard, President's Address, "The Past, Present and Future of the Roentgen Ray," *Transactions of the American Roentgen Ray Society*, Sixth Annual Meeting, 28, 29, 30 September 1905 (Pittsburgh: Press Murdoch, Kerr and Company, 1906), 31, Hathi.

6. H. G. Wells, *The War of the Worlds* (London: William Heinemann, 1898), 39, Internet Archive.

7. "The Scientific Novel, A Talk with Mr. H. G. Wells," *The Daily News* (London), 26 January 1898, p. 6, BNA.

8. Clement Shorter, "Mr. Wells's 'War of the Worlds,'" review of *The War of the Worlds*, by H. G. Wells, *The Bookman*, vol. 7, March-August 1898, May, 246.

9. The first edition in book form came in 1947.

10. Garrett Putman Serviss, *Edison's Conquest of Mars* (Los Angeles: Carcosa House, 1947), 14, Hathi.

11. Wirt Gerrare (William Oliver Greener), *The Warstock: A Tale of Tomorrow* (London: W. W. Greener, 1898), Hathi. One reviewer found it a little too bizarre, adding that "it is the product of a Royal Institution lecture, a heavy supper, and a nightmare." See "Fantastic," *Pall Mall Gazette*, 5 December 1898, p. 4, BNA.

12. Fred T. Jane, *The Violet Flame: A Story of Armageddon and After*, 1899 (New York: Arno Press, A New York Times Company, 1975). See also the review in *The Queenslander* (Brisbane), 4 November 1899, p. 903 [total pages 48, beginning with 885 and ending with 932 S], Trove.

13. Full name George Chetwynd Griffith-Jones (1857–1906)

14. George Griffith, *The World Masters* (London: John Long, 1903), 243–246, GB. This novel also appeared in serial form in several Australian newspapers, among the first being the *Bendigo Advertiser* of Bendigo, Victoria, beginning 22 February 1902, Trove. The basis for the novel came from Griffith's short story entitled "A Corner in Lightning," which appeared in *Pearson's Magazine* in 1898. This version did not include any war or involvement by foreign governments, and the important term "death ray" was also absent. After exerting its mysterious force throughout much of Europe, the electrical storage facility in Canada explodes and the inventor dies. See volume 5, January to June, 264–271, Hathi.

15. Griffith, *The World Masters*, 296, 297, GB. The review by John Long in *The Athenaeum* makes no reference to the "death rays." See Literature, *The Athenaeum*, 11 April 1903, 460, Hathi.

16. The alignment of nations in Griffith's scenario differs somewhat from that of the First World War, for he has Russia becoming disillusioned with France and returning to the fold of the alliance that Bismarck tried to maintain under the framework of the Three Emperors' League and subsequent agreements: Germany, Austria-Hungary, and Russia. This becomes the new Triple Alliance, Italy having withdrawn and joined with France and Britain. Griffith also places Turkey on the side of the Western democracies.

17. George Griffith, *The Lord of Labour* (London: F. V. White and Company, 1911), Internet Archive.

18. George Griffith, *The World Peril of 1910* (London: F. V. White and Company, 1907), 14, GB.

19. C. S. Raymond, "The Wireless Death," *Technical World Magazine*, February 1906, 742–750, Hathi. It reappeared three years later in an Australian newspaper. See "The Wireless Death, A Fascinating Story," *North-Western Advocate and Emu Bay Times* (Devonport and Burnie, Tasmania), 20 March 1909, p. 8, Trove.

20. Jack London, *The Complete Short Stories of Jack London*, ed. Earle Labor, Robert C. Leitz, III, and I. Milo Shepherd, vol. 2 (Stanford, California: Stanford University Press, c. 1993).

21. Hollis Godfrey, *The Man Who Ended War* (Boston: Little, Brown, and Company, 1908), 54, Internet Archive.

22. Ibid., 246.

23. "Notable Autumn Fiction," *Des Moines Capital*, 5 November 1908, p. 8, NA. P. D. Smith suggests that Godfrey, a lecturer in engineering at M.I.T., was influenced by stories in the press regarding radium and its power to "blow the British navy out of the sea." See *Doomsday Men: The Real Dr. Strangelove and the*

Dream of the Superweapon (New York: St. Martin's Press, 2007), 113.

24. After Japan's victory over Russia in 1905, some Americans began to view that Asian country as a threat to their interests in the Far East. Relations between the United States and Japan worsened in 1906 over racial issues, these involving primarily the treatment of people of Japanese ancestry living in California, as well as Japanese immigration. Foreseeing the possibility of a future war, President Theodore Roosevelt instructed the army and the navy to draw up a plan on how to fight and defeat Japan. See Kathleen Dalton, *Theodore Roosevelt: A Strenuous Life* (New York: Alfred A. Knopf, 2002), 333.

25. Rowan Stevens, "Sorakichi,—Prometheus," in Rowan Stevens et al., *The Battle for the Pacific and Other Adventures at Sea* (New York: Harper and Brothers Publishers, 1908), 22–23, GB.

26. F. D'A. C. De L'Isle, "The Strange Adventures of Bailey Catford, Scientist and Inventor," *The Queenslander* (Brisbane), 18 June 1910, p. 43, Trove. Installments ran from 11 June to 23 July.

27. Ibid., 23 July 1910, p. 43, Trove.

28. C. J. Cutcliffe Hyne, *Empire of the World*, 1910 (New York: Arno Press, 1975). See also the book review in *The Register* of Adelaide, under the heading "A Benevolent Pirate," 28 January 1911, p. 4, Trove.

29. Edward Stewart White, *The Sign at Six* (Indianapolis: The Bobbs-Merrill Company, Publishers, 1912), 209–214, GB.

30. Ibid., 223.

31. "The 'Death Ray' and the Next War," *San Antonio Light*, 15 December 1935, p. 20 [97], NA.

32. Arthur B. Reeve, "The Terror in the Air," in *The Silent Bullet: The Adventures of Craig Kennedy, Scientific Detective* (New York: Grosset and Dunlap, Publishers, 1910), 254–285. This story also appeared in *The Salt Lake Tribune*. See Arthur B. Reeve, "The Terror—In the Air," 3 November 1912, Magazine, pp. 4–5 [44–45], NA.

33. Arthur B. Reeve, *The Exploits of Elaine* (New York: Harper and Brothers, Publishers, 1914), 169, GB.

34. Ibid., 173–174. See also 182.

35. The success of this movie serial led to two sequels: *The New Exploits of Elaine* in 1915 and *The Romance of Elaine* in 1916. Pearl White, who had starred in the forerunner serial, *The Perils of Pauline*, played the heroine in all three versions.

36. Arthur B. Reeve "The Sixth Sense," *Cosmopolitan*, Vol. 58 December-May 1914–1915, (May) 704, GB.

37. Regis Gignoux and Roland Dorgelès, *La Machine à finir la guerre* (Paris: Albin Michel, Éditeur, 1917), 225. It first appeared as a supplement in the Parisian magazine *L'Heure*. According to Maurice Rieuneau, it was written in fifteen days, the first half of the book by Gignoux, the other by Dorgelès. See Rieuneau, *Guerre et révolution dans le roman français de 1919 à 1939* (Paris: Klincksieck, 1974), 32–33, GB.

38. Sir William Crookes (1832–1919) was an English scientist famous for his work with cathode rays.

39. Gignoux and Dorgelès, *La Machine à finir la guerre*, 226–228. For a contemporary view of the novel, see Louis Latzarus, "La Machine à finir la guerre," *Le Figaro*, 7 July 1917, p. 1, Gallica.

40. Bernard C. White, "A Pawn in the Game," *The Wireless World*, March 1914, 764, Hathi.

41. Ibid., February 1914, 702, Hathi.

42. Victor Appleton, *Tom Swift and His Electric Rifle or Daring Adventures in Elephant Land* (New York: Grosset and Dunlap, 1911), 17, Internet Archive. Different writers were used but all employed the name "Victor Appleton."

43. Guido Horvath and Dean Hoard, "The Isolated Continent: A Romance of the Future," *The Rake Register* (Rake, Iowa), 18 December 1913, p. 3, NA. Installments ran from 16 October 1914–12 March 1915.

44. M. P. Shiel, *The Yellow Peril* (London: Victor Gollancz Ltd., 1929), 304.

45. Arthur Train and Robert Williams Wood, *The Man Who Rocked the Earth*, 1915 (New York: Arno Press, 1974, The Project Gutenberg EBook #19174), Internet Archive. This is the same Robert Wood of Johns Hopkins University mentioned in Chapter 3.

46. "Zudora," *Victoria Daily Advocate* (Texas), 21 January 1915, p. 4, NA. Installments ran from 10 December 1914-February 1915. See also "The Million Dollar Mystery," *Ogden Standard* (Ogden City, Utah), 27 June 1914, p. 9, NA, as well as "Notes Written on the Screen," *NYT*, 25 October 1914, 7:7.

47. William Le Queux, *The Mystery of the Green Ray* (London: Hodder and Stoughton, 1915), 241–242, Internet Archive. Le Queux's best known and most successful work was *The Invasion of 1910* (1906), describing a German invasion of Britain.
48. William Le Queux, *The Zeppelin Destroyer: Being Some Chapters of Secret History* (London: Hodder and Stoughton, 1916), 173, Internet Archive.
49. William Le Queux, "Hushed Up at German Headquarters, Amazing Confessions of an Aide-de-Camp of the Crown Prince," *The Cumberland Argus and Fruitgrowers' Advocate of Parramatta* (New South Wales), 30 January 1918, p. 4, Trove.
50. Sax Rohmer, *The Golden Scorpion* (New York: McKinlay, Stone and Mackenzie, 1920), 82, GB.
51. Ibid., 258. See also the review in the *New York Times*, "Russia's Master of the Short Story: A New Collection of Yarns by Anton Chekhov—Latest Works of Fiction by Edgar Wallace, Sax Rohmer, B. M. Bower and Others," 27 June 1920, 5: 22.
52. For a compendium of French science fiction writing, see Jean-Marc Lofficier and Randy Lofficier, *French Science Fiction, Fantasy, Horror and Pulp Fiction: A Guide to Cinema, Television, Radio, Animation, Comic Books and Literature from the Middle Ages to the Present* (Jefferson, North Carolina: McFarland and Company, Publishers, c. 2000).
53. For a fuller treatment of this type of literature in Weimar Germany, see Dina Brandt, *Der deutsche Zukunftsroman 1918–1945: Gattungstypologie und sozialgeschichtliche Verortung* (Tübingen: Max Niemeyer Verlag, 2007), and Peter S. Fisher, *Fantasy and Politics: Visions of the Future in the Weimar Republic* (Madison, Wisconsin: The University of Wisconsin Press, 1991.
54. A number of newspapers during this time published articles about clandestine activities in which Germans were allegedly preparing for another war. Probably the most important was a series in the *Times* containing "indisputable proof" obtained from sources in Germany. See "German Secret Army Plans," 19 October 1921, p. 11; 22 October 1921, p. 9; and 24 October 1921, p. 11. See also the subsequent articles "German Army Plot," 19 November 1921, and "German Military Plans," 27 October 1921, p. 13.
55. F. E. Solf, *1934 Deutschlands Auferstehung* (Naumberg: Carl August Tancré Verlag, 1922). See also the review "1934" in *The Daily News* (Perth), 19 January 1922, p. 7, Trove.
56. Hans Dominik, *Die Macht der Drei: Ein Roman aus dem Jahre 1955* (Leipzig: Ernst Keils Nachfolger (August Scherl) G.m.b.H., 1922), 95, 135, Internet Archive.
57. Ibid., 147.
58. Ibid.
59. Hans Dominik, *Vom Schraubstock zum Schreibtisch: Lebenserinnerungen* (Berlin: Verlag Scherl, 1943), 192–193.
60. "Ray-Sender to End War," *Charleston Daily Mail* (West Virginia), 15 July 1923, p. 28, NA.
61. Summaries of many of these German works can be seen at Geopolitical Fiction, Inhaltsangabe anzeigen, www.cafegroessenwahn.net/gf.
62. Brandt, *Deutsche Zukunftsroman*, 152.
63. Joseph Delmont, *Die Stadt unter dem Meere* (Leipzig: Verlag Fr. Wilh. Grunow, 1925).
64. See Brief Reviews, *NYT*, 29 July 1928, 3: 14.
65. H. Ashton-Wolfe, "Allivi: The Bogus Death Ray," in *Warped in the Making: Crimes of Love and Hate* (London: Hurst and Blackett, Ltd, 1928), 191–212. Internet Archive. For more on questions of Ashton-Wolfe's credibility, see Rick Lai, "The Legacy of Hanoi Shan," http://pjfarmer.com/woldnewton/Hanoi_Shan.pdf, 48. Accessed 7 July 2014.
66. "Almost Perfect Crimes, No. V.—The F-Ray," *San Antonio Express*, 16 February 1930, 4B [38], NA.

Chapter 6

1. Henry de Graffigny, *Voyage de cinq Américains dans les planètes: roman astronomique* (Paris: Librairie Gedalge, 1925), 296, Gallica.
2. Gordon Sussex, "Jezzard of the Mill," *Oakland Tribune*, 23 May 1926, Sunday Magazine Section, p. 9 [87], NA.
3. Francis Beeding, "Little White Hag," *Billings Gazette* (Montana), 30 December 1926, p. 4, NA. See also "New Books, The

Little White Hag," review by Florence Sanden, *Helena Daily Independent*, 14 February 1926, p. 14, NA. The title refers to opium.

4. Albert Bailly, "L'Éther-Alpha: grand roman d'aventures," *Lectures pour tous*, August 1929, 115, Gallica. This novel appeared in three installments, August-October 1929, and won for Bailly the coveted Jules Verne Award for that year.

5. Reinhold Eichacker, *Der Kampf ums Gold* (Munich: Universal-Verlag, 1924), 171–173.

6. Ibid., 193.

7. Eugène Thébault, "Radio-Terreur: Grand Roman de Mystère," *L'Aventure*, 23 June 1927, 13, Gallica. Thébault's work first appeared as a serial in the magazine *L'Aventure*, beginning with the 23 June 1927 issue, before being published in book form in 1929. It was later translated into English and included in *Wonder Stories* as installments in the June, August, and October 1933 issues. The "polar chill" and the broadcasting of threats echo to an extent Edward Stewart White's *The Sign at Six* described in Chapter 5.

8. This first appeared in a Russian magazine in 1925 and 1926. As time passed, Tolstoy revised the story until it was finally published in book form in 1934. See Maria and Elena Kozyreva (Kazan), "H. G. Wells and A. K. Tolstoy," in Elmar Schenkel and Stefan Welz, eds., *Lost Worlds & Mad Elephants: Literature, Science and Technology 1700–1990* (Cambridge, Massachusetts: Galda and Wilch, 1999), 195.

9. Alexei Tolstoy, *Engineer Garin and His Death Ray*, trans. George Hanna (Moscow: Raduga Publishers, 1987), 60–61. Tolstoy and others who referred to "Rindel Matthews" may have obtained their information about the English inventor from German-language newspapers. The *Neue Freie Presse* of Vienna, for example, carried a story on 10 April 1924 from the *Berliner Tagblatt*, entitled "Eine angebliche englische Erfindung zur Verhinderung von Luftangriffen" (An alleged English invention for the prevention of air attacks), in which Grindell Matthews is referred to as "H. Rindell Mathews." *Die Neue Zeitung* of Vienna spelled his name "Rindell-Matthews." See "Eine angebliche englische Erfindung zur Verhinderung von Luftangriffen," *Neue Freie Presse* (Vienna), 10 April 1924, pp. 8–9, ANNO. See also "Gibt es noch einen Zukunftskrieg?" (Will there be another war in the future?), *Die Neue Zeitung* (Vienna), 10 April 1924, p. 2, ANNO.

10. Tolstoy, *Engineer Garin*, 72.

11. This event, minus the death ray, evokes the 1921 gas explosion at the Badische Anilin Werke in Oppau, Germany, in which more than five hundred people died. This later became the famous BASF company, or Badische Anilin-und Sodafabrik.

12. O. Hanstein, *Radiopolis*, Adaptation Tancrède Vallerey (Paris: Fernand Nathan, Éditeur, 1933), 106.

13. Ibid., 149.

14. Ibid., 201–202.

15. H. Allorge, *Les rayons ensorcelés* (Paris: Fernand Nathan, Éditeur, 1935), 204, 206.

16. Professor A. M. Low, "The Great Murchison Mystery," *Townsville Daily Bulletin* (Townsville, Queensland), 3 December 1936, p. 9, Trove. Weekly installments in this Australian newspaper ran from 25 September 1936 to 27 January 1937. The novel was then published in 1937 as a book by Herbert Joseph Limited of London. The title was *Mars Breaks Through, or, The Great Murchison Mystery*.

17. Ibid., 10 December 1936, p. 9.

18. Edwin L. James, "Book on German War of Revenge Stirs Paris," *NYT*, 24 February 1924, 8:18.

19. "Fierce 'War of 1930' Pictured by German," from the *Chicago Tribune*, *NYT*, 3 August 1924, p. 6. See also "À travers journaux et revues: Les prophéties d'un général allemand," *Le Gaulois*, 9 October 1924, p. 3, Gallica.

20. Generalmajor Freiherr Paul von Schoenaich, *Der Krieg im Jahre 1930* (Berlin-Hessenwinkel: Verlag der Neuen Gesellschaft G. m. b. H., 1925), 15. *Vom vorigen zum nächsten Krieg* (Fichtenau bei Berlin: Verlag der Neuen Gesellschaft, 1924).

21. Ibid., 18–19.

22. See Revue des Livres, *L'Aéronautique* (Paris), August 1926, No. 87, 284, Gallica.

23. Pierrepont B. Noyes, *The Pallid Giant: A Tale of Yesterday and Tomorrow* (New York: Fleming H. Revell Company, 1927), Hathi. The *New York Times* review was mixed, faulting the author for the

somewhat awkward juxtaposition of the two stories but praising it as an interesting work. See "A Prehistoric Story," *NYT*, 11 September 1927, 3: 14.
 24. George S. Schuyler writing as Samuel I. Brooks, *Black Empire* (Boston: Northeastern University Press, 1991), 256. This novel first appeared as a serial in the *Pittsburgh Courier*, running from October 1937 to April 1938.
 25. Ibid., 248–249.
 26. George S. Schuyler, *Ethiopian Stories*, compiled and edited with an introduction by Robert A. Hill (Boston: Northeastern University Press, 1994), 121. This short story also appeared first as a serial in the *Pittsburgh Courier*, October 1935-February 1936.
 27. Édouard Adenis, "Tu mourras le...," *Tribune de Lausanne* (Switzerland), 2 May 1937, p. 5, Scriptorium. Installments ran from 29 March–22 May.
 28. "Marconi's New Wave May Lead to Perfection of Television," *The World's News* (Sydney), 2 August 1933, p. 9, Trove.
 29. Agatha Christie, *The Big Four*, 1927 (New York: HarperCollins Publishers, EPub edition, August 2011 [Kindle]), 193. See also the commentary by Jerry Speir in Dick Riley and Pam McAllister, eds., *The Bedside, Bathtub & Armchair Companion to Agatha Christie* (New York: Frederick Ungar Publishing Company, 1979), 30–31.
 30. Christie, *Big Four*, 41–42.
 31. Ibid., 160.
 32. Books and Their Writers, "Russian Invasion," review of *Drake's Mantle*, in *The Courier and Advertiser* (Dundee, Scotland), 4 August 1928, p. 8. BNA. See also Books of the Week, *Brisbane Courier*, 6 October 1928, p. 22, Trove.
 33. Kay Burdekin, *The Rebel Passion* (New York: William Morrow and Company, 1929), 246. See also the review "The Last World War," *The Sunday Mail* (Brisbane), 7 July 1929, p. 2, Trove. Born Katharine Penelope Cade, she wrote also under the name Kay Burdekin and the pseudonym Murray Constantine.
 34. Arthur Russell, "The Ether King," *Central Queensland Herald* (Rockhampton, Queensland), 7 April–2 June 1932, pp. 4–5 in every installment.
 35. Erle Cox, "Out of the Silence," *The Argus* (Melbourne), 9 August 1919, p. 10, Trove.

 36. Ibid., 20 September 1919, p. 12, Trove.
 37. Erle Cox, "Out of the Silence," No. 92, *The Courier-Mail* (Brisbane), 20 November 1934, p. 11, Trove. The installments in *The Argus* version ran from 19 April–25 October 1919, with those in *The Courier-Mail* from 4 August–1 December 1934.
 38. L. Bamburg, "Septimus March Again," *The Sunday Times* (Perth), 8 December 1929, p. 19 S, Trove.
 39. John Kirke, "Captain Midnight," *The Argus* (Melbourne), 14 November 1935–9 April 1936, Trove. This "Captain Midnight" is not to be confused with the radio and movie serial American hero who first appeared in 1938.
 40. Gregory Baxter, *Blue Lightning* (London: Cassell and Company, Limited., 1926), 146. See also J. Penn, "The Library Table," *The Advertiser* (Adelaide), 19 March 1927, p. 4; and "Recent Publications" in the 16 October 1926 issue of *The Advertiser*, p. 20, Trove. The title is derived from a quotation with the words "blue lightning" from Shakespeare's *Julius Caesar* (Act I, Scene iii) included in the front matter.
 41. Maryse Rutledge, *The Silver Peril* (New York: Walter J. Black, Inc., 1931).
 42. E. Phillips Oppenheim, *The Dumb Gods Speak* (Boston: Little, Brown, and Company, 1937), 290–291.
 43. Book Reviews, "The Dumb Gods Speak," *Albany Advertiser* (Western Australia) 12 May 1938, p. 6, Trove.
 44. Egypt had been a protectorate of Britain from 1914 until 1922, when it gained partial independence. British troops and officials still occupied the country until 1952.
 45. Maurice Boué and Édouard Aujay, "Le masque de feu," *Feuille d'Avis de Lausanne*, 26 August 1938, p. 8, Scriptorium. Installments ran from 26 August–17 December.
 46. Peter Cheyney, "The Gold Kimono, A Great Mystery Story," *The Sunday Times* (Perth), 5 October–28 December 1930, Trove.
 47. Léon Groc, "L'impossible rançon," *Le Petit Parisien*, 16 April 1937, p. 4, Gallica. Installments ran from 30 March–9 May.
 48. Warwick Deeping, "Trelawney's Z-

Rays," *The Queenslander* (Brisbane), 8 January 1921, p. 35, Trove.
49. Robert L. Hadfield and Frank E. Farncombe, *Ruled by Radio*, 1925 (Vancleave, Mississippi: Ramble House reprint, 2008).
50. Percy F. Westerman, *The War of the Wireless Waves* (London: Oxford University Press-Humphrey Milford, 1930, first published in 1923).
51. Edmund Snell, *The Z Ray* (Philadelphia: J. B. Lippincott Company, 1932). See also Isaac Anderson's review "New Mystery Stories," *NYT*, 24 April 1932 4: 16.
52. Harry Stephen Keeler, *The Black Satchel* (London: Ward, Lock and Company, 1931), 16.
53. It should be noted that Fairlie served as the model for Sapper's detective "Bulldog Drummond," a proto-James Bond character, and wrote some of the stories after his death. Fairlie attended the Royal Military Academy at Sandhurst and served in the Scots Guards. While in the army he was a boxing champion.
54. Gerard Fairlie, *Scissors Cut Paper* (New York: A. L. Burt Company, Publishers, 1928), 252.
55. Mark Channing, "King Cobra," *The Courier Mail* (Brisbane), 25 November 1933–8 February 1934, Trove. It was first published in book form by Hutchinson and Company of London in 1933.
56. Charman Edwards, *Fear Haunts the Roses* (London: Ward, Lock and Company, 1936), 289.
57. Madge Macbeth, *Wings in the West* (London: John Hamilton Limited, Publishers, 1937), Internet Archive.
58. Ignazio Silone, *Bread and Wine*, trans. Gwenda David and Eric Mosbacher (New York: Harper and Brothers Publishers, 1937), 192. First published in Zurich under the German title *Brot und Wein* in 1936, an extract that included this passage appeared in *The Living Age*. See Ignazio Silone, "Mobilization Day," trans. Eric Mosbacher, from the *Left Review*, *The Living Age*, October 1936, 116–122. The first Italian version, *Pane e Vino*, came out in 1937.
59. Silone, *Bread and Wine*, 211.
60. Julie Anne Moore, "Interrupted Romance," *Mansfield News-Journal* (Ohio), 15 July–18 August 1937, NA.
61. Arthur Gask, "The Fall of the Dictator," *The Advertiser* (Adelaide), 12 January 1939, p. 10, Trove. Installments ran from 22 December 1938–20 February 1939.
62. William J. Makin, "The Silver Assassin," *The Northern Star* (Lismore, New South Wales), 30 July 1937, p. 13, Trove. Installments ran from 25 June–1 September.
63. Jean d'Agraives, *La Cité des sables* (Paris: Hachette, 1935), 110–112. This book was originally published in 1924 by Chaix and went through several editions.
64. This sounds similar to the "dilithium crystals" required for the warp-drive engines in *Star Trek*.
65. N° 12, Jean d'Agraives, *Le Rayon Swastika*, *Revue des Lectures*, 15 February 1930, 193, Gallica. The 1929 edition used "Swastika" instead of the original "Svastika."
66. Les Grandes aventures, *Revue des Lectures*, 15 December 1927, 1244, Gallica. He followed this up with *Le Dernier pirate*, a semi-sequel to *Le Sorcier de la mer*.
67. Edmond Romazières, "Le sommeil qui tue," *L'Aventure*, 1928, June–18 October, Gallica. Issues of this magazine can be found online at Gallica, but the one with the first installment of the story is missing. Although it would have to be in Number 52 since Number 53 (21 June, pp. 13–15) has a synopsis of Chapter 1, the exact date is in question. The magazine is advertised as appearing every Thursday, but Number 51 is dated 4 June and Number 53 is 21 June. A further note is that this work should not be confused with the novel bearing the same title by Jacques Desvosges published in 1913.
68. Bernard Newman, *Armoured Doves: A Peace Book* (London: Jarrolds, Limited, 1931), 160.
69. Novels of the Day, "Scientists Wage War upon War," *Sydney Morning Herald*, 17 April 1931, p. 6, Trove.
70. Michael Arlen, *Man's Mortality* (Garden City, New York: Doubleday, Doran and Company, Inc., 1933), 54, 222, 233.
71. Book Notes, *NYT*, 22 March 1933: 15; Latest Works of Fiction, "War in the Air," *NYT*, 26 March 1933, 5: 16.
72. Ralph Trevor, "The Ghost Counts Ten," *Queensland Times* (Ipswich, Queensland), 24 August 1937, p. 3, Trove. Installments ran from 24 August–2 October. The weapon itself is described as harmless

to people, affecting only metal, which melts when subjected to the ray.

73. Claude Farrère (Frédéric-Charles Bargone), *Les condamnés à mort* (Paris: Ernest Flammarion, Éditeur, 1921), 258–259, Google Livres (French Google). It was first published in serial form in the French magazine *L'Illustration* from 9 October through 6 November 1920.

74. Sax Rohmer, "The Day the World Ended," *Collier's*, 6 July 1929, 50. Installments ran from 4 May–20 July. It was published as a book in 1930 by Doubleday, Doran and Company for the Crime Club.

75. Edmund Snell, *The Sound Machine* (London: Skeffington and Son, Limited., c. 1932), 65.

76. Manuel Ugarte, *El Camino de los Dioses (novela de la próxima guerra)* (Barcelona: Sociadad General de Publicaciones, c. 1926), 139, 141.

77. Latest Works of Fiction, "The Next War," *NYT*, 13 November 1927, 4: 36.

78. Arthur Conan Doyle, "The Disintegration Machine," in *The Best Science Fiction of Arthur Conan Doyle*, ed. Charles G. Waugh and Martin H.Greenberg. Carbondale: Southern Illinois University Press, 1981), 163.

79. Austin J. Small, *The Avenging Ray* (Garden City, New York: Doubleday, Doran and Company, 1930). See also Novels of the Day, "Death Ray Story," *Sydney Morning Herald*, 24 January 1930, p. 8,Trove.

80. Junius, "Broadcasting the Tea Race," *Central Queensland Herald* (Rockhampton), 8 November 1934-January 1935, Trove. Rhodes was a prolific Australian writer born in England who attended school in New Zealand and served in the Royal Navy during the First World War. He later followed several pursuits, including journalism.

81. Ibid., 17 January 1935, p. 54.

Chapter 7

1. "Pawns of Mars," *Feilding Star* (New Zealand), 1 June 1916, p. 3, and "Everybody's Continuous Pictures 'The Pawns of Mars,'" *Wanganui Chronicle* (New Zealand), 13 April 1916, p. 6, Papers Past.

2. Public Amusements, Town Hall, *Albany Advertiser* (Western Australia), 11 May 1918, p. 4, Trove. See also the review in *Variety Film Reviews, 1907–1920*, Vol 1, 20 October 1916. This publication has no page numbers.

3. "Pearl White Says 'Good-Bye,'" *The Sunday Times* (Perth), 10 August 1924, p. 6, Trove.

4. There is some confusion about the year of release of this movie, ranging from 1923 to 1925, as well as its French title. The earliest mention found by this writer was an announcement in *Le Matin* dated 16 November 1923 describing some of the coming films from the company of Henri Diamant-Berger. One was *Paris qui dort*. But not until October 1924 was there mention that the film was coming soon to Paris, which it did the following month. See "Un programme français," *Le Matin*, 16 November 1923, p. 3, as well as Présentation, *Les Spectacles*, 24 October 1924, 13. Some of the French reviews did not refer to the film as *Paris qui dort* but as *Rayon diabolique* instead. See Jacques Vivien, "Le cinéma à Paris," *Le Petit Parisien*, 22 November 1924, p. 6, and "Le Cinéma," *Journal des Débats politiques et littéraires*, 20 December 1924, p. 3. Gallica.

5. For an in-depth summary, see "La Cité Foudroyée," *Les Spectacles*, 9 January 1925, 13–14. See also the review by Robert Trévise in the French magazine *Cinéa-Ciné pour tous*, 15 November 1924, 26, and La Semaine au Ciné, *Le Matin*, 5 December 1924, p. 4, Gallica.

6. Around the Film World, *NYT*, 5 October 1924, 8: 5. The description of the movie referred to it as *A Story Without a Name*, but the ad for the Rialto Theater billed it as *The Story Without a Name* and carried the contest's challenge: "You Name It and Share in Photoplay Magazine's $5,000 Prize." Ibid., 8: 4.

7. "$25 for a Name," *The Saturday Spectator* (Terre Haute, Indiana), 25 October 1924, p. 26 [25], NA.

8. Arthur Stringer and Russell Holman, *The Story Without a Name* (New York: Grosset and Dunlap, 1924). While filming off Long Island, the actors and crew on board a yacht were stopped by two revenue agents who suspected them of being bootleggers. The director, Irvin Willat, convinced the government agents only by having Ayres and Moreno act out one of the scenes. See "Paramount Players Mak-

ing 'The Story Without a Name' Mistaken for Rum-Runners," *The Morning Herald* (Hagerstown, Maryland), 2 December 1924, p. 5, NA.
  9. *The Story Without A Name*, Paramount Pictures, 1924; Stringer and Holman, *The Story Without a Name*, 109–110.
  10. Amusements in Derby, "Cosy," *Derby Daily Telegraph* (Derby, England), 12 October 1926, p. 3, BNA.
  11. Notes on Current Events, "Central Hall Cinema," *Derby Daily Telegraph*, 9 February 1926, p. 2, BNA. See also "Lone Wolf's Last Adventure," *The Daily Mail* (Hull, England), 31 July 1925, p. 6, BNA.
  12. "The Mystery of Lost Ranch." Turner Classic Movies, www.tcm.com/tcmdb/title/497626/The-Mystery-of-Lost-Ranch/full-synopsis.html.
  See also "Mysterious Death Ray in Picture at DeLuxe," *Hutchinson News* (Kansas), 5 June 1926, p. 13, NA.
  13. The fascist agents identify one another by folding a piece of paper creating a black swastika which faces to the right and therefore more identifiable with the Hakenkreuz on the Nazi flag, formally adopted by Hitler in 1920.
  14. An English transcript of the Russian subtitles can be found at the University of California at Berkeley. See The Death Ray, CineFiles, Berkeley Art Museum & Pacific Film Archive, http://cinefiles.bampfa.berkeley.edu/cinefiles/DocDetail?docid=307. The film itself is available for viewing on YouTube. Search for Lev Kuleshov, and the title appears in the Russian Cyrillic letters "Луч Смерти" (luch smerti).
  15. See "Code of the Air at Jefferson Sunday," *Jefferson City Post-Tribune* (Missouri), 12 January 1929, p. 11 [7], as well as "Bright Sketch Tops New Bill," *Galveston Daily News*, 26 January 1929, p. 18, NA.
  16. *Air Hawks*, Columbia Pictures, 1935, Sony Pictures Choice Collection DVD, 2012. For a contemporary review, see Andre Sennwald, The Screen, "At the Criterion," *NYT*, 4 June 1935, p. 26.
  17. "Kilmore Talkies," *Kilmore Free Press* (Kilmore, Victoria), 17 September 1936, p. 2, Trove. See also "Electric Ray Featured," *The Daily News* (Perth), 9 January 1936, p. 9, Trove.
  18. *Ghost Patrol*, Excelsior Pictures—Puritan Pictures, 1936, FMO.
  19. Entertainments, Edmonton Regent Theatre, *Cairns Post* (Queensland), 10 July 1939, p. 3, Trove. See also *Variety Film Reviews*, vol. 6, 14 December 1938.
  20. *Q-Planes*, Irving Asher Productions, 1939, YouTube. For a review of this film, see Frank S. Nugent, The Screen in Review, *NYT*, 16 June 1939, p. 31, as well as the review in the *Times*, "Entertainments. New Films in London," 10 July 1939, p. 10. Both gave it good marks and praised especially the performance of Richardson. The American version had the title *Clouds Over Europe*.
  21. This fact was made clear by French diplomats at the time that Grindell Matthews had become the center of attention with his death ray. See "The Death Ray," *The Register* (Adelaide), 31 May 1924, p. 9, Trove.
  22. *Blake of Scotland Yard*, Victory Pictures Corporation, 1937, FMO.
  23. *Murder at Dawn*, Big 4 Film, 1932, Internet Archive.
  24. Motion Picture Notes, *NYT*, 22 February 1920, 4: 8. It appears that this movie is lost.
  25. "The Story of 'The Flaming Disk,'" *San Saba News* (Texas), 24 February 1921, p. 5, NA.
  26. "At the Idle Hour," *Sheboygan Press* (Wisconsin), 2 April 1926, p. 15, NA. "Screen Stars and Films," *Auckland Star*, 1 August 1925, p. 28, Papers Past.
  27. Several islands bear this name, with only one remotely connected to the South Pacific. This Halfway Island, however, lies only a few miles off the coast of Queensland and belongs to Australia.
  28. *The Fighting Marines*, Mascot Serial, 1935, YouTube.
  29. *The Fighting Devil Dogs*, Republic Pictures, 1938, YouTube.
  30. This 1926 novel featured the unconventional British detective and crime-fighter Bulldog Drummond, as mentioned above, a character created by Herman Cyril McNeile. Having served in the Royal Engineers during the Great War, the author chose to write under the pseudonym "Sapper."
  31. Frank S. Nugent, The Screen, *New York Times*, 12 January 1939, p. 27.
  32. *Arrest Bulldog Drummond*, Congress Films, Inc., 1939, *Internet Archive*. See also *Variety Film Reviews*, Vol. 6, 1938–1942, 23 November 1938.

33. *The Whispering Shadow*, Mascot Pictures, 1933, YouTube. This film was released in France in 1937 under the title *L'Ombre qui tue* (The Shadow That Kills). See Emmanuel Jacob, Cinéma, "L'Ombre qui tue…, dans onze cinémas de quartier…," *La Semaine à Paris*, 14 January 1937, 21. Gallica.

34. *The Vanishing Shadow*, Universal Pictures, 1934, Internet Archive.

35. *The Phantom Empire*, Mascot Pictures Corporation, 1935, FMO.

36. *The Lost City*, Super-Serial Productions, Inc., 1935, FMO. A gaff occurred in the opening scene when the lead character pinpoints the source of the disturbances. He declares that it lies "along the twenty-eighth meridian ten degrees south of the equator in the heart of Africa," but he places his finger on a globe on the spot that looks close to the modern-day boundary separating Mali from Niger—north of the equator.

37. *Undersea Kingdom*, Republic Pictures, 1936, FMO.

38. *Ace Drummond*, Universal Pictures, 1936, FMO.

39. *The Phantom Creeps*, Universal Pictures. 1939, Internet Archive.

40. Editorial Comment, *The Catholic World*, March 1936, 649. *The Invisible Ray*, Universal Pictures, 1936, YouTube.

41. "Have They Found the Death Ray?," *The Daily News* (Perth), 21 July 1936, p. 4. Trove.

42. *Chandu the Magician*, Fox Pictures, 1932, YouTube.

43. "Death Ray," *Northern Star* (Lismore, New South Wales), 14 April 1933, p. 12, Trove.

44. *The Mask of Fu Manchu*, Metro Goldwyn Mayer, 1932, YouTube.

45. *Variety Film Review*, vol. 5, 18 December 1934.

46. *Sherlock Holmes*, Fox Film, 1932, YouTube.

47. Entertainments, "New Films in London," *Times*, 9 January 1933, p. 10. See also William K. Everson, *The Detective in Film* (Secaucus, New Jersey: Citadel Press, c. 1992), 12.

48. For reviews and synopses, see Film Reviews, "The Girl from Scotland Yard," *Sydney Morning Herald*, 26 July 1937, p. 5; "What's On at Brisbane Shows," *The Courier-Mail* (Brisbane), 25 September 1937, p. 6; and New Shows, "Story of Death Ray at Rex," *The Advertiser* (Adelaide), 24 January 1938, p. 7. Trove.

49. "Film Shows 'Death Ray' in Operation," *Gastonia Daily Gazette*, 8 May 1937, p. 8, NA.

50. "Vaudeville Acts Full of Speed," *Winnipeg Free Press*, 1 May 1937, p. 18, NA.

51. *Dick Tracy*, Republic Pictures, 1937. YouTube. The movie, released in February 1937, depicts the San Francisco-Oakland Bay Bridge, which opened in November 1936 six months before the Golden Gate Bridge was completed.

52. "The God of War," *The Era* (London), 23 April 1898, p. 15, BNA.

53. Cicely Hamilton, *The Old Adam*, The British Drama League of Modern British Drama No. 13 (New York: Brentano's, 1927), n.p.

54. *Alfred Hitchcock Scholars Meet Here!*, 'The McGuffin' Web Page. http://labyrinth.net.au/~muffin/index.html.

55. "The London Stage," *NYT*, 6 January 1929, 4: 1. See also Ernest Marshall, "Notes of London Screen, A 'Bloodless Revolution' in Britain's Film Industry—New English Pictures," *NYT*, 13 July 1930, 8: 4.

56. Local Amusements, *Nottingham Evening Post*, 24 March 1925, p. 6, BNA.

57. "The Council of Seven," *The Argus* (Melbourne), 6 October 1930, p. 15, Trove.

58. "Refreshingly Rare," *Aberdeen Press and Journal* (Scotland), 9 April 1929, p. 7, BNA.

59. Little Theatre, Review of *Before Midnight*, *Times*, 9 April 1929, p. 14.

60. "Death Ray Play in London," *NYT*, 8 October 1935, p, 26.

61. Gossip of the Rialto, *NYT*, 5 November 1939, 9: 1–2.

62. "A World War of the Future," *Nineteen-Sixty-Four*, by H.E.M. Flinn. Reviewed by "Polygon," *The Western Australian* (Perth), 14 March 1932, p. 10. Trove.

63. After losing control of *Amazing Stories* in 1929, Gernsback went on to start others, including *Science Wonder Stories* and *Air Wonder Stories*. He also contributed his own science fiction stories, most notably *Ralph 124C 41+* in 1911.

64. George Frederic Stratton, "The Poniatowski Ray," *The Electrical Experimenter*, January 1916, 473.

65. Ibid.
66. Ibid.
67. Ray Cummings, "The Fire People," *The Argosy-Allstory Weekly*, 21 October 1922, 485. PMP. The subsequent installments appeared in the 21 and 28 October issues as well as in those of 4, 11, and 18 November.
68. Ray Cummings, *The Fire People*, eBook # 25780, 13 June 2008, 36, Project Gutenberg.
69. Philip Francis Nowlan, *Armageddon 2419 A. D.*, Project Gutenberg of Australia eBook No. 0601821.txt, Edition 1.
70. Hugo Gernsback, "The Magnetic Storm," *Amazing Stories*, July 1926, 351, Internet Archive.
71. Ibid.
72. Louis Buswell, "Clouds of Death," *Amazing Stories*, June 1929, 272–276.
73. Morrison F. Colladay, "The Return of the Cosmic Gun," *Wonder Stories*, October 1931, 586, PMP.
74. Félix Celval, *Le rayon infernal*, Romans pour la jeunesse (Paris: F. Rouff, Éditeur, 1935), 12.
75. Lowell Howard Morrow, "The Blue Demon," *Air Wonder Stories*, December 1929, 487, PMP.
76. R. V. Happel, "The Triple Ray," *Amazing Stories Quarterly*, Fall 1930, 529.
77. "The Saint Closes the Case," *The Saint with Vincent Price*, Internet Archive.
78. Everett F. Bleiler and Richard J. Bleiler, *Science-Fiction: The Gernsback Years* (Kent, Ohio: The Kent State University Press, 1998), 18.
79. Jack Barnette, "The Purple Death," *Amazing Stories*, July 1929, 370.
80. Ibid., 373.
81. P. Schuyler Miller, "Dust of Destruction," *Wonder Stories*, February 1931, 925, PMP.
82. Bleiler, *Science-Fiction*, 55.
83. Ibid., 9.
84. Eando Binder, "Static," *Thrilling Wonder Stories*, December 1936, 38.
85. Allan K. Echols, "The Island of Doctor X," *Thrilling Wonder Stories*, December 1936, 95.
86. The Lighter Side, "A Radio 'Thriller,'" *Nottingham Evening Post*, 11 September 1928, p. 4, BNA.
87. "The Mystery of the Death Ray Tube," 12 Feb. 1936, *Phyl Coe Mysteries*, recording from Internet Archive.
88. Régis Gignoux, "La Machine à finir la guerre," *Le Figaro*, 13 April 1924, p. 1.
89. "Olympic=City," Revuette de paravente, by Fursy and Mauricet, *Les Annales politiques et littéraires*, 6 July 1924, 22. Gallica.
90. Ibid.
91. Georges-Armand Masson, "Vers un monde meilleur," *Les Modes de la Femme de France*, 25 May 1924, 9. Gallica.
92. "Les Échos d'Henriot," *Le Journal amusant: journal illustré, journal d'images, journal comique, critique, satirique, etc.*, 14 June 1924, 2. Gallica.
93. M. Radiguet, "Revue en vitesse de l'Année 1924," *Le Journal amusant: journal illustré, journal d'images, journal comique, critique, satirique, etc.*, 3 January 1925, p. 11, Gallica.
94. The incident occurred on 27 November 1923 when Asquith spoke at a rally in Paisley. The story was carried in numerous newspapers and repeated for quite some time afterward. See "Mr. Asquith Heckled," *The Western Morning News and Mercury* (Devon, England), 28 November 1923, p. 5, BNA; as well as British Politics, "The Election," *The West Australian* (Perth), 24 October 1924, p. 9. Trove.
95. "Robin Red-Flag," *Punch*, 4 June 1924, 611.
96. "A Death Ray Challenge," *The Courier* (Dundee, Scotland), 31 May 1924, p. 4, BNA.
97. Science, *Punch*, 4 June 1924, 618.
98. Ibid., "The Death-Ray in Antiquity," 617.
99. "The Death Ray Glance," *The West Australian* (Perth), 1 August 1924, p. 6. Trove.
100. Henry McLemore, "Hank to Sell Helmet As Women Calm Down, Death Ray Glances Gone From Gals' Golf Tourneys," *Oakland Tribune*, 10 March 1936, p. 25, NA.
101. Gossip from the Garages, "Motor Tragedy," *The Advocate* (Burnie, Tasmania), 23 April 1924, p. 10. Trove.
102. John Galsworthy, *A Modern Comedy* (New York: Charles Scribner's Sons, 1929), 386, Hathi.
103. "Pins and Needles, Comedy on the Pavement," *The Mercury* (Hobart, Tasmania), 14 August 1931, p. 4. Trove.

104. "Le rayon fatal," *L'Aéro*, 3 May 1935, 9. Gallica.

105. "The Chain Store Menace," *The Southern Mail* (Bowral, New South Wales), 24 January 1936, p. 1, Trove.

106. Advertisement, *New Zealand Herald* (Auckland), 5 July 1927, p. 5, Papers Past.

107. Frank Reid, "Invisible Ray," *Townsville Daily Bulletin* (Queensland), 21 August 1939, p. 3. Trove. Installments ran from August to late September.

108. The COLYUM, Let's Not Be Too D___d Serious, "Suggestion for Movie Bedtime Story," *Kossuth County Advance* (Algona, Iowa), 24 August 1937, p. 8 [Editorial Page], NA.

109. Gene Ahern, "Our Boarding House," *Manitowoc Herald Times* (Wisconsin), 2 September 1933, p. 16, NA.

110. Monte Barrett and Frank Ellis, "Jane Arden," *Oakland Tribune*, 25 September 1930, Daily Magazine, p. 4 M [34]; Al Capp, "Li'l Abner," *Oakland Tribune*, 30 October 1938, 1st Comic Section, p. 2 [48]; and Harry J. Tuthill, "The Bungle Family," *The Chronicle-Telegram* (Elyria, Ohio), 29 February 1932, p. 13, NA.

111. Harry J. Tuthill, "The Bungle Family," *Frederick News Post* (Maryland), 1 March 1932, p. 6, NA.

112. E. C. Segar, "Sappo," *Port Arthur News*, 11 March 1934, Comics Section, p. 1 [25]. NA.

113. "Inspector Post and His Junior Detective Aides," *San Antonio Light*, 14 August 1932, Comic Weekly Section, p. 11 [65], NA.

Bibliography

This bibliography is divided into eight sections: Books—Nonfiction; Books—Fiction; Serial Novels and Short Stories in Newspapers and Magazines; Pulps; Journals and Magazines; Films; Radio; and Miscellaneous.

Books—Nonfiction

The American Library Annual for 1913–1914. New York: R. R. Bowker Company, 1914. GB.

Anderson, Charles R. *Giulio Ulivi; The Inventor Who Might Have Ended Wars.* Ebook, Charles R. Anderson, 2013.

Applied Physics. Science in World War II. Edited by C. G. Suits, George R. Harrison, and Louis Jordan. Boston: Little, Brown and Company, 1948.

Bakeless, John. *The Origin of the Next War: A Study in the Tensions of the Modern World.* London: Jonathan Cape, 1926.

Bleiler, Everett F., and Richard J. Bleiler. *Science Fiction: The Gernsback Years.* Kent, Ohio: The Kent State University Press, 1998.

Bond, Brian. *Liddell Hart: A Study of His Military Thought.* London: Cassell, 1977.

Brandt, Dina. *Der deutsche Zukunftsroman 1918–1945: Gattungstypologie und sozialgeschichtliche Verortung.* Tübingen: Max Niemeyer Verlag, 2007.

Breuer, William B. *Secret Weapons of World War II.* New York: John Wiley and Sons, 2000.

Brown, Louis. *A Radar History of World War II: Technical and Military Imperatives.* Bristol: Institute of Physics Publishing, 1999.

Chesterton, G. K. "The End of the Armistice," in *The Collected Works of G. K Chesterton,* Vol. 5. San Francisco: Ignatius Press, 1987.

Churchill, Winston S. *The Dardanelles Campaign and the Fall of the Cabinet,* Vol 2. of *The World Crisis.* New York: Charles Scribner's Sons, 1923.

Clark, Ronald W. *Tizard.* Cambridge, Massachusetts: The M.I.T. Press, 1965.

Clarke, I. F. *The Tale of the Next Great War, 1871–1914: Fictions of Future Warfare and Battles Still-to-Come.* Syracuse, New York: Syracuse University Press, 1995.

———. *Voices Prophesying War 1763–1984.* London: Oxford University Press, 1966.

D'Albe, E. E. Fournier, *The Moon-Element: An Introduction to the Wonders of Selenium.* New York: D. Appleton and Company, 1924. Hathi.

Dalton, Kathleen. *Theodore Roosevelt: A Strenuous Life.* New York: Alfred A. Knopf, 2002.

Doberer, Kurt. *Elektrokrieg: Maschine gegen Mensch.* Vienna: Saturn-Verlag, 1937.

———. *On the Way to Electro War.* London: John Gifford, 1943.

Dominik, Hans. *Vom Schraubstock zum Schreibtisch.* Berlin: Verlag Scherl, 1943.

Douglas, Sir George, and Sir George Dalhousie, eds. *The Panmure Papers,* Vol. 1. London: Hodder and Stoughton, 1908. Hathi.

Dupuy, R. Ernest, and George Fielding Eliot. *If War Comes*. New York: Macmillan, 1937.

Ellenborough, Lord. *The Guilt of Lord Cochrane in 1814: A Criticism*. London: Smith, Elder and Company, 1914.

Everson, William K. *The Detective in Film*. Secaucus, New Jersey: Citadel Press, c. 1992.

Fanning, William J., Jr. "The Historical Death Ray and Science Fiction in the 1920s and 1930s." In *Vintage Visions: Essays on Early Science Fiction*. Edited by Arthur B. Evans. Middletown, Connecticut: Wesleyan University Press, 2014.

Fisher, Peter S. *Fantasy and Politics: Visions of the Future in the Weimar Republic*. Madison, Wisconsin: The University of Wisconsin Press, 1991.

Foster, Jonathan. *The Death Ray: The Secret Life of Harry Grindell Matthews*. Gloucester, United Kingdom: Inventive Publishing, 2009.

Franklin, H. Bruce. *Future Perfect: American Science Fiction of the Nineteenth Century—An Anthology*. New York: Oxford University Press, 1968.

Gannon, Charles E. *Rumors of War and Infernal Machines: Technomilitary Agenda-Setting in American and British Speculative Fiction*. Lanham, Maryland: Rowman and Littlefield Publishers, 2005.

Gilbert, Martin. *The Prophet of Truth: 1922–1939*. Vol. 5 of *Winston S. Churchill*. Boston: Houghton Mifflin Company, 1977.

Grunden, Walter E. *Secret Weapons and World War II: Japan in the Shadow of Big Science*. Lawrence, Kansas: University Press of Kansas, 2005.

Hecht, Jeff. *Beam Weapons: The Next Arms Race*. New York: Plenum Press, 1984.

Irwin, Will. *The "Next War": An Appeal to Common Sense*. New York: E. P. Dutton and Company, 1921.

Kozyreva (Kazan), Maria and Elena. "H. G. Wells and A. K. Tolstoy." In *Lost Worlds & Mad Elephants: Literature, Science and Technology 1700–1990*. Edited by Elmar Schenkel and Stefan Wels. Berlin: Galda and Wilch, 1999.

La Stella, Mario. *Il Raggio della Morte*. Rome: Istituto per L'Enciclopedia de Carlo, 1942.

Lefebure, Victor. *The Riddle of the Rhine: Chemical Strategy in Peace and War*. London: W. Collins Sons and Company, 1921.

Lofficier, Jean-Marc, and Randy Lofficier. *French Science Fiction, Fantasy, Horror, and Pulp Fiction: A Guide to Cinema, Television, Radio, Animation, Comic Books and Literature*. Jefferson, North Carolina: McFarland & Company, Inc., Publishers, 2000.

Lytton, Earl of. *The Life of Edward Bulwer First Lord Lytton*. Vol. 1. London: Macmillan and Company, 1913. GB.

MacKenzie, Norman, and Jeanne MacKenzie, *H. G. Wells: A Biography*. New York: Simon and Schuster, 1973.

Marvin, Carolyn. *When Old Technologies Were New: Thinking About Electric Communication in the Late Nineteenth Century*. New York: Oxford University Press, 1988.

Méric, Victor. *Guerre qui revient fraîche et gazeuse!* Paris: Éditions Sirius, 1932. Gallica.

Miessner, B. F. *Radiodynamics: The Wireless Control of Torpedoes and Other Mechanisms*. New York: D. Van Nostrand Company, 1916. GB. *New York Times Current History: The European War*. Vol. 17. New York: New York Times Company, 1919. GB.

Pirolo, Nicholas. *Babylon: Political and Ecclesiastical, showing characteristics of Anti-Christ and False Prophet considering Mussolini and the Pope with their respective "VV Il Duce" and Vicarius Fili Dei" 666*. Milwaukee: Word Publishing Company, 1937. Hathi.

Rieuneau, Maurice. *Guerre et révolution dans le roman français de 1919 à 1939*. Paris: Klincksieck, 1974. GB.

Riley, Dick, and Pam McAllister, eds. *The Bedside, Bathtub & Armchair Companion to Agatha Christie*. New York: Frederick Ungar Publishing, 1979.

Rynin, N. A. *Radiant Energy: Science Fiction and Scientific Projects*. Translated by IPST Staff. First published in Leningrad, 1931. Vol. 1, No. 3 of *Interplanetary Flight and Communication*. Jerusalem: Published for the National Aeronautics and Space Administration and the National Science Foundation, Washington, D.C., by the Israel Program for Scientific Translations, 1971.

Schachtman, Tom. *Terrors and Marvels: How Science and Technology Changed the Character and Outcome of World War II*. New York: William Morrow, An Imprint of HarperCollins-Publishers, 2002.
Seifer, Marc J. *Wizard: The Life and Times of Nikola Tesla, Biography of a Genius*. Secaucus, New Jersey: Carol Publishing Group, 1996.
Seydewitz, Max, and Kurt Doberer. *Todesstrahlen und andere neue Kriegswaffen*. London: Malik-Verlag, 1936.
Smith, Denis Mack. *Mussolini*. New York: Vintage Books, A Division of Random House, 1983.
Smith, Don G. *H. G. Wells on Film: The Utopian Nightmare*. Jefferson, North Carolina: McFarland & Company, Inc., Publishers, 2002.
Smith, P. D. *Doomsday Men: The Real Dr. Strangelove and the Dream of the Superweapon*. New York: St. Martin's Press, 2007.
Speer, Albert. *Inside the Third Reich: Memoirs by Albert Speer*. Translated by Richard and Clara Winston. New York: The Macmillan Company, 1970.
Stephenson, Charles. *The Admiral's Secret Weapon: Lord Dundonald and the Origins of Chemical Warfare*. Woodbridge, United Kingdom: The Boydell Press, 2006.
Variety Film Reviews 1907–1980. 16 vols. New York: Garland Publishing, Inc., 1983.
Waloschek, Pedro. *Todesstrahlen als Lebensretter*. Norderstedt: Books on Demand, GmbH, 2004. GB.
Weart, Spencer R. *Nuclear Fear: A History of Images*. Cambridge, Massachusetts: Harvard University Press, 1988.
Zimmerman, David. *Britain's Shield: Radar and the Defeat of the Luftwaffe*. The Hill, Stroud, Gloucestershire, United Kingdom: Amberley Publishing, 2001, electronic edition 2012.
Zimmern, Helen. *Italy of the Italians*. Rev. ed. New York: Charles Scribner's Sons, 1914. GB.

Books—Fiction

Agraives, Jean d.' *La Cité des sables*. Paris: Hachette, 1935.
Allorge, H. *Les rayons ensorcelés*. Paris: Fernand Nathan, Éditeur, 1935.
Appleton, Victor. *Tom Swift and His Electric Rifle, or Daring Adventures in Elephant Land*. New York: Grosset and Dunlap, 1911. Internet Archive.
Arlen, Michael. *Man's Mortality*. Garden City, New York: Doubleday, Doran and Company, 1933.
Ashton-Wolfe, H. "Allivi: The Bogus Death Ray," in *Warped in the Making: Crimes of Love and Hate*. London: Hurst and Blackett, Ltd., 1928. Internet Archive.
Baxter, Gregory. *Blue Lightning*. London: Cassell and Company, 1926.
Burdekin, Kay. *The Rebel Passion*. New York: William Morrow and Company, 1929.
Christie, Agatha. *The Big Four*. New York: HarperCollins Publishers, EPub edition, August 2011 [Kindle]; London: Collins, 1927.
Conan Doyle, Arthur. *The Best Science Fiction of Arthur Conan Doyle*. Edited by Charles G. Waugh and Martin H. Greenberg. Carbondale: Southern Illinois University Press, 1981.
Cummings, Ray. *The Fire People*, eBook # 25780, 13 June 2008. Project Gutenberg.
Delmont, Joseph. *Die Stadt unter dem Meere*. 6th ed. Leipzig: Verlag Fr. Wilh. Grunow, 1925.
Dominik, Hans. *Die Macht der Drei: Ein Roman aus dem Jahre 1955*. Leipzig: Ernst Keils Nachfolger (August Scherl) G.m.b.H., 1922. Internet Archive.
Edwards, Charman. *Fear Haunts the Roses*. London: Ward, Lock and Company, 1936.
Eichacker, Reinhold. *Der Kampf ums Gold*. Munich: Universal-Verlag, 1924.
Fairlie, Gerard. *Scissors Cut Paper*. New York: A. L. Burt Company, Publishers, 1928.
Farrère, Claude. *Les condamnés à mort*. Paris: Ernest Flammarion, Éditeur, 1921. Google Livres (French Google).
Galsworthy, John. *A Modern Comedy*. New York: Charles Scribner's Sons, 1929. Hathi.
Gerrare, Wirt. *The Warstock: A Tale of Tomorrow*. London: W. W. Greener, 1898. Hathi.
Gignoux, Régis, and Roland Dorgelès, *La Machine à finir la guerre*. Paris: Albin Michel, Éditeur, 1917.

Godfrey, Hollis. *The Man Who Ended War*. Boston: Little, Brown, and Company, 1908.

Graffigny, Henry de. *Voyage de cinq Américains dans les planètes: roman astronomique*. Paris: Librairie Gedalge, 1925. Gallica.

Griffith, George. *The Lord of Labour*. London: F. V. White and Company, 1911, Internet Archive.

_____. *The World Masters*. London: John Long, 1903. GB.

_____. *The World Peril of 1910*. London: F. V. White and Company, 1907. GB.

Hadfield, Robert L., and Frank E. Farncombe. *Ruled by Radio*. 1925. Vancleave, Mississippi: Ramble House, 2008.

Hamilton, Cicely. *The Old Adam*. The British Drama League of Modern British Drama No. 13. New York: Brentano's, 1927.

Hanstein, O. *Radiopolis*. Adaptation Tancrède Vallerey. Paris: Fernand Nathan, Éditeur, 1933.

Hyne, C. J. Cutcliffe. *Empire of the World*. 1910. New York: Arno Press, 1975. GB.

Irving, Washington. *Knickerbocker's History of New York*. Author's Autograph Edition. Vol. 1. New York: G. P. Putnam's Sons, 1895. GB.

Jane, Fred T. *The Violet Flame: A Story of Armageddon and After*. 1899. New York: Arno Press, 1975.

Keeler, Harry Stephen. *The Black Satchel*. London: Ward, Lock and Company, 1931.

Le Queux, William. *The Mystery of the Green Ray*. London: Hodder and Stoughton, 1915. Internet Archive.

_____. *The Zeppelin Destroyer: Being Some Chapters of Secret History*. London: Hodder and Stoughton, 1916. Internet Archive.

London, Jack. *The Complete Short Stories of Jack London*. Vol. 2. Edited by Earle Labor, Robert C. Leitz, III and I. Milo Shepherd. Stanford, CA: Stanford University Press, 1993.

Lytton, Edward Bulwer. *The Coming Race*. Edinburgh: William Blackwood and Sons, 1871. Hathi.

Macbeth, Madge. *Wings in the West*. London: John Hamilton Limited, Publishers, 1937. Internet Archive.

Newman, Bernard. *Armoured Doves: A Peace Book*. London: Jarrolds, 1931.

Nowlan, Philip Francis. *Armageddon 2419 A. D.* Project Gutenberg of Australia eBook No. 0601821.txt, Edition 1.

Noyes, Pierrepont B. *The Pallid Giant: A Tale of Yesterday and Tomorrow*. New York: Fleming H. Revell Company, 1927. Hathi.

Oppenheim, E. Phillips. *The Dumb Gods Speak*. Boston: Little, Brown, and Company, 1937.

Reeve, Arthur B. *The Exploits of Elaine*. New York: Harper and Brothers, Publishers, 1914. GB.

_____. "The Terror in the Air," in *The Silent Bullet: The Adventures of Craig Kennedy, Scientific Detective*. New York: Grosset and Dunlap, Publishers, 1910.

Rohmer, Sax. *The Golden Scorpion*. New York: McKinlay, Stone and Mackenzie, 1920. GB.

Rutledge, Maryse. *The Silver Peril*. New York: Walter J. Black, 1931.

Sapper [Herman Cyril McNeile]. 1935. *Bulldog Drummond at Bay*. A Project Gutenberg Australia eBook.

Schoenaich, Paul Freiherr von. *Der Krieg im Jahre 1930*. Berlin Hessenwinkel: Verlag der Neuen Gesellschaft G.m.b.H., 1925.

Schuyler, George S., writing as Samuel I. Brooks, *Black Empire*. Boston: Northeastern University Press, 1991.

Schuyler, George S. *Ethiopian Stories*, complied and edited with an introduction by Robert A. Hill. Boston: Northeastern University Press, 1994.

Serviss, Garrett P. *Edison's Conquest of Mars*. 1898. Los Angeles: Carcosa House, 1947. Hathi.

Shiel, M. P. *The Yellow Peril*. London: Victor Gollancz, 1929.

Silone, Ignazio. *Bread and Wine*. Translated by Gwenda David and Eric Mosbacher. New York: Harper and Brothers Publishers, 1937.

Small, Austin J. *The Avenging Ray*. Garden City, New York: Doubleday, Doran and Company, 1930.

Snell, Edmund. *The Z Ray*. Philadelphia: J. B. Lippincott Company, 1932.

_____. *The Sound-Machine*. London: Skeffington and Son, c. 1932.

Solf, F. E. *1934 Deutschlands Auferstehung*. Naumberg: a. d. S. Carl August Tancré Verlag, 1922.

Stevens, Rowan. "Sorakichi,—Prometh-

contemporain." Livre II. *Revue militaire française* 24 (April-June 1927): 34–50.
Caresse, Philippe. "The *Iéna* Disaster." *Warship* 2007, 121–138. GB.
Churchill, Winston S. International Relations Section, "Shall We Commit Suicide," *The Nation*, 3 December 1924, 608, 610.
"La Cité Foudroyée." *Les Spectacles*, 9 January 1925, 13–14. Gallica.
"Civilization Must Abolish War or War Will Destroy Civilization." *Popular Science Monthly*, December 1921, 26–27.
D'Albe, E. E. Fournier. "The Myth of the Death Ray." *The New Republic*, 16 July 1924, 207–208.
Dash, Mike. "The Amazing (If True) Story of the Submarine Mechanic Who Blew Himself Up Then Resurfaced as a Secret Agent for Queen Victoria," 30 June 2014, Smithsonian.com.
Davis, Watson. "Cathode Ray a New Tool of Science." *Current History*, December 1926, 392–396.
———. "Momentous Discovery in the Science of Radiation." *Current History*, January 1926, 552–554.
"Death-Dealing and Labor-Saving Rays." *Scientific Monthly*, January 1925, 108–111.
"The Death of the Death Ray." *Scientific American*, December 1934, 287.
"Death Ray Again." *The Pathfinder*, 28 July 1934, 14.
"The Death-Ray in Antiquity." *Punch*, 4 June 1924, 617.
"'Death Ray' Is Carried by Shafts of Light." *Popular Mechanics*, August 1924, 189–192.
"'Death Ray' May Outlaw War." *Modern Mechanix and Inventions*, October 1936. http://blog.modernmechanix.com/death-ray-may-outlaw-war/
"Death Ray, of What?," *The Pathfinder*, 11 August 1934, 14.
"Death Rays Deferred." *Time*, 2 December 1946, 99.
"Death Rays from Silent Sounds." *Modern Mechanix and Inventions*, May 1932, 67. http://blog.modernmechanix.com/death-rays-from-silent-sounds/.
"Death Stroke." *Time*, 10 August 1925, 22–23.

Delano, Frederic Mortimer. "Man's Most Terrible Invention." *Popular Science Monthly*, August 1924, 33–34.
"Did the British Admiralty Decline to Use Burning-Glasses?" and "Lord Cochrane's 'Horrible' War Device." *Munsey's Magazine*, October 1919, 126. Hathi.
Dowd, George Lee, Jr. "Getting Ready for the Next War." *Popular Science Monthly*, December 1927, 26–27.
"Dundonald's Destroyer." *The North American Review*, November 1914, 656–660.
"Les Échos d'Henriot." *Le Journal amusant: journal illustré, journal d'images, journal comique, critique, satirique, etc.*, 14 June 1924, 2. Gallica.
"Edison Out-Edisoned." *Lightning*, 6 February 1896, 111. In Marvin, Carolyn. *When Old Technologies Were New: Thinking About Electric Communication in the Late Nineteenth Century*. New York: Oxford University Press, 1988, 146.
Editorial Comment. *The Catholic World*, March 1936, 649.
"Electrical Engines of War." *The Literary Digest* (from *Electricity*), 7 May 1898, 554.
"Electricity in Warfare, and Telegraphing Without Wires." *Chambers's Journal of Popular Literature, Science and Arts*, 9 October 1897, 655–656, GB.
"Electro-Tank Shoots Lightning Rays." *Modern Mechanix and Inventions*, August 1935, 81.
"England." *The Independent*, 7 June 1924, 323.
Fanning, William J., Jr. "The Historical Death Ray and Science Fiction of the 1920s and 1930s." *Science Fiction Studies* 111, Vol. 37, Part 2 (July 2010): 253–274.
French, Donald G. "Unlimited Power from the Sun." *Illustrated World*, December 1917, 511-512, Hathi.
"German Death Ray Pistol Stuns Animals at Mile Range." *Modern Mechanix and Inventions*, January 1935. http://blog.modernmechanix.com/german-death-ray-pistol-stuns-animals-at-mile-range/#more.
Les Grandes aventures. *Revue des Lectures*, 15 December 1927, 1244, Gallica.
Hart, Joseph K. "The Next War." *The Survey*, 21 May 1921, 234–235.

"High-Frequency Sound Waves Destroy Life." *Popular Mechanics*, February 1927, 241.

Honoré, F. "L'arrêt des avions par ondes hertziennes." *L'Illustration*, 29 December 1923, 689.

"Inventor Hides Secret of 'Death Ray.'" *Popular Science Monthly*, February 1940, 117.

"Invisible Death." Science, *Time*, 21 April 1924, 19.

"'Invisible Dust' Curtain to Halt War Planes." *Popular Mechanics*, November 1934, 693.

"Kills Animals with Noises." *Science News Letter*, 5 May 1926, 9.

Lai, Rick. "The Legacy of Hanoi Shan." http://pjfarmer.com/woldnewton/Hanoi_Shan.pdf.

"Lightning as a Weapon." *Popular Science Monthly*, January 1924, 61.

Low, A. M. "How We Shall Fight in A. D. 2023." *The Nineteenth Century and After*, September 1923, 354–358.

Maclay, Edgar Stanton Maclay. "'Burning-Glasses,' Dundonald's Destroyer?," *The North American Review*, March 1915, 434–438.

Marva, José. *The Sciences and War. Memorial de Ingenieros* (Madrid) 15 November 1915. The inaugural discourse of the 5th Congress of the Spanish Association for the Progress of the Sciences, in Valladolid, 17–22 October 1915, "XI.—Intervention of Science to Diminish the Evils of War," in Cornélis De Witt Willcox, *The International Military Digest Annual: A Review of the Current Literature of Military Science for 1916*. New York: Cumulative Digest Corporation, 1917. GB.

Masson, Georges-Armand. "Vers un monde meilleur." *Les Modes de la Femme de France*, 25 May 1924, 9. Gallica.

Maxim, Hiram Percy. "The Next War in the Air." Part I. *Popular Mechanics*, January 1936, 66–73.

_____. "The Next War on the Land." Part II. *Popular Mechanics*, February1936, 194–201.

Mayer, Douglas W. F. "The Truth About Death Rays." *Science Digest* (from *Discovery*), August 1940, 44–48.

Miller, Jay Earle. "New Weapons for the Next War." *Modern Mechanix and Inventions*, November 1931, 46–51.

http://blog.modernmechanix.com/new-weapons-for-the-next-war/.

"The Mystery of Lost Ranch." Turner Classic Movies, www.tcm.com/tcmdb/title/497626/The-Mystery-of-Lost-Ranch/full-synopsis.html.

"Neutrons, Tool of Physics, Deadly Biological Menace." *Science News Letter*, 14 March 1936, 163.

"A New Death-Dealing Ray." *Literary Digest*, 7 June 1924, 27–28.

"New Ray Makes Cold Stones Glow." *Popular Mechanics*, January 1927, 1–2.

"New Scientific Discovery." *The Ohio Architect, Engineer and Builder*, October 1913, 22: 4. GB.

N° 12, Jean d'Agraives, *Le Rayon Swastika*. *Revue des Lectures*, 15 February 1930, 193, Gallica.

Notes. *Nature* 78 (24 September 1908): 513.

O'Callaghan, Frank. "New Ray Destroys Zeppelins." *Popular Mechanics*, May 1917, 679–680.

"Oh Dear! Another War Terror." *Answers* (London), 30 July 1897, 182. In Marvin, Carolyn, *When Old Technologies Were New: Thinking About Electric Communication in the Late Nineteenth Century*. New York: Oxford University Press, 1988.

"Olympic=City." Revuette de paravente, Fursy and Mauricet. *Les Annales politiques et littéraires*, 6 July 1924, 18–23. Gallica.

Parsons, Charles L. "Humane Chemical Warfare." *Literary Digest*, 19 September 1931, 28.

"Power from the Invisible World." *Popular Mechanics*, June 1933, 890–893.

President's Address. "The Past, Present and Future of the Roentgen Ray." *Transactions of the American Roentgen Ray Society*, Sixth Annual Meeting, 28, 29, 30 September, 1905. Pittsburgh: Press Murdoch, Kerr and Company, 1906, 29–39. Hathi.

"Radio Death Force." *Science News Letter*, 8 January 1927, 17.

Radiguet, M. "Revue en vitesse de l'Année 1924." *Le Journal amusant: journal illustré, journal d'images, journal comique, critique, satirique, etc.*, 3 January 1925, 11, Gallica.

"Ray of Death Kills at 6 Miles." *Modern Mechanix and Inventions*, August 1935, 31.

Bibliography 263

"Le rayon fatal." *L'Aéro*, 3 May 1935, 9. Gallica.
"Le rayon invisible et son inventeur." *L'Illustration*, 24 May 1924, 512.
"Le rayon mortel." *Les Spectacles*, 20 June 1924, 16.
"Rays That Can Blow Up Battleships." *Current Opinion*, January 1914, 36–37.
Renseignements Divers. *Revue d'Artillerie* 71 (December 1907): 184. Gallica.
Review of George Griffith's *The World Masters*. *The Athenaeum*, 11 April 1903, 460. Hathi.
Revue des Livres. *L'Aéronautique*, August 1926, No. 87, 284, Gallica.
"Robin Red-Flag." *Punch*, 4 June 1924, 611.
Science. *Punch*, 4 June 1924, 618.
Science. "Welder at Work." *Time*, 10 August 1936, 29–30.
Secor, H. Winfield. "The Tesla High Frequency Oscillator." *The Electrical Experimenter*, March 1916, 614–615.
"Secret Ray to Stop Planes Is Seen in Accidents." *Popular Mechanics*, December 1923, 931.
Selden, Charles A. "World Destruction." *The Ladies Home Journal*, September 1923, 6.
Serrigny, General Bernard. "L'organisation de la nation pour le temps de guerre." *Revue des Deux Mondes*, 1 December 1923, 583–601.
"Shall We Commit Suicide?" *The American Review of Reviews*, November 1924, 537–538.
"Shattering the Atom." *The Literary Digest*, 31 January 1925, 23.
Shorter, Clement. "Mr. Wells's 'War of the Worlds.'" *The Bookman*, Vol. 7, March-August 1898, May, 246–247.
"Some Scientific Hoaxes." *Chambers's Journal of Popular Literature, Science and Arts*, 12 June 1880, 376–378. GB.
Stevens, Truman. "Manless Monsters to Decide Future War." *Popular Science Monthly*, August 1925, 24–25.
Stimson, Thomas E. "The Wonders of High Frequency." *Popular Mechanics*, December 1935, 860.
"Tesla: Inventor Has Scheme for Dealing Out Death Wholesale." *News-Week*, 21 July 1934, 25.
"Tesla at 75." *Time*, 20 July 1931, 27.
"Tesla's Ray." *Science, Time*, 23 July 1934, 48–49.
Things Scientific. "Sh! That Mysterious Ray of Light." *The Pathfinder*, 3 May 1924, 12.
Thone, Frank. "A New Magic." *Century Magazine*, February 1927, 449–456.
_____. "Death Rays? No!," *Science News Letter*, 23 March 1935, 186–188.
"Thunderbolts Made to Order." *Current Opinion*, August 1923, 169.
Trévise, Robert. Review of *La Cité Foudroyée*, *Cinéa-Ciné pour tous*, 15 November 1924, 26. Gallica.
"Ulivi's Experiments in Exploding Bombs with Infra-Red Rays." *The Labor Digest*, July 1914, 7: 6, 31–32. GB.
Urbain, Georges. La vie scientifique. "Considérations sur le Verre et l'État Vitreux; Le 'Rayon Invisible' de M. Grindell Matthews." *Les Annales politiques et littéraires*, 20 April 1924, 458. Gallica.
"A Violet Ray That Kills." *Current Opinion*, June 1924, 828–829.
"'Viper' Weapons." *Literary Digest*, 24 December 1921, 8–9.
"War Engines of Future to Be Electric." *Popular Mechanics*, November 1923, 757.
"Warfare of the Future: The Radium Destroyer." *The Electrical Experimenter*, November 1915, 315.
Wilkins, Harold T., "War Secrets Revealed." *Popular Mechanics*, June 1927, 978–984.

Films

Ace Drummond. Universal Pictures, 1936. FMO.
Air Hawks. Columbia Pictures, 1935. Sony Pictures Choice Collection DVD, 2012.
Arrest Bulldog Drummond. Congress Films, 1939. Internet Archive.
Blake of Scotland Yard. Victory Pictures Corporation, 1937. FMO.
Chandu the Magician. Fox Pictures, 1932. YouTube.
The Death Ray ("Луч Смерти"). 1925. YouTube.
Dick Tracy. Republic Pictures, 1937. YouTube.
The Fighting Devil Dogs. Republic Pictures, 1938. YouTube.
The Fighting Marines. Mascot Serial, 1935. YouTube.

Ghost Patrol. Excelsior Pictures-Puritan Pictures, 1936. FMO.
The Invisible Ray. Universal Pictures, 1936. YouTube.
The Lost City. Super-Serial Productions, Inc., 1935. FMO.
The Mask of Fu Manchu. Metro Goldwyn Mayer, 1932. YouTube.
Murder at Dawn. Big 4 Film, 1932. Internet Archive.
The Phantom Creeps. Universal Pictures, 1939. YouTube.
The Phantom Empire. Mascot Pictures Corporation, 1935. FMO.
Q-Planes. Irving Asher Productions, 1939. YouTube.
Sherlock Holmes. Fox Film, 1932. YouTube.
Undersea Kingdom. Republic Pictures, 1936. FMO.
The Vanishing Shadow. Universal Pictures, 1934. Internet Archive.
The Whispering Shadow. Mascot Pictures, 1933. YouTube.

Radio

"The Mystery of the Death Ray Tube." *Phyl Coe Mysteries*, 12 February 1936. Internet Archive.
"The Saint Closes the Case," *The Saint with Vincent Price*, n.d. (recordings between 1944 and 1951). Internet Archive.
"Sounds Historical Hour One–30 August 2009, Radio New Zealand National. www.radionz.co.nz/national/programmes/soundshistorical/audio/2050197/sounds-historical-hour-one-30-august-2009. Accessed 11 June 2014.

Miscellaneous

The Death Ray, CineFiles, Berkeley Art Museum & Pacific Film Archive, http://cinefiles.bampfa.berkeley.edu/cinefiles/DocDetail?docid=307.
Geopolitical Fiction, Inhaltsangabe anzeigen, www.cafegroessenwahn.net/gf.
"Official Guide Souvenir Program, California Pacific International Exposition, San Diego," 1936, Hathi.
Phil's Old Radios, June 1928, http://www.antiqueradio.org/welcome.htm. Accessed 21 November 2014.
"Weird Weapons—The Axis." *Modern Marvels. The History Channel*, Season 12, Episode 8.
Weitert, Anna, Forschungsdienst, Sekretariat BiG. Email to author, 2 April 2014.

Index

Abbey Theatre 200
Ace Drummond 195
Adenis, Édouard 161
aero-chemical warfare 9, 12–16
Agraives, Jean d' 177–178
Ahern, Gene 215
Air Defence Committee 117
Air Hawks 190–191
Alfani, Guido 36, 147–148
Algin, Sergius V. 86–87
Allenby, Field Marshal Edmund 13
"Allivi: The Bogus Death Ray" *see Warped in the Making: Crimes of Love and Hate*
Allorge, Henri 154, 156
Allsop, Raymond 51
"Almost Perfect Crimes, No. V.—The F-Ray" 147–148
"alphabet rays" *see* individual alphabet rays under their own headings
American Institute of Electrical Engineers 52
"American Sherlock Holmes" *see* Kennedy, Craig
Anderson, Charles R. 226–227n106
Anderson, L.G. 81
Anderson, Thomas W. 24
Aniline Chemical Works 153, 246n11
Appleton, Victor 137
Aquidaban 31
Archimedes 21, 31, 42, 45, 125
Arlen, Michael 179
Armageddon 2419 A.D. 203
Armoured Doves: A Peace Book 178
Army Institute of Scientific Research 119
Arrest Bulldog Drummond 194
Arsonval, Jacques-Arsène d' 94
"artificial lightning" 23, 67
Ashton-Wolfe, H. 146–147
Asquith, Prime Minister Herbert 211–212, 252n94
Atlantis 195

"Attempt to Sell the Death-Ray" *see* "Dicing with Death"
Aujay, Édouard 167
Australia: and allegations of death-ray in the First World War 73–74; soldier's hoax 44
Autry, Gene 194–195
The Avenging Ray 182
Ayres, Agnes 187, 249n8

Bacon, J.M. 28
Bailly, Albert 151, 246n4
Bakeless, John 15, 84
Baldwin, Hanson 87
Baldwin, Oliver Ridsdale *see* Hussingtree, Martin
Baldwin, Stanley 15, 106–107
Balfour, Arthur 59, 231n44
"Balkania" 174
Bamberg, L. 164
Bamberger, Dorothy 40
Barlow, Lester P. 103–104
Barnes, Arthur K. 208
Barnette, Jack 207
"Batman" 233n96
The Battle of Dorking 11
Bauer, Ludwig 15
Baxter, Gregory 165
Beckwith, O.L. 207
Becquerel, Henri 21, 124
Beeding, Francis 150
Before Midnight 200
Bellamy, Ralph 190–191
Benjamin, Park 24, 33, 126
Bennett, Charles 199–200
Bennett, W.R. 74
Bennington, Arthur 40
Benson, Thomas 231n46
Bentley, Norman K. 162
Berliner, Emile 26
Bernhardi, Gen. Friedrich von 11

The Big Four 161–162
Bigney, M.F. 22
Bijou Theatre 200
Billows, Charles F. 42
Binder, Eando 208
Birchall, Frederick T. 110
Birkenhead, Lord 64
Birmingham Repertory Theatre 199
Black, Ladbroke 16
Black Empire 160
The Black Satchel 171–172
Blake of Scotland Yard 192
Blanco, Iglesias 41
Blondlot, René 224–225n69
"The Blue Demon" 206
Blue Lightning 165–166
"The Blue Ray" 141
Bond, James 195
Boué, Maurice 167
Bowen, T.A. 63
Boyka, A.N. 80
Brandt, Albert 115, 242n69
Brandt, Dina 144
Branly, Édouard 30, 65
Bratt, K.A. 15
Bread and Wine 175–176
Brettmon, Jacques 95–96
British Institute of Radiologists 85
"Broadcasting the Tea Race" 182–183
Brook, Clive 197
Brooks, Samuel I. *see* Schuyler, George S.
Brosnan, Gerald 200
Brown, Cyril 54–55
Brühahn, Albert 80
"Buck Rogers" 184, 203
"Bulldog Drummond" 248n53
"The Bungle Family" 215
Burdekin, Katharine 162
Burney, Admiral Sir Cecil 13
"burning glasses" 45–46, 104, 144, 193, 207
"'Burning Glasses,' Dundonald's Destroyer?" 45
Burns, Albert G. 104
Buswell, Louis 204
Buw (American inventor) 39
Byrd, Ralph 198

Caldine (French inventor) 74
El Camino de los Dioses (novela de la próxima Guerra) 182
"Campaign of 1919" 14
Campbell, John W., Jr. 208
"canned lightning" 39
Canonge, Gen. Frédéric 84
Capp, Al 215
"Captain Midnight" 164–165
Carnarvon, Lord 168
cars stopped by rays: in Britain 114; in Denmark 114; in France 56; in Germany 54, 56–58, 109–110; in Italy 113; in the United States 82; by Victor Penny 196

Carter, Howard 168
Castelnau, Gen. Curières de 34
"Catford Death Wave" 132
cathode rays 89, 101, 207–210
The Catholic World 196
Celval, Félix 205
Chadfield, R.C. 85
Chandu the Magician 197
Channing, Mark 173
Chantiers du Rhône Company 61–64
Charbonneau, French inventor 74
Charlottenburger Technische Hochschule 111
Charlton, Adm. Edward 35
Charlton, L.E.O. 15
Charteris, Leslie 206
Chesney, George 11
Chesterton, G.K. 17
Cheyney, Peter 168
Christie, Agatha 161–162
Christmas, Edmond de 93
Churchill, Winston 15, 35, 61, 109, 178, 228n137, 231n44
La Cité des sables 177–178
La Cité foudroyée 185–186
Clair, René 185
Clarke, I.F. 11
Claudel, Henri 99
"Clouds of Death" 204
"Club of the Harmless" *see 1934 Deutschlands Auferstehung*
Cochrane, Thomas *see* Dundonald, Tenth Earl of
Code of the Air 190
Colladay, Morrison F. 204–205
Colorado Springs 68, 223n31
Comedy Theatre 199
The Coming Race 16, 32, 123–124
Conan Doyle, Sir Arthur 182, 197
Les condamnés à mort 159, 179–180
Congreve brothers 228n137
Conquest City 164
Conrad, Otto 71
Coolidge, W.D. 89, 99, 101; in fiction 207–210
Coonley, Howard 91–92
Coontz, John L. 99
"A Corner in Lightning" 243n14
Corr, Alexander 42
Corrigan, Ray "Crash" 195
"The Cosmic Gun" 204–205
Cosmotania 185
The Council of Seven 200
La Couronne 38
Cowperthwaite, A.C. 42
Cox, Erle 163
Cox, Harry 31, 224n54
Coxen, Maj. Gen. W.A. 200
Coxhead, Arthur 83, 235n40
The Crazy Ray see Paris qui dort
"The Creeping Death" 206–207

Index

Cristallia 126–127
Crookes, Sir William 136, 244n38
Cummings, Ray 202
Cummings, W.L. 40–41
Curie, Marie 30
Curie, Pierre 30
Curzon, Lord 64
Cyrania 176
Czech Crisis 105

"Dagonet" 27, 223n34
D'Albe, E.E. Fournier 59, 65–66, 231n43
Darius, Captain 111
Daugherty, William T. 79
Davis, Bergen 66
Dawn 60
"The Day the World Ended" 180
"death-noise" 90
"Death Ray" (poison) 214
"death ray" (term) first used 25; first appearance in fiction 128, 203
The Death Ray (1925 film, Soviet Union) see *Luch Smerti*
The Death Ray (1931 film, Britain) see *Murder at Dawn*
The Death Ray (1931 play) 200
"Death-Ray Argument" 17
"death-ray cannons" 119
"Death Ray Co." 214
"Death Ray Glances Gone from Gals' Golf Tourneys" 212
"The 'Death-Ray' in Antiquity" 212
"death stroke" 165–166
"death whisper" 103
Debeney, Gen. Eugène 51
"Deep Island" 155
Deeping, Warwick 169
"defensive curtain" 94, 106
de Forest, Lee 59
Delano, Frederic Mortimer 67
Delattre, Antoine-Joseph 98
De L'Isle, F. D'A.C. 131
Delmont, Joseph 144
Denain, Gen. Victor 81
"Desert City" 153–154
Desmond, Shaw 43
Desvosges, Jacques, 248n67
"detective defective" 214
"devastator" 164
Diamant-Berger, Henri 249n4
"Dicing with Death" 85–86
Dick Tracy 198
Dies Irae 144
diesel engines: and death rays 110, 205
"The Disintegration Machine" 182
Division 13 see National Defense Research Committee
Dixon, Thomas 96
Doberer, Kurt 100–102, 242n69
Dominik, Hans 143–144, 159
Il dominio dell'aria 15

Dorgelès, Roland 135, 210
Douhet, Giulio 15
The Dragon see *The Yellow Peril*
Drake's Mantle 162
The Dumb Gods Speak 166–167
du Mond, J.W.M. 85
Dundonald, Tenth Earl of 46–48, 73, 104, 228n137
Dundonald, Twelfth Earl of 228n137
"Dundonald's Destroyer" 47
"Dundonald's Plan" 47
Dunikowski, Zbigniev 98, 101
Dupuy, R. Ernest 7–8
"Dust of Destruction" 208

Echols, Allan K. 209
Edgewood Arsenal, Maryland 14
Edison, Thomas 9, 21, 23, 44, 83, 124–125
Edison's Conquest of Mars 39, 125–126
Edward VII 85, 128
Edward VIII 198
Edwards, Charman 174–175
Eichacker, Reinhold 151
The Electrical Experimenter 201, 231n16
Elektrokrieg: Maschine gegen Mensch see *On the Way to Electro War*
Elektropolis: Die Stadt der technischen Wunder 153–154
Electro-tank 83–84
Elettra 161
Eliot, George Fielding 7–8
Elliott, J.W. 200
Empire of the World 133
Engineer Garin and His Death Ray 152–153
Esau, Abraham 89, 101
L'Éther-Alpha: grand roman d'aventures 151
"The Ether King" 163
"The Ethiopian Murder Mystery" 160
Exmouth, Lord 228n137
The Exploits of Elaine 135, 184–185, 193
"explosion by concussion" 28

F-rays 33–41, 46, 58, 135–137, 142, 144, 147, 150–151, 171, 202
Faccioli, Giuseppe 67
Fairlie, Gerard 172–173
Falcoz, André 141
"The Fall of the Dictator" 176
Farncombe, Frank E. see Hadfield, Robert L.
Farrell, Charles 191
Farrère, Claude 159, 179
Fear Haunts the Roses 174–175
Ferrié, Commandant Gustave 34
Fighters from Mars 125
The Fighting Devil Dogs 193
The Fighting Marines 193
Filippov, Mikhail Mikhailovich 99–100
"The Fire People" 202–203

Fisher, Adm. Lord 59
Fitch, Herbert T. 85–86
Fitzgeorge, Col. Sir Augustus 97
The Flaming Disk 193
Flamm, Oswald 58–59
"Flash Gordon" 184
"fleet destroyer" 29
Fleur, Henry 94–95
Flight to Fame 191
Flinn, H.E.M. 201
Der Flug zur Sonne 159
Foch, Marshal Ferdinand 15
Fornari, Maria Luisa 36
Fornari, Adm. Pietro 36, 38
Forster, John 123
Foster, Jonathan 231*n*49
France: airplanes forced down over Germany 53–54, 56–58; allegations of death-ray development in 56, 68, 73–74, 79, 81, 84, 92–93
Francill, Maurice 76–77
Franco, Gen. Francisco 82
Franco-Prussian War 23
Freeman, Air Marshal Sir Wilfred 109
French airplane mystery 53–59, 73, 111, 144, 150–151, 159, 162, 190–194, 204–205
French Indochina 161
Fuldheim, Dorothy 109
Fuller, Col. J.F.C. 14

Galsworthy, John 213
Gask, Arthur 176
Geake, Captain 73
General Electric Company 89, 103
George V 85
Germany: allegations of death-ray development 33, 38, 41, 45, 53–60, 62, 66, 71–73, 77, 79–80, 102, 109–112, 114–117, 230*n*41, 240*n*24, 241*n*34; secret death-ray projects in World War II 118–119
Germany and the Next War 11
Gernsback, Hugo 201–203
Gerrare, Wirt (W.L. Greener) 126
"The Ghost Counts Ten" 179
The Ghost Patrol 191
Gibbon, American inventor 39
Gignoux, Régis 135, 210
Gilchrist, Maj. Gen. H.L. 84–85
Girenas, Lithuanian pilot *see* Darius, Captain
The Girl from Scotland Yard 197–198
Glastonbury Abbey 162
"Gloomy Sunday" *see* "Hungarian Suicide Song"
The God of War 198
Godfrey, Hollis 130, 243*n*23
"The Gold Kimono" 168
The Golden Scorpion 141
Goldfinger 195
Goldman, Russian professor 92

Goldsmith, Alfred N. 67–68, 110, 112
Goliah 130
Göring, Herman 102, 240*n*26
Graffigny, Henry de 150
Graichen, Erich 87–88
Grammachikoff, Russian inventor 71, 80
Grantham, Cyril Henry 78
Grassegger, Werner 144
Great Britain: allegations of death-ray development 29, 31, 35, 42, 45–46, 63–64, 85–86, 97, 107–109, 113–114, 232*n*68, 235*n*35; death ray and radar; and military hoaxes 44–45
The Great Murchison Mystery 156–157
The Greater Power 209
Green, Mr. (member of Parliament) 232*n*58
Greener, William L. *see* Gerrare, Wirt
Gregory, Sir Richard 64–65
Grenfell, Russell 15
Griffith, George 127–130, 243*n*14
Grindell Matthews, Harry 9, 72–74, 79, 90–91, 99, 102, 117, 250*n*21; address at Café Royal 60; and Chantier du Rhône Company 61–64; and Churchill 61; criticism of 64–66, 90; demonstration for British military 62–63; demonstration of wireless telephone 59, 231*n*42; demonstration with *Dawn* 59–60; discussed in House of Commons 64; and film of the death ray 69; and Harry E. Wimperis 63, 117; incident at Croydon airport 63; influence in fiction 149–154, 156–157, 160, 171, 186–192, 199, 203, 206, 208, 210; influence in humor 212; interview in Paris 61–62; and "light-o-mine" 231*n*45; meeting with Salmond 62; named in "Olympic-City" 211; in poem "Motor Tragedy" 212–213; and "Rindel Matthews" 153–154, 246*n*9; in satire by Régis Gignoux 210; and *The Story Without a Name* 186–187; support for 66–68; and the United States 68–70
Grinnell, New Jersey inventor 23
Groc, Léon 168
Guarini, Émile 29
"Guarini Thunderbolt" 29
La Guerre de 1924 157–158

Hadfield, Robert L. 169
Halsbury, Earl of 16, 221*n*12
Hamill, John H. 73
Hamilton, Cicely 16, 199
Hanstein, Otfrid von 153–154
Happel, R.V. 206
Harhorn, Victor 41
Harlan, Kenneth 190
Harrison, G. Russell 85
Hart, Joseph K. 50
Hartman, John 25, 29, 125, 128, 190
Hartmann (German inventor) 41

Hartwell, Wilson 30
Harvey, W.J. 42
Hassell, Hector M. 77
"The Heat Ray" 207
heat rays 26, 125, 199, 207
Heinkel H-60 112
Helders, Maj. von 16, 221*n*13
"heliotaueb" 79, 165–166
Hencocque, V.A. 74
Hensingmüller, Rudolf 38
Der Herr der Welt 197
Hertz, Heinrich 21, 124
Hicks, Cuthbert 50, 91
Hillersleben 118
Hilzinger, Adolfo 40
Hitchcock, Alfred 199
Hitler, Adolf 100, 112, 115, 250*n*13
Hoard, Dean *see* Horvath, Guido
Holder, Anthony 97
Holman, Russell *see* Stringer, Arthur
Honoré, F. 55, 65
"Hoople Ray" 215
Horvath, Guido 137
House of Commons 9, 47, 59, 62, 64, 106–107, 230*n*22
Howard, William K. 197
"Hungarian Suicide Song" 234*n*16
"Hungarian woman" 54, 58
Hunley 22
"Hushed Up at German Headquarters" 140
Hussingtree, Martin 16, 221*n*11
"hydro-electrocutor" 52
Hyne, C.J. Cutcliffe 133

Ibbotson, English inventor 97
Iéna 31, 38, 140
If War Comes 7
imaginary war 10–11, 16; in film 185; in novels and short stories 126–133, 135–146, 151–152, 157–160, 162–163, 170–171, 178, 201–204, 206; in the theater 199–201
L'impossible rançon 168–169
Inskip, Sir Thomas 107–109
"Inspector Post" 215–216
Interallied Disarmament Commission 53
"Interrupted Romance" 176
The Intrigue 185
The Invisible Ray (1920) 193
The Invisible Ray (1936) 196
"Invisible Ray" (1939) 214
"The Invisible War of 1950" 43
Irving, Washington 123
Irwin, Will 11–12, 50, 228*n*144
"The Island of Doctor X" 209
Island of Funen 114
"The Isolated Continent: A Romance of the Future" 137–138, 169
Italy: and Ethiopian War 107; and Giulio Ulivi 36, 39–40; in fiction 160, 175; and Marconi 113

J-ray 168–169
Jane, Frederick Thomas 38, 127
"Jane Arden" 215
Japan: alleged interest in British claims 72; alleged interest in German claims 73, 242*n*69; alleged interest in Ulivi 38; death-ray announcement 117; in fiction 131–132, 141, 155, 165, 167, 178, 182, 201; secret projects 119
Javor, Lazlo 234*n*16
Jellicoe, Admiral John 13
"Jezzard of the Mill" 150
Joffre, Gen. Joseph 33–34, 37
Johns Hopkins University 89–91
Johnson, Bernays 41, 111, 137
Jules Verne Award 246*n*4
Jungfrau Research Institute 85
"Junius" (Fred Rhodes) 182
"Jupiter moderne" 61

Kalsey, John 78
Der Kampf ums Gold 151–152, 168
"Kappa Rays" 190
Karloff, Boris 196–197
Keck, Lt. Col. John A. 118
Keeler, Harry Stephen 171–172
Keith, Lord 228*n*137
Kennard, Trevor 111
Kennedy, Craig 134–135
Khaki 200
Khokkim 178
"King Cobra" 173–174
"King's Shadow" 85
Kirke, John 164
"Klepton-Holorif" 160
"knockout Blow" 15
Kokai, Etienne *see* Papp, Ladislas
Kosmosoli Rays 170–171
Der Krieg im Jahre 1930 158–159, 180
Kruger, P.G. 88
Kuleshov, Lev 189–190
Kurtz, Daniel Webster 86

Lady Henrietta 34–35
Langevin, Paul 65, 89, 115–116
Lartaud, Émile 200
The Last Hour 199–200
Latouche-Tréville 38
Laue, Max von 67
Laughing at Danger 188–189
"Lavender Ray" 138
Leach, William 62, 64
League of Nations 12; in fiction 157, 162, 192
Le Bon, Gustave 28–30
Lefebure, Maj. Victor 51
Lenard, Philipp 101
Lenglen, Suzanne 64, 232*n*69
Leonard, Charles Lester 124
Le Queux, William 139–140, 245*n*47
Lewisham Hotel incident 213

Ley, Robert 119
Liddell Hart, Basil 15, 108
"light" gun 93
"light-o-mine" 231n45
"light" weapons 50
"Li'l Abner" 215
Lindemann, Frederick Alexander 61
Little Theatre 200
"The Little White Hag" 150
Lloyd George, David 230n22, 231n42
Lodge, Sir Oliver 56, 58, 193
London, Jack 130
Lone Wolf's Last Adventure 189
Longoria, Antonio 104–105
Loomis, Alfred E. 90–92, 103, 237n69
The Lord of Labour 128–129, 181
The Lost City 195
Low, A.M. 52, 58, 79, 156
Loy, Myrna 197
Luch Smerti 189–190
Luckner, Count 53
Lugosi, Bela 194–197
Lytton, Edward Bulwer 16, 32, 123–124

M-rays 36, 38
MacArthur, Gen. Douglas 119
Macbeth, Madge 175
MacGrath, Harold 139
La Machine à finir la guerre 135–136, 210
Die Macht der Drei 143–144, 159
Maclay, Edgar Stanton 45–48, 50, 141, 207, 227n134
MacNeile, Paul Humphrey 108
"The Magnetic Storm" 203
magnetron 119
USS *Maine* 31
Le Maître de la Foudre 141
"Major Hoople" 215
Makin, William J. 176
The Man Who Ended War 130–131
The Man Who Rocked the Earth 138–139
Mangin (French professor) 116
Mann, Arthur E. 66
Manning, Frank 78–79
Man's Mortality 179
Mapadonia 185
Marchant, Maj. Arthur W. 105
Marconi, Guglielmo 21, 24, 92, 112–113, 124, 241n43; and fiction 161, 176, 196
Marlowe, June 190
Martin, John T. 77
Martin brothers 77
Marva, José 39
Mary, Queen 59, 97
The Mask of Fu Manchu 197
Maskelynes 28, 223n38
Mason, E. 74
Mason, George *see* Mason, E.
"Le masque de feu" 167–168
Masson, Georges-Armand 211
Maxim, Hiram Percy 93, 237n90

May, Harry 99
Mayer, Douglas W.F. 93, 116
McClintock, James R. 22, 222n6
McCormick, Langdon 200
McCoy, Samuel J. 67–68
McCoy, Tim 191
McIvor, Roy 81
McKenna, Reginald 59
McLemore, Henry 212
McWhorter, Milton 96
Melsone-Smith, C.H. 77
Menschlichkeit 144
Mesny, Commandant 230n26
microwaves 8, 102
Miessner, B.F. 39
Mikasa 31–32, 147
Milch, Field Marshal Erhard 118–119
Miller, Col. Jay Earle 84
Miller, P. Schuyler 208
The Million Dollar Mystery 139
Minister for Coordination of Defence 107
Mitchell, Gen. William 13
Miyoshi, Takoyi 242n69
A Modern Comedy 213
Mohr, Otto H. 115
Moldinke, Richard 77
"The Mole Men of Mercury" 208
Mong, William V. 190
Montgomery-Massingberd, Field Marshal Sir Archibald 44–45
The Moon Element 59
Moore, Julie Anne 176
Moreau, Marcel 73
Moreno, Antonio 187, 249n8
Morgan, Charles 200
Morley, Karen 197
Morrow, Lowell Howard 206
Moseley, Oswald 178
Moselli, José 141
"Motor Tragedy" 212–213
Mott, Francis J. 209
Mpiki 170
Mu *see* Murania
"le mur invisible" 107
Murania 195
Murat, Henri 35, 38
Murder at Dawn 192
Murray, A.F. 118
Mussolini, Benito 104, 107, 112–113, 160, 241n43
The Mystery of Lost Ranch 189
"The Mystery of the Death Ray Tube" 210
The Mystery of the Green Ray 139

N-rays 43, 155, 180, 224–225n69
"Nameless Force" 21
National Defense Research Committee 118
National Inventors' Congress 82, 104–105
National League of Health 97
Nauen incident 57, 67, 144
"Negative Ray" 199

Index 271

Neues Tagebuch 242*n*69
New Zealand 26; and Victor Penny 82
Newell, O.A. 97
Newman, Bernard 178
Nicolet, E. 55
Nicholson, Capt. W.C.M. 35
Nineteen-Sixty-Four 201
1934 Deutschlands Auferstehung 142
Nixon, Lewis 32
Nordmann, Charles 55, 226*n*85
Novak, Eva 188
Nowlan, Philip Francis 203
Noyes, Pierrepont B. 160
Nudl, Ludwig 78

The Old Adam 199
"old gent from Maoriland" 26
Olivier, Laurence 191
"Olympic-City" 210–211
On the Way to Electro War 100–101
Oppenheim, E. Phillips 166–167
USS *Oregon* 32
O'Reilly, Mary Boyle 47, 228*n*144
The Origin of the Next War: A Study in the Tensions of the Modern World 84
Orlando 26
Osborne, John Hall 34
"Our Boarding House" 215
"Out of the Silence" 163–164

Painlevé, Paul 109–110
Pakington, Mary 200
The Pallid Giant: A Tale of Yesterday and Tomorrow 160
Palmerston, Lord 47
Panmure, Lord 47
Paphlagonia 199
Papp, Ladislas 78
Paris Peace Conference 11
Paris qui dort 185
"A Pawn in the Game" 137
Pawns of Mars 185
Peenemünde 116
Penny, Victor 82, 196, 235*n*35
The Perils of Paris 185
"Perpetual Death" 212
Pétain, Marshal Philippe 93
Peyvel, Lieutenant 74, 137
The Phantom Creeps 195
The Phantom Empire 194–195
Photoplay 187, 249*n*6
"Phyl Coe" 210
Phyl Coe Mysteries 210
Pirate Mallory 200
Pirolo, Nicholas 113
plague ray 97
Poirot, Hercule 161–162
"The Poniatowski Ray" 201–202
Post, Wiley 191
Poulsen, English inventor 31
"Power by Radio" 103

Price, Vincent 207
Princess Irene 38
Prior, William 72, 212
Progress 16
Pupin, Michael I. 28, 67
"The Purple Death" 207–208

Q Planes 191–192
Q-ray 168, 215
"?-ray" 53

Die rächende Stünde. Englands Schicksalstag: Ein Zukunftsbild 144
radar 106, 108, 117
Radiant Energy: Science Fiction and Scientific Projects 99–100
radio death ray (radio gun) 76, 97, 102–103, 113
Radio Nazionale Agency 112
Radio Singapore 117
"Radio-terreur, grand roman de mystère" 152
radioballistica 40
Radiopolis 154
radium 10, 21, 30–31, 88, 128–129, 196
Radium Destroyer 43
RAF 97, 198
Raffe *see* Prior, William
Ramsey, Margaret 234*n*16
Randall, F.H. 39
Rapallo, Treaty of 54, 71, 229*n*22; in fiction 158
Rathbone, Basil 197
Ravn, Danish inventor 101–102
"El Ray" 208
Raymond, C.S. 130
Le rayon de la mort 200
rayon destructeur 84
Rayon diabolique 249*n*4
Le rayon infernal 205–206
Le Rayon phi 141
Le Rayon Svastika 177–178
rayon thermique 60
Les rayons ensorcelés 154
The Rebel Passion 162–163
Reber, Charles 85
Red Army *see* Soviet Union
"Redlike Ray" 138
Reeve, Arthur B. 17, 134–135
Reichswehr 54
Reid, Frank 214
"The Return of the Cosmic Gun" 204
Rhodes, Henry *see* "Junius"
Rialto Theatre (London) 69
Rialto Theatre (New York) 249*n*6
Richardson, J. Frederick 69
Richardson, Ralph 191–192
Rickenbacker, Eddie 195
Riesa, Saxony 109–110
"Rindell-Matthews" 153–154, 246*n*9
Robards, Jason 191

Roberts, A.J. 91
"Robin Red Flag" 211–212
Robinson, Henry 124
Rogers, Will 191
Rogue's March 200
Rohmer, Sax 141, 180, 198, 200
Romazières, Edmond (Édouard de Keyser) 178
Roosevelt, Theodore 244n24
Rota, L.G.V. 53
Royal Institution 31
Royal United Service Institution 50
Royer, Eugène 61
Ruhr: French occupation of 53; in fiction 158
Ruled by Radio 169–170
Ruritania 199
Russell, Arthur 163
Russell, G. (Australian inventor) 52
Russell, William 33
Russo-Japanese War 31, 244n24
Rutherford, Ernest 45
Rutledge, Maryse 165–166
Ryan, Harris J. 52
Rynin, N.A. 99–100

Saager, Adolf 144
Saentis, Guber de 85
"The Saint" 206–207
St. Ange, Oskar von 80
The Saint Closes the Case see "The Creeping Death"
St. John Irvine 16
St. Quentin, Gen. Gaston de 157
Salmond, Air Vice-Marshal Sir Geoffrey 62–63
Sapper (Herman Cyril McNeile) 194
"Sappo" (E.C. Segar) 215
Sarnoff, David 80
The Scarlet Streak 193
Schiebold, Ernst 118–119
Schimkus, Kurt 81, 207
Schlosz, Josef Karl 78
Schmidt, Henri see Hencocque, V.A.
Schoenaich, Freiherr Paul von 158–159
Schuyler, George S. 160
Scientific American 8
Scissors Cut Paper 172–173
Scotland Yard 163–164, 170, 176, 192, 197–198
Scotoscopia 40
Scott, E.R. 165
Scott, James K. 80
Secor, H. Winfield 28
"The Secret Cypher" see "Septimus March Again"
Seely, J.E.B. 231n42
Segar, E.C. see Sappo
Selassie, Haile 235n34
Selden, Charles A. 13
Le Semeur de feu 141

Sennacherib 32
"Septimus March Again" 164
Sergi, Eugene T. 77
Serrell, Gen. E.W. 25–26
Serrigny, Gen. Bernard 51
Serviss, Garrett P. 39, 44, 125–126
Severinghaus, W.L. 65, 67
Seydewitz, Max 100–102, 242n69
"Shall We Commit Suicide?" 61
Shanks, Edward 16
The Shape of Things to Come see *Things to Come*
Sherlock Holmes 197
Shiel, M.P. 138
Short, S.H. 26
Shorter, Clement 125
Sibley, Robert 52
Siemens Company 87, 116, 143
sigma ray 156
The Sign at Six 133–134
"Signor Planta," 40
The Silent Bullet: The Adventures of Craig Kennedy, Scientific Detective 134
Siljak, Rajko 101
Silone, Ignazio 175
"The Silver Assassin" 176–177
The Silver Peril 165–166
Simon Templar see The Saint
Sinclair, Charles 78
"The Sixth Sense" 135
Skowronnek, Fritz 144
Sky Racket see *The Ghost Patrol*
Slessor, Group Captain Jack see Freeman, Air Marshal Sir Wilfred
Small, Austin J. 182
"smiling death" 200
Smith, Harry 96
Smuts, Gen. Jan 13
Snell, Edmund 171, 180–181
sodium 37, 147, 226n85
Solf, Ferdinand Eugen 142
Somaini Cotton Mill 40
"Le sommeil qui tue" 178
Sonnengewehr (sun gun) 118
Le Sorcier de la mer 178
"Sorokichi—Prometheus" 131, 202
sound (as a weapon) 90–93, 103, 242n63; in fiction 125, 179–181, 198
The Sound Machine 180–181
Soviet Union 71, 80, 104
Spanish-American War 27, 198
Speer, Albert 119
Die Stadt unter dem Meere 144–146
Stalin, Joseph 104
"Static" 208–209
Steiger, Judge George 95
Stevens, Rowan 131, 202
Stevens, Truman 79
Stimson, Thomas E. 92
The Story Without a Name 150, 187–188, 249n6

Strahlenzieler 143
Strahler 143–144
"The Strange Adventures of Bailey Catford, Scientist and Inventor" 131–133
Stratemeyer, Edward *see* Appleton, Victor
Stratton, George F. 201
Stringer, Arthur 150, 187
Sudetenland 105
"Suggestion for Movie Bedtime Story" 214
"super-radium death rays" 116
Sussex, Gordon 150
Sutter, Walter 232*n*62
Swinton, Gen. Ernest 50–51
Switzerland 85
Symes, John Morgan 92

Tabouis, Geneviève 112
Talmadge, Richard 188
Tangye, Nigel 111
Tarkhanoff, Prince Ivan R. 30–31, 224*n*52
Taylor, H.E. 82
Tempelhof Airport 81, 116
Terpsichore 35
"The Terror in the Air" 134–135
Tescovich, Capt. Emo 66
Tesla, Nikola 9–10, 21, 26–28, 31, 66, 73–74, 124, 196, 223*n*31; and "defensive curtain" 93–94, 106; in fiction 135, 203
Thébault, Eugène 152
Thieme, Paul 159
Things to Come 16
Thomas, Phillips 99, 103
Thomson, Lord 13, 232*n*68
Thone, Frank 92
Thuillier, Henry 15
"thunderbolt-wielder" 25
Times Square 68
Timpson, Lawrence 69
Tizard, Henry 117
To-Ray 166
Todesstrahlen als Lebensretter 118
Todesstrahlen und andere neue Kriegswaffen 100, 242*n*69
Die Todgeweihten see *Les condamnés à mort*
Tolstoy, Alexei 152–153
Tom Swift and His Electric Rifle or Daring Adventures in Elephant Land 137
Train, Arthur 138
"Trelawney's Z-Rays" 169
Trévise, Robert 249*n*5
Trevor, Ralph 179
"The Triple Ray" 206
Truss, Thomas Frederick John 72
"Tu mourras le ..." 161
Tuohy, Ferdinand 44
Turpin, Eugène 41, 221–222*n*1
Tutankhamun 168
Tuthill, Harry J. 215
Tyndall, John 72

Udet, Ernst 240*n*26
Ugarte, Manuel 182
Ulivi, Giulio 9, 43; allegations of fraud 36–37, 226*n*85; dealings with the British 35–36, 225*n*70, 225*n*81; demonstration for the French 33–34; demonstration in Rome 39; demonstrations in Florence 36–38; elopement 36; influence in film 192, 194, 202, 205–206; influence in novels and short stories 135, 136, 140–148, 151–152, 156–157, 170–171; mentioned in the works of Arthur B. Reeve 135; remote detonation patterned after 81; Scotoscopia 40; at Somaini Cotton Mill 40; support for 38–40, 58, 230*n*29
Ullmo, French naval officer 230*n*31
ultrashort wave 101–102, 112
Undersea Kingdom 195
United States: and alleged death-ray development 25–26, 80, 84–85, 91–92, 105, 115; alleged interest in other death-ray inventors 73, 81–83, 91, 96, 104–105; Army Chemical Warfare Service 14, 84, 91; Bureau of Standards 94; and German death rays 79, 81; and Grindell Matthews 64, 68–69; investigation of death rays during Second World War 118; and Nikola Tesla 94; research with ultrashort and shortwave radio waves 101, 103
Urbain, Georges 65

V-rays 40
V-weapons 116–117, 119
Vallery, Tancrède 154
Van Carneghem 71
Vance, Louis Joseph 189
Van deGraff, Robert J. 84
The Vanishing Shadow 194
Versailles, Treaty of 11, 45, 50
The Violet Flame: A Story of Armageddon and After 127
Vom vorigen zum nächsten Krieg 158
Voyage de cinq Américains dans les planètes: roman astronomique 150
"vril" 32
"VXO" Accumulator" 192

"W-rays" 151–152
Walker, Col. William H. 14
Wall, T.F. 71–72
Waloschek, Pedro 118
The War in the Air 10
The War of the Wireless Waves 170–171
The War of the Worlds 16, 26, 50, 124–125, 150, 202
Ward, Arthur Henry *see* Rohmer, Sax
Wardenclyffe 28, 223*n*35
Warped in the Making: Crimes of Love and Hate 146–147
The Warstock: A Tale of To-Morrow 126–127

Watson-Watt, Robert A. 117
"waves of detonation" 29
Way, Charles Sidney 82–83
Weitert, Anna 236n53
Wellington, Duke of 50
Wells, H.G. 10, 16, 26–27, 32, 42, 124–125, 150, 179, 198
Wells, Linton 107
Westbury, Lord 168
Westerman, Percy F. 170–171
Westervelt, Col. W.I. 68
Westinghouse Company 52, 101, 103
"When the Atoms Failed" 208
The Whispering Shadow 194
White, Bernard C. 137
White, Pearl 185, 244n35
White, Stewart Edward 133, 246n7
Whitlock, Charles 198–199
Wilhelm II, Kaiser 166; in fiction 128–129, 131, 140
Wilkins, Arnold "Skip" 117
Wilkins, Harold T. 45, 111
Willat, Irvin 249n8
Williams, H.C. 83
Williams, Wythe 51
Wimperis, Harry E. 63, 117

Wingard, James C. 21–22, 24, 133, 222n2
Wings in the West 175
"The Wireless Death" 130
Without Warning see *Photoplay*
Wood, R.W. 65, 67, 89–92, 99, 103, 138, 238n108, 244n45
The World Masters 127–128, 203
The World Peril of 1910 129
The World Set Free 10
Wright, S. Fowler 16
"Wright brothers" 86
Wulle, Reinhold 71

X-rays 10, 21, 80, 88, 119, 185

Yanistan 174
The Yellow Peril 138
"yellow peril" 141, 178
York, Duke of 228n137

The Z Ray 171, 180
Z-rays 41, 110–111, 137–138, 169–172, 201, 215
The Zeppelin Destroyer 139
Zudora 139
Zukunftsroman 142, 153, 159

www.ingramcontent.com/pod-product-compliance
Ingram Content Group UK Ltd.
Pitfield, Milton Keynes, MK11 3LW, UK
UKHW041930140426
5217IPUK00014B/406